IMPERIALISM
TODAY

IMPERIALISM

TODAY

An Evaluation of
Major Issues and
Events of Our Time

by GUS HALL

INTERNATIONAL PUBLISHERS
New York

To Elizabeth

For her encouragement and criticism

and

As a tribute to the many thousands of heroic working
class fighters throughout the world in the struggle
against U.S. imperialism and for Socialism.

ISBN (cloth) 0-7178-0303-1; (paperback) 0-7178-0304-X
Library of Congress Catalog Card number: LC 72-90500
Printed in the United States of America

CONTENTS

PART THREE

THE STRUGGLE AGAINST OPPORTUNISM

PART FOUR

AN HISTORICAL NECESSITY

AUTHOR'S NOTE

The material in this book has been in the course of preparation over a period of ten years during which time Presidents Kennedy, Johnson and Nixon served in the White House. Each of their administrations in its turn pursued policies dictated by the dominant sections of monopoly capital. In their basic essence they are policies of imperialism. The inevitable consequence of such policies has been acts of military, economic and political aggression.

What is unique about this period is that U.S. imperialism has pursued the policies of imperialist aggression at a moment when the basic currents and social forces of history have turned against imperialism.

For U.S. imperialism this ten-year period has been an explosive turning point. During these years it reached the very apex, the floodmark of its development. We have witnessed the meteoric rise of a ruthless dollar-dominated world empire of exploitation and profits, enforced by an unprecedented military power. We are now seeing it in a deep crisis of disintegration.

This analysis does not, of course, include accounts of all the manifestations of imperialist aggression or of neo-colonialism in this decade, but I believe that the historical events discussed are representative. They are studies of social, economic and political currents and trends as they surfaced in the context of current situations. This material was not prepared with a book in mind. Much of it is the essence of political reports and articles, dealing with analyses of specific moments and events. For the most part I have retained the dates and figures that prevailed at the time when they were written.

The analyses and assessments are not from the viewpoint of one who is a detached observer. Rather these are reflections of an active participant and a partisan in the struggle against imperialism. They were intended to strengthen the struggle against imperialism.

To clear the ideological decks I want to say a few words about the overall approach to the analyses in this book. As a guide I have drawn on the revolutionary science of Marxism-Leninism. It is the most trustworthy instrument in probing for the root causes, and in getting a deeper understanding of the dynamics of life's realities. It is a science that provides a rounded-out, a many-sided world outlook. It is a science of the general laws of development of nature, of society, and of human thought. It is the science of the revolutionary transition to socialism. It is the science for the liberation of human society from oppression and exploitation. Marxism-Leninism is inseparable from reality. Its premises are the premises of life. It is a continuing reflection of objective reality. In writing about their approach, the two giants of human thought, Marx and Engels, observed:

> This method of approach is not devoid of premises. It starts out from the real premises and does not abandon them for a moment. Its premises are men, not in any fantastic isolation and rigidity, but in their actual, empirically perceptible process of development under definite conditions. As soon as this active life-process is described, history ceases to be a collection of dead facts . . . or an imagined activity of imagined subjects. . . .
> Where speculation ends—in real life—there real positive science begins. . . .[1]

In its basic essence human society is not a conglomerate of accidents. It is not a treadmill of blind changes, of isolated, disconnected events. Like all phenomena or "happenings" human society is basically influenced by objective laws of development.

History has a direction. There are setbacks, there are zigs and zags, there are areas of uneven development, there are moments of retrogression, but they take place within the overall framework of advancing from a lower social structure to a step up the ladder.

The defenders of capitalism go to great lengths to deny this truth. This is understandable because the direction of history

[1] Karl Marx and Frederick Engels, *The German Ideology* (New York: International Publishers, 1970), pp. 47-8.

condemns capitalism as an obstacle to all human progress. They see the handwriting of history on the walls of life.

To be fully effective in the struggle against imperialism it is necessary to know the laws of capitalist development. In the words of Engels:

> The forces operating in society work exactly like the forces operating in Nature—blindly, violently, destructively, so long as we do not understand them and fail to take them into account. But when once we have recognized them and understood how they work, their direction and their effects, the gradual subjection of them to our will and the use of them for the attainment of our aims depends entirely upon ourselves. And this is quite especially true of the mighty productive forces of the present day. . . . But once their nature is grasped in the hands of the producers working in association they can be transformed from demoniac masters into willing servants. It is the difference between the destructive force of electricity in the lighting of a thunderstorm and the tamed electricity of the telegraph and the arc light. . . .[2]

Movements can become fully effective only when they become aware of the objective laws of capitalist development.

The science of Marxism-Leninism is a necessary tool to understanding the class nature of capitalism, the class nature of the exploitation. It provides one with the understanding of the historic role of the working class.

It is the only solid base for a revolutionary program of struggle against imperialism. It is the only base for a correct line of tactics.

Marxism-Leninism embodies the best in human thought. It is the accumulated experience of the history of struggle against oppression and exploitation the world over. In these studies the basic theoretical point of reference is Marxism-Leninism. They express the Communist point of view.

The shortcomings and limitations in these studies should not be placed at the doorstep of the science. They must be chalked up against the author. The shortcomings are not the result of poor tools, they are weaknesses of craftsmanship.

June 1, 1972   GUS HALL

[2] Frederick Engels, *Anti-Dühring* (New York: International Publishers, 1970), p. 305.

IMPERIALISM:

History's Greatest Obstacle to Human Progress

We have landed men and equipment on the moon, we are putting instruments on Venus and Mars. We are seriously discussing establishing human communities on other planets, we can now produce more food than the inhabitants of the world can eat. We can now tap a power source that has no limits, we now have the medical know-how for putting an end to most dreaded diseases. We can make the deserts bloom, harvest the oceans, and build cities in the skies above us. Yes, we the human race have now advanced in science and technology to a point where we can raise and produce enough of all the necessities for every man, woman and child who inhabits the world. We have it made.

This is not a dream beyond the reach of reality. It is physically and technically possible now. It is possible, but it is not being done. Instead of experiencing this possible reality, most of the human race lives a nightmare reality. The number of ill-fed, ill-housed and ill-clothed people continues to grow each week. The latest reports are that 540 million people are on the verge of death from starvation.

One-third of all children born in Africa die before the age of five—from hunger related causes.

In colonial Angola 97.3 percent of the population and 98.7 percent of the people in colonially oppressed Mozambique are illiterate.

One-fifth of the people in these United States live in poverty. Over 34 percent of Black Americans live in poverty. Over 30 million Indians in Bolivia, Brazil, Mexico, Peru and Ecuador live now as they did during the colonial rule of Spain and Portugal. Not the life of abundance but the nightmare of unemployment is the reality for increasing millions of workers in the capitalist world.

Life is not security, abundance and peace. Instead, hunger, insecurity, military aggression, threat of wars and nuclear disaster are the reality for most of the earth's inhabitants.

The obvious question is, why? Why this discrepancy between what is possible and what is in fact the ugly reality? What is the hang-up? Who is responsible? Some keep saying it is because of a flaw in human character. Some say it is because of a "lack of leadership."

In the past most have accepted the nightmare with its sense of values, morals and priorities as inevitable, as a normal way of life. Many thought that was the best life could offer. Others thought their plight was the result of an unfortunate set of circumstances plaguing their family or nation. In history this period will be referred to as the moment of the great awakening. The fairy tales of the inevitability of hunger and oppression are now rejected by the millions. The human race is now fighting to restructure society and is determined to build a structure in which human needs will have the top priority.

It is becoming obvious that the problem has deeper roots, more basic causes than a lack of leadership or weakness in human nature. The roots of the problem are in the socio-economic system. The explanation is in one word—"imperialism." It is imperialism that is the obstacle to social progress. Imperialism is not only the obstacle, it is the threat to all people. Imperialism makes the difference between reality and the potential.

Imperialism is not the product of human nature. It is a product of the inherent nature of capitalism. It is the offspring of the objective laws of capitalism. Imperialism cannot be separated from capitalism. Imperialism is what capitalism has become. It is capitalism in its last stage of development. It is capitalism, decaying, but trying by wars, by racism, by brutal oppression, to turn back the clock of history. It is a socio-economic system trying to avoid the judgment of history by brute force.

Imperialism is the ugly monster, spawned and bred in the incubator of capitalism, nurtured by the greed for private profits, fattened on the exploitation of millions, gorged on the blood, sweat and tears of hundreds of millions of people in all of the continents.

The roots of imperialism are not in people. The propelling force that drives imperialism is the endless, gluttonous pursuit by privately owned corporations for private profits. This determines its inherent inner nature. This is its heart. Cut it out and it dies.

Imperialism has left a long bloody trail. It stands as the most ruthless bloodthirsty oppressor and human butcher in all of human history.

Wars and events in history are labeled many things. As a rule, the labels do not indicate the causes or who the culprits are. Apologists for imperialism are not concerned about labels as long as the finger does not point to imperialism. They prefer to number the wars—World War I, II and III. These numbers do not indicate imperialism to be the cause. The imperialists do not mind being called "super powers." They do not mind speaking about "anti-Americanism" as long as it is not anti-imperialism. The crimes of imperialism are endless. During the century of our times, 60 million people have been killed in wars imperialism is responsible for. One hundred ten million have been crippled, tens of additional millions have died from disease and epidemics, all resulting from wars of imperialism. Eleven million known men, women and children have been murdered in gas chambers, shot or hanged. At least three million have been slaughtered by air raids, by napalm bombs. Besides the military casualties, over 350,00 South Vietnamese children have been killed by napalm bombs. Seven hundred fifty thousand South Vietnamese have been crippled for life. Over one million have been killed, wounded or tortured to death in U.S.-supported South Vietnamese concentration camps. Since 1870 imperialist powers have conducted 121 wars and military operations against the peoples of Africa. In the process they have murdered 5,300,000 inhabitants of Africa.

Aggression is a way of life for imperialism. Here is a list of some of the military acts of aggression during the last 15 years:

France against Laos and Cambodia (1945-54)
France against Vietnam (1946-54)
Britain against Oman and Aden (since 1946)

USA against the Korean People's Democratic Republic (1950-53)
Britain against Kenya (1952-54)
USA against Guatemala (1954)
France against Algeria (1954-62)
USA against Laos (since 1954)
Britain against Cyprus (1955-59)
France against Tunisia (1956-58)
Britain, France and Israel against Egypt (1956)
USA and Britain against Jordan and the Lebanon (1958)
USA against China (the Taiwan Strait) (1958)
USA against Panama (1959)
Britain against Nyasaland (1959)
The actions of several imperialist states against the Congo (1960-62)
USA against the National Liberation Front in South Vietnam (since 1960)
USA against Cuba—since Cuba won independence
Britain and USA against Yemen (since 1962)
France against Tunisia (Bizerta) (1961-63)
USA against Panama (1964)
USA against the Democratic Republic of Vietnam (since 1965)
USA against the Dominican Republic (1965)
Israel against Arab countries (1967-71)

The casualty list of U.S. youth carrying out the aggression in Vietnam grows. Over 50,000 have been killed in action. Over 300,000 have returned crippled. These are the physically crippled.

These are casualties related to military actions. How this brutal, unjust war, a war opposed by most in the military services, has affected these youth mentally only time will tell. But the list of the victims of capitalism does not end there. Millions die unnecessarily in industrial accidents, from diseases related to jobs; hundreds of millions are crippled in industry, because maximum private profits is the only criterion regulating work and health standards. There have been over 100 million serious industrial accidents in the United States alone since 1920. Between 1941 and 1945, 11 million workers in the United States were killed and injured. This was 11 times as large as the U.S. casualties sustained in World War II. These millions are no less victims of imperialism. The irresponsible destruction of the earth's environment must be added to the list of crimes committed by imperialism.

The struggle against imperialism is therefore a struggle to remove a threat, to remove the central log jam to social progress.

There are only two possible waterways for the products of human social activities. One can be a waterway through which the products of human endeavor will flow mainly into private preserves owned by about one percent of the population while only a trickle goes to 99 percent of the people. This is the waterway of capitalism. Or there can be a social order in which the products and achievements of society will flow along waterways from which all of the people can draw the necessities of life. This is socialism. The private waterway is imperialism. It is now getting polluted, corroded, like Lake Erie or the Hudson River.

The struggle against imperialism is a struggle to divert a bigger share of the products created by the people into the mass channels. The struggle is to close the polluted waterways of imperialism, and to open up the waterways to social progress.

Compared with slavery and feudalism, capitalism was a step forward. But it was born with a built-in cancer. It adopted the basic evil of slavery and feudalism, that of the few exploiting the many, as a way of life.

It continued the basic evil of slavery and feudalism, a system where the few exploit and oppress the many. Capitalism was a new economic system—but in a basic sense it was a continuation of the old. Exploitation remained. Society continued to be divided between a class of oppressors and a class of the oppressed. As in past economic and social systems, the capitalist political and social superstructures, governments, constitutions, priorities and values were all geared to protect and facilitate the system of exploitation.

In its day the U.S. Constitution was a progressive document. But in its basic essence it sanctified a system of exploitation.

Exploitation of the many for private profits is the basic law of capitalism. Workers work and produce commodities. The capitalist class takes these products and pays the worker for only a very small share of what he has produced. The lion's share of the value of the products the boss keeps as profits. It is this system that placed capitalism on the rails of no return, on the track of its imperialist development.

Capitalism as a system is planless. No one had preconceived plans of how capitalism should develop. Capitalism has reached its present stage of decay and corrosion because of the unalterable laws of its development. No one had plans, but those who understand the laws of its development could foresee where it was going. Lenin's brilliant analysis of imperialism as the last stage of capitalist development stands as one of the monumental contributions to human thought. Based on his insight of the laws of capitalist development, he wrote, "The rise of monopolies, as the result of the concentration of production, is a general fundamental law of the present stage of development of capitalism."

Based on these same laws he saw the rise and concentration of economic power in the hands of financial conglomerates. He saw the expansion of capital investments breaking through national boundaries into an avalanche of export of capital resulting in the growth of worldwide monopolies, into the present multinational corporations. Based on these same laws he foresaw a situation where the major imperialist powers could continue to expand only at the expense of some other imperialist power—leading to struggles for redivision—to wars of imperialism. On the basis of these laws of capitalist development it has been possible to foresee the rising struggle of the people who have been the victims of the "capital export" of capitalism. This is a world struggle against imperialist domination.

Based on an understanding of these same inherent laws it has been clear that the victim of the class exploitation—the working class—will be forced to raise the struggle to new levels. It is these struggles that set the stage for a revolutionary struggle to put an end to capitalism and to all economic and social systems based on exploitation for the profits of the few.

Thus imperialism as the last stage of capitalist development has set the stage for the transition from capitalism to socialism.

Imperialism is to human society what cancer cells are to living matter. In both cases it is growth. But in imperialism, as it is with cancer, the growth is uncontrolled and destructive. Both distort, mutilate and block healthy growth, and unless stopped or cut out they lead to death. Imperialism is never benign. The drive for maximum profits drives the corporation to overtake, to destroy, or to seize its competitors. The result is the growth of huge monop-

[1] Lenin, *Selected Works,* Vol. 1 (New York: International Publishers, 1967), p. 688.

olies. Banks moved in to get a piece of this action. Banks and other financial institutions took over. They become a dominating factor. Bigger banks took over small banks and so there emerged on the scene a few monopoly banks controlling and dominating an industrial-financial complex. There are no limits to the greed of the corporate drive for profits. When the domestic scene was covered with this cancerous growth it broke through the national boundaries. Weaker nations were enslaved and oppressed. Imperialism became a system of worldwide private corporate networks with their tentacles grasping endlessly for more raw materials, markets and cheap labor. The struggle to destroy its competitors became a worldwide struggle. It is this drive for profits that has resulted in colonial oppression, in racist enslavement and wars of aggression. This is imperialism. It is a cancerous growth.

The escalation of the war against the peoples of Indochina has cast a powerful spotlight on U.S. imperialism. The protracted devastation in Vietnam has revealed—to millions for the first time—the ruthlessness of U.S. imperialism. As the truth about the war becomes clearer to masses of the world's people, it becomes a greater and greater factor in all economic, social and political alignments, and gives rise to extensive anti-imperialist movements and struggles the world over.

The people's indictment charges specifically that the United States at this stage in history is the most warlike and predatory of all nations; that it represents the most extended military and economic penetration of imperialism; that it is the most flagrant practitioner of neo-colonialism. It is the very center, the bulwark and the main beneficiary of neo-colonialism. In the last decade it has been the single most stubborn obstacle to world peace. It is the military, financial and political pillar of every reactionary, oppressive movement and government throughout the world. It is the most formidable obstacle to human progress.

It has become apparent that U.S. imperialism, far from relinquishing war as a means of settling international problems, plans its military alliances and armaments programs with increased reliance on war and the possible use of nuclear weapons, especially against underdeveloped or potentially revolutionary sectors. And far from being geared to national defense, these programs are all too clearly geared to aggression. The one obstacle to arms reductions is U.S. imperialism. The one obstacle to ending the deadly arms race is U.S. imperialism.

Because of the present balance of world forces, the other capitalist powers who have aggressive designs and would be inclined to resort to war, lack the military or economic capabilities to do so on their own. Therefore the United States constitutes the shock troop of world imperialism; it is the monetary clearing house and the partner in every warlike adventure. U.S. imperialism is tied in with the Belgian operations in the Congo; it has a growing piece of the slave-based industries of South Africa; it is the dominant imperialist force in Latin America; it is part owner of domestic industries in all other advanced capitalist countries— England, West Germany, Italy, France, Spain, Belgium, Japan, Australia, and Canada. In Latin America, investments in oil, fruit, iron and copper mining and a host of other industries bring in an especially gluttonous harvest of super-profits sweated out of the Latin American masses, whose per capita income is less than one-tenth of that in the United States, and who live in indescribable poverty. In many of the countries mentioned, virtually every important industry, including telephone companies, public transportation facilities and other public utilities, is owned or controlled by U.S. monopolies, and each extracts its toll from the working people.

Because much of American imperialist expansion took place during a period when resistance to foreign domination was on the rise, it was found necessary to develop a special craftiness in camouflage and deception. Thus U.S. monopoly capital became the chief practitioner of the policy of aggression carried on under the slogan of "anti-imperialism." Indeed, there are no limits to this hypocrisy. U.S. forces, for example, went into the Dominican Republic as aggressors, but President Johnson could say at the time to the 20th anniversary meeting of the United Nations: "I now call upon this gathering of the nations of the world to use all their influence, individually and collectively, to bring to the tables those who seem determined to make war." President Roosevelt used anti-imperialist slogans in his policies against imperialist rivals. He was for the breaking up of the old imperialist empires— Germany, Japan and Great Britain—only to enable U.S. imperialism to pick up the pieces. When the corporations of other capitalist countries lost control, U.S. corporations grabbed the reins. This unconscionable gap between righteous pronouncements on the right of all nations to self-determination and peace, and actual policies of imperialist manipulation and aggression has become the hallmark of the United States.

The warlike posture of imperialism is an inherent characteristic that impels it to go on the prowl, seeking the weak spots. But this characteristic is forced to operate within the realities of the new world balance of forces. It must take into account the forces of anti-imperialism—the growing economic, military and political might of the socialist third of the world, the thrust of national liberation forces, and the political awareness of the working class and other people of the capitalist world. And it must deal with its imperialist rivals.

To understand how imperialism operates within the present balance of forces is basic in working out policies and tactics to oppose and destroy it. It would hardly be realistic to aim at changing what is an inherent characteristic of imperialism. To think it is possible to change the basic nature of imperialism is a dangerous illusion. What needs to be done is to curb and quarantine imperialist aggressors, to fight to free territories from oppression, and to force imperialism to retreat within its own national boundaries. This is also the pathway to its total destruction.

There are some specific developments that influence U.S. imperialism in this epoch. After World War II it expanded its operations almost at will and became geared to a seemingly endless process of expansion. Today, in some parts of the world the pathways to this expansion are contracting or already are closed. The easy pickings are disappearing and this at a time when unprecedented profits at home and abroad have resulted in massive accumulations of idle capital with no place to go. And with each dollar of unused capital the pressure for imperialist expansion grows.

Viewing the pressures for foreign investment and aggression within the framework of the increasingly ominous signs on the economic horizon of world capitalism, it is clear they point to intensified inter-imperialist rivalries. But, interestingly enough, these factors also increase the pressures for capitalism to seek a way out through closer trade relations with the socialist countries and other parts of the world on a basis of equality and mutual benefit. The national liberation movement will continue along the path of independence, while U.S. forces always and in every country will line up with the most reactonary forces of counterrevolution in the attempt to crush the people's revolutionary movement. Thus we have this paradox in the present stage of U.S. imperialism.

Hubert Humphrey referred to all this as "a bold new form of aggression which could rank in military importance with the discovery of gunpowder . . . 'the war of national liberation'—this new sophisticated form of warfare [which] is becoming the *major challenge to our security." (Italics mine.)* In this logic, the victim of the robbery when he resists becomes a "major challenge" to the security of the thief. The time when nations and peoples permit themselves to be robbed and enslaved is fast becoming past history.

The struggle against imperialism does not proceed smoothly from one victory to the next. There are setbacks, there are moments when the forces of anti-imperialism must absorb past experiences. As it is with all phenomena there are ebbs and flows. It is necessary to take careful note of these developments. But it is just as important to be conscious of the overall direction. There have been setbacks in Ghana, Congo, Sudan, Greece, Spain and in other specific countries. But they have not reversed the overall trends— they have not changed the basic nature of the epoch. These are short-term shifts and should not lead us to confuse what are the surface waves on a body of water with the direction of its flow.

To quote from Lenin:

Here we have important historical epochs; in each of them there are and will always be individual and partial movements, now forward, now backward; there are and will always be various deviations from the average type and mean tempo of the movement. We cannot know how rapidiy and how successfuly the various historical movements in a given epoch will develop, but we can and do know *which class* stands at the hub of one epoch or another, determining its main content, the main direction of its development, the main characteristics of the historical situation of that epoch, etc. Only on that basis, i.e., by taking into account, in the first place, the fundamental distinctive features of the various "epochs" (and not single episodes in the history of individual countries), can we correctly evolve our tactics. Only knowledge of the basic features of a given epoch can serve as the foundation for an understanding of the specific features of one country or another.[2]

In this light, we can readily see that the crisis of imperialism has greatly sharpened all relationships. Although the dangers of world war have increased, the forces of imperialism have not gained new strength. The dangers have increased but the opportunities for victories have also greatly increased. This is the two-sided nature of most critical moments.

We all know the penalties of underestimating the strength of a foe. But we also know what it means not to see his weakness, not to see the opportunities for struggle. Without creating illusions about U.S. imperialism, it is necessary to see both sides; it is ugly, aggressive, but it is over-extended, it is in deep crisis.

A cancerous growth reaches a point of crisis. Imperialism, the cancer on human society, has reached a crisis point. There is only one fundamental cure for it. If a surgeon does not cut out the roots, the growth will reappear. The roots of imperialism are in the system of capitalism. It is here where the surgery must take place. This is the epoch of the crisis of imperialism, the epoch of anti-imperialist surgery. Once the cancer is removed, the human society can build a healthy body called socialism, a body in which the greedy drive for private profits has been removed. Once this is removed the human race can settle down and work full time on turning the fruits of science and technology toward the good of all.

Almost one century ago, Karl Marx noted:

> The discovery of gold and silver in America, the extirpation, enslavement and entombment in mines of the original inhabitants, the beginning of the conquest and looting of the East Indies, the turning of Africa into a warren for the commercial hunting of blackskins, signalized the rosy dawn of the era of capitalist production.[3]

Since these words were written capitalism has entered its im-

[2] V. I. Lenin, "Under a False Flag," *Collected Works,* Vol. 21 (Moscow: Progress Publishers, 1964), p. 145.

[3] Karl Marx, *Capital,* Vo.l 1 (New York: International Publishers, 1967), p. 751.

perialist stage and other new features have developed. But it has lost none of its traditional butchery, none of its "rosy," blood-stained history. And in the van of this bestial heritage has marched U.S. imperialism. The destruction of imperialism is a precondition for social progress.

1972

PART ONE

*Emergence of U.S. Imperialism
to the Center of World Imperialism*

I

TRENDS IN AMERICAN CAPITALISM
DURING THE PAST HALF CENTURY

1. Overall Pattern

The French have a saying: "The more things change, the more they remain the same." (*"Plus ça change, plus c'est la même chose."*) To complete the thought one must add: "The more things seem to remain the same, the more they in fact are changing." By itself the expression does not encompass the significant new developments that have occurred in American capitalism over the last half century; nevertheless, it does convey one side of the basic reality, namely, the growing stranglehold over the economy, the nation, the people, and, especially, the increasing exploitation of the working class by finance capital.

Capitalism has changed but it remains capitalism. The changes were inevitable and predictable. The changes are momentary solutions to problems, but they dig the inevitable grave for capitalism. The changes are beneficial to a narrowing sector of the capitalist class. They are solutions at the expense of the people.

There is no returning to the old capitalism. There is no way one can escape the tentacles of monopoly capitalism in the United States. Dropping out is an illusion. One can drop out from the struggle against monopoly capitalism but one can not escape its clutches. There are only two choices. One can become a willing slave or one can unite with the majority who are the victims of monopoly oppression.

Capitalism has been a miserable failure for the U.S. working class. Between World Wars I and II output per man-hour in manufacturing doubled, vastly increasing corporate profits at the expense of the workers, while unit labor costs, a measure of wages and salaries to the capitalist class, declined by 40 percent—all according to conservative government data—and similar trends have continued since that time. Since 1957-59 labor's share of production in manufacturing has declined by over 25 percent while capital's share has increased correspondingly.

While labor's share of production has been declining, the share of taxes paid by workers has been greatly increasing. In the 1940s workers paid only one-third of all federal income taxes. Today the situation has been more than reversed: 70 percent of all federal income taxes are paid by workers. In 1970 the farm population was the lowest on record, less than one-third the size of 1920, as agricultural workers and small farmers have been driven out by the monopolies which have vastly increased their domination. Between 1959 and 1964 alone the number of large farms with $40,000 in sales increased by 40 per cent while the number of small farms declined by 30 percent.

And the overall impact of capitalism today on the population as a whole has been catastrophic. In 1950 there were 55,000 heroin addicts. Today there are 560,000 and this is only a small percentage of the millions who resort to various types of drugs (cocaine, etc.), and other types of escape from the realities of "people's capitalism." Between 1955 and 1968 the number of known mental patients has doubled as millions of people today have been beaten senseless by imperialism's life style. And in only seven years from 1962 to 1969 there was a 100 percent increase in the number of murder victims—those who have been butchered by the cannibalism of our system.

Capitalism remains capitalism but the changes are preparing the foundation for socialism. The huge production complexes are more suitable for a planned economy. The increased role of the state has more meaning for a society in which the public organizes plans and controls production through a state apparatus. The changes within capitalism result in a socialization of production. The scientific-technological revolution is new proof that capitalism is a social and economic system suited for a period of life now being bypassed and that only socialism can turn this leap in science to the benefit of society as a whole.

The changes will continue. The changes that have taken place in the last half century are indicative of the changes to come. The same processes will continue. The crises will deepen. The need for revolutionary change will become more urgent.

By the end of the 19th century, the power of the big corporations had been established, the domination of finance capital had been achieved, and with the U.S. invasion of the Philippines in 1898, U.S. capitalism's "graduation" to the imperialist stage had become an incontrovertible fact.

The aftermath of the first imperialist world war was crowned by the achievement of the Bolshevik revolution, and the birth of the first socialist state in history ushered in the general crisis of world capitalism. As a result of the general crisis the economies of most of the major imperialist powers faced a series of crises. Greater use of the government to bail out the monopolies and repress revolutionary movements was required by the ruling classes. The era of state-monopoly capitalism, a feature of imperialism noted by Lenin,[1] became especially pronounced. And in the United States, state-monopoly regulation, as an instrument to save capitalism, became particulary necessary during the Great Depression when U.S. capitalism suffered its worst economic crisis.

In the imperialist stage of its development four main interrelated developments in U.S. capitalism have been apparent: 1, the growth of finance capital which has permeated all of these developments; 2, new features of state-monopoly capitalism, particularly its military impact on the nation; 3, the emergence of the scientific-technological revolution as a new productive force; and 4, the growing export of U.S. capital resulting in the U.S. dominated multi-national corporations.

2. Growth of Finance Capital

Stimulated in particular by the scientific-technological revolution

---

[1] "Imperialism—the era of bank capital, the era of gigantic capitalist monopolies, the era of the development of monopoly capitalism into state-monopoly capitalism—had demonstrated with particular force an extraordinary strengthening of the 'state machine' . . . ." V. I. Lenin, *The State and Revolution* (New York: International Publishers, 1971), p. 29.

by which certain highly specialized tasks could be accomplished by small companies, there may have been a small real growth in the total number of businesses over the past five decades; however, their overall importance to the economy has diminished. Superficially, it appears that there was a large increase. Thus in 1918 there were 1,708,000 businesses in operation while in 1968 there were 11,672,000, but fully 10,130,000 consisted of proprietorships and partnerships which tend to be the smallest of small business. The population in 1918 was 103,203,000 while in 1968 it was 200,619,000. In 1939 there were 470,000 corporations but in 1968 there were 1,542,000.[2] However, these figures are very misleading because of the widespread use of dummy corporations and businesses as tax dodges for the concealment of actual profits by the plutocracy.[3] Most of the small companies are in retail and service fields.

Under monopoly capitalism the existence of small businesses reaffirms the position of the monopolies which stand above the mass of non-monopolized businesses and obtain the super-profits. Hence, it is not surprising that while there may have been a real increase in the number of corporations, the share of the national wealth owned and controlled by the monopolies has vastly increased, worsening the relative position of small business. The concept of "People's Capitalism" is a myth.

Thus the former chief economist of the Federal Trade Commission in testimony before the Senate Subcommittee on Antitrust and Monopoly stated in November, 1969:

You may recall that I testified before this Committee in 1965 that, should post-war trends in aggregate concentration continue, by 1975 the 200 largest manufacturing corporations would control 2/3 of all manufacturing assets. Unhappily, we have reached this level ahead of schedule. Today the top 200 manufacturing corporations already

[2] U.S. Department of Commerce: *Statistical Abstracts of the United States, 1971,* pp. 5, 459; *Historical Statistics of the United States, Colonial Times to 1957,* p. 570.

[3] "Another device for income splitting, thus obtaining lower taxes, is to establish many corporations in place of one. In one of many instances a finance business split into 137 corporations to avoid $433,000 of taxes annually, and a retail chain divided itself into 142 corporations to avoid $619,000 annually." Ferdinand Lundberg, *The Rich and the Super Rich* (New York: Lyle Stuart, Inc., 1968), p. 343.

control about 2/3 of all assets held by corporations engaged primarily in manufacturing.[4]

In fact, the 100 largest corporations today have a greater share of manufacturing assets than did the 200 largest in 1950, the year Congress passed the Celler-Kefauver Act supposedly designed to stop the trend toward concentration. And the top 200 corporations today control the same share of assets held by the 1,000 largest in 1941, the year the Temporary National Economic Committee (TNEC) issued its last report to Congress recommending an investigation of corporate economic power.[5]

Even more revealing are developments in the American plutocracy, the rule of the wealthy, particularly the financial oligarchy that dominates the nation's economy. There are now 90 families each of which owns a personal capital of at least $75 million. Of these, 36 families make up the "old core" of the financial oligarchy in the sense that their fortunes, although greatly increased and totaling far more than the others, were amassed prior to the 1929-33 crisis. These include such names as the Rockefellers, DuPonts, Mellons, Fords, and Morgans. More than half of the wealthiest families, however, make up a new generation of the American plutocracy; their fortunes were amassed almost exclusively between the 1930s and the 1950s, and include such names as Getty, Kaiser, Dillon, Moody, Sloan, Kettering and Pratt.

There is only one source for these riches. Every last nickel comes from the blood and sweat of workers. The values these sums represent are values produced by workers. They are the stolen products of exploitation. Whether the old rich or the newly rich, they are rich because they are thieves.

Never in the history of the United States have new multimillion fortunes grown as rapidly as in the last 25 years. In conditions of the scientific-technological revolution, those who were the first to get into new industries and utilize the monopoly of their patent rights made their fortune faster than others. But again, science and patent rights by themselves are not a source of profits. In the

---

[4] Cited in Center for Study of Responsive Law ("Nader's Raiders"), *The Closed Enterprise System,* Vol. 1, pp. 12-13.

[5] Center for Study of Responsive Law, Vol. 1, p. 13.

hands of private corporations they are a means of greater exploitation, and therefore of greater profits. In addition, while the old wealth was accumulated at a time when the role of the state in the U.S. economy was small, the new fortunes are a natural product of state-monopoly capitalism including the growth of the military industrial complex. Furthermore, with the growth of U.S. imperialism since World War II there was an expansion of U.S. capital abroad which resulted in the receipt of enormous profits to the capitalist class.

Thus one-third of the new multimillionaires grew up in the oil and gas industry where U.S. holdings in the Middle East are a vital part of the economic structure of U.S. imperialism while the remainder has been amassed mainly from various sectors of the manufacturing, construction, and mining industries other than oil and gas, particularly aircraft, electronics, and chemicals[6]—industries where the application of science and technology as well as the federal dole of prime military contract awards have been most pronounced.

In 1966 each of the 400-odd members of the top financial oligarchy had a declared annual income of $1 million or more but at that time there were 71.8 million wage and salaried workers, including managerial, engineering, technical and office personnel, whose per capita annual earnings averaged $5,500. In fact, in 1953 less than one percent of the population owned over one-quarter of all personal wealth in the United States,[7] and this situation has greatly worsened since that time. Today the same one percent now own over one-third of all assets, and 200 corporations now do over 50 percent of all business in the United States. Thus Lenin's words about the abyss between the handful of multimillionaires and the millions of working people are vividly confirmed by the reality of U.S. imperialism.[8]

Carrying on the tradition of the old plutocracy, whose capital long ago became fully intertwined with and integrated into the

[6] Based on S. Menshikov, *Millionaires and Managers, Structure of U.S. Financial Oligarchy* (Moscow: Progress Publishers, 1969), pp. 55-6.

[7] Robert J. Lampman, *The Share of Top Wealth-Holders in National Wealth, 1922-56* (New Jersey: Princeton University Press, 1962), p. 202

[8] See, for example, V. I. Lenin, *Imperialism, The Highest Stage of Capitalism* (New York: International Publishers, 1971), p. 29.

main financial groups, most of the vultures of profits in the new plutocracy have become part of the existing system of financial conglomerates which dominates the country.

Lenin defined finance capital as

... the bank capital of a few very big monopolist banks, merged with the capital of the monopolist associations of industrialists. . . . The concentration of production; the monopolies arising therefrom; the merging or coalescence of the banks with industry—this is the history of the rise of finance capital and what gives the term "finance capital" its content.[9]

In the United States a handful of banks have become the directorate of the imperialist conglomerates.

Under conditions of capitalism the private owners of the means of production exploit the workers through the appropriation of labor they do not pay for. Under monopoly capitalism the private property of a capitalist preserves this main attribute, but at the same time, the finance capitalist, in contrast to the simple capitalist, has a new attribute. The finance capitalist increasingly appropriates not only the labor of the proletariat deprived of the means of production and the mass of small businessmen who subsist on the fruits of their own labor, but also the private capitalist property of a large group of people who are not finance capitalists. Thus, for example, between 1947 and 1971 the amount of corporate stocks and bonds used by the commercial banks for investment purposes rose from about $3.7 billion to $19.4 billion,[10] and currently 47.4 percent of the value of all stock in circulation has been bought up by the banking institutions,[11] compared with 35 percent in the mid-1950's.[12] And most of this is controlling stock. Between 1941 and 1971 the amount of loans by the com-

[9] V. I. Lenin, *Ibid.*, p. 47, 89.

[10] U.S. Board of Governors, Federal Reserve System, *Federal Reserve Bulletin*, November, 1971, p. A24.

[11] By "banking institutions" is meant what is commonly termed "financial institutions": commercial banks, life insurance companies, savings and loan associations, etc., because all of them fulfill the chief, intrinsic, common feature of bank capital, namely, the fulfillment of the function of a loan capitalist, that is, a banker. See S. Menshikov, p. 140.

[12] Victor Perlo, *The Empire of High Finance* (New York: International Publishers, 1957), p. 62; S. Menshikov, p. 161.

mercial banks alone, multiplied 14 times from $22 billion to $318 billion, the latter amounting to about one-third of the total 1970 gross national product. What is not controlled through stocks is controlled through loans. But in 1941 total commercial bank loans only amounted to 17 percent of the gross national product.[13] Thus the banks appropriate a lion's share of the unpaid labor in the form of interest on the loans and profits through direct control via ownership of stocks.

And about 43 percent of all bank capital in the United States is concentrated at 102 of the biggest bank companies which comprise about 0.4 percent of the total number of banking institutions. Of these 102, most are mammoth commercial banks and life insurance companies which constitute the main core of the banking segment of American finance capital. One-half of all bank capital in the United States is held by 300 of the biggest banking institutions comprising 1.3 percent of the total.[14]

The merging of industrial and banking capital is a feature of the overall development of monopoly capitalism. This merger has given rise to a top level corporate-banking syndicate with unprecedented powers. It has a power of veto over all economic matters. It is the political boss over all two party politics. It is the decisive force behind the whole state-monopoly capitalist structure. I.T.T. got its Nixon Administration to approve a new merger for itself and it is paying half a million dollars of the expenses of its Republican Party convention. The syndicate usually has its candidates run for president of the United States on both Republican and Democratic Party tickets.

The financial-industrial syndicate places corporate profits as the only important item on the list of priorities. The most signifi-

---

[13] *Federal Reserve Bulletin,* November, 1971, pp. A20, A70; *Economic Report of the President, 1971,* Table C-1.

[14] S. Menshikov, p. 147. Since all banking institutions attract the money savings of the population as a whole, the increased domination by finance capital has resulted in its greater use of the savings of the working class and its allies for profit-making purposes. In 1917 there were approximately 30,000 banking institutions but by 1971 this had diminished to about 15,000. Their capital, however, increased more than 590 percent from $150 billion in 1929 to over one trillion dollars in 1971. *Historical Statistics of the United States from Colonial Times to 1957,* pp. 623, 672; *Federal Reserve Bulletin,* November, 1971, pp. A20, A39-40; Menshikov, p. 144.

cant development of the last 50 years is that the syndicate has taken over. It is a syndicate of imperialism.

As in the case of sick industries such as munitions, nationalization of the banks, including the life and property insurance companies, the investment and savings banks, savings and loan associations, etc., is long overdue. Why should private institutions make high profits for handling money that is issued by the government? But such nationalization must be democratic in content, subject to real control by the majority of the people, and, in practice, must divert profits from the monopolies to the working class and its allies. Only under socialism can this be fully guaranteed.

Under the conditions of the general crisis of world capitalism the gold standard was abandoned. The banking system, via the Federal Reserve, was allowed to emit billions of dollars of worthless paper notes, without regard to the actual requirements for the circulation of commodities, mainly for the purpose of financing imperialist wars and monopoly-priced goods. The capitalist class as a whole, and particularly finance capital, was able to redistribute the national income in their favor at the expense of the working class. This is the real meaning of the inflation that has spiraled to gigantic dimensions both in the United States and throughout the capitalist world.

The Federal Reserve System is the chief organ of state-monopoly regulation and control of the banks. It has the power to issue billions of dollars of debt, chiefly in the form of bonds and other securities, which, due to acounting practices, show up as reserve assets in the commercial banks, and become the base upon which these banks can increase their loans and investments. In 1939 the public debt purchased by the Federal Reserve amounted to $2.5 billion. By 1970 it multiplied 25 times to over $62 billion.[15] When the commercial bank increases its reserves it is then entitled to make loans up to approximately six times the amount of increases in its reserves. These banks get their currency as needed from the Federal Reserve System itself. The Federal Reserve System has become an instrument of the banking thieves. It manipu-

---

[15] *Federal Reserve Bulletin,* May, 1971, p. A 42.

lates interest rates and the amounts of money in circulation in a manner that best suits the corporate-banking syndicate.

Those who rely on relatively fixed incomes—pensions, public and private, recipients of social security and public assistance benefits, as well as people who depend on their savings—in other words, the working class, the poor and super-exploited Afro-Americans, Chicanos, Puerto Ricans, and Indians, find that their incomes buy less and less. Also, their incomes do not rise sufficiently. But the big capitalists are successful in increasing their profits faster than their costs. The result is an ever increasing rate of exploitation.

Illustrative of this redistribution of the national wealth in favor of the rich, are a few facts hidden in a study of inflation by an ardent admirer of the capitalist system, Albert E. Burger, which was published by the Federal Reserve Bank of St. Louis, an organ of finance capital.[16] Burger found that the real wealth of common stockholders rose 30 percent in 1964 over 1960 and 8 percent in 1968 over 1964 compared with 9 percent and 4 percent respectively for unskilled workers.[17]

But these figures, which among other defects, fail to take into consideration the effect of the increase in state and local taxes on workers, greatly understate the redistribution of the national wealth in favor of the rich as a result of inflation. Thus, for example, between 1947 and 1970, adjusted for price increases, corporate profits (including amounts hidden in depreciation accounts) increased almost 50 per cent faster than unit labor costs, a measure of wage costs in the production process. And a main reason for the huge corporate profit increase has been the price-hiking by the monopolies which is implied in the phrase "administered pricing" used by economist Gardner Means.

This is not surprising. Karl Marx demonstrated in *Capital,* written over 100 years ago, that workers receive wages about equivalent to their socially necessary means of subsistence,[18] contrary to the claims of admirers of capitalism, including many trade union leaders. Illustrative is the fact that in the United States, as

[16] *Review,* November, 1969.
[17] Based on *Economic Report to the President, 1971,* Tables C-34, C-73.
[18] See, for example, Karl Marx, *Capital,* Vol. 1 (New York: International Publishers, 1967), p. 193.

late as 1970, the Department of Labor budget for a moderate standard of living for a family of four in the urban United States was $205 a week, but in that year the average factory wage in the total private economy was $120 a week, less than 60 percent of the Department of Labor standard

And of course, these figures do not speak directly to the plight of the millions of very poor, especially the super-exploited Afro-Americans, Chicanos, and Puerto Rican-Americans. The magnitude of their grim poverty due to the profit-grabbing of U.S. capitalism is illustrated in the disclosure by a Department of Agriculture report in 1968 which found that one-fifth of the total population, or about 40 million people in the United States, suffer from malnutrition.[19]

3. State-Monopoly Capitalism

The growth of state-monopoly capitalism especially since World War II, and the alignment of class forces since that time, has resulted in a massive shift in the federal tax burden from the capitalists to the workers. This is shown by the fact that while corporate income taxes increased over 30 times from $1 billion in 1940 to $33 billion in 1970, individual income taxes jumped almost 90 times during this period from $1 billion to $90 billion.[20] In addition there has been a massive growth of individual state and local taxes which bear most heavily on workers.[21]

The result has been that the state has become a major means for the appropriation of super profits on behalf of finance capital. In the main it does not do this directly because surplus value is created at the point of production in the unceasing economic war between the worker and the capitalist. In short order a large

[19] U.S. Department of Agriculture, Agricultural Research Service, *Dietary Levels of Households in the United States, Spring, 1965.*

[20] U.S. Department of Commerce, *Historical Statistics of the United States, Colonial Times to 1957,* p. 713; *Fereral Reserve Bulletin,* May, 1971, p. A41.

[21] For example, in fiscal year 1969, 46 percent of all state and local revenues consisted of sales taxes, licenses and other flat charges which hit workers the hardest while only 3 percent consisted of corporate income taxes. *Economic Report of the President, 1971,* Table C-72.

sum of his "take home pay" is taken in federal, state, county and city taxes. A lion's share of these moneys goes back to the monopoly corporations in the form of war orders, tax deductions and subsidies. But it should be noted that the Pentagon, as of June, 1969, directly owned some 202 billion dollars of property in land, buildings, productive equipment, offices, communications facilities, airports and military equipment.[22] This is a huge sum, amounting to one-fifth of the nation's current gross national product. Here the exploitation is more direct. Frequently much of the government-owned plant and equipment obtained by the government largely from the taxes paid by the workers is operated by the monopolies at no or minimal cost to them. Thus economist Robert J. Gordon has found:[23]

. . . a $45 billion treasure chest of plant and equipment which the U.S. government has purchased for the use of private firms since 1940, but which has never been counted as part of the private U.S. capital stock. . . . Even today, 123,000 employees of private firms work in plants and laboratories owned by the Atomic Energy Commission, having a gross book value of over $8 billion. Much of the aircraft and ordnance production for the Vietnam war has been carried on by private firms with government-owned plant and equipment.

Because of the shifting federal tax burden and the monetary policies of the Federal Reserve System, much of the exploitation is indirect, taking the form of robbing from the worker a part of his socially necessary means of subsistence and transferring this amount to the monopolies.

Marx, in *Capital,* demonstrated that even under conditions of competitive capitalism, the worker was exploited thru the appropriation by the capitalist of a surplus value created by the worker. This is a value above and beyond the value of the socially necessary labor time for the production of the worker's means of subsistence. The value of this necessary labor time is paid by the capitalist in the form of wages. Marx also noted that in actual practice the capitalist frequently pays the worker a value below the

[22] Seymour Melman, *Pentagon Capitalism: The Political Economy of War* (New York: McGraw-Hill, 1970), p. 72.

[23] *American Economic Review,* June, 1969; cited in Victor Perlo, "Arms Profiteering," *New Republic,* February 7, 1970, p. 24.

value of his or her means of subsistence.[24]

Under the conditions of state-monopoly capitalism in the United States, this tendency is greatly intensified even though there are pressures in the other direction such as the degree of success of the working class struggles in the fight against super-exploitation by the monopolies and the relatively small tribute that the ruling class siphons off to a section of the workers as a result of its super-exploitation of the workers and peoples of foreign nations.

With the development of state-monopoly capitalism in the United States there have been increasing attempts by the ruling class to regulate the economy. Until 1971 with the establishment of wage-freeze controls by the Nixon-Agnew regime, during the post World War II period, this attempt at regulation has chiefly taken the form of government expenditures. Since 1962, for example, U.S. government expenditures for goods and services each year exceeded $100 billion, and in 1970 reached $200 billion.[25] The projected budget for 1971-72 is about $250 billion.

4. Militarism

But the overriding, dominant effect on the economy by the state, illustrated by the federal borrowing for imperialist war financing, and the ensuing spiraling inflation, has been the military impact.

Absolutely and relatively, military spending in the U.S. vastly exceeds that of any other country. U.S. military expenditures account for more than 40 percent of the world total. It is more than the gross national product of all but six countries. The *U.S. News and World Report* (February 3, 1969) estimated that U.S. military outlays were 2¼ times the combined total of spending by its "allies," including 14 NATO countries, seven SEATO countries and others, such as Japan which have mutual defense treaties with the U.S. In relation to gross national product, U.S. military expenditures are over 9 percent compared with 5

[24] Karl Marx, *Capital* (New York: International Publishers, 1967), Vol. 1, pp. 186-94, 314-15.

[25] *Economic Report to the President, 1971,* Table C-66.

percent for Britain, 4 percent for West Germany, and 1 percent for Japan. U.S. military expenditures amount to almost 1.5 times USSR military expenditures even according to U.S. government figures, and 1.3 times the entire military expenditures of the Warsaw pact countries.[26] The military orientation has significantly distorted economic developments. It tends to further unbalance that which is already out of kilter.

A special group of war industries has developed, stimulated by the scientific-technological revolution, such as aerospace and electronics whose main customer is the Pentagon, and whole areas have become heavily dependent on these industries. In Southern California military dollars account for about 25 percent of the economy, in Connecticut for 20 percent. Cities like San Diego, Seattle, Baltimore and many others are heavily dependent on military production. Research and development, whether in universities or in private corporations, is almost wholly financed by the Pentagon and is oriented toward military technology.[27]

The mushrooming of this vast military establishment maintained in both war and peace is a post World War II phenomenon. Before World War II, military spending was relatively much smaller than today. In the years between the Civil War and World War I direct outlays as a rule did not rise above 1 percent of the gross national product. The same is true of the twenties. In 1929 the figure was 0.8 percent, and in 1939 it was 1.3 percent. Since World War II, on the other hand, such expenditures have run in the neighborhood of 10 percent, rising during the Korean War to 14 percent.[28]

However, this represents much more than a mere quantitative jump in military spending; it represents an extremely important qualitative change. Imperialism, as Lenin noted, breeds war, and with this it breeds militarism. Thus the rise of militarism has been a characteristic of imperialist powers generally, the United States no less than others. But the post World War II militarization of

[26] Hyman Lumer, "Imperialiasm and Militarism," *Political Affairs*, June, 1970, p. 40; U.S. Arms Control and Disarmament Agency, *World Military Expenditures, 1970,* Table II.

[27] Lumer, *ibid.,* p. 41.

[28] Lumer, *ibid.,* p. 41.

the economy is something new in U.S. history. It represents the establishment of a permanent war economy, a modern counterpart of the Hitlerian Wehrwirtschaft of the thirties. And basic in the picture are the giant monopolies, outposts of finance capital, the main recipients of military contract awards, which profit from the foreign aggression, from the manufacture of arms, and from the interest on the government bonds through whose sale much of the military operation is financed.[29]

5. Scientific-Technological Revolution

As a result of the scientific-technological revolution which refers to the totality of the major scientific discoveries of the last 20-30 years in mathematics, physics, chemistry, biology, cybernetics, and in other technical fields of knowledge, science has become a direct productive force of society. The formerly insignificant sphere of research and experimentation has itself developed into a sector of social production no less important than industry or agriculture.

6. Regional Patterns

While Midwest and North Central U.S. traditionally has been the industrial heartland, and continues to be so, the scientific-technological revolution has stimulated the shift in manufacturing by finance capital to the Southern and Western states, while the importance of manufacturing as a whole to the economy increased from 25 percent in 1929 to 30 percent in 1967.[30] Especially effected by changes in air transport and weapons technology, the South and West have become main areas of missile, aerospace and atomic energy development, as well as of the military establishment. Because of this industrial growth, the growth of the working class in the South and West is producing the decisive force for combat against the ultra-right, reactionary

[29] Lumer, *ibid.*, p. 44.

[30] U.S. Department of Commerce, *1967 Census of Manufactures, General Summary*, p. 3.

Dixiecrats and Republicans who have counted among their strongholds the South as a whole and sections of the West Coast. The acceleration of the all-national character of the working class across the entire nation is thus being achieved with the aid of the scientific-technological revolution.

At the turn of the century the Middle Atlantic and East North Central states, which include New York, Pennsylvania, Ohio and Illinois, accounted for 60 percent of all U.S. manufacturing employment, but by 1970 this had fallen to 47 percent. Together with the New England states, these regions accounted for 60 percent of all U.S. capital expenditures in manufacturing in 1947, but for only about 50 percent in 1967.[31] U.S. manufacturing employment in New England fell from 20 percent of the U.S. total at the turn of the century to 6 percent in 1970.[32] States such as Massachusetts and New Hampshire now abound with ghost towns, the remnants of textile and garment manufacturing centers that have fled South.

In contrast, manufacturing employment in the Southern states increased from slightly over 15 percent in 1899 to over 25 percent today. By 1967 over 30 percent of all capital expenditures in manufacturing was in the South. The most dramatic rise in factory employment has been in the Western states which accounted for 4 percent of the total in 1899 but by 1967 this had jumped to 12 percent. All told, in 1899, 52 percent of U.S. manufacturing employment was in the Northeast, 29 percent in the North Central states, 16 percent in the Southern states, and 4 percent in the Western States. In 1967 the percentages were 30, 33, 25, and 12 respectively.[33]

7. Agriculture

Aided by the new developments in technology, such as the increased mechanization in agriculture resulting in the mass migration

[31] Based on *General Summary*, Table 7; U.S. Department of Labor, *Manpower Report of the President, 1971,* Table D-2.

[32] *General Summary,* Table 7; *Manpower Report of the President, 1971,* Table D-2.

[33] *General Summary,* p. 5.

of millions of Afro-Americans from the farmlands of the South, the monopolization of agriculture has proceeded at a rapid pace. In 1970 the farm population of 9,712,000 was the lowest on record, less than one-third the size in 1920, while the average size per farm multiplied 2.5 times during this period. In the five year period between 1959 and 1964 the number of very large farms with $40,000 in sales increased by 40 percent, the number of small farms with $50-$4,999 in annual sales declined by almost 20 percent, while those in the $2,500-$4999 subcategory declined by 28 percent.[34] Needless to say, the federal government's farm support program, based on agricultural output is a bonanza to the farm monopolies which individually account for the largest amounts of farm produce.

The government farm income support program which awards farmers on the basis of agricultural output is a bonanza to the large monopolistic farms. In 1970 the federal government spent $5 billion in "farm income stabilization" mainly for "farm commodity support, price support and supply adjustment programs." But about half the total value of farm sales goes to the largest farmers who sell $40,000 or more worth of farm products annually.[35] Most of the small farms are weighted down with mortgage payments.

New impetus was given to the historic transformation of Black Americans from an agrarian to a proletarian people by the technological revolution. Hastened by World War II, this process has turned the majority of Afro-Americans into working people residing mainly in the great industrial centers of the South and North. Chicago today has a population which is over 32 percent Black compared with 22 percent in 1960. The steel city of Gary, Indiana is 53 percent Black compared with 38 percent in 1960, and this has become typical of industrial centers.

All the problems of work, living, health and education fall with particular force on the Black and Spanish-speaking population crowded into stifling ghettos. To these are added the crushing burdens of racist discrimination in employment, upgrading of

[34] *Statistical Abstracts, 1971*, pp. 572-3.

[35] *Statistical Abstracts, 1971*, p. 574; Office of the President, *The U.S. Budget in Brief, Fiscal Year 1972*, p. 36.

skilled, higher-paying jobs in industry, the professions and in all walks of life.

8. Impact on Finance Capital

The high cost of using the new technology has given new impetus to the merging of corporations into immense concentrations of capital. In the first six months of 1969 no less than 2,815 corporate mergers took place, an increase of 65 percent over the same period of 1968, while the amount of merged corporate assets among major corporations during the last decade has been greater than in the previous 40 years.[36]

9. Impact on Working Class

Although the scientific-technological revolution opens the possibilities for untold wonders for all of mankind, finance capital, whose only real interest is maximum profits, withholds use of the new technology if maximum profits can not be obtained. One example out of many that can be chosen is the automobile. Notes auto expert, Ralph Nader: "Auto manufacturers, with a corporate brutality unsurpassed since the railroads in post-Civil War days, have been steadily rejecting a life-saving technology that could reduce our annual highway death toll from 40,000 a year to 12,000 or less."[37] And of course, a main cause of this wanton slaughter of human life which each year almost equals the total number of American soldiers who have died as a result of the Vietnam atrocity is the way the auto monopolies construct the vehicles. Thus a study headed by a Harvard scientist, Dr. Buxbaum, has found that mechanical failure of automobiles may be responsible for as many as one-half of the motor vehicle deaths that occur in this country each year. [38]

The cost to the worker of the revolution in technology in the

36 *Statistical Abstracts, 1970,* p. 483.

37 Ralph Nader, "Fashion or Safety," *The Nation,* October 12, 1963, p. 214.

38 *The New York Times,* April 20, 1966.

heartland of world imperialism has amounted to more intensification of labor and exploitation, less real take-home pay, less time with his family and more members of his family compelled to seek work. And the cost can also be counted in workers' mental and physical health.

Between 1958 and 1969 alone, the disabling work injury rate in manufacturing rose by 30 percent. For munitions workers the rise was 90 percent. For rubber and plastic workers where the introduction of synthetics has been greatly stepped up, the rise was 100 percent. In the primary metals industry which includes blast furnaces and steel making the rise was over 70 percent. In aluminum rolling and drawing the increase was 157 percent. But for the bankers there was a one percent decline in the work injury frequency rate during this period, and the federal government bureaucracy showed a 17 percent decline.[39] Ironically a Labor Department news release (April 8, 1968) has noted:

If you're a logger, your chances of escaping an accident on the job are not so good. If you're a banker, they're extremely good.

As a banker, you can expect 217 accident-free years on the job. In other words, you could work five lifetimes before suffering a disabling injury.

As a logger, however, the statistics give you only 8 years before being felled by an occupational accident. A coal miner has 11 years.

Thus finance capital uses the scientific-technological revolution to intensify its murderous exploitation of the working class. The epoch of the scientific-technological revolution in the United States has brought about the sharpest increase in the rate of exploitation of the working class in all recorded history, increasing by more than 70 percent since the end of World War II.[40]

Heart disease death rates in the United States rose from 510.8 per 100,000 in 1950 to 521.4 in 1966. Mental patients increased from 715,000 in 1950, to 1,248,000 in 1966. The 1966 figure is 121 percent above that for 1935, a year in the midst of the economic crisis. At the same time, the cost of hospital daily service charges in 1967 was eight times higher than in 1940; while all

---

[39] Based on U.S. Department of Labor, *Handbook of Labor Statistics, 1971*, Table 153.
[40] Based on *General Summary*, p. 26.

medical costs taken together rose 2.7 times in the same period.

The deterioration in workers' health and working conditions occurs amidst the deterioration of the physical surrounding and living conditions. Decay and blight spread unabated in working class neighborhoods, slums, and ghettos; the physical plant of the public schools undergoes continuing rot, while pollution of air and water by industry and the internal combustion engine has cast a monstrous poisonous pall of growing danger to human life over all industrial centers.

Certain industries have been decimated by automation and mechanization, leaving workers homeless and jobless, forcing them to relocate and take lower paying jobs. This is particularly true in coal mining where the continuous mining method has slashed employment by 73 percent between 1940 and 1966. But between 1947 and 1969 productivity in the coal mining industry has more than tripled with a greater than 25 percent jump between 1962 and 1966 during the Vietnam war period.

In the professions, teaching machines, hospital beds controlled by the patient, automatic analyzers in health laboratories and information storage and retrieval systems are doing some of the work formerly done by teachers, nurses, medical technologists, and librarians. Repetitive and less skilled aspects of professional jobs continue to be taken over by machines or lower skilled workers.

The high-speed machinery responsible for much of the increase in productivity and profits in the post World War II period has increased the noise level to unbearable levels in factories. Workers increasingly have reported greater nervous and psychological fatigue because of the care and accuracy needed in handling expensive equipment as well as performing detailed, terrifically fast-paced operations. In places where a few workers are able to handle a considerable number of machines or labor-saving devices there are numerous complaints of isolation and resentment at the monotony of work. Fear of displacement by the installation of automated machinery has also affected the mental health of workers.

Jobs which are typically low-skilled and routine have been a prime target for elimination by automation. Although unskilled and semi-skilled jobs remain, the number is not sufficient to satisfy the heavy demand of 6 million youth aged 16 to 24 years who entered the labor force between 1960 and 1969.[41] In such industries as insurance and banking, the relative loss of low skilled jobs has been especially hard on young women and other inexperienced and untrained workers, and has helped keep teenage unemployment at Depression levels.

The enemy is not the new automated machines. The enemy is the class that takes the benefits, the values produced by the machines as its private profits. The enemy is the corporation that uses the automated equipment to speed up the production lines to the breaking point. The enemy is a social system that discards the workers who are displaced by machines.

Finance capital has used the scientific-technological revolution and its consequent unemployment and speedup to intensify its divide and conquer policy, pitting whites against Blacks, young against old, men against women. By reducing the relative number of unskilled jobs heretofore required by American industry, American capitalism is thus adhering to a policy of economic genocide against Afro-Americans and other U.S. racial minorities.

While the scientific-technological revolution has reduced the number of heavy industrial workers relative to the working class as a whole, it has not changed the basic nature of the working class as the single most exploited class and the grave digger of capitalism. In fact the working class has become more proletarianized during the period of the scientific-technological revolution than ever before. Including professional and technical workers and bottom-rung managers, in 1958 the number of wage and salary workers comprised 80 percent of the employed civilian population but by 1971 this had topped the 85 percent mark.[42]

And, of course, the working class has not been sitting idly by in the midst of this onslaught by finance capital. The period 1965-69 witnessed the greatest strike wave in any other five year period beginning with 1950 both in amount of time away from the job due to strikes and in number of strikes.[43] In 1970 there were more

[41] *Manpower Report of the President, 1971,* Table A-6.
[42] Based on U.S. Department of Labor, *Employment and Earnings,* February, 1971, pp. 139, 148, 151; February, 1972, pp. 150, 159, 162.
[43] *Economic Notes,* October, 1970, p. 8.

strikes than in any year since the end of World War II.[44]

Proof of the failure of finance capital's policy of using the scientific-technological revolution to drive the workers into submission is seen in the increase in strike activity of government and professional workers including teachers, many of whom owe their jobs to the developments in science and technology. In 1955, for example, there was an average of 1,000 government workers on strike, but in 1970 this figure had grown to 334,000. The backbone of the strike wave, however, has been and continues to be the most highly organized workers in basic industry. A typical news release from the Department of Labor is illustrative (March 7, 1969):

> About 320 stoppages, involving 182,000 workers, began in January, 1969. These were the highest levels for the month since 1953. . . . The largest stoppage affected the petroleum refining industry; the second largest, which continued from the previous month, involved longshoremen in Atlantic and Gulf Coast ports. The remaining large strikes were reported at the Louisville and Nashville Railroad, McDonnell-Douglas Corp. and the Westinghouse Electric Corp., and two at General Motors Corp. plants.

And working class militancy continues despite the wage-price controls heavily stacked against labor that have been imposed by the Nixon-Agnew regime even though there has been a reduction of strike activity in the face of this all-out attack against labor led by the government.

10. Impact on Business Cycles

The scientific-technological revolution and militarily dominated state-monopoly capitalism have altered the previous pattern of the U.S. capitalist production cycle. Before World War II, the depression phases of the production cycle were extremely deep and protracted. In the 1921 economic crisis, for example, industrial production fell by 29 percent in one year's time. And in the Great Depression, industrial production declined by almost 50 percent.[45]

---

[44] U.S. Department of Labor, *Monthly Labor Review*, December, 1971, p. 125.

[45] Based on Board of Governors, Federal Reserve System, *Federal Reserve Index of Industrial Production*, October, 1943, p. 45.

Since World War II, economic crises have not been so sharp and severe in terms of production, although their impact on workers continues to be catastrophic. But the accumulation of unresolved contradictions in the capitalist economy opened up new areas of crisis such as in the financial sphere which had not seen such intensity since the Great Depression, e.g., the bankruptcy in 1971 of such a leading U.S. corporation as the Penn Central railroad. And in the epoch of the deepening general crisis of capitalism the possibility persists of a spillover from these areas of crisis to the production sphere itself, and of a great general economic crisis of the magnitude of the Great Depression of 1929-33.

11. Natural Resources and Raw Materials

Finance capital has turned the fruits of the scientific-technological revolution into poisons which pollute and destroy our environment and fail to solve the nation's requirements.

With only 6 percent of the world's population, the United States uses one-third of the total world production of energy. Under present conditions it will be necessary to triple available energy supplies from coal, oil, natural gas, hydropower and nuclear fuels, and on this basis the U.S. will have depleted its present low-cost energy reserves within the next century or less and all foreseeable conventional energy resources within 150 to 200 years.[46]

Amidst the immense water pollution by the monopolies which will require up to $45 billion to rectify according to a government study, the nation's water requirements may well exceed the current supply during the next decade. The main air pollutants released each year total 125 million tons according to a 1966 report by the National Academy of Sciences. These pollutants cast a killing pall over all of the nation's cities where most people live. Automobiles, trucks and buses made by the transportation monopolies are the major emitters of carbon monoxide, oxides of nitrogen and hydrocarbons. The nation's factories are the next greatest offender, and the burden of principal pollutants emitted by these and other sources is expected to double by the year

[46] *The American Federationist,* January, 1969, p. 14.

2,000.[47]

The noise pollution which is particularly catastrophic to factory workers subjected to unbearably loud levels continues unabated. Dr. Vern O. Knudsen, a pioneer in acoustics, has recently stated that "the loudest noises to which we are exposed have increased some 20 decibels in the past 20 years and if this rate of increase continues for another 20 years, they will become lethal."[48]

The United States has been forced to import industrial raw materials, and at an accelerated rate during the past 20 years. Of the 36 most important industrial raw materials, U.S. manufacturing industries are self-sufficient in only ten, notes Dr. Raymon Ewell of the State University of New York. The United States must import all or part of the requirements of 26 materials.[49]

Dr. Ewell finds that more reliance on foreign imports of basic raw materials with the ensuing balance of payments problems may result in an actual decline in the U.S. standard of living within the next two or three decades. He notes that while the raw materials position of the United States is declining, that of the Soviet Union is becoming stronger. Since 1955 it has exceeded the United States in known mineral and forest resources. Of the 36 major industrial raw materials, the Soviet Union is self-sufficient in 29 and needs to import only seven.[50]

The Soviet Union now greatly exceeds the United States in such basic mineral resources as petroleum, natural gas, iron ore, aluminum ore, lead/zinc ore, chromium, and manganese, in addition to the other vital materials such as gold, platinum, and diamonds.

12. Export of Capital and Growth of the Multi-national Corporations

Of great significance has been the huge proliferation abroad of

[47] *The American Federationist,* January, 1969, p. 9.
[48] Harry Conn, "The Ear Pollution Noise," *The American Federationist,* October, 1971, p. 13.
[49] Raymond Ewell, "U.S. Will Lag USSR in Raw Materials," *Chemical and Engineering News,* August 24, 1970, p. 42.
[50] Raymond Ewell, p. 42.

U.S. branches and subsidiaries of home corporations. The output of these today amount to some $200 billion or about five times current U.S. exports, a truly massive invasion of U.S. capital abroad, exceeding the value of exports of all industrially developed countries in the world in 1969.[51] And the results of this foreign investment has been the loss to American workers of over a million jobs. All of the largest corporations have significant capital outlays abroad. All have become "multi-national," which is the current phrase denoting their increased foreign capital outlays and economic imperialism.

In the past 25 years, particularly in the 1960's these U.S.-based multi-national corporations have set up about 10,000 new foreign subsidiaries, mostly in manfacturing. Seventy per cent of all multi-national corporations is now owned by U.S. capital. And about 50 percent of what is called American foreign trade is about equally divided between exports and imports among U.S.-based multi-national corporations[52] and between their foreign licensees, patent holders, and other foreign companies with which they have an arrangement.[53] Thus a minimum of 25 percent of American foreign trade now consists of inter-company transactions.

In the past the foreign subsidiary of a major U.S. corporation was more or less an appendage. Today they represent a new higher stage in the capitalist division of labor and are more indispensable

[51] See United Nations, *Monthly Bulletin of Statistics,* October, 1971, p. 111.

[52] "Though globe-girdling business concerns are at least as old as the British Empire's East India Company, the multinational corporation is largely a phenomenon of the post-World War II era, and its emergence has become spectacular in the past decade. There's no universally accepted definition, but the multinationals generally are agreed to be those companies having production facilities in many lands, having access to capital world-wide and having a "global outlook" among their managements. That encompasses some 200 U.S.-based multinationals, including General Motors, RCA, IBM, Dow Chemical and other blue chips." *The Wall Street Journal,* January 13, 1972.

[53] Nat Goldfinger, "Multinational Companies and their Effect on the American Economy," *Developing Crisis in International Trade, 1970* (Washington, D.C.: Industrial Union Department, AFL-CIO, 1970), p. 10.

to the monopolies.[54] Thus while the U.S. monopolies, with finance capital at their helm, have become more international and mobile they have also become more vulnerable and penetrable, more susceptible to lasting defeats by the anti-imperialist forces all over the world.[55]

The increased capital expansion abroad by finance capital has provided it with additional super-profits with which to bribe certain sections of the working class, particularly top trade union leaders. But even if all of the profits from capital investment abroad each year were used in this manner, they would total only about 5 percent of the wages and salaries that are paid out in the United States.[56] And of course, finance capital makes these profits primarily only for its own use, using only the leavings for bribing labor leaders and workers.

The operation of the law of the uneven development of capitalism has been unfavorable to U.S. capitalism during the decade of the 1960's following the post World War II recovery of the European capitalist powers and of Japan. Growth rates of a number of capitalist powers, particularly Japan and West Germany have far outdistanced the United States. Symbolic of this trend has been two key events in 1971: the devaluation of the U.S. dollar for the first time since 1933 and the balance of payments deficit of some $18-23 billion which is several times the amount of any previous annual deficit in the post World War II period. Furthermore, the U.S. balance of trade deficit which refers specifically to the export and import of merchandise of some $1.5 billion for the first three quarters of 1971 alone, was the worst ever in all U.S. history. Thus the net of internal and external contradictions continues to close in on U.S. imperialism.

[54] International Telephone and Telegraph (ITT), notes its annual report: ". . . is constantly at work around the clock—in 67 nations on six continents," in activities extending ". . . from the Arctic to the Antarctic and quite literally from the bottom of the sea to the moon . . ." *The American Federationist,* August, 1970, p. 3.

[55] "On the foreign front, the specter of expropriation haunts the multinationals, especially in Latin America." *The Wall Street Journal,* January 13, 1971.

[56] Victor Perlo, *American Labor Today* (New York: New Outlook Publishers, 1968), p. 12.

The direction of the processes is clear. They lead to a further growth of the monopolies toward a greater concentration of economic and political power in the hands of the rich, to a further increase in the rate of exploitation, to prolongation and sharper class confrontation. The trend is toward increased militarization. Monopoly domination increases the danger of reaction and fascism.

These trends will continue as long as capitalism will be on the scene. But these trends also create the objective factors that stimulate mass struggles. They help to create a counter force. It is this force led by the working class that will not only resist capitalism, but will exchange it for socialism.

The past half century has been a period of industrial growth for the monopoly corporations. But it has been growth at a great cost for the working class. It has been a period of growth but it has also been a period when the processes of decay set in. We are now beginning to see the effects of this decay in the crises— the crises of the cities, the ghettos, the crisis in education, transportation, medicare. It is evident in the collapse of the dollar as a world currency. In the period ahead it is the crises that will become the dominant factor in our capitalist reality. The collapse of the capitalist world's post-war structure signalizes a new stage in the overall crisis of world capitalism.

1972

2

FAR-FLUNG EMPIRE OF U.S. IMPERIALISM

"You don't really know why we are so concerned with the far-off southeast corner of Asia. . . . All of that position around there is very ominous to the United States, because finally if we lose all that, how would the free world hold the rich empire of Indonesia?"

The words "the free world," is a Madison Avenue alias for monopoly corporations. In plain words what President Eisenhower was saying is we must have a government policy that makes it possible for the corporations to steal the natural resources from the people of Indonesia.

These words were spoken by President Eisenhower in 1956, and not so many years later, with the help of the CIA, the anti-imperialist coalition that supported the Sukarno government of Indonesia was smashed. For the moment the powerful Communist Party of Indonesia, an effective force for social progress, was destroyed. This catastrophe, in which hundreds of thousands were slaughtered in cold blood, opened the floodgates for imperialist penetration into Indonesia. The forces of imperialism carefully prepared the soil for counterrevolution. They used the backwardness of parts of Indonesia. They used the difficulties of an underdeveloped nation. They took advantage of nationalism, of religious differences and the fact that most of the people were farmers, serfs, petty artisans, civil servants and professionals. The working class is small. The imperialist forces secretly prepared the cadre of the counterrevolution. They corrupted the military leaders. They used the weaknesses of the Sukarno forces and the errors and weaknesses of the Communist Party of Indonesia.

Many of the leaders of the Communist Party of Indonesia followed the ideas of Mao Tse-tung. They repeated far out radical phrases but in life followed right opportunist policies. The extreme left phrases were demagogically used by the right wing forces to mobilize the masses against the Sukarno government. The Party did not build a solid political following on the basis of a militant struggle against all exploiters, including a struggle against the exploitation of the big land owners. The Party was satisfied with repeating abstract anti-imperialist slogans. Instead of relying on mobilizing masses for struggle, it played around with Mao's idea that all power comes from the barrel of a gun. The enemy became a "paper tiger." The masses were not ideologically prepared for a class struggle. The enemy used these weaknesses. They destroyed a people's government that came to power in the sweep of the national liberation movement. The C.I.A. used the various forces of imperialist counterrevolution. The C.I.A. spearheaded the counterrevolution because the monopoly corporations in the United States wanted the "rich empire of Indonesia." They won a momentary victory. In August of 1970, the *Magazine of Wall Street* stated:

Every square mile of exploration territory on and around Indonesia's main islands of Sumatra, Java, Borneo, the Celebes and West Irian has now been nailed down, primarily by American oil companies. These corporations included Atlantic Richfield, Caltex (Standard Oil of California and Texaco), Union Oil Co. (engaged in a 'joint' Japanese consortium venture), Cities Service Co., Gulf Oil, Continental Oil and Getty Oil Company. The area accounts for over 50 percent of all crude oil production in the Far East.

Thus within a period of months the oil parasites of imperialism stripped the mineral riches of "that far off southeast corner of Asia" about which Eisenhower was so concerned. That is the very meaning of imperialism. U.S. imperialism has followed the same pattern of conquest in country after country.

This global highway robbery takes place behind the sign "the free world." It is a free world for the corporations who plunder, but it is slavery and oppression for the people who are the rightful owners of these resources provided by nature. It is in support of this global piracy that the government spends 80 billion dollars a year on the military. The C.I.A. and the State Department are all instruments of imperialist looting.

Imperialism in its basic essence does not change but it is forced to operate in a changing world. It is forced to make tactical changes, structural changes, changes of emphasis. Imperialism tailors its policies to fit the moment in a specific country or continent. For example, while the U.S. corporate investments have increased in all continents and in all industries, there is a significant new emphasis towards investments in the heavy manufacturing areas of Europe and Canada. This is a relative shift away from the areas of only raw materials, and of low wages. U.S. imperialism feels more secure from the danger of expropriation in areas of higher industrial development. Much of these new investments go into the expansion of U.S. owned corporations and subsidiaries. It is also evident that U.S. imperialism's capacity to apply the new process of the scientific-technological revolution most profitably is in the industrially developed countries. An exception to this trend is the increased investments in the hard to find minerals of Africa. But this shift brings with it new contradictions. It is a big factor in widening the gap between the industrially developed countries of capitalism and the developing countries. There are also serious political repercussions.

The application of the new technology in the underdeveloped countries would entail larger investments. So U.S. imperialism wants it both ways—to use the new technology to penetrate and extract huge profits from the industrially developed areas, and to continue holding the underdeveloped areas economically under developed, politically oppressed while it robs them of their natural riches.

Thus the share of developed capitalist countries in direct U.S. investment rose from 48.3 percent in 1950 to 67.2 percent in 1967, and the share of developing countries fell from 51.7 percent to 32.8 percent, with Latin America showing a drop from 38.8 to 20.1 percent. These are percentages of investments that have continued to grow.

U.S. private direct investment in Europe multiplied 4.7 times between 1957 and 1968, it is higher there than in any other continent. Europe accounted for 16.4 percent of all U.S. direct private imperialist investment abroad in 1957, but by 1968 this had almost doubled. Canada remains the largest single area for U.S. investment, accounting for 30.0 percent of the total in 1968, while Latin America's share dropped from 31.9 percent in 1957 to 20.1 in 1968. The imperialist investments in Asia remained relatively stable.

U.S. investment in Africa multiplied 4.0 times between 1957 and 1968, showing the second highest increase next to Europe. U.S. imperialism has important designs for Africa. Between 1963 and 1968, U.S. private investment in Africa grew at an average annual rate of 14 percent, with mineral and petroleum development accounting for nearly three-fourths of the total. This is the reason that one administration after another supports the racist governments of countries like South Africa and Rhodesia, in spite of the growing popular movement against such policies. The interests of the Rockefellers, DuPonts and Morgans come first. The racism in Africa, as it is in the United States, is profitable for the Rockefellers and DuPonts.

Studying these figures, it can be seen that Asia and Africa, which in 1968 accounted for 11.3 percent of all U.S. direct private foreign investment, nevertheless accounted for 42.6 percent of all U.S. profits from direct foreign investment abroad in 1969! No wonder U.S. imperialism is so concerned with being a "Pacific power."

Latin America, Asia and Africa accounted for over two-thirds of all U.S. imperialist profits from foreign countries in 1969.

U.S. imperialism now aims, above all, to penetrate the manufacturing industries, which account for 50 percent of all its private direct investment in Western Europe. Between 1958 and 1968, this sector of investment increased 202 percent, compared with 191 percent for trade, 91 percent for petroleum development and 136 percent for the all-industry average. In 1968 the manufacturing investment was greatest in Western Europe and Canada.

The output of U.S. subsidiaries and branches outside the United States is now well over $200 billion, or about five times U.S. exports abroad.

The significance of this investment shift goes beyond the facts and figures. It has resulted in a new internationalization of capital and has set off new economic and political processes. The specific industrial and financial empires in West Germany, Japan, France and Italy, which are active partners, and have tied their fortunes to the U.S. dominated monopolies, are emerging on the top of the heap in their respective countries. Many are partners in U.S. imperialist ventures in Asia, Africa and Latin America. This is a two-edged sword. Besides penetrating the economies of those capitalist countries, the shift is opening the doors for U.S. penetration of their respective colonial setups. When a U.S. corporation or a bank obtains an interest in a West German, Japanese or a French corporation, it also becomes a partner in their foreign colonial operations. When they can not enter through the front door they are going through the side door. Through this means U.S. capital takes full advantage of the special arrangements— preferred tariff treatment, etc.—existing between these countries. And it is largely a one-way street. The U.S. colonial empires are not open to the foreign partners. These joint imperialist-colonial ventures are adding a further component to neo-colonialism. And they are a growing threat to the capitalist interests in their respective countries which are not affiliated with multi-national corporations.

These new alignments have given U.S. imperialism great political leverage in the affairs of industrially developed capitalist countries. But they are also creating new tensions, new contradictions, between U.S. imperialism and the other industrially developed capitalist countries. They lead to complicated trade wars. Goods produced by U.S. owned corporations overseas compete with goods produced in home plants frequently *their own* home plants.

Because of the high rate of profits, corporations build new plants, furnishing them with the latest production processes in foreign countries in preference to enlarging or modernizing their domestic plants. The greater part of the production facilities of some corporations are in foreign countries. Over 52 percent of the assets of Standard Oil of New Jersey is in foreign lands. The United States is not a formal member of the Common Market, but U.S. corporations are in the very heart of its production and markets processes.

Moreover, with most of its resources for reseach and development siphoned off into military application, U.S. imperialism is losing ground in the race for the economic stimulus afforded by the scientific-technological revolution. As noted by U.S. Pentagon Director of Defense, Research and Engineering, John S. Foster, Jr., Japan's growth rate in technologically intensive manufactured products was 22.5 percent during 1955-65, compared with 3.9 percent for the United States and 8.4 percent for West Germany. Says Foster: ". . . our past national position of technological leadership is being eroded and is being challenged seriously by both our friends and our potential enemies."

Nevertheless, U.S. imperialism is a wily and cunning foe and accounts for over 40 percent of world capitalist industrial production. It remains very powerful and dangerous. In Latin America, for example, it resorts to greater behind-the-scenes use of local police forces to achieve its aims of domination as well as to achieve overall increase in its own military activities. It assumes the function of gendarme for world imperialism; it is the world center for counterrevolution, supplying a major service in the international capitalist division of labor for combating the forces propelling the world revolutionary processes.

U.S. imperialism banks on the use of the scientific-technological revolution to serve its interests and to this end spends ten times as much as its nearest West European rival, Great Britain. Technological-scientific breakthroughs have also set off economic and political processes. We are now seeing this phenomenon only in its initial stage of development. A technological-scientific breakthrough means the appearance of new materials, synthetics, plastics, fibers and fabrics. Formerly the might of the monopolies was determined by the scale of their raw materials resources, but scientific and technological progress has reduced the consumption of nature's ready to use raw materials per unit by 75-80 percent in value as compared with the pre-war level.

"In 1969 in the United States the consumption of major raw materials per net ton of pig iron produced resumed a downward trend that has persisted during most of the last two decades," notes the American Iron and Steel Institute (*Steel Facts,* July 1970, p. 3), and some experts now predict that with the development of composite materials of extremely high stiffness and high-strength filaments bonded together with a soft plastic matrix, the volume of steel, aluminum and wood currently used in structures today may be reduced by as much as 50 percent in the near future.

Thus the technological and scientific revolution rather than bringing new hope for progress has become a new disaster to the industrially underdeveloped countries of the world, and in large measure, to workers in capitalist countries. In the hands of the big monopolies the new technology turns into a nightmare for the workers under capitalism. It raises the question of job security as a critical problem. And it has become a decisive new factor in creating an ever wider gap between the industrially developed countries and those which are either newly liberated or still under the heel of world imperialism.

The substitute materials developed—such as the new families of plastics and fibers—have generated a new problem for countries that exist mainly by selling natural raw materials. This problem will become ever more critical.

The scientific breakthroughs have resulted in the development of new industries and new concepts of production. These technological advances are more readily adaptable to the production processes of the industrially developed countries. Thus the scientific breakthroughs have become an important factor in shifting the export of capital to the industrially developed zones of world capitalism. All in all, these factors have resulted in a new imperialist squeeze, cutting back on the use of raw materials and on capital expenditures in the less developed areas. This has greatly sharpened the contradictions between imperialism and the oppressed nations and peoples, adding new difficulties to their ability to develop their economies and to raise their standards of living.

To break out of the bonds of imperialism, the developing countries not only face the task of building an industrial base, but they must break the scientific and technological stranglehold of imperialism. This adds a new dimension to many questions. Can this be done while following the path of capitalist development? It raises in a new way the significance and the role of socialist power that can match and surpass the technological levels of the United States. The socialist countries not only become the source of capital for industrial development of the developing countries, but also the source for the new technology.

The position of newly liberated and other underdeveloped countries whose economies are tied to imperialist powers continues to deteriorate; their public debt has multiplied while interest rates have increased at a prodigious rate. Much of the "aid" and "loans" goes now into paying the interest on past loans.

Thus the capitalist path of development for the newly liberated countries is a tightening noose—economically and politically.

If imperialism penetrates wherever the profits are the highest, it does not necessarily give up its exploitation in other areas.

The leap in U.S. penetration into the very heart of European capitalism is partly traceable to the scientific revolution. Today, U.S. capital in Western Europe controls 80 percent of the production of electronic computers, 50 percent of the output of transistors, 15 percent of radio and TV sets and 95 percent of the market for integrated circuits. U.S. monopolies dominate the auto industry in Europe. Seventeen of the biggest industrial corporations own more than two-thirds of the total U.S. investment in West European countries.

American business, however, has penetrated even more deeply into key sectors of the Canadian economy—holding one-half the total assets of Canada's largest companies, 90 percent of the automobile industry, 80 percent of rubbber, 75 percent of chemicals, 65 percent of electrical apparatus—as well as over 50 percent of the mining, smelter, petroleum and natural gas industries.

U.S. imperialism designs its policy to fit each specific situation. Canada is a next door neighbor extremely rich in national resources. U.S. imperialism has an iron grip on Canada's industry, raw materials and sales outlets. U.S. corporations have built factories in Canada. But most of them are related to the production process in the United States. It is a special system that robs Canada of its riches, uses Canada's labor force, blocks the development of an independent capital base. It is a system of imperialist extortion. The corporations use the leverage to cut wages, they use it to extort special tax and tariff concessions.

The technical revolution brings with it new patterns of penetration; the big profits are in the areas where the new technology is both an instrument of penetration and opportunity for high profits. All this has greatly affected the nature of world capitalist formations, facilitating the rise of what Lenin called "super-monopolies . . . a new stage of world concentration of capital and production incomparably higher than in the preceding stages." Worldwide conglomerates, worldwide industrial and financial empires are in a new stage of development; the new technology grinds industries based on outmoded techniques to the ground. This has become a powerful threat, forcing capitalist formations into world conglomerates. The "super-monopolies" pool their efforts and create world areas for their private exploitation. The revolutionary forces must take cognizance of the changing patterns and develop tactics in the struggle against these monster conglomerates.

In its December 1971 issue *Fortune* reports that the total production of multi-national corporations outside of the countries in which they are based has now reached an annual figure of $450 billion dollars. This is more than the gross national product of any country outside of the Soviet Union and the United States. Of the total, $200 billion is the share of the United States-based corporations. This is the fastest growing sector of the U.S. economy. Since 1950 it has grown at the rate of 9 percent a year.

This development is also an outgrowth of the technological breakthrough. But the chickens of the multi-nationals are coming home to roost. There is a growing resistance to their economic storm trooper tactics in most of the capitalist countries. In the United States there is a growing demand for closing the tariff and tax loopholes now enjoyed by these corporations.

We must take into account, too, that new contradictions and divisions within world capitalism are in process, giving new dimensions to its uneven development and necessitating the redistribution of the loot among imperialist countries.

These important changes have profoundly affected the struggle over the question of what path the liberated countries should take—socialist or capitalist. No matter what aspect of the problems of their relationship to imperialism one studies, the increasing bankruptcy of capitalism as a solution to their problems becomes apparent. The emergence of state-monopoly capitalism, the scientific-technological revolution in the control of monopoly corporations, neo-colonial methods and solutions—none of these can resolve their problems. What does become clearer and clearer to the new millions is that capitalism in the imperialist stage of its development has become the main obstruction to human progress. The two opposite world processes will continue, each in its own direction and orbit. The contradictions of imperialism will continue, and capitalism as a system will continue to decay.

At this stage of capitalist development it is almost impossible for a newly independent country to succeed along the capitalist path and also to remain politically and economically independent. Imperialist governments, or private corporations are not going to support or help build the industries of independent countries. The new countries face the same problems as the new corporations. It is almost impossible to launch a new corporation in the field of production, or a new farm. There are no available sources for the prohibitive initial capital that is needed because of the new level of technology.

The forces propelling the world revolutionary process are, on the other hand, growing and maturing. The historic transition from capitalism to socialism is a reality; the world will turn more and more to socialism as the solution to its problems. Socialism has opened the gateway to mankind's new stage of social existence. People in the newly liberated countries and those still under exploitive imperialist rule will accelerate their struggle against all forms of oppression. As the class forces become more differentiated, confrontation will become ever more unavoidable in the capitalist countries. The development of state-monopoly capitalism will of necessity continue to sharpen class relationships.

The results of these processes can be seen in the events of the past few months; they are clearly evident in countries like Peru, Egypt and Libya. The message comes loud and clear in the election of a Marxist as the President of Chile. The same processes are moving West Germany to consider more realistic policies in its relationships with its socialist neighbors. The world revolutionary process will successfully complete its historic march because it is on the right side of history.

The economic gap between the countries of imperialism and the countries it has been and is oppressing keeps getting wider. The gap between the class of capitalist exploiters and the U.S. working people also keeps getting wider. The name of this game is exploitation and profits—that is what imperialism is all about.

It is true that the cost of empire building has gone up, but the burden of this cost does not come out of the profits of the monopolies who are the beneficiaries. The transfer of these costs onto the backs of other sectors—especially the working class and the poor—is peculiarly a function of the state within the state-monopoly capitalist setup. The transfer is effected mainly in the form of ever increasing taxes and through inflationary price spirals. It is estimated than an average U.S. family pays $2.65 per day in taxes and inflation to keep the wars of U.S. imperialist aggression going.

The officially reported unemployment rate in 1971 was 5.9 percent the highest in 10 years. The jobless rate among the

Black people is at Depression levels and stands at about twice that for whites, while the teenage unemployment rate is over 14 percent. In some cities (Seattle, Detroit, Houston, Los Angeles, New York and Chicago) unemployment rates of 30-50 percent for youth are not uncommon. Women comprise slightly more than one-third of the employed labor force, but more women are unemployed than men, and unemployment has been rising among professional and technical workers and even among business executives.

In 1971, output, in terms of percentage of capacity in manufacturing, dropped to 74.5, which at an annual rate was the lowest since the Korean War. The stock market has been in one of its steepest slumps of the post-World War II period. For the first time since the 1929 depression, a major corporation, the Penn Central Railroad, for instance, accounting for 20 percent of all tonnage carried on the railways, went bankrupt, and others are teetering on the brink.

State and local government bonds for school construction and other vital community needs find few buyers, and schools all over the country are closing down or curtailing services due to lack of funds.

Thus the militarization of the economy intensified by the Vietnam war has resulted in a permanent war economy similar to Hitler's *Wehrwirtschaft* of the 1930s. This has greatly augmented the role of the state in the economy—it accounts for one job out of every three. In real terms the Nixon administration has reduced social welfare spending to an even lower level than during the previous administration. In a throwback to the Hoover days, it has declared open economic warfare against the poor.

Interest rates have been at their highest peaks since the Civil War and, during the cold war period, consumer debt, which amounted to $6 billion in 1945, has skyrocketed to $137.2 billion in 1971—equivalent to over 30 percent of the gross wages paid to all workers in the private economy. Military spending in the current fiscal year is greater than that of the same period in the preceding year, and the Pentagon, waiting in the wings, has 130 weapons-development projects costing over $140 billion.

The economic recession in the United States, which had continued despite massive government deficit spending and expansionist monetary policy to stimulate investment in an election year, had profound reverberations throughout the capitalist world. The Organization for Economic Cooperation and Development (OECD), a Marshall Plan by-product, reported that the real output for capitalist countries rose by an annual rate of only 1.75 percent in the first half of 1970, sharply down from 5 percent in 1969 and 5.5 percent anually during 1958-67.

As a result of the Vietnam war, the United States finds itself in increasing political isolation throughout the world. In contrast to previous wars, U.S. imperialism has had to bear the brunt of the cost of this one alone. Today the U.S. share in world capitalist industrial output has dropped from 56 percent in 1948 to 44 percent in 1969. U.S. domination of the "club" of 100 super monopolies of the capitalist world has shrunk from 79 in 1956 to 67 in 1968. The U.S. share of world capitalist exports has fallen from 25 percent in 1948 to 13 percent in 1969. Foreign capitalist inroads into the U.S. home market have been growing at a far faster rate than U.S. imperialist penetration abroad. In 1948, the profit on U.S. investments abroad was 4.8 times the foreign profit on investments in the United States. In 1968 it was down to 2.6 times. In contrast, foreign holdings in the United States have grown by 55 percent over the past five years, compared with a 35 percent growth in U.S. investments overseas.

From the above it is obvious the foreign policy of imperialist aggression cannot be separated from domestic developments. The 80 billion dollar military budget is an imperialist war budget. This is a heavy millstone affecting all domestic processes. It is directly responsible for the crisis of the cities, the crisis of welfare, crisis of education, medicare, transportation, and the crisis of housing.

The imperialist policy of aggression warps moral standards. It feeds on the ideology of racism and chauvinism. The policy of imperialism is immoral, unjust and criminal. A nation permitting such policies will have to pay the price.

1972

3

U.S. IMPERIALISM IN THE WORLD

United States imperialism is the headquarters of world imperialism. It is aggressive and brutal. But the West German, Japanese, British, Portuguese and Italian imperialists are not benevolent, misguided powers. They have not shed their basic plundering and pillaging nature. They are not innocent dupes. They are partners, even if junior partners, in the crimes of imperialism. They are not just "militarists." They are imperialists. In each of these countries the acid test of anti-imperialism is how one places the question and fights against the imperialism of one's own country.

The world imperialist structure has been like a pyramid standing on its sharp point. The pyramid has become unstable. There are cracks in its walls. This pyramid has been and is dominated by U.S. imperialism. This fact has carried with it built-in contradictions. These inter-imperialist contradictions have reached the point where they are now important factors influencing world events.

The dream of the "American Century" is turning into a U.S. imperialist nightmare. It was based on a myth. The attempt was a hundred years too late. After the successes of conquest following the Second World War U.S. imperialism became dizzy with success. Anything it touched turned to profits. But the roots of the new problems were evident already in the post-Second World War structure. As we know, the struggle over redivision of their ill-gained holdings is also an inner law of imperialism. This is the cause for wars between them. Even periods of peace are periods of struggle for redivision. This struggle results in an uneven development of capitalism. One makes a gain at the expense of the other. It has become a law of uneven decline and decay.

World War II resulted in a number of historic changes in the correlation of world forces. The conflict acted as a trigger that released pent up forces that had accumulated and gathered force beneath the surface. These shifts generally accelerated the world revolutionary process and pushed the general crisis of capitalism to a new stage.

If World War II had been only a war between opposing imperialist blocks, the peace would have been an imperialist peace. The loot would have shifted from one imperialist lion to another. What made the qualitative difference, of course, was the world role of the Soviet Union. It proved to be the main force for destroying the most reactionary feature of imperialism, the fascist axis. But it did much more, it became the stimulant, the arsenal and the armed guard, the force that held back the incursions of imperialism while those of national liberation and socialism marched to new victories in one country after another. This was as true for Asia as it was for Europe. The post-World War II years resulted in a qualitative leap, a decisive shift in the balance of forces against world capitalism. In all this the role of the Soviet Union was the most decisive factor.

Thus World War II resulted in the smashing of the military machine of the fascist powers and set the stage for a struggle that undermined the old colonial powers. In quick succession 70 countries won political independence. But it also resulted in a redivision of the imperialist holdings. The old imperialist powers were forced to retreat—they did not change their inner nature but they did retreat—a development that resulted from the shift in the balance of world relationships. But it also provided the United States with an opportunity to move in on its allies and vanquished foes. The weakened industrial capitalist states, because of the war, needed capital for postwar reconstruction. U.S. capitalism was glad to be of service but for a price. The price was the right to plunder and loot. It was extortion.

Each redivision, however, sets the stage for a new struggle between the imperialist powers. Far from being an ordinary shift, World War II resulted in the remaking of capitalist world relationships: in place of an axis or alliance of capitalist powers, there was a capitalist world in which one country became the dominant force.

Thus U.S. imperialism became top dog. NATO, SEATO, and CENTO were set up as instruments of U.S. domination over the non-socialist world just as they were instruments of aggression against the socialist world. They became tools of imperialism against the forces fighting for national liberation. Following this major reshuffle, for a period, world imperialism settled down to a shaky existence of accommodation to the reality of U.S. domination. During this period United States capitalism was further bolstered by being the world banker for the postwar reconstruction as well as by the accelerated scientific-technological revolution. This has given the industrial capitalist powers a relatively long period of favorable economic development. But it was a distorted development. It was a development with new contradictions.

The capitalist countries needed capital for postwar reconstruction, and the United States had huge accumulated stockpiles of unused capital. These factors, and the relative stability of U.S. internal conditions, were the underpinnings of a period of economic expansion in the camp of world imperialism. U.S. monopoly capital, to be sure, took full advantage of the situation. It was piracy without precedent. It evolved the Marshall Plan, which based assistance to other capitalist countries on their readiness to make further "concessions" and a readiness to accept a position of increased subservience. World capitalism became a junior partner to U.S. imperialist operations. Thus U.S. capitalism became the "savior" of world capitalism, the "guardian" that stole and robbed while it protected. What it really did was to save world capitalism for U.S. imperialism. As a result it became a power with the largest imperialist holdings in world history.

These relationships of accommodation to one-nation domination, however, carried within them the seeds of their destruction. When the other capitalist countries, having overcome the ravages of war, entered into a period of growth and expansion, the U.S. share of production and trade began to decline. A chronic balance-of-payments deficit set in, and the dollar lost its charmed status. Antagonisms in the imperialist camp grew sharper and sharper.

To this situation, U.S. imperialism reacted with a new offensive. Not satisfied with grabbing industrially underdeveloped areas from the old colonial empires, it moved into the capitalist world's industrial centers, penetrating them as a virus penetrates the host cell. Initially the penetration took the form of buying into industrial and banking firms. They needed money for expansion. But slowly the "host" firms have become junior partners. Some have been completely swallowed up. The decisions are made by the parent Executive Board operating from Wall Street. Thus, for all the major industrial capitalist nations, U.S. imperialism has become a rival at home, a domestic foe, as well as a foreign competitor.

U.S. corporations are now the direct exploiters of tens of millions of workers in all of the leading capitalist countries, directly challenging the existence of millions of small and medium-size businesses. They have become a major factor in banking, manufacturing and retail merchandising in all of the capitalist countries. In these operations, they are willing to work with local partners-in-crime. But they want silent, permissive partners.

U.S. production in countries abroad has now become a major factor in its operations. U.S.-owned production facilities in other countries annually turn out 200 billion dollars worth of products that are sold abroad, while U.S. exports from its domestic factories amount to 43 billion dollars. One firm, the General Electric Corporation, has production facilities in over 100 countries of the world; for an increasing number of corporations, domestic production has now become smaller than production abroad. While opening up new factories in other countries General Electric and others are closing factories in the United States.

During the early postwar years this new twist in inter-imperialist relations, and the struggle for a redivision of holdings generally, did not emerge as clearly as they do now. Postwar reconstruction and other factors tended to ease the contradictions arising from one-nation domination. But we are now in a new stage; the centrifugal force generated by bourgeois national interests are increasingly weakening the threads that hold the capitalist world together; U.S. imperialism is losing its place on the pinnacle of the pyramid.

As U.S. imperialism sinks into the quagmire of its aggression in Indochina, the centrifugal forces within the capitalist world gain new momentum and the pressures for redistribution become ever greater. The element of inter-imperialist contradictions that was one source of U.S. strength in the postwar years has now turned into its Achilles' heel. The growing trend towards United States isolation and the rising tide of anti-U.S. sentiment in the world are fed by these contradictions.

There have been other moments in history when specific national interests have overshadowed the overall world class interests of capitalism. This does not mean that worldwide class interests have disappeared. For the moment the contradictions within the global class have greater force than the appeal for worldwide class unity.

All this takes on a qualitatively new significance when seen in the context of, and in relation to, the existence of the world system of socialism and the rising national liberation movements. In fact, divisions among the capitalists show themselves over the question of how they should relate to the reality of the present-day world revolutionary process. How to use the new divisions that arise from the new situation in the capitalist world, has emerged on a new level for all forces of the world revolutionary process.

This new factor must of necessity be taken into account in a new way in the struggle against imperialism in general, and especially in the struggle against U.S. imperialism. Centrifugal forces are forces of dispersal and when they tend specifically to pull away from the U.S. imperialist orbit, their overall effect will be to weaken the position of imperialism in general.

All tactical questions must be reexamined to see how they fit into the strategic framework that emerges from these developments within the pyramid of world imperialism.

The problems of U.S. imperialism in all parts of the world are affected by these new inter-imperialist contradictions. Because of the heroic struggles of the people of Vietnam, the "conquest" that was to be effected by a few puppet troops with a few U.S. "advisors" has turned into a major war, with serious internal consequences. It is a war U.S. imperialism cannot win. It is the most unpopular war in our country's history. U.S. capitalism has extracted profits out of all past world conflicts, but the cost of the Vietnam aggression cannot be transferred to "allies." There are sections of monopoly capital who are angry not because it is a destructive war, not because it is killing Vietnamese or Americans but because successive administrations have permitted it to become "an American war" with the United States footing the bill. In the Middle East war of aggression United States imperialism has an ally—Israel.

In spite of the military setbacks and temporary loss of territory suffered by the Arab countries, Israel or U.S. imperialism have not come out with a strengthened position in the Middle East. The main aim of the aggression was to overthrow the anti-imperialist governments of Syria and Egypt. This did not happen. Instead, the act of aggression did much to expose to millions the nature of U.S. imperialism and it became more isolated than ever. Israel will be forced to give up the stolen territories. The oil monopolies are not at all happy with the present stalemate.

This specific phase of relations within the capitalist world has direct significance in the struggle to drive the forces of U.S. imperialism out of Vietnam. The inability of the United States to acquire other major partners of crime in its aggression is a reflection of the centrifugal pull within the imperialist camp, and it has been a very positive factor internally in the struggle against the war.

It is also now quite clear that the momentum resulting from the postwar reconstruction and the subsequent economic boom has run its course in the United States, and that the periods of economic slowdown tend to get longer. Capitalist countries find increasingly that they cannot rely on the expansion of capital outlays from the United States as a means of resolving their difficulties. The inherent weaknesses that hitherto were somewhat covered up by the postwar boom are now coming into sharper focus.

The centrifugal force pulling away from the U.S. imperialist orbit is having a number of important side effects. Trade relations are sharpening, and there is a slowdown in the rate of consumption of a number of raw materials and a corresponding decline in their prices. This has broadened and deepened the anti-imperialist movements in countries that are dependent on imperialist buyers. It has especially affected miners and workers in the countries exploited by imperialism in South America, Africa and Asia. The number of strikes in foreign U.S.-owned industries is on the increase.

These developments are propelling new class elements into political and economic struggles and adding a new quality to the national liberation struggles. They are also sharpening the relations between capitalist countries; the unprecedented struggles now going on in the United States over tariffs and trade restriction are only the initial skirmishes.

The rise of the "production abroad" features of U.S. imperialist operations has had a number of effects; it has developed new divisions within monopoly circles and added a new quality to the development of world financial and industrial empires. The growth of runaway overseas industrial facilities is causing great turmoil in the U.S. domestic economy.

In addition to the 200 billion dollars worth of goods produced in monopoly-owned industries in foreign lands and sold abroad, an appreciable part of their output is shipped back to the United States to compete with U.S.-made products. Some reactionary trade union leaders are going in for tariff and import restrictions, but more important, this development has engendered a new high in international consciousness among U.S. workers, opening up completely new opportunities for approaches to international trade union unity. This is not a movement under the leadership of the State Department or the CIA. Wherever U.S. trade unions are forced to fight the monopolies with large overseas shops, they are also breaking with the Meany-Lovestone-CIA position on relations with trade unions abroad.

The new level, the new forms of global monopolies call for a new look at forms and priorities of the class struggle. For example, what about new initiatives for worldwide trade union committees of common struggles? What about a world drive to nationalize U.S.-owned industries? Is not the demand for laws limiting foreign capital involvement within any one corporation a basis for broad worldwide campaigns?

There is deep anti-imperialist consciousness here at home; millions feel the policy of military aggression is unjust, while others are convinced it is not in the best interests of our people. Workers go on strike, Black Americans and the poverty-stricken rebel because they know the war policy threatens their meager programs of relief, job-training and the like. The full coercive force of the state machinery has not been able to force the masses into war-supporting patterns of behavior.

And there has emerged a deep conviction—for many, a rude awakening—that the resources, the reserves of the United States are not unlimited. For the majority of the people, the war and its horrendous expenditures for murder are not on the list of priorities. And there is a basis for their broad apprehensions. Putting aside the fact that capitalism always puts as much of the burdens of war as possible on the backs of the people, the truth is that U.S. resources are not unlimited. Because of this, the ability of U.S. capitalism to maneuver both at home and in the four corners of the globe is narrowing down. Because of this, and because of the people's struggles, the ruling circles are facing a dilemma. The cut in foreign aid has already narrowed down the ability of U.S. imperalism to maneuver in certain parts of the world.

The government is spending and borrowing at an unprecedented rate; the national debt and the interest on it are reaching new highs; the federal budget deficit is astronomical; there is an inflationary spiral in prices, taxes and rents. The cost of a bed in a hospital room is now over $100 a day.

The inflation is weakening the competitive position of the United States in the world market. Much of the opposition to the war among certain business and monopoly circles is based on the conviction that U.S. capitalism is losing more in other parts of the world than it can gain in Southeast Asia even if its aggression should succeed. This is not to state that U.S. imperialism is about to collapse, but it is important to understand that there is much more instability than appears on the surface.

To be able to use the division in the ranks of world capitalism it is necessary to understand the centrifugal forces that are in operation. It is necessary to fully understand the new contradictions that arise from the U.S. policies of dominating the capitalist world.

1971

4

THE PATH OF UNEVEN DEVELOPMENT

When there were continents to enslave, the struggle between developing imperialist powers took the form of a rush to establish their political and economic domination over conquered lands. Expansion, acquisition, to take possession, was the imperialist order of the day. But the day came when there were no new continents to enslave. The struggle between the imperialist powers turned to a battle for a redivision of the stolen loot.

Imperialist aggression is an extension of the inherent aggression within each corporation. No imperialist power, as is the case with each monopoly corporation, is ever satisfied with either the rate of profits or the accumulated wealth from past exploitation. When there were no new lands to conquer they fought for each other's loot. This has led to imperialist wars. The countries have gone to war behind slogans of defending "God," "country," "democracy" and "peace," but the real reason has been the corporate interests of each country. It is a sad commentary that people have been and still are seduced and tricked to kill each other in wars in which they had absolutely no self-interest, wars from which they could not gain or win anything, wars that were fought, so one group of thieves waving one flag, could steal the stolen riches of another group of thieves waving another flag. The struggle between the imperialist bandits for redivision goes on. It leads to wars and to an uneven development within world capitalism. It is a law of its development.

After the Second World War U.S. imperialism established its domination over most of the capitalist world. The defeat of fascism was a historic necessity. Different class forces had different reasons for taking part in the anti-fascist struggle. People generally supported it because fascism was a threat to democratic rights. The Soviet Union carried the main burden because fascism was a direct threat to socialism and because fascism was a threat to all concepts of social progress. Some monopoly groups gave their support because German imperialism by using fascism threatened to take over their holdings. This was true for monopoly groups in France and England. But, of course, they did not join in the struggle until their game of using fascist Germany against the Soviet Union had backfired. The monopoly corporations in the United States also joined in the struggle when the game of using fascist Germany backfired and when they were convinced that they had more to gain than lose. Their policy was to save the world for U.S. imperialism.

Being the top dog on the pyramid of world capitalism has given the United States unprecedented advantages. But it has also resulted in unusual commitments, expenditures and counterrevolutions. Everything has not turned to gold. United States domination has not put an end to either the struggle for redivision or to the uneven development of capitalism. For a period the struggle has been muffled, but it has simmered beneath the surface. Some have quietly built their reserves while accepting the domination and protection of the big brother.

In a period when the current of history is generally running against imperialism, a war-oriented economy such as the United States has built since World War II also becomes a factor in the operation of the law of uneven development among capitalist countries. For most of the post-war years the overseas expenditures have annually turned the U.S. trade balance against itself, with a resultant negative effect on the U.S. economy. Thus U.S. imperialism is caught in the vise of its policy of worldwide aggression and simultaneous competition for world markets. It has over-extended itself. It must now either retreat or keep spending billions of dollars to maintain the operation of its more than 3,000 overseas military bases, while its chief imperialist rivals spend relatively small amounts for their military establishments. This is now adding a new dimension to contradictions between imperialist powers. For example, this, among other factors, has drastically changed the position of Japan in the imperialist pyramid. During the past ten years the U.S. industrial growth rate has been about 5½ percent per year; the growth rate for Japan during the past 15 years has been 13½ percent. In the past eight years it rose to 14.7 percent, rising during the past three years to 16.5 percent. In 1960, Japan's industrial, manufacturing output was 20 percent of the U.S. level and 85 percent of the West German level. But in 1968 it was 36 percent of the U.S. level and 157 percent of West Germany's level. Thus Japan has by-passed West Germany and has now become the second industrial producing nation in the capitalist world. As is the case with other capitalist countries the Japanese growth rate is not on solid ground.

This has shifted many of the imperialist rivalries. The contradictions between U.S. imperialism and Japanese imperialism have greatly sharpened; the struggle to return Okinawa was only symbolic of more far-reaching antagonisms between them. It is an antagonism between monopoly interests in their drive for profits.

The growth rate of the capitalist world is closely tied to its relationship with U.S. imperialism. After World War II, U.S. capital investments were helpful to the war-ravaged economies of a number of capitalist countries. Many apologists for U.S. imperialism hailed this "benevolence." They boasted that foreign capital investments coming into an industrially developed country would not have the negative effects of colonial "investments." Life has shattered this illusion; U.S. investment has become a dead weight on the industrial growth rate of these industrially developed countries.

Perhaps no other group of defeated capitalists was so thoroughly at the mercy of U.S. imperialism as the Japanese. Yet while the capitalists of Western Europe felt obliged to open the doors wide to penetration by U.S. monopolies, the Japanese held them at arm's length. They continue to tightly limit U.S. investments, thereby retaining essential control of all major industries except oil and—to some extent—computers. And they are challenging the U.S. grip even in these areas. The figures in billions of dollars concerning U.S. direct investments in the leading countries of imperialism are indicative: Britain, 72; West Germany, 43; France, 20; Italy, 1.4; and Japan, 1.2. These figures are reflected in the growth rate of these countries; generally, the larger the investment, the slower the growth rate.

The 15-year annual growth rates are: Japan, on one end, with a 13.5 percent rate; then Italy with 8.8 percent; West Germany, 6.4 percent; France, 5.4 percent, and Great Britain, with a 2.9 percent rate on the other end.

The industrial growth rate in Japan is closely related to the designs of U.S. imperialism. After the war the United States became an occupation force in Japan. It was able to dictate the terms of the military settlement and the direction of economic and political developments. So the developments in Japan have not been without the agreement of U.S. imperialism. Germany in Europe and Japan in the East have had a special place in the plans of U.S. imperialism. Before the Second World War, including the period when Hitler fascism was in power, the United States armed Germany, and then through loans and gifts built its industrial and military might. The game was to use Germany as the shock troop against socialism, the Soviet Union. It almost worked. Hitler went along with the game but on his own terms. This created divisions in the ranks of world imperialism. The Soviet Union took advantage of these divisions. They signed the German-Soviet treaty. This stripped the gears in the neatly built anti-Soviet machine of world imperialism.

Before the pact the Soviet Union proposed to the United States, England and France an alliance against the Berlin, Rome, Tokyo axis. The offer was turned down. They played the game till the last moment. When the fascist troops were marching through Europe and the bombs were falling on London, only then did Britain and the United States give up their game of pushing Hitler to fight the Soviet Union.

In Europe the United States has returned to the old plan that failed. The United States has never given up its plans to use Japan against People's China and the Democratic Republic of Korea. U.S. imperialism has never given up its efforts to destroy socialism. While not openly involved, Japan has been and is a base of operation against the people of Indochina.

As is the case with Germany, the U.S. policy in Japan creates contradictions. The ruling circles of Japan go along but they have their own imperialist ambitions. They have become partners in the crimes of U.S. imperialism. But they have used the game plan to build their own forces. Japan has re-emerged as an imperialist power. Japanese imperialism has significantly increased its overseas investments. It has had a policy of hiding and understating the nature of these holdings. But the fact is that its overseas operations have climbed from a total of 94 million dollars in 1960 to 668 million in 1969 and over 3 billion dollars in May of 1971. A graphic illustration of these operations is in Indonesia. Japan was very much involved in the imperialist conspiracy to destroy the people's government of Indonesia. Hundreds of thousands of Indonesian Communists and progressives were slaughtered. For U.S. and Japanese imperialism the defeat opened up new avenues for exploitation. Now the United States has 58 projects with an investment of 528 million dollars. Japanese imperialism has 65 projects with an investment of 259 million dollars. The guess is that these figures are understatements.

Japanese imperialism is now the number one foreign exploiter in Thailand, number two in Hong Kong, and number one in Malaysia. Similar rankings can be given for its holdings in Laos, South Korea, Taiwan, etc. The buildup of its military forces has kept up with the buildup of its foreign investments. The Japanese military has grown from a force of 75,000 in 1950 to 243,000 in 1962 and the plans call for a force of 336,000 regular and 662,000 reservists by 1975. This is a feature of the uneven development of imperialism. Behind each imperialist move is the drive to redivide the loot. This remains a factor in all relationships. But it is now forced to operate in a new world—in a world where the balance of forces has tipped against imperialism. It is now forced to operate in a world where one-third is building socialism, where capitalism has been discarded. So U.S. imperialism wants to dominate and exploit the capitalist world, but it wants to stop the revolutionary processes that are moving to eliminate capitalism from the rest of the world. It wants to dominate the capitalist world but it wants to destroy the socialist countries and the national liberation movements. This explains the contradictory nature of its game plans in dealing with its rival countries of imperialism like West Germany and Japan.

This uneven development is undermining the hegemony of U.S. imperialism in the world of capitalism in all phases, economic, political and military. The drive of the fastest growing imperialists for a larger share of investment opportunities, markets and sources of raw materials brings to the fore elements of rivalry between the imperialists. This economic rivalry contributes to growing weaknesses in such systems as NATO and SEATO, the main systems of bases and alliances of U.S. imperialists. The U.S. military grip on Latin America is being seriously challenged; the United States and its military advisers are being driven slowly but steadily from foreign bases in one country after another.

The law of the uneven development of capitalism is not only related to economic growth rates in the capitalist camp. It has a bearing on the advance of the socialist revolution in the citadels of capitalism. The uneven development of capitalism has resulted in the uneven development of socialism in the fortresses of imperialism and throughout the world. This is yet another vindication of the truth of the ideas of Lenin who more than anyone brought about the signing of the peace treaty with Germany in 1918 precisely because, in fact, there was no world socialist revolution in the West, and because defending the USSR from foreign invasion was in the best interests of the world revolutionary movement, contrary to the views of Trotsky and others.

The relative strengthening of the socialist camp and especially the growing economic, military and political might of the Soviet Union increase the risk to any capitalist power in being involved with the Pentagon planners. It is, nevertheless, a continuing part of reality that the centripetal forces tending to bring the imperialist powers together against the "menace" of communism remain strong. We cannot take for granted the continuation of any given split among the imperialists; on the contrary, they have a tendency to try to patch things up and to restore relative unity among themselves. To ignore the possibility of an imperialist military unity directed against either the socialist sector or the forces of national liberation, or both, would not only be an illusion about the nature of imperialism, it would be a misreading of what is the main contradiction of our time. And there is always the element of desperation and irrationality inherent in this period of imperialism with the consequent danger of the annihilation of mankind.

1970

5

THE COLD WAR

Background of Imperialist Aggression

A dominant feature of this moment of history is the shift in the relationship of the forces that determine the social, political and economic events of the world. The significance of this shift cannot be understood if viewed within the narrow limits of momentary changes in the fortunes of any single country, the changes that result from the usual power politics or the redivision of markets and resources such as take place periodically between imperialist powers. We are concerned, rather, with the fundamental facts of our epoch, the historic movement of forces that is determining and molding all major human events.

Today a potential force exists on every continent. There is a combination of the dynamic and progressive forces on the world scene that can, and to a growing degree does determine the course of history.

It consists of: First: the world system of socialist states comprising over one billion people; this is a powerful political, economic, ideological and military base.

Second: the legions of organized people who are for peace and democracy in the capitalist world, in the first place the working class—this includes the trade unions and the powerful Communist parties in the capitalist countries. In the United States, the Black Liberation movement, those of other disinherited and disfranchised, specially oppressed minorities, the surge of youth and of women for full participation, are also forces propelling an historic world revolutionary process.

Third: hundreds of millions of people who inhabit the countries that have won independence and are moving away from imperialist domination and towards independence and freedom in Africa, Asia and Latin America.

It is this combination of parallel forces and movements, each acting in its own self interest but traveling in the same direction, that is increasingly determining trends in world affairs. These are the progressive, the revolutionary forces of our epoch. No major development takes place in any part of the world that is not influenced in some degree by this "high pressure system" of the world's political climate. Those who would influence the course of events in our land cannot fail to take into account and act upon this new relationship of world forces. The wheels of history get their head of steam from these dynamic forces.

In the old center in the world of capitalism and big business, undertakings with high-sounding names like "new frontiers," the "Common Market," "Alliance for Progress" become increasingly tangled in the webs of contradictions. Each attempt of imperialism to find a way out only brings new problems to the surface. Capitalism is losing its "head of steam."

It is true that many phenomena in the capitalist world have been modified in this new stage of history, but its basic nature has not changed. The timing of crises and their duration differ but they remain crises of overproduction typical of capitalism. While the new world relationships make war as an instrument of national policy more difficult (and no longer inevitable), with thermonuclear conflict the unthinkable last resort, still the struggle for redivision and conquest by capitalist countries goes on.

In a general sense, for the United States this has been a period of decline both in relation to the world as a whole and to the capitalist world. The era hailed by many imperialist spokesmen as the "American Century" has in fact turned into an era of decline. The masses of the American people are not responsible for this turn of events. The accomplishments and aspirations of the people of our land are not in decline. Who then is responsible?

The cold war policies of imperialism, as applied at home and abroad, have continued to sacrifice the interests of the people and the nation to those of a few monopolies. The decline in our relative position is the direct result, and their continuance can only lead to new disasters.

Cyrus Eaton, writing from a capitalist viewpoint in the *Chicago Sun Times,* put it this way: "The United States is riding for a fall by basing its foreign and domestic policies on war. Continuation of the cold war can only lead to the creeping impoverishment and eventual bankruptcy of every country concerned."

What we need to understand is that solutions to our problems cannot be found in the cold war. On the contrary, many of these problems either emerge from or are aggravated by these policies. Developments, both internally and externally, have now reached a point where an effective mass campaign can be launched to change the direction of cold war strategies. There are sufficient forces in our country who can see the dead-end character of the cold war policies.

Winston Churchill made his famous "iron curtain" speech in 1946 in Fulton, Missouri. He said: "The United States stands at this time at the pinnacle of world power. . . . Opportunity is here now, clear and shining." He was, of course, an unabashed imperialist. During the course of World War II, he never hesitated to maneuver against his allies. And when he came to Fulton with President Truman, he coolly calculated the ensuing call for the cold war, with the U.S. and Great Britain in a partnership against the Soviet Union. Monopoly capital in our country could not quite rely on President Harry Truman to do the job and called on Churchill to help. Cold war opportunities looked "clear and shining" not only to Churchill but also to the financial overlords in our country.

The U.S. plan of world conquest was based on the assessment

that, because the rest of the world was weak and had to rebuild after the war, because the United States had a monopoly on the atomic bomb, because the United States had become the pivotal center for the capitalist world—this was going to be the American Century. Everything that has followed since has been in line with that master plan. Hiroshima, the cold war, the Marshall plan, the McCarthy hysteria, the attack on North Korea, the Indo-China aggression, the CIA actions in Iran and Guatemala, the murder of Lumumba, the U.S.-dominated system of alliances (NATO, SEATO, etc.), were all related to the master plan of aggression.

The anti-Soviet campaign, the counter-insurgency program, the plans of ideological and political penetration—these were all features of the plan for U.S. domination of the world. The anti-Soviet campaign has been in the center of this drive because militarily, politically and ideologically the Soviet Union has been and is the pivotal force on which the master plan of aggression has foundered.

Five administrations have adopted the master plan of aggression as the framework for their policies.

Winston Churchill espoused it at Fulton, Missouri in 1946. In 1951—during the aggression against Korea and when the first steps in the aggression against Vietnam were being taken—Henry Jackson, Eisenhower's speech writer and then the editor of *Fortune* magazine, called it "U.S.A.'s Permanent Revolution." He was, of course, talking about U.S.A.'s permanent counter-revolution. It is worth recalling some of his statements now when that era is coming to an end. After openly saying war with the Soviet Union is almost inevitable, Jackson wrote editorially in *Fortune* (February 1951):

> But today, though we again have allies, though we have the U.N., though we have access to resources all over the world, it is *we* who must shape the struggle: *we* must make the mold. . . . The shape of things to come depends on us: our moral decision, our wisdom, our vision, and our will. . . .
>
> It seems as likely that we shall be required to fight a series of partial wars . . . over remote terrains and over a long period, to maintain the principles of freedom, law and balance. That may be the hardest test of all: to fight without national hatred or national fear. . . .

Yet the U.S. has it in its power to put something better in sight: to demolish these autocracies, undermine all their dead-end dreams of state socialism, and set their extraordinary citizens on a new and more promising economic path.

That was the design, the master plan. U.S. monopoly capital was united behind this plan of aggression. But it was a plan based on a historic miscalculation.

It is obvious that Churchill and the American architects of the cold war did not understand the moment nor the forces of history. They reckoned without the newly developing realities. What Churchill projected was a continuous increase in the expansion of capitalism. It was a plan of imperialist aggression. It was a plan for United States domination of the world. It was a plan for dominating the world by nuclear terror. It was based on still another myth—of the United States having an atomic bomb monopoly. British imperialism was planning to ride on the coat-tails of United States imperialism. Thus the cold war was foisted on the American people.

What should be remembered is that World War II had already changed the balance of world forces, had shaken the old empires to their very foundations. The United States and the Soviet Union emerged as the two most powerful states, the centers of the two opposite poles of the two world systems of capitalism and social-ism. A realistic approach at that time would have been an American-Soviet agreement based on the peaceful coexistence of countries with differing social systems. A mutually beneficial trade policy and a cut in war expenditures would have benefited all concerned. But deluded by a belief that their long atomic monopoly would continue, the leaders of our nation ignored pro-posals for peaceful coexistence and followed Churchill's call for a cold war—the grand design for turning back the wheels of history. They did not understand the power behind the world revolu-tionary process.

As far as our nation and its people are concerned the grand design has backfired. After all these years and after spending billions of dollars in various "aid" programs and hundreds of billions of dollars in war budgets, by 1960 the U.S. share of capitalist world production had already declined from 58 percent to 45 percent and the decline continues. And as to the U.S. share of capitalist world exports, another declining barometer of considerable proportions is in process. This includes automobile and steel production.

One of the prime features of the cold war has been the U.S. self-blockade from large sections of the world, especially the socialist world—an example, perhaps the only one, of self-blockade in history. The blockade has become a victim of its own success. The blockader has become blockaded.

The cold war has been the main instrument of monopoly capitalism in its overseas expansion. In no other sphere is the intertwining of the state and monopoly capital so clearly manifest as in overseas operations; it is difficult to determine where one ends and the other begins. Government appropriations are in fact used directly in every way to assist the grabs by finance capital. This cold war drain is the principal cause for the balance-of-payments deficit that resulted in the run on U.S. gold reserves and the devaluation of the U.S. dollar.

This is not to say that U.S. capitalism as a result of these developments has reached a dead-end or that it has no further capacity to maneuver. But there are a number of processes and developments taking place in which slow quantitative changes continue, and these will necessarily reach the point where a quantitative change will have to take place. There are already some indications of such changes, in addition to the run on the gold reserve. The same few financial syndicates who own and dictate the policies of wages and prices in U.S. industries are those who export capital overseas and are the beneficiaries of the money that is spent on the cold war.

Overseas investments have become a club wielded by big business to demand more concessions from the U.S. government and greater sacrifices in the form of lower wages from the workers. As *Life* magazine reports: "More than a few smart investors have been switching from U.S. to foreign securities for better profits." This galloping process of capital export is reaching a point where some substantive qualitative change must of necessity take place. It is quite realistic to pose the question: Has this trend reached a point where Wall Street is the center of world financial empires reaping profits from expanded foreign production, surrounded by a withering U.S. economy with its resultant misery and unemployment? Rockefeller is the governor of New York but 82 percent of his Gulf Oil employees are in foreign lands, 44.4 percent of General Motors workers, and 45.9 percent of Ford's workers are in foreign lands.

It must be emphasized that while the U.S. share of capitalist production has declined, this does not mean that the "take" of the few multibillion corporations has also declined. The contrary is true.

The imprint of these "monopoly first" policies is clearly stamped on the domestic scene. The interests of our people and nation are ignored; the sole concern is for maximum profits at the expense of the people of our nation and those of every country involved.

The more than five million permanently unemployed begins to appear as a minimum low for the army of victims in the United States. After each recession the number of those who never do get back on the job continues to grow. In addition, it is officially estimated that each year automation now replaces well over a million human hands.

Roosevelt, in his day, spoke about one-third of the nation being ill-housed, ill-fed and ill-clothed. Now, after two decades the situation is still deplorable. Approximately 36 million people live in poverty. For those who work, the fear of layoff has become a permanent lifetime companion. For the American who does not have a job—whether because of layoff, automation, runaway shop, or because he is a youth just entering the labor market—the prospect of a job has become hopelessly bleak.

Since World War II, war production has served as one of the major methods of economic pump-priming, as well as an integral factor in the cold war imperialist policies of expansion. War production contracts have always been a source of fabulous cost-plus profits, a reckless plundering of public funds, needless to say, at the hands of the same few monopoly interests.

As the instruments of war have changed the emphasis from tanks to missiles, from planes to rockets, this new war production has become less and less effective as an economic stimulator.

The cost of war production and the profits are high but the number of workers employed is relatively low. The shortsighted and opportunistic argument that war orders mean more jobs has had the rug pulled from under it. The billions of our tax dollars that the government spends for war orders do not result in a corresponding increase in jobs, since the new engines of mass destruction do not depend to the same extent on the job-making materials and processes called for in earlier wars. The highest rate of unemployment is now in the cities and states where war production is a dominant industry.

Where does the money go? To Boeing Aircraft, for example, which has made a 105 percent profit on its missile investment—a species of modern robbery. The huge public funds go into the coffers of a small group of financiers who use it only to augment their huge piles of accumulated capital. This hoarded wealth taken from the public treasury cannot serve to stimulate the economy; a growing portion of it goes into overseas investments for private corporate profits.

Thus one can justly say that these war orders amount to pilfering the public purse. War orders are obtained on the fraudulent claim of making new jobs, aided and abetted by false war propaganda. Profits used for overseas investments add to the unemployment at home. Thus not only are they used for private profit but they also aggravate the condition of the domestic economy. An economy built on war production is bound to be an economy in constant crisis.

American automobile trusts have created a far-flung network of plants abroad that has resulted in a steep reduction of cars exported from the United States, while the auto trusts in Britain have grown considerably stronger. The sale of small West European cars in the United States produced by American-controlled enterprises is one of the factors that explains the great increase in American imports of light passenger cars.

One of the dramatic examples of the dead-end practices arising from the cold war is the huge, wasteful stockpiling of raw materials and finished goods in warehouses, in open fields and caves.

There simply are no benefits at all for the people in any phase of the cold war. The cold war corrosion of our home front looms up in the rising national debt. The total indebtedness, private and public, has now risen into the stratosphere of over two trillion dollars! There is a false notion held by many that it does not matter how large this incubus becomes. But it does matter, if for no other reason than that the interest must be paid annually—again to the same monopolists—and each year it fattens by what it feeds on. The annual interest on these debts is now in the neighborhood of 50 billion dollars. More and more of the tax dollars go to pay interest on the national debt.

Industrial overcapacity, accompanied by the severe restriction in consumption due to low wages, has been and continues to be a drag on our economy. The attempt by the administration to extend this capacity further by giveaway subsidies from public funds such as tax write-offs (needless to say, to the small group of monopoly forces) only aggravates the problem. Automation is speeded up at a time when there are no solutions to the economic hardships that already flow from it. Further expansion when there is already idle capacity cannot solve the economic problems; in fact, devices that do not result in an expansion of buying power on the home market are not solutions. This is another of the quantitative processes that is reaching a point of no return.

Thus, the cold war drains the resources of the economy and aggravates all social and political contradictions. There is a direct relationship between these policies and the fact that the rate of economic growth of the U.S. economy lags considerably when compared to the other capitalist countries and the world as a whole. These are some of the factors that explain why our economy works its way in and out of a continuous series of economic recessions and crises.

As U.S. capitalism has lost ground economically, it has also slipped in its political preeminence in the capitalist world. This is a predictable result of cold war policies, because in the very heart of these policies there has always been the concept of building up every possible reactionary center. It is a continuation of the twice-bankrupt attempts to build these same centers as arms depots to be used against the socialist world.

The cold war includes the strategy of attempting to restore

the very West German lords of high finance who built up the Hitler war machine. While the U.S. government spent billions of our tax dollars on military expenditures and directly refinanced these war lords, the Wall Street monopolies led the conspiracy to rebuild West German industry—much of it in joint projects.

So, while for the average American the cold war has been a nightmare, for the men who were behind Hitler fascism it has been a highly profitable business. During all these years since the Second World War, the United States has been spending 12 percent of its national income for military goods while West Germany has been spending 5.4 percent of its national income for this purpose. The Common Market has only added fuel to the flames. Without exception, all the proposals to meet this challenge follow the same line. All the bargaining concessions to the Common Market countries call for sacrifices from the non-monopoly sections of industry, from small retail business, from the farmers and, above all, from the workers of the United States. On the other hand, all the gains would again go to the same cold war monopoly circles. Each of the countries joining the setup expects to get a share of the other's loot; inevitably someone is bound to be disappointed.

The cold war advocates have not drawn any lessons from these developments. Instead of reversing course, they are swinging our nation further into the web of monopoly intrigue. In the attempt to offset the decline in the relative economic status of the U.S., they have increasingly shifted the emphasis to military domination. The unheard of increase in military buildup is for the purpose of advancing the policies of imperialist expansion and is intended as a threat to the socialist world. This push toward military domination keeps the world on the brink of nuclear disaster.

From all this, one arrives at the inescapable conclusion that what has been good for Morgan and Rockefeller has been exceedingly harmful to the interests of our people and our nation. The cold war policies have cut across the two-party system. A Rockefeller is Republican governor of New York, but the Rockefeller empire, the greatest beneficiary of the cold war, is completely bipartisan. It has control of the most sensitive cold war posts in every Federal administration. John Foster Dulles and Dean Rusk, our recent secretaries of state, both emanated from the Rockefeller stable. Allen Dulles and his successors as heads of the CIA were also tied to the same financial oligarchy. John McCloy was the High Commissioner in the postwar years, followed by General Lucius Clay; both were connected with the Rockefeller empire.[1]

The house of Morgan has its own direct representatives in key posts. Indeed, the whole cold war setup is truly state-monopoly capitalism in the raw. About these policies one can truthfully say that never have so many been forced to sacrifice so much for the interest of so few for so long.

The pent-up mass resistance building up against the cold war policy is going to force changes. It is important, however, to note that the changes will not necessarily or automatically move only in one direction. Demagogic use of the frustrations can lead toward a reactionary direction. The key is an alliance of the victims, an understanding of the nature of the cold war hoax, the forces behind it, and the projection of realistic alternatives to it.

A reversal of cold war policies is in the most fundamental interest of our people. Such a change could result in a large-scale cut in taxes, could divert billions from wasteful expenditures on war production to useful, peacetime, job-providing construction. "Let the cold war fade and the world will trade" has been suggested as a slogan, and its very simplicity makes it apt.

A decisive development of our times has been the fact that the old colonialism is dying; the old colonial empires are forced to bow out under the pressure of people for independence. U.S. imperialism seems to think it can unilaterally reverse the course of history, but it will find out otherwise. The waves of history will wipe out the beachheads of U.S. imperialism in Indochina, in Taiwan, in Latin America, in Africa. No policy based on myths of the past can succeed.

There is no end to ideas for a useful program, one that will serve our nation, once we have been released from the

[1] Now in the Nixon administration the direct Rockefeller representative is Mr. Kissinger.

prison of the cold war. A major step must be an end to all nuclear testing and a start on the road to total disarmament; it must include the withdrawal of our armed froces from around the world and the withdrawal of support from all reactionary puppets and regimes.

With such changes, friendly relations and trade the world over could be established and war tensions would subside. Colonial and underdeveloped countries would continue along the path of independence and liberation, and with realistic programs of aid, could begin to reap some of the benefits of the scientific-technological revolution.

The financial circles that make most from war orders and have the largest overseas investments are also the biggest contributors to cold war and fascist war funds. The cold war and domestic reaction are two sides of one reactionary coin. Four of the founding leaders of the Birch Society were also former presidents of the National Association of Manufacturers. The oil, motor, aircraft and electronic industries spend millions on promoting the native wing of fascism. The Rockefeller empire through its regional outlets siphons millions into these groups— witness the donations of General Dynamics to the most reactionary and fascist-like movements.

In spite of the irresponsible, fanatical statements by Robert Welch of the Birch Society, he continues to be a favored speaker at clubs throughout the country where big business executives gather, and the sinister hand of the military brass is also discernible in the workings of the ultra-right.

All one has to do is to watch how ultra-right congressmen and senators, their newspaper columnists and news reporters, their radio and TV commentators simultaneously move into action on specific questions with identical lines. It is clear that the cold war policies improve the climate for the work of the ultra-right. The ultra-right slogan against the so-called "no-win" policy in Vietnam is in fact a call for nuclear war. For any force that cries for a victory in smashing the socialist and anti-imperialist peace forces of the world will of necessity have to decide in favor of, and reckon with, a nuclear war. The politics of "victory in the cold war," of nuclear suicide, must be countered by an end to the cold war as the only way out for the United States.

1970

PART TWO

Reactions to Specific
Issues and Events

I

IMPERIALISM AND ITS ACCOMPLICE, THE STATE

The purpose of a study of imperialism is to formulate a policy, a tactical line of struggle, in order to build forces to oppose it, to compel it to retreat and, finally, to bring about its total destruction. As we have seen on close examination, imperialism appears neither as a paper tiger nor a Frankenstein. It is a formidable foe of progress but a foe fighting against odds, against the direction of history and as a foe that will succumb to the full mobilization of the forces that struggle against it.

Any study of the subject, if it is to serve the purposes of this struggle, must take into account the inner contradictions, the rivalries and divisions within its ranks; it must include a continuous and current assessment of the forces of anti-imperialism and the changing balance between the two camps. Unity in the ranks of the progressive opposition and the constant exposure of imperialism's demagogy are indispensable for a successful anti-imperialist campaign.

What may seem new in the field of political thought very often is a repetition of old concepts under new conditions. Even if life and experience lead to a rejection of certain ideas, they have a way of appearing on the stage of history again and again. Such is the case with certain erroneous conceptions concerning the role of the state. In 1872, Frederick Engels said, in discussing the approach of Bakunin (the leading anarchist of his day):

. . . Bakunin maintains that it is the *state* which has created capital, that the capitalist has his capital *only by the grace of the state*. As, therefore, the state is the chief evil, it is above all the state which must be done away with and then capitalism will go to blazes of itself. We, on the contrary, say: Do away with capital, the concentration of all means of production in the hands of the few, and the state will fall of itself. The difference is an essential one. . . .[1]

Since that day scores of variations on the Bakunin theme have appeared, each time as brand-new ideas. The concept emerges today once more as a roadblock to struggle, as a misleading detour sign on the roadway to effective action. The question has a new significance because the capitalist state has a new significance. The development of state-monopoly capitalism has given the state a front and center presence. The role of the state in imperialist operations has greatly added to its importance. It is a direct factor in the monopoly drive for maximum profits.

Speaking to the Congress of American Industry, Virgil B. Day, Vice President of General Electric Company, said:

> . . . American industry has a catch-up problem of long standing which is why *our government should maintain a continuing program of depreciation allowances and investment credit competitive with that of other nations. Competitive government is a requisite for competitive industry.* (December 3, 1971)

In plain words it means that the government will pay for all of the research, for all of the new machinery and for the new buildings.

The "new" narrow and mechanical interpretation of the role of the state starts with the correct enough assertion that the state is an instrument of the ruling class; but they say from this it logically follows that it has no distinct existence of its own. In this concept the role of the state is reduced to a simple one-to-one relationship with the ruling class, thus ignoring the many-sided, contradictory factors that have weight and influence with the decision-makers of state power.

The capitalist state has no existence without the capitalist class. It is its instrument. The state is not some neutral force of arbitration superimposed to mediate between the classes. It is an instrument of the ruling class. It carries out its general man-

---

[1] Karl Marx and Frederick Engels, "Engels to T. Cuno in Milan," (letter) London, January 24, 1872, *Selected Works,* Vol. 2 (Moscow: Progress Publishers, 1969), p. 425.

date. How it carries out its class tasks, what factors influence its decisions are important questions for the revolutionary movement. It is in this sense that it has some life of its own.

One of the factors that influence the actions of the state are the decisions and differences within the ranks of monopoly capital—reflecting the specific self-interest of different sections. If the revolutionary movement is going to use these differences then it is necessary to understand how they are reflected in the role of the state.

If, to the true proposition that imperialism is inherently reactionary and warlike, we add the concept that the state has no existence apart from carrying out its dictates, there are no openings for the intervention of mass struggles. It leads to such unrealistic and pessimistic conclusions that nothing can be done about imperialism that is frozen in state power, nothing can be done about its policies of war and aggression, or about any of the evils of monopoly, that is, nothing short of a socialist revolution. But when the situation is not ripe for a socialist revolution, shouting abstract slogans about revolution is simply a way of doing nothing. It is a form of political self-hypnosis.

It is not necessary or fruitful to counterpose which of the two will have to be destroyed first. This counterposing has significance only because it leads to one-sidedness as tactical and strategic concepts.

The simplistic view of the role of the state rules out all democratic struggle, including the struggle for civil rights. On this basis, some of today's "radicals" seek to excuse their lack of support for the struggles of the working class for social legislation, for laws protecting the legality of unions and the right to strike, for laws restricting the monopolies—all efforts which seek to use the state for working class ends. One must add that these are struggles that are not without historic victories.

This concept of the relationship between the state and monopoly leads to other shortsighted conclusions. It leads to an underestimation of electoral struggles. Because on the surface it seems logical if an election campaign or the act of electing people to bodies of government is meaningless—if such activities have no effect on the struggle against imperialism, or on the struggle against racism, and if they have no meaning for the class confrontation then, of course, to take part in such activities is a waste of time. But such an assessment does not correspond to current reality of today.

On the other hand a one-sided emphasis on the separate and independent role of the state, or a denial of its basic class role, leads to other errors. It leads to forceful concepts of a welfare state, to classless and reformist electoral policies, to a one-sided emphasis on the role of electoral struggles.

Such one-sidedness downgrades the direct struggles against monopoly capital. It leads to a minimizing of basic class questions, to downgrading of the role of the working class, and to a belittling of the importance of trade unions as instruments of the class struggle.

This one-sidedness is not necessary. From a correct undestanding of the dialectical unity between the two will flow correct tactics and strategic concepts of struggle.

With the development of state-monopoly capitalism, the struggles against monopoly lead to a progressive increase in activities in the political and legislative spheres. If this places a higher priority on political movements, it in no way minimizes economic struggles and it does emphasize the close relationship between the two.

With the further development of state-monopoly capitalism all struggles tend to move into the political sphere. As monopoly capitalism increasingly surrounds and insulates its activities with an ever larger bureaucratic state structure the masses need a political atom smasher of their own to break the political crust.

It is true that the state is an instrument of the dominant class, and in present-day capitalism it is a tool of the monopoly groups. But this is not the full story; beyond this role it has a certain degree of relative independence. It is also influenced by other factors such as contradictions in the ranks of monopoly and by situations in which the interests of one monopoly group are in conflict with the interests of the capitalist class as a whole.

The tie-in between the superstructure of a society and its economic base is an intricate, involved, interdependent network. The political machinery, the ideological arsenal, the massive government-servicing community, which are all components of state power, do not function in an isolated, monopoly-run reservation. They serve monopoly but they are of necessity also enmeshed with the rest of the real world; they are forced to deal with the contradictions, the currents, crosscurrents and countercurrents of their surroundings.

The situation in the U.S.A. with regard to the war in Indochina is a classic example of this dilemma. The state is influenced by mass political trends and is forced at times to act contrary to the interests of some monopoly groups. Thus, in spite of its overall subservient role, it can be influenced, can even be curbed, by mass political struggles.

People learn about the need for working class state power in the process of struggling against capitalist state power.

The danger of illusions about the state being above classes, about its being neutral, should not be permitted to undercut the importance of struggling to influence its actions; indeed such flimsy illusions disappear in the fires of struggle.

As we all know, elections are not the be-all and the end-all of the democratic process. They do not create the issues, the trends or even the prime movements, but they are very important reflections of trends and issues and they are important referendums on how people understand the problems presented by objective reality. They also serve as instruments for the further crystallization of forms of struggle and as important phases of political education.

The most influential issue that has determined voting patterns and molded trends during recent years has been and remains the issue of war and peace and, with it, all the endless problems affecting the everyday lives of our people.

When we assess the implications of the war, it is always necessary to include the fear of its escalation into a world or even a nuclear conflict. The existence of vast nuclear power has made it a very personal, life-and-death issue for the people of the world. And this is a relatively new horror added to the other serious impacts on their daily lives. Its economic and social effects are in inverse ratio to where one stands on the economic ladder; the lower one stands, the heavier the burden.

Increased taxes, prices and rents; reduced anti-poverty funds; inadequate housing; cutbacks in construction—all the hardships fall on the poor. And the principal victims are the Blacks, the Puerto Ricans, the Chicanos, the unemployed, the old, the working class as a whole.

Mass pressure for de-escalation, divisions in the ranks of the ruling class, student rebellions, minority demonstrations of greater and greater intensity—all these present U.S. monopoly state power with a serious dilemma. While the pressure of the masses is for de-escalation, the pressure of the war forces is for further escalation.

The propensity of imperialism towards wars of aggression does not close the door to victories for the people. The totality of the present objective situation—starting with the growing power of the forces of anti-imperialism and including the contradictions within the world of imperialism and the many-sided political developments in the U.S.—can spell de-escalation and a defeat for U.S. imperialism. The time for the right of self-determination of nations has arrived. This is the direction of history and all the military power in the world cannot reverse this trend. The policy of imperialist aggression can be defeated, but it must be met by the united forces of anti-imperialism. The political mass pressure of necessity must be directed at the instruments and forces of the state.

In all of the imperialist countries, the state has become an increasingly important factor in economic life, with a new and many-sided influence on production processes. It is one of the principal factors behind the changes in the development of economic crises and boom cycles. Concomitantly, it assumes a greater role in the development of world conglomerates. Its activities have been extended to carrying out the policies of neo-colonialism, and its class assignments have increased in dealing with the world system of socialism. And the imperialist state is the instrument for the militarization of the economy and of life in general, to which we must add that in the United States it is an increasing factor in capital-labor relations and a formidable participant in the field of technology and science.

The growth of the U.S. massive bureaucratic state apparatus, military and civilian, parallels the growth of U.S. imperialism. It has been and remains a main instrument of greater profits at home and abroad.

Above all, what is coming into ever sharper focus is the *persistent U.S. policy of imperialist aggression and war*. More than any other factor it now molds and shapes all external as well as internal policies. We are in the midst of a war-induced inflation, runaway prices and rents, wartime taxes, war-disguised attacks on standards of social security, war-camouflaged attacks on civil rights and civil liberties, war-induced attacks on labor and the right to strike.

It is this focal point in U.S. history that gives rise to specific political trends and moods. That U.S. capitalism follows a policy of imperialist aggression is not unique or new; what is new is the kind of world in which that policy is being pursued. It is here that we find some unique by-products.

In all past wars of this century in which the United States was a combatant, the main burden was carried by other nations, by other peoples. Wars in which the effort and the loot were one-sidedly distributed not only worked to change the relationship of forces between the victor and the vanquished but also changed the relationships among allied capitalist states. Thus, in the past, U.S. capitalism has always been on the light end of war sacrifices but on the heavy end when the imperialist loot was redistributed. Indeed, past war periods have been moments of its greatest opportunities to expand productive facilities, markets, investments, sources of raw materials.

Even during World War II, U.S. capitalism found that "defending democracy" was above all else a very profitable business. The Marshall Plan and all the government foreign aid programs that followed were geared to take full advantage of the openings created by the war. They may have been "moments of patriotic glory" for some, but for U.S. capitalism, they were always and above all "moments of profitable opportunity." Within the overall historic task and effort to defeat fascism which was the greatest threat of the moment, U.S. capitalism was able to both take part in these efforts but also satisfy its greedy profit interests.

What is new, what is more unique for U.S. imperialism, is that this formula based on the old world relationships is no longer working. The moment of opportunity is turning into a period of isolation; capitalist governments that have even ordinary dealing with the U.S. find it necessary to apologize to their own people. This feeling of moral shock at the present policies of the U.S. is the result of a serious miscalculation—a miscalculation of the present stage of history, of the direction of events molding the 20th century.

In this dirty war in Indochina, it is the U.S. that must carry the burden; it is U.S. imperialism that is preoccupied with war production, mobilization, economy, finances, and investments. And as a result, the nation is in the midst of wartime inflation, taxes and shortages. And it is sinking ever deeper into the quagmire of a policy that cannot win.

General DeGaulle saw this as an opportunity for French capital. The U.S. policy of aggression, more than any other factor, aggravates and sharpens the contradictions between the imperialist powers.

During past war periods, because of expanded foreign markets as well as the need for war production for domestic and foreign purposes, the United States experienced a shortage of industrial capacity. Now, because of automation, war induced inflation and new world relationships, an unprecedented over-capacity is developing.

The U.S. balance of trade has always turned favorable in time of war; now we have a trend in the opposite direction. The new situation forces the U.S. increasingly to import strategic materials to be used in its own war production that will not go into exportable items to offset the adverse trend in the balance of trade. And war-stimulated inflation has created a price situation that works to the advantage of the competitors of U.S. capitalism.

To be sure, war production remains very profitable for the monopoly groups that are involved in it. But it has not turned into a moment of opportunity for all sections of U.S. capitalism.

Because U.S. capitalism is finding it difficult to shift the burdens of the war onto the backs of other nations and peoples, it is forced to place them on the backs of its own people. This explains why the domestic consequences of the war escalation appeared so swiftly and dramatically.

Thus, *the new world relationships have changed the nature and the weight of the burden carried by our people.*

If this helps us to understand the domestic effects of the war, it also provides a basis for estimating the magnitude of the war burdens to come. Such an understanding helps to explain the mass reactions of different sectors of our people to the war and its burdens.

1972

2

THE MILITARY-INDUSTRIAL COMPLEX

The "military-industrial complex" may not be the most accurate term, but it is a feature of our present day reality. It is a popular term for state-monopoly capitalism. It is a description of the high level of militarization. It has resulted in the intertwining of the huge military establishment with the massive banking and industrial monopoly corporations. It is a powerful complex. It dominates every phase of life in the United States. It is not a healthy influence. It distorts and corrodes all processes. It reflects the decaying element of capitalism. It is the militarization of life. Militarization is not only the growth of the armed forces. Karl Liebknecht, the German Marxist, at the turn of the century said militarization was a "system which embraces the whole society through a network of militarist and semi-militarist institutions." In the United States the "system" is the military-industrial complex. The rise of the complex, the process of militarization, has been a creeping process. Wartime government budgets have become peacetime budgets.

The rise of the military-industrial complex is an element of the policies of imperialist aggression. The struggle against this complex, the struggle against militarization is an important feature of the struggle against the policies of imperialist aggression.

The urge by some to play soldier is not the cause for militarization and the mere existence of an armed force is not militarization. The fundamental question about militarism is, to what use is the military force put? In a capitalist society the military is an instrument of class rule, the rule of a minority over the majority. In the present day United States it is an instrument of class rule and imperialist aggression. It is an attempt to place the military into a position where it dominates all of society. Militarization is a way of bypassing constitutional and democratic rights. It is an instrument of a police state. From this viewpoint, the rise of militarization and the military-industrial complex are closely and dangerously related to the dangers of fascism. The military-industrial complex of Germany was the power base of Hitler fascism.

The military-industrial complex is a new and higher level of the process of militarization. Within capitalism the military has always been closely related to industrial corporations. With the development of state-monopoly capitalism this relationship has become even closer. The production of military hardware has become a decisive factor both for the capitalist economy and for the military. This production has created a huge military-industrial community. The self interests of the monopoly corporations and the military staff merge in war goods production. It provides an opportunity for huge profits and easy payoffs. The secret agreements are turned into cash when members of the military brass take early retirement and step into executive titles in the big corporations. The payoff is in the form of big salaries and stock dividends.

War production is a source of huge profits and it has become an accepted form of priming the economic pump of capitalism. As the time for Presidential elections approaches the rate of letting out contracts for war orders increases. Military production is an accepted form of economic stimulation. If not for the 100 billion dollar war budget countless huge corporations would go under. If not for the research grants from the military, most private re-

search centers and most research departments in colleges and uni-
vesities would close their doors. Most so-called "think tanks"
would stop thinking if the monies from the military were cut off.
Five thousand three hundred cities in the United States would
become immediate ghost towns if the military funnel was cut.
Some of these cities are rather large. Many states would be in
serious crisis if the military institutions closed. About 13 percent
of the labor force is employed by the military complex. If not for
the military money thousands of authors, television newscasters,
newspaper columnists, scientists and professors would be on welfare. Ninety percent of all government allocations for science goes
to the military. The Pentagon owns more property than 50 of the
largest corporations put together. The endless list of people who
are "beholden" to the military because they are on the "take"
includes labor leaders, comedians, small businessmen, and the
clergy. Thus the militarization has become a "system" affecting
all places of society. It has become a decisive factor in the economy and in the political, cultural, ideological and social life of our
country.

The military is a reactionary influence. In a sense, fascism is
militarism in full bloom. The military is a political base for the
ultra-right. Most ultra-right and fascist organizations are led by
retired military brass. They are the direct link between the ultra-
right, the military and the monopoly corporations. They form a
political network for a state-military-industrial complex. This network is intertwined with the C.I.A. and the F.B.I. apparatus. They
all are components of the invisible government coordinated and
institutionalized in the National Security Council.

Each of the military branches has set up large scale intelligence
departments. Their main activity is to snoop around and gather
information on the civilian population. Each of these departments
has units composed of infiltrators and units that work on creating
provocations. The organization of these units has greatly increased
the dangers that flow from the process of militarization.

The military is a racist influence. Racism is one of its ideological
pillars. Wherever there is a U.S. military base, racism has become a factor in the surrounding areas. The military has become
a worldwide carrier of racism.

The military is a conduit for the big lie anti-Communism. This is its main ideological pillar. Each request for additional billions of dollars is backed up by some news story about the rising danger of "Communist aggression." Thus the military complex exists on a total falsehood. To sustain the military build-up, the falsehood, the big lie must be made even bigger. Military buildup is always hidden behind rhetoric about the needs of national defense. Whenever the Pentagon wants new billions from the United States Congress, its spokesmen take to the air waves to talk about the dangers of other countries surpassing the United States in arms technology and in arms buildup. They have specialists who plant such stories especially in foreign magazines. These articles are then put into the Congressional Record. This is then quoted as coming from "official government sources." The process of arms buildup is endless. It has its own created momentum. It has no relationship to national defense. The United States has a stockpile of nuclear weapons that could wipe out the population of the world many times over. But the military brass pushes for more overkill. It has nothing to do with national defense.

The process of militarization is related to policies of imperialist aggression. It is related to the growth of fascism, to racism. As capitalism decays, it increasingly relies on military power. Therefore a successful struggle against imperialism, against racism, against fascism, a struggle to safeguard democratic rights, the struggle to break the grip of monopoly capital demands a struggle against the creeping militarization, against the military-industrial complex.

1970

3

AN INTRODUCTION TO THE NEW EDITION OF LENIN'S "LETTER TO U.S. WORKERS"

Written from the barricades of the first successful socialist revolution, Lenin's letter to U.S. workers is one of history's most illuminating documents. It was written at a moment when human society took its greatest leap; the first beachhead against world imperialism was a reality; the working class had attained state power. As the head of a workers' state, he wrote to workers of another land in the spirit of mutual confidence between class brothers and sisters. It is a report to the United States' people on the nature of a most critical moment in the history of the world, and an exposure of the criminal activities of U.S. imperialism. And it is particularly relevant today when many people, especially the young, are particularly interested in knowing how things were at the moment of victory, how Lenin saw the relationship of forces and what he had to say about the inner essence of the first socialist state.

If Lenin wrote at the moment of a great victory, it was also a moment when the new socialist republic faced the serious danger of imperialist foreign invasion. The United States, Great Britain, France, Italy and eleven other capitalist states had started their military onslaught on the Soviet Union. His letter was geared to influence U.S. workers. It used the reality of the new working class power in the Soviet Union to heighten their class consciousness. It highlighted the international significance of the victorious socialist revolution to deepen their internationalism, clearly characterizing the reactionary role of the world imperialist powers, especially that of the United States. Lenin said:

"The American workers will not follow the bourgeoisie. They

will be with us for civil war against the bourgeoisie. The whole history of the world and of the American labor movement strengthens my conviction that this is so."

Both on a short-term and a long-term basis this confidence was well founded. The rising mass actions by U.S. workers in defense of the Soviet Republic and the actions by U.S. troops at the Archangel and Siberia fronts were important factors in forcing U.S. imperialism to give up its criminal aggression. The rise of socialist consciousness and the birth of a revolutionary socialist movement in the United States are witness to Lenin's insight and the correctness of his confidence in the United States workers. During the 1920's, over one third of the local unions of the American Federation of Labor passed resolutions which called for recognition of the Soviet Union.

Lenin sought out the areas where the self-interests of our two peoples merged. He tied the nerve ends of our own revolutionary traditions to those of the new socialist revolution. Our war for independence, the Civil War, the sharp class warfare, the struggle against racism and slavery and for Black liberation linked us to history's first socialist revolution. Thus he tapped the progressive wellsprings of our revolutionary traditions and injected a new life into the currents that carried the power of our own historic development. "The American people," he said, "have a revolutionary tradition which has been adopted by the best representatives of the American proletariat."

Cutting through generalities and petty bourgeois fears, he wrote:

And so it will be in the eyes of world history, because for the first time not the minority, not the rich alone, but the real people, the vast majority of the working people are themselves building a new life, are by their own experience solving the most difficult problems of socialist organization.

Blasting the "hypocrisy of formal equality," he rejected the concept of abstract, classless "freedoms and democracy." And many of his concepts were new revolutionary concepts for the entire world.

The sharpest expression of the basic class contradictions of our time is the life-and-death opposition of world capitalism to working-class state power. Reflected in capitalist ideology, in its economic and diplomatic policies, it was nakedly expressed in the military attack on the new socialist state and in the anti-Soviet economic blockade. Today it is expressed in the never diminishing anti-Soviet drive by U.S. imperialists. But it was the birth of the first socialist state that was the beginning of the end for the imperialist powers and engaged these powers in a life-and-death struggle to destroy the one great hope of humanity.

Liberals, and many classless radicals as well, during the past half-century have also had difficulties in accepting the concept of working-class state power. They hide their disdain behind general and abstract concepts of "democracy"; they set up abstract concepts of "individual rights," in opposition to working-class rule. It is difficult for them to accept the concept that when a social structure serves the best interests of a majority class, it serves the best interests of society. For the historic period of revolutionary transition, the rule of the majority class, the interests of the working class are considered the yardstick for measuring what are the best interests of society. In a socialist revolution, for the first time, the interests of the majority are made primary. Revolution demands class priorities and concepts, and Lenin states these clearly and cogently. Without such class priorities, the socialist revolution would have failed. Lenin placed all "rights" and "interests" squarely within the framework of the interest of the revolution:

When it is a matter of overthrowing the bourgeoisie, only traitors or idiots can demand formal equality of rights for the bourgeoisie. "Freedom of assembly" for workers and peasants is not worth a farthing when the best buildings belong to the bourgeoisie. Our soviets have confiscated all good buildings in town and country from the rich and have transferred all of them to the workers and peasants for their unions and meetings. This is our freedom of assembly—for the working people. This is the meaning and content of our soviet, our socialist constitution.

Lenin used the lessons of the U.S. war of liberation:

In their arduous war for freedom, the American people also entered into "agreements" with some oppressors and thereby strengthened those who were fighting in a revolutionary manner against oppression.

I shall not hesitate one second to enter into a similar "agreement" . . . Such tactics will ease the task of the socialist revolution; will hasten it, and will weaken the international bourgeoisie.

Lenin was not writing about agreements in general, but about those that were based on the use of contradictory differences between imperialist powers when such a tactic would be in the best interests of the revolutionary movement. This concept has remained a guiding principle of the Soviet Union in its relationships with and its struggle against world imperialism. Thus, in 1939, when the United States, France, and Great Britain refused an alliance with the Soviet Union against the Rome-Berlin-Tokyo axis and were maneuvering for a united world imperialist front against the Soviet Union, it used the contradictions between these powers, split their ranks, and defeated the conspiracy of a united imperialist world front. This was the meaning of the Soviet-German non-aggression pact of 1939; the basis for this action is clearly stated in Lenin's letter to American workers.

In addition to the letter from which we have been quoting. there is another very interesting message Lenin addressed to the American people. President Wilson for his own reasons had sent a message to the Russian people by way of a communication to the Congress of Soviets. In March, 1918, Lenin wrote the following resolution in reply:

> The Congress expresses its gratitude to the American people, and primarily to the working and exploited classes of the United States of America, in connection with President Wilson's expression of his sympathy for the Russian people through the Congress of Soviets at a time when the Soviet Socialist Republic of Russia is passing through severe trials.
> The Russian Soviet Republic, having become a neutral country, takes advantage of the message received from President Wilson to express to all peoples that are perishing and suffering from the horrors of the imperialist war its profound sympathy and firm conviction that the happy time is not far away when the working people of all bourgeois countries will throw off the yoke of capital and establish the socialist system of society, the only system able to ensure a durable and just peace and also culture and well-being for all working people.[1]

Through all the years the Soviet Union has been the greatest source of strength, the strongest supporter, the bastion of the

[1] Lenin, *Collected Works,* Vol. 27, (Moscow: Foreign Languages Publishing House, 1962), p. 171.

world revolutionary process. It is the protective umbrella for all the developing socialist states and for all peoples and nations fighting for independence from world imperialism. It is the pivotal force in the world struggle for social progress and peace.

Lenin's remarkable "Letter to U.S. Workers" should serve to introduce millions of Americans to others of his monumental works, now exceeding 40 volumes, their 290 different translations exceeding the Bible's 202. The content of his writings is fresh, meaningful and totally relevant to our struggles in the United States today. The resistance to U.S. imperialist aggression in Vietnam, the never ending battle for Black liberation and the sharp class struggles of our workers who reject the brutal system of exploitation and racism must draw strength from a knowledge of the world revolutionary process.

Lenin had penetrating insight into the laws of objective processes, but he became a great revolutionary because he was a master craftsman in the art of using these objective processes to stimulate, accelerate and propel revolutionary developments. He viewed all things in their ever-changing interrelationships because to him surface manifestations were only one minor aspect of the elements of reality. There are no books of sage-sounding scriptures or axioms authored by Lenin, and his writings are never abstract formulas.

Lenin's revolutionary concepts remain the guide, the challenge to all forces fighting against imperialism, for he set high standards of anti-imperialism. He was unrelenting towards both open opportunists and those who said the right things about imperialism but did not back up their words with deeds. To the new, rising Communist Parties, he said, "There must be no toleraton of the verbal condemnations of imperialism while no revolutionary struggle is waged."

Life continues to bear witness to the deep wisdom of that warning. General condemnations of imperialism can be a convenient cover for accommodation to its policies. The struggle against imperialism must be pinpointed on its nerve center, U.S. imperialism. For us, the most urgent test is the struggle against U.S. aggression in Indochina. This policy is reaching a new crisis point. The ability of the United States to maneuver with token troop withdrawals is fast coming to an end.

Even though Lenin's policies of struggle must be translated into today's realities, his underlying concepts remain fully valid. It would be an error, however, for revolutionary forces, especially those in other capitalist countries, to limit themselves to this; their efforts against U.S. imperialism will be fully effective only when they combine them with the struggle against the imperialism of their own countries.

We keep coming up against this incontrovertible reality: U.S. imperialism is the largest oppressor and exploiter in human history. It directly exploits over 100 million workers; draws profits from 80 million U.S. workers; holds nearly 40 million U.S. citizens in a special racist vise of oppression.

The centennial of Lenin's birth is an appropriate moment for all revolutionary forces, on all levels, to raise to new heights the revolutionary banner of Lenin; for each national force basing itself on its own circumstances to accept both its national and international responsibility. The revolutionary path opened by Lenin is the path to victory.

1970

4

KISSINGER'S FOLLIES

This was written two years before Mr. Kissinger made his first trip to China, two years before Nixon announced his plans to visit Peking and Moscow. What has happened since only adds spice to these observations.

Defenders of a dying system are always perturbed and tormented about the nature and the direction of historical processes. Henry Kissinger, one of the foremost of the new breed of ideologists of U.S. imperialism and one of Nixon's closest advisers, recently wrote:

> The essence of Marxism-Leninism is the view that objective factors
> such as the social structure, the economic process and, above all, the
> class struggle are more important than the personal convictions of
> statesmen. [And so, he continued] If personal convictions are "subjec-
> tive," Soviet security cannot be allowed to rest on the *good will* of
> other statesmen, especially those of a different social system.[1]

What he and his fellow-defenders of U.S. policies of imperialism
devoutly yearn for is the day when socialist countries rest their
security "on the good will of . . . statesmen . . . of a different
social system," whose benevolence at this moment extends from
Vietnam to all of Indochina to Africa, from My Lai to U-2 fighters,
and whose humanitarian goodwill ambassadors feature the CIA
and the Pentagon.

Mr. Kissinger's "convictions" are the convictions of U.S. imperialism. He may have some sane secondary thoughts of his
own—but if they run contrary to the basic interests of monopoly capital he will not dare express them even to his girl
friends. Kissinger is in the position of power only because before
his appointment he publicly expressed his total agreement with
the policies of U.S. imperialism. Yes, Kissinger is four square on
the imperialist side of the class struggle. As long as he expects to
stay in the Nixon administration these "objective factors" are going
to be not only "more important"—they are going to be the determining factors in his behavior.

The bridge-building policies of Johnson's and now Nixon's
administration are transparent attempts to convince leaders of the
socialist countries and the newly liberated lands that they must
overlook mere class factors and the greedy aims of U.S. imperialist
policies and instead rest their security on the "good will of statesmen," that is, Nixon, Agnew, Westmoreland and the whole
military-industrial crew.

And, of course, Kissinger distorts the role of objective processes
in the Marxist-Leninist position, which does not view them in a
vacuum but as developments that create the material conditions
and the framework in which struggles take place. There is a continuous flow and inner relationship between these processes and

[1] *American Foreign Policy*, p. 35.

the forces and movements that develop in struggle. New obstacles and contradictions are always looming up and must be taken into account in the continuing struggle against imperialism. It would, of course, be self-defeating to assume that imperialism will collapse on its own, and the constant challenge is how best to use the materials and conditions that objective processes present. This involves evaluation and analysis of facts that have a bearing on the issue.

For example, it must never be forgotten that in opposition to imperialism there is the rising torrent of world revolutionary movements—a powerful worldwide confluence from the three cardinal sources that power social progress. First, the one-third of the world that is building a socialist society; second, working class movements within the capitalist countries; third, the national liberation movements against colonial oppression. At the root of these world forces is the class struggle—between the working class and the capitalist class, reflected on a world scale in the contest between the socialist and capitalist states. The shift in the balance of world forces has been a historic process.

The first qualitative, revolutionary shift in the balance between these two systems took place in 1917, and working class power in the Soviet Union was the beginning of the end for imperialism.

In 1917, the six leading imperialist powers and their colonies accounted for 44 percent of the world's territory and 58 percent of its population; by the end of 1969, the figures were 9 percent of the world's territory and 15 percent of its population. At the end of 1969, the population of all the remaining colonies came to only 1 percent of the world's total, compared with 69.4 percent in 1919. There are, however, 35 million people still languishing in colonial bondage in the most inhuman conditions. By the end of 1969, socialist countries accounted for one-third of the world's industrial capacity; their volume of industrial output had increased 6.3 times since 1950, compared with 2.7 times for the highly developed capitalist countries. These are some of the data concerning the two world processes that the Kissingers are so alarmed about.

The second qualitative balance shift was triggered by and related to World War II. The war itself had reflected the new contradictions and the new level of the objective processes of its time. To be sure, it had extended the contradictions between the imperialist powers, but the new factor was the changed relationship between the world revolutionary forces and those of imperialism. Without the power of the new revolutionary forces, the war would have been just another device for dividing the loot between the imperialist powers.

In this area, the decisive factor was the role and power of the Soviet Union and its ability to aid the world working class and national liberation movements. This made it possible for countries like Poland, Hungary, China, Czechoslovakia, Bulgaria, Romania, North Korea, North Vietnam and Albania to cross the dividing line and start the tasks of building socialism.

After the war this new balance of relationships became the background, the umbrella for the anti-colonial explosion that literally wrecked the old colonial empires. As a result, most of the oppressed nations won political independence. Imperialism had lost its power to dominate and unilaterally decide the direction of world events.

All this was truly a giant step for mankind. History saw its greatest mass upheaval. Hundreds of millions of people from all sectors and classes of society moved into the political arena. The walls of imperialist Jericho came tumbling down.

There were those who drew hasty conclusions at the new turn of events; they thought this was the end of imperialism and that what remained could be toppled by small groups of armed men. Others wishfully thought it was now possible to depend on the "good will and understanding" of imperialist statesmen. And still others saw imperialism as a "paper tiger." All these attitudes fostered illusions that became the basis for irresponsible tactics that led to a number of serious setbacks.

In the underdeveloped countries where the anti-imperialist mass upsurge took place, the working class was small or non-existent. Leadership was therefore taken over by other than working-class elements and this engendered a rash of petty bourgeois radical theories. Some unfurled the banner proclaiming that "only the peasants are a revolutionary class." This became the basis for the Maoist claim that the center of the world revolution had shifted to the "peasant" countries of the East. Thus the door was opened to such petty bourgeois radical slogans as "surround the cities with small, peasant-based military guerrilla units."

Franz Fanon gained a certain amount of influence when he said, "The starving peasant, outside the class system, is the first amongst the exploited to discover that only violence pays. For him there is no compromise, no possible coming to terms."

To deny these conclusions is not in any way to deny the militant role of the peasants and other non-working class elements in the struggle against imperialism. But the first stage of the struggle for national liberation does not primarily involve the concept of doing away with private property. In fact, for most of the non-working-class participants, the need and the urge that spurs the struggle is for land. In the struggle against imperialism this is indeed revolutionary, but it is not yet revolutionary in the sense of fundamentally changing the nature of the economic and political system. Some who are revolutionary in the struggle against foreign expropriators are not yet revolutionaries when the struggle effects a shift to socialism, which is a struggle against the expropriation of one's own country. The first drive of the peasant is to acquire land as private property, and in a sense the degree of his revolutionary spirit is gauged by that historic task. In the struggle against imperialism the hunger for land is associated with the struggle against a foreign oppressor.

The role of the working class is, however, conditioned by a different class position. Involved in social production, its basic problem cannot be resolved by the private expropriation of the means of production whether it is land or factories. It is forced to think in terms of class expropriation—the form of class struggle alone capable of fundamentally changing the very basis of society. It is a propelling objective factor that pushes them far past the effort to effect reforms.

New theories have cropped up, among them petty bourgeois radicalism that rejected reality and arrived at an illusory assessment of the existing forces. These theories saw no need for concepts of class struggle; they saw only "hothouse" shortcuts to revolution. It is difficult to minimize the price the revolutonary forces have had to pay for these follies.

These unrealistic deductions emanated from the correct enough assessment that the shift in the balance of forces had made it impossible for imperialism to regain its lost historical initiative or to reverse the direction of the accelerating world process. This led to the dangerous illusion that imperialism was dead, but it remains a dangerous foe, changing its tactics to meet realities, and it has many lives. Old colonial empires have been smashed, but colonialism remains very much a cruel reality.

1971

5

INDOCHINA:

The War U.S. Imperialism Cannot Win

The very heart of today's grim world reality is the U.S. war of aggression against Vietnam. In murder, torture, and destruction, U.S. imperialism has never extracted a more horrifying toll than in Indochina. Not only from the innocent men, women and children of this far-off land but from our own young men who die by the thousands and are maimed by the hundreds of thousands. In terms of human lives, lost or crippled, this is now the second most destructive of all U.S. wars.

The nature of U.S. imperialist designs in Indochina has now emerged into full view. The aim is to turn Indochina into a U.S. military complex from which to enslave, exploit, harass the Asian mainland, to make it a military-political beachhead of U.S. imperialist aggression. The goal of the "limited war" was never limited; it has at all times been the complete subjugation of Indochina. The aggressors' only miscalculation has been to believe that they could achieve total victory by limited warfare. Only if **we** understand that the aim of U.S. imperialism from the very beginning has never changed, does it become clear why the U.S. has rejected all proposals that would have led to de-escalation and eventually to peace. Nixon refuses to set a date for ending the war because U.S. imperialism has not decided to end it.

James C. Thompson, Jr., who was in a policy-making position as assistant to McGeorge Bundy in the Kennedy Administration, wrote in *The New York Times* (June 4, 1967):

> The Vietnam conflict is a needless war—one that could and should have been avoided. . . . My six years in the Federal Government revealed a melancholy truth that seems pertinent today: *that at each stage of the Vietnam conflict, from 1961 onward, constructive alternatives have, in fact, been available and proposed, both within the Government and outside it; that at each stage such alternatives have been rejected as unpalatable.* . . . I can attest that they were in fact proposed at the time. . . . (Emphasis added.)

Many new "constructive alternatives" have appeared since 1967. They have appeared in the realistic and constructive proposals made by the delegations of the Democratic Republic of Vietnam and by the delegate of the Vietnam Revolutionary Council. U.S. representatives have turned them down because U.S. imperialism has not given up on its aggression.

U.S. imperialism is not the reluctant aggressor who is caught in the web—in the logic of events—not knowing how to break away, as some would like the world to believe. Military conflict has its logic, but the primary propellant in Vietnam is a fully-thought-out political, economic and military policy of imperialist aggression.

The nature of U.S. imperialism is such that it will move along this path as long as it thinks it will get away with it; it will retreat only when the path of aggression becomes politically, diplomatically and militarily untenable at home and overseas.

Years ago U.S. imperialism secretly and arrogantly placed nuclear weapons in the very heart of Europe; the public announcements came after the fact. The people of Europe, as well as our own people, were told of this act of aggression years later. U.S. imperialism is following the same course today in Indochina. U.S. spokesmen are publicly talking against the "proliferation" of nuclear weapons, while they go full steam ahead to establish such weapons on every continent. After the crime has been committed, the story will then be "leaked" out. Without the consent of the people of Puerto Rico, U.S. imperialism has built a base for nuclear arms there.

The so-called limited war has now been escalated into a world struggle. The proclaimed "anti-insurgency tactic" is now a full-scale land and air war. The policies of neo-colonialism have given way to open, ruthless imperialist warfare and open colonial oppression. The Indochinese war now constitutes the sharpest expression of the contradiction between imperialist aggression by the capitalist world and support of the struggle for national liberation and the right of self-determination by the socialist world, between oppression and freedom, between progress and retrogression.

The policy of U.S. aggression is being propelled along to a collision course by all the forces of progress. The danger of a world armed conflict remains clear and present. The odds in favor of a world nuclear confrontation have, in fact, increased.

But the forces of aggression are not winning the war. Therefore, U.S. imperialism faces three possible alternatives: 1) it can seriously open up the path toward a negotiated withdrawal; 2) it can continue its present level of military activity, which can at best lead to a stalemate in which active fighting continues; 3) it can take the very dangerous step of initiating the kind of escalation that *will* qualitatively change the nature of the war.

All other options, including the option of a military victory are closed.

The hard fact remains that this is a war U.S. imperialism cannot win. All the war declarations in the world are not going to erase the miscalculation as to the nature of the war, and they will not in the least change the balance of the forces involved. Continued escalation will bring on new dimensions in both resistance and retaliation by the forces of anti-imperialism.

This critical point in the military struggle coincides with a critical point of political frustration on the home front. The mass resistance to the war has continued to grow; it has changed the traditional relationships between elections and wars. Masses are fast learning to distinguish just wars from unjust wars. The realization that this is an unjust war is now possibly the primary ideological force propelling the peace movement. Not all know *why* it is unjust, but that it is unjust is accepted by millions.

The Vietnam war emerges increasingly as the dominant factor in all phases of life in our country. The price our people are paying is only partially revealed in mounting budget deficits and growing national debt. Rising prices, rents and taxes take an increasing bite from the worker's income. The status of the poorest sections of the population—the poor in the ghettos and on the farms, those on welfare rolls—becomes increasingly desperate as funds for social purposes are cut back and living costs rise. More and more the minimum necessities of life move out of the reach of millions of Americans.

Besides the immediate bread-and-butter effects, the expansion of the war-related sector speeds up all the processes of deterioration in the capitalist system. War economy accelerates the bloating of the monopolies, while the new war technology sharply reduces the participation of non-monopoly firms in war production. The 200 largest corporations own over two-thirds of all manufacturing assets and the trend was moving to an even greater share for the monopolies who are the arms manufacturers. The military-industrial complex, through the state-monopoly junta, casts an ever uglier shadow over the affairs of our nation. An economy dominated by a war psychosis provides the materials for the speedier development of state-monopoly capitalism. The process of militarization goes on at a prodigious pace. The top military echelons, together with top corporate executives of finance and industry, have become an extremely dangerous force in our society, since they have the last word in the spending of tens of billions of dollars in war contracts. They furnish the power behind putsches against democratic governments, the setting up of reactionary juntas, the creation of conditions that can lead to fascism.

Such institutions as the Pentagon, the National Security Council, the CIA, the FBI—all the various other "invisible" government agencies beyond the reach of democratic controls—become the primary decision-making bodies. Even the Cabinet as a collective body has virtually disappeared. The traditional processes of democratic rights, institutions and safeguards are being corroded at an alarming rate. The invisible government has become institutionalized.

This is a body with disturbing powers. Although its activities are hidden from the people, it has the power to instigate wars of aggression. Headed by the National Security Council, it tends to usurp the authority of the Cabinet, which plays less and less of a role. The President's Cabinet has become largely a ceremonial body. The emergence of this behind-the-scenes center of political power, closely linked to the centers of financial-industrial combines and to the Pentagon, the CIA, and the FBI, is a most serious threat to the whole democratic structure.

The emergence of the invisible government is a new form of the capitalist dictatorship that corresponds to its state-monopoly capitalist stage of development. This is a process of chipping away at the powers of state bodies that must go through the electoral processes. The members of the Senate and the House of Representatives cannot totally ignore mass sentiment. But with the rise of the invisible government and its increasing powers of making decisions that constitute basic direction of policies, the electorate will continue to go through the process of electing people to governmental bodies that have less and less "say-so" about the basic policies of government.

In this scheme of things the monopoly corporations have direct control of governmental policies through bodies that are invisible to the people, while the people have access to bodies with a declining influence. Monopoly capitalism finds it necessary to establish this direct control over the affairs of the state because the gap between what are the self-interests of the people and the policies of state-monopoly capitalism becomes more unbridgeable. This development is the basic cause for the sharpening Constitutional crisis. It is the cause for the credibility gap.

The rise of the invisible government is a step towards a police state. It adds to the dictatorial powers of the Presidency. The new dictatorial powers are introduced as special war powers. But they become accepted and institutionalized. They change the essence of the democratic institutions while permitting the structure to stand.

Dictatorial powers and invisible government bodies are instruments of anti-people, anti-democratic policies. These policies affect all sections of the people.

This process is most tragically visible in the ghettos. The war on poverty has by and large been replaced by a war against the people. Instead of programs to relieve extreme poverty, there are now secret blueprints for military containment, calling for co-ordinated attacks by city, county, state and federal forces. The areas have been subdivided very much as has been done in the plans of war and "pacification" in Vietnam.

The plans call for surrounding and closing off "affected" areas. In cities like Los Angeles, where police officials have close relations with racist and ultra-right groups, fascist elements are part of the strategy and have been given assigned tasks. Among their assignments are the promotion of racist propaganda among white Americans, spreading rumors and creating incidents and provocations. The old Pinkerton strike-breaking manuals have been taken off dusty shelves for instruction in provocation, "preventive" action and the use of the "surprise element." The concern of state legislatures is not poverty but, as in Ohio, the passage of laws that fit into the "containment" policy. And, of course, the FBI's high command is in the very center of the act to sound the alarm and point the accusing finger at the Reverend Martin Luther Kings and others who have called for action to end the war and relieve poverty.

Life has joined the problems of everyday existence with the issue of war and peace. The dominance of war orientation has become the primary obstacle to social progress; indeed, it has become the primary factor underlying the deterioration of economic, political and social conditions, seriously corroding progress.

This is the Achilles' heel of the war policy: the growing realization of the cause-and-effect relation between the accelerating war sector and the neglect of burning social issues. In this inescapable reality lies the primary incentive for a victorious struggle for peace. This was dramatically demonstrated in Dr. King's stand on peace, which reflected the truth that the war policy had developed to a point where it was a primary obstacle to the further development of the struggle for civil rights.

The growing domination of the war does not mean that victories on social issues are impossible—only that such victories are possible if they are combined with a struggle for peace. This is the vulnerable area of imperialist aggression if it is clearly recognized as such by the anti-war forces. When it is not understood, it can be a serious break in the armor of the progressive forces—a lesson that sections of the trade-union leadership are beginning to learn. Unfortunately, this is not true of the top leadership.

Labor leaders who support the war policies are going in only one direction—toward a policy which is anti-labor in its basic orientation. The Nixon administration pursues policies of high prices, high rents, anti-union actions in the name of "public interest" as it proceeds to scuttle programs for health, education, and the fight against poverty. To support the war while trying to fight against its negative effects on the home front is to go in two directions at the same time.

This is a new experience for our people. Because of the special situation of the United States in past wars, there is a popular concept that war is associated with economic boom, good times for all, shortage of labor, lots of overtime, high farm prices and greater opportunities for small business. Many have waited for such economic effects, but they have not appeared and they are not coming. Instead, dairy farmers have had to pour their milk into the sewers to keep the prices they get from sinking to nothing; instead of wartime boom, there is wartime economic decline. For the first time in our history we have wartime economic crisis, a wartime 75 percent use of industrial capacity.

The understanding of this question—and this bears repeating— is the key to developing a victorious struggle against the war policy, to getting new sectors of the people to join the forces for peace. For these negative economic effects are only just beginning. As this process develops further, it will truly become the soft spot in the U.S. policy of aggression. When we speak about the war policy becoming untenable, it is this objective process of our own deteriorating economy that is helping to make it so. It is one of the trump cards against U.S. imperialism.

There are a number of important changes taking place in the struggle for peace, in fact, the phrase is less and less expressive of the nature of this mass current. The generalized pacifist appeal for peace has been and remains an important sentiment behind the peace movement. The rejection of war as a means of settling differences has deep roots in our society. But other concepts have emerged that are increasingly taking over as important propellants toward mass action. Mass concepts have shifted from a mere desire for peace toward a sharp condemnation of U.S. policies of aggression, toward placing responsibility on the United States as an aggressor. This mass sentiment increasingly recognizes the nature of U.S. policy, and it has moved in the direction of seeing the U.S. policy of aggression as the *basic* source of the conflict.

There are important shifts in thinking on questions concerning just and unjust wars. This is evident in the renewed interest in the nature of the Nuremberg verdicts and their possible application to today's war criminals. There those who argue that it is not enough to have the right to refuse to support this war or refuse to be drafted because of opposition to wars in general, but that there must be the overall right to refuse to support *a particular war*. This clearly differentiates between just and unjust wars. It is a rejection of the old jingoistic slogan, "My country, right or wrong."

That this discussion has taken root among the masses is indicated by important changes in outlook among major sectors of our people, especially among the youth and Black Americans. It is evident in the new developments of the anti-draft movement. Black youth are very effectively tying this in with the struggles for civil rights, including the exclusion of Blacks from draft boards. What is new here is not only the growing numbers who are refusing to be drafted, but also the growing popular sentiment that because the war in Vietnam is immoral, illegal and unjust, the youth have a moral, legal and just right to refuse to serve.

Many diverse forces have contributed to the development of a broad peace movement in the past few years. During the struggle around the issue of nuclear weapons, the scientists were very much in the forefront. At another point, religious leaders were prominent in the daily struggle, especially when the encyclical *Pacem in Terris* was issued by the late Pope John XXIII. With the birth of the "teach-in," the academic community reached out to the public, and the professor and student came to the forefront. However, the movement has involved masses at all times, and the prominence of specialized groups has been in relation to mass movements.

The Communist Party made peace the central issue in all its work, and now every Communist is in one way or another involved in some phase of this struggle. Through participation in the mass actions for peace, new sections of our people have for the first time acquired some understanding of the nature of imperialism. We cannot claim, however, that anti-imperialist consciousness is the motive power that stirs the broadest sections of the opposition to wars of aggression. The struggle against the war policy cuts across many movements, classes and levels of development; it will not limit itself to any one preconceived form.

Anti-Communism still plagues some leaders of the peace movement. This is a self-defeating policy. In order to achieve the maximum mobilization of the people it is necessary to expose the smokescreen of anti-Communism behind which the administration hides its war policy. The reversal of an over-all aggressive orientation can only start with a reversal of policy in Vietnam.

The development of anti-imperialist consciousness must be seen in this context. To be anti-imperialist is more than being anti-war. Anti-imperialism stands for the right of complete self-determination, for a correction of the injustices of years of imperialist robbery. It is not the monopolies that should get compensation when industries are nationalized. It is rather the victims of imperialism who must be compensated for the years during which their resources have been looted. Anti-imperialism advocates policies that combat all economic, political and social inequality. It represents the most advanced of a wide range of levels of understanding, each expressed in a form of organization that corresponds to it. All of these levels need to be mobilized, involved increasingly in common effort, and helped to advance further along the road to ideological consciousness.

The invisible section of the government contains within it the dangers of fascism. It is an attempt to force policies of class unity.

It would be incorrect, however, to assume that even this sector of government is united; there are inner struggles within the ranks of U.S. capitalism. But at this moment the outstanding feature of this phase of imperialism is that the most warlike forces have become the dominant voices in determining foreign policy. Nevertheless, their position is precarious, as is the whole policy of aggression they promote, for there are powerful forces within and around the government who oppose the present policies.

For example, there are important sections of big business which, in the face of sharpening competition with West European and Japanese capital, are pressing for the opening up of trade with the Soviet Union and other socialist countries and find the administration policy in Vietnam an obstacle to this. They are not men of peace, but they see the present policy of aggression as creating unnecessary difficulties for them.

Such opposition is important when it coincides with the more basic anti-war and anti-imperialist sentiments among the people. It is especially significant when these sentiments have their reflections in governmental councils.

For the moment U.S. policy remains that of endless escalation in Vietnam and is based on the demand for unconditional surrender. While it is a fact that even the forces that dominate U.S. foreign policy do not at this moment want to run the risk of a world war or a nuclear war, it does not follow that the world is not on the path that can lead to both. And there are new factors related to the influence of the laws of military movements on the overall scene. These are the new dimensions of the destructiveness of nuclear weapons and the hairline difference between a calculated launching and the accidental triggering of atomic destruction.

1968

6

WHO GETS THE SUPER-PROFITS?

Imperialism is aggressive, it pursues its policies of expansion and oppression because the "export of capital" is profitable. The United States is an imperialist country because imperialism is profitable for the corporate interests. There is no "people's capitalism" and there is no people's imperialism.

U.S. capitalism has become rich from the sweat and blood of the U.S. working class. Of course, it was also aided by its internal situation. Capitalism in this country has had at its disposal a very large home territory. It has stolen and gorged itself on the vastness of our natural wealth. It has had a constant source of labor through immigration, and the defeat of chattel slavery in the Civil War released former Afro-American slaves to the capitalist production market.

All these favorable features for its development turned to profits on the production line. U.S. capitalism has broken all records in the rate of exploitation. It devours human beings in a shorter period of time than any society in all of history. It discards people at 40 years of age as "used up." It practices industrial slaughter.

A glimpse of this slaughter, in the interest of capitalist profit, is revealed in on-the-job death and accident statistics that the government has compiled.

For example, between 1941 and 1945, there was a total of 11,200,000 workers killed and injured in major manufacturing and non-manufacturing industries, or approximately *eleven times as large* as total U.S. casualties of 1,058,000 sustained in World War II.[1]

[1] U.S. Department of Labor, *Handbook of Labor Statistics,* 1947, Bulletin, No. 916; cited in Boyer, Richard O., and Morais, Herbert M., *Labor's Untold Story* (New York: Cameron Associates, 1955) p. 336.

And this is no wartime aberration. Thus a report prepared for the U.S. Department of Labor which was shelved with great haste states:[2]

Each year 15,000 workers are killed—more than the total number of United States battlefield fatalities in any year of the Vietnam war—and *2.2 million workers* are injured on the job. Over a million workers are disabled by occupational diseases from the effects of asbestos, beryllium, carbon monoxide, coal dust, cotton dust, cancer-causing chemicals, dyes, unusual fuels, pesticides, radiation, and other occupational hazards such as heat, noise, or vibration. Each working day brings 55 dead, 8,500 disabled and 27,000 injured. (emphasis added)

These figures do not include the workers who die after they have been layed off or retired.

This is the basic source for the profits of the monopoly corporations. When considering other questions one must never lose sight of this basic fact. To lose sight of this fundamental question leads to erroneous concepts of classlessness.

United States capitalism has extended this brutal exploitation across our national boundaries. It is a policy of imperialist aggression. The exploitation, the oppression is even grimmer.

This results in super-profits for the corporations. Where do these profits go has always been an important question. Who gets these super-profits?

It is generally accepted that the lion's share of the extra profits derived from imperialist colonial exploitation are confiscated by the imperialist lions—the large corporations and banks directly involved in these operations. These corporate thieves are not Robin Hood-like characters. They do not voluntarily give up, or pass on, any of their loot to anyone. But there are some benefits traceable to the super-profits of imperialism that trickle down to other sections of the population within the imperialist countries. The super-profits help to create a special reserve for the monopolies. These financial reserves then make it possible and easier for the corporations to maneuver, under pressure to make concessions. In a sense these reserves are a fund for a "payoff" in the same manner as a thief pays off the cop or the "lookout." Thus the

[2] Delphic Systems & Research Corporation, "An Evaluation of the National Industrial Safety Statistics Program," September 30, 1970, p. 1.

"payoff" in the first place trickles down to other non-monopoly sections of the capitalist class, to sections of the middle class. In one way or another they have become attached to the imperialist "syndicates." Sections of the technical, professional and civil service personnel are also on the "take." And some of it reaches as "influence money" into the ranks of the working class.

The services rendered by those on the "payoff" lists are political and ideological support for the policies of imperialism. In the ranks of the working class the task of those on the receiving end of the special concessions is to give leadership in the promotion of policies of class collaboration—to paper over the basic contradiction between the class of exploiters and profiteers and the class of the exploited. Their task is to keep the working class politically tied to the two parties of capitalism. This section in the ranks of the working class is the main purveyor of racism. Their ideological task is to block the development of class and socialist consciousness. They are the chief propagandists for anti-Communism.

When compared to the lion's share going to the imperialist corporations this "payoff" money is but a mere trickle. But it is big enough to influence class relations, class politics, and class ideology. It is a corrupting influence.

This phenomenon is a source of endless debate and confusion within radical and revolutionary groups. It is especially a subject of confusion within non-working class radical groups. Its significance is either overstated or its existence is denied. Those who want to downgrade or to totally deny the historic progressive role of the working class take the trickle and magnify it into an illusory gushing well of working class enrichment. This then makes the workers "partners in the imperialist profits." Of course, when one accepts this basically erroneous concept, it does not take too much creativity to see the working class as the "partners in crime," as the "main enemy," the "base for reaction" and even the "mass base for fascism." These are some of the full-blown anti-working-class concepts that have been expressed on the left. But there are others—less open, less extreme expressions that flow from the same wrong assessment of the trickle. This has been and remains the most persistent and widespread of the two errors. This other is a denial of the "payoff" and its effects. And it leads to a blind spot. When one does not see the problem, one does not deal with it. The trickle creates ideological and political problems that cannot be ignored.

Because of the extra profits from its colonial exploitation U.S. capitalism is able to create a well-to-do section of the middle class. This is the source for the affluence of the "upper middle class." Because of these extra profits it is also able to place another significant grouping of the intellectual community, people from the world of science and culture, people in the field of mass communications into a status of being the "aristocrats of their professions."

It is in these sectors where imperialism gets its highest dividends for its "payoffs," because they are in the best position to carry the ideological message of imperialism. They are the ideological apologists. They are the main conduits for imperialism's message. It is in this context one must view the special concessions capitalism makes to a section of the working class. But it must be seen in the framework of the class struggle, in the context of the class exploitation that is the main source of U.S. corporate profits.

It cannot be denied that U.S. workers put up a militant struggle for every last concession they get. They get nothing on a silver platter. The rate of exploitation is the highest in the world. They are the victims of one of the highest industrial casualty rates in the world. But it also cannot be denied that U.S. corporations have special reserves, because of the super-profits from imperialist operations, from which they can make concessions to some sections of the working class. Therefore, these super-profits are a factor influencing the class relationships in the United States. The Meany-Lovestone support for the policies of U.S. imperialism is the open side of the "payoff."

So the "payoffs," by and large, go to a small section of the class. But it has an indirect influence on the class relationships generally.

Within the working class these "payoffs" from the super-profit reserves, in the main, go to the more skilled and craft sectors of labor. They helped to create a small privileged sector of the working class. Lenin spoke of this group as the "aristocrats of labor." They have some special privileges but remain as workers. In a sense they are what "trustees" are in the prison system. In return for some privileges they work for the prison authorities—but they remain prisoners. Their assigned role is to keep the class prisoners in prison.

These "payoffs" also come as a result of struggles; they are concessions to struggle. With the exception of a few years and the exception of some unions, these workers with privileges have politically and ideologically dominated the American trade union movement. They are a corrupting influence on the trade unions. The "privileges" are granted for getting the trade unions to openly support capitalism as a system, the "payoff" is granted for getting the trade unions to support the candidates of the two capitalist parties, and for openly supporting U.S. imperialist acts of military aggression. The "payoff" is granted for helping to mislead, to divide and to destroy the working class movements in countries where U.S. corporations are getting their super-profits. The "payoff" accrues from helping to administer the system of racist discrimination against some 25 million Black Americans, 5 million Chicanos and 2 million Puerto Ricans.

The emergence of the broad militant working class rank-and-file movement is preparing the working class for putting an end to the system of "payoffs." Once the elements who have accepted the special privileges are isolated in the working-class movement they will become worthless, and the ruling class will stop the "payoffs." This will close the spigot of political and ideological corruption.

In a general sense the "payoff" system continues. But like everything else, it now operates within a new set of realities. New factors have emerged that significantly modify and complicate these relationships. In these new circumstances, a reapplication of the old "payoff," namely, the "labor aristocracy" formula yields very little practical knowledge. All assessments must start with an examination of the concrete factors. For us that calls for an examination of the specifics of U.S. imperialism in today's world and how they affect the system of "payoffs."

What are these specifics? U.S. imperialism is forced to operate in a world reality in which imperialism is not the unchallenged master. It is forced to deal with powerful bastions of anti-imperialism. Since the birth of the Soviet Union the main contradiction has been between the two opposite social systems—capitalism and socialism. It is one thing to sail into light breezes or an occasional gust of wind, but it is another matter when you are forced to buck the hurricane-like forces of history.

Because of these changes in objective conditions for sailing, imperialism has been forced to maneuver, to tack or to retreat to a safe haven. It has been forced to make concessions to the peoples and nations it has oppressed. Because of the revolutionary hurricanes of history the costs of imperialist operations have gone up. This in turn is having its effects on the system of "payoff" at home.

The costs for the policies of imperialist aggression have never come from the super-profits. While the costs have gone up, the super-profits continue to escalate. The increased costs are paid mainly by U.S. workers. The 1969 corporation profits from their foreign operations reached the record sum of an estimated 35 to 40 billion dollars. The lion's share of these profits go to the corporations, but the lion's share of the costs are paid by the people of the United States. The cost of imperialist operations is in the escalating cost of living. The cost of living index now stands at 130 percent of ten years ago.

The dollar costs of U.S. aggression in South East Asia are an estimated 35 to 40 billion dollars each year. This is paid for by the high tax load.

In 1969 the Federal Government spent an admitted 81 billion dollars on the military hardware it needs to continue its imperialist policies throughout the world. This expenditure is the cost for the 35-40 billion dollars the U.S. corporations take by way of profits from these operations. The corporations take 95 percent of these extra profits. But the U.S. workers pay 70 percent of these costs in federal government income taxes.

This is increasingly an important new factor in today's world reality. In 1941 when the total income tax load was a small fraction of what it is today, the corporations paid 55 percent of the total. Now in 1970 when these taxes have escalated to keep in step with the expansion of U.S. imperialist operations, the corporations pay 32 percent and the workers pay 68 percent of this load. This is significantly affecting the "payoff" system. If we could return to the 1941 tax ratio, the U.S. workers could collect 45 billion dollars each year.

The corporations not only receive the 35 to 45 billion in super-profits but they also get the super-profits that come from production of military hardware at home. These profits go mainly to the same corporations that get the super-profits from overseas operations.

In the five years between 1965 and 1969, years when the aggression against Vietnam was at a high point, the real weekly wages of U.S. production workers declined by $1.02 while the production per man hour rose by some 46 percent. For most U.S. workers the "trickle" is a drain in the opposite direction. The changes in the nature of the export of capital are having their influence on the "payoff" relationships.

The shift is towards the production of goods in foreign countries. It is an extension of the "runaway shop" across the borders to lower wage areas. For example, U.S. corporations have moved their operations to South Korea, Taiwan and Hong Kong. The workers there are forced to work under inhuman conditions, long hours, no standards of health protection or social security. Their wage scale is about $15 to $20 per month. The U.S. government guarantees these corporate investments and gives them additional incentives by granting special tariff concessions based on a number of gimmicks. Some 3,400 corporations now have 23,000 separate businesses abroad. They produce ove 200 billion dollars worth of goods.

The products of these "runaway shops" now enter the U.S. market in an increasing volume. This is a new factor in the U.S. worker relationship to U.S. imperialist exploitation in foreign lands. This has also turned the direction of the "trickle."

The shift in U.S. investments towards countries with a highly developed industry also affects the U.S. workers. Canada and capitalist Europe now account for 60 percent of all U.S. investments abroad. In this process the export of capital has become automated. Over 25 percent of all manufactured imports into the United States come from plants totally owned by United States corporations. When U.S. imperialism imported raw materials, there was no direct problem created for U.S. workers. The trickle was in one direction. The shift in the export of capital to set up industrial production and now to automate production has created a new contradiction between imperialism and the workers of the imperialist country. The competition and the threat of U.S. overseas production is replacing the "payoff" system. The policy of the corporations is, "If you have a club—why hand out carrots!" This has given the class confrontation in the United States a new dimension.

The cost of imperialist aggression in human lives has also escalated. U.S. imperialism has sent 50,000 young Americans to their deaths in South Vietnam. Some 350,000 are maimed and crippled. The aggression has now become the second most costly war in U.S. history.

The postwar period in which the United States was the "favored" capitalist nation has come to an end. The crisis of the dollar reflects the deeper crisis of the world capitalist setup. Monopoly capitalism does not give up on its drive for profits. If it has a crisis in its world operations it demands a higher rate of productivity, higher taxes, rents and prices at home. The corporations are on a "binge" to "cut off excessive fat." In many cases this hits the "paid off" sections. More and more the special concessions are going to be considered "excessive fat."

These are some of the new factors making up the new reality in which the system of imperialist "payoff" now operates. It is a period when the material base for granting "privileges" is wearing thin—a period when the sacrifices and costs are greater than the "privileges."

There is no question that U.S. imperialism still draws on the reserve fat which it accumulates from the super-profits that it gets from its imperialist operations. A small sector of the working class continues to get some special privileges, as a "payoff" that comes from these reserves. The "payoff" continues to influence class developments. They continue to be a source of opportunistic trends. But the new factors are making significant changes in this picture. The new factors are resulting in a sharpening class confrontation. Instead of "paying off," the ruling class is shifting the cost, including the new costs of imperialist operations, onto the backs of the working class.

In analyzing the "payoff" system of British imperialism, Lenin placed great emphasis on the source of the reserve funds. He said British imperialism was able to do it because of: "1) exploitation of the whole world by this country; 2) its monopolist position in the world market; 3) its colonial monopoly."[3]

Earlier Engels had placed the same emphasis:

> The truth is this: during the period of England's industrial monopoly the English working class have, to a certain extent, shared in the benefits of the monopoly. These benefits were very unequally parcelled out amongst them; the privileged minority pocketed most, but even the great mass had, at least, a temporary share now and then.[4]

From this it follows that when there is a change in the objective picture there is a change in how the "payoff" comes off.

This is the significance of the new factors now appearing on the stage of U.S. imperialism. It cannot now "exploit the whole world,"—"its monopolies" are not now "the masters of the capitalist world," and it does not now have a "colonial monopoly."

We have not seen the last of opportunism in the working class movement. The policies of class collaboration are not dead. United States capitalism will continue its policies of special concession. But it is necessary to take note of the changed set of objective conditions that do and will influence class relations and class forces.

What we are witnessing in the United States now more closely fits into what Lenin said at a later date: "The distinctive feature of the present situation (1916) is the prevalence of such economic and political conditions which could not but increase the *irreconcilability* between *opportunism* and the *general* and *vital interests* of the *working class movement*."[5]

For us the "distinctive feature" of the present movement is that as U.S. imperialism suffers defeats, as it is forced to retreat, as the cost of pursuing the policies of imperialist aggression go up, the material basis for the system of "payoffs" declines. The contra-

---

[3] V. I. Lenin, *Imperialism, The Highest Stage of Capitalism:* (New York: International Publishers, 1970), p. 108.

[4] Frederick Engels, "England in 1845 and in 1885," London *Commonweal*, March 1, 1885; cited in Frederick Engels, "Preface to Condition of the Working Class in England," Marx and Engels, *Selected Works*, Vol. 3 (Moscow: Progress Publishers, 1970), p. 450.

[5] V. I. Lenin, *Imperialism, The Highest Stage of Capitalism* (New York: International Publishers, 1970), p. 108.

diction between the system of "privileges" and "payoffs" and the vital interests of the U.S. working class becomes sharper. These changes in the objective scene have narrowed down the source and the base of opportunism within the working-class movement.

These changes are now showing up in the sharpening of the class confrontation. It is an important propellant for the rising rank-and-file movements. The new class relationships come to the surface in the labor-management contract negotiations. Gone are the days when the corporations presented ever new "package deals" that became the base for new contracts. The "package deals" in the past were a form of granting "privileges."

As U.S. imperialism's world position deteriorates, as it sinks into new crises at home, it moves from the carrot to the club, from concessions to policies of no concessions, from "payoffs" to pay cuts. This is creating serious problems for the trade union leadership that continues to serve the paymaster—U.S. imperialism. The gulf between such leaders and the rank-and-file becomes ever more impassable. The material base for opportunism narrows down. This is the new "distinctive feature" of the present moment.

When U.S. corporations were expanding their holdings all over the capitalist world, "foreign competition" in the domestic market was never an issue in the United States. Both the corporations and the class collaborationist trade union leaders were strong advocates of a "free trade" policy. As long as the U.S. corporations had the upper hand they were for free trade. Now when the shoe is shifting to the other foot, "free trade is idiotic" and they have started a "buy American" campaign. From the self-interest viewpoint of the workers in the United States the "buy American" campaign is self-defeating. I. W. Abel, the present head of the Steelworkers Union has developed further the bootlicking, crawling, class-collaborationist policies of the past leadership. Most of his speeches are concerned with the profits of the steel corporations.

I am sure, that we of the labor movement and we who work for a living will have the standard of life that the industries for whom we work can provide. We are tied together, and we either sink or we swim together. You know as well as I do that you can't go to a well that has gone dry and get a bucket of water, nor can you go to an industry nor a company and demand and receive improvements in the way of wages and benefits unless first that industry is a stable industry and a profitable industry.[6]

Abel either lies or he is childishly naive when he tells the steel-workers: "I remind you that over the past ten years the steel industry has enjoyed approximately a two percent year improvement factor." It simply is not true, and even if it were, the profits of the steel corporations were too high already ten years ago. This pro-corporation policy of Abel led to a disgraceful open sellout section in the 1971 steel contract.

The corporations use the "foreign import" issue to cut down the standards of the American workers. With Abel's connivance they used it to keep the wage increases at a minimum and then used it to start a joint corporation and union speedup drive in the steel industry. The contract states:

The parties are concerned that the future for the industry in terms of employment and return on substantial capital expenditures will rest heavily upon the ability of the parties to work cooperatively to achieve significantly higher productivity trends than have occurred in the recent past. . . . Thus, it is incumbent upon the parties to work cooperatively to meet the challenge posed by principal foreign competitors in recent years. It is also important that the parties cooperate in promoting the use of American-made steel.

In order to implement this expression of purposes, a joint advisory Committee on Productivity shall be established at each plant. . . . The Company and Union members of the Committee shall meet at mutually agreeable times, but no less than once a month. The function of the Committee shall be to advise with plant management concerning ways and means of improving productivity, and developing recommendations for stimulating its growth . . . to achieve uninterrupted operations in the plants, to promote the use of domestic steel and to achieve the desired prosperity and progress of the Company and its employees.

Abel reads the section to a steelworkers meeting and then adds:

Now, let me repeat there, the purpose is to "stimulate the growth of the industry." . . .
So I say to you that if you have visions of our shop stewards and our committeemen carrying blacksnake whips and special clubs, you can forget about it. . . .

[6] (Remarks of I. W. Abel at the Basic Steel Contract Briefing Conference, Sept. 29-30 and Oct. 1, 1971, p. 3).

Again I say we enlist your cooperation. . . .

1. It shall be the responsibility of the Joint Union-Industry Committee at the International Office-Company level to install the guidelines and oversee their operation. . . .

   A. Assuring continuity.

   B. Administration.

   C. Disseminating information and data relating to improving productivity.

   D. Reporting outstanding plant achievements on productivity. . . .

It provides us all with an opportunity to share in the responsibility of our own future. I don't think anybody in their right mind can quarrel with that. . . .

I would like at this meeting to suggest that you give a lot of serious thought; that you go back home and talk to your fellows about it, that you talk to your fellows about these other things—not just productivity. It's the problems of the steelworker and the steel industry —the problem of advancing our products and our jobs. . . .[7]

The steel corporations like this policy because it is their policy. They are the only ones who will benefit from this policy. The wage increases will be kept to a bare minimum. It will lead to wage cuts. It will result in further speeding up of production. Safety standards will be shelved and the profits will continue to rise. This is not only a matter of collaboration; this is a policy that destroys the union as an instrument fighting for workers' rights. This turns the workers into serfs, and trade union officers into speedup, efficiency experts.

The "buy American" campaign is self-defeating. Imports and exports are not a one-way street. Abel speaks about 20 percent steel imports. What he does not say is that more than 20 percent of steel goes into the products that the United States exports: What he does not say is that the campaign to cut off imports will result in a corresponding cut in exports and a corresponding cut in jobs.

The campaign to "buy American" is playing the bosses' game. The working class faces new problems. They will not be solved by policies of toadying capitulation. To become a partner in tightening the bonds of slavery is no solution.

The workers of all capitalist countries face these same new problems. They are the offsprings of the new stage of the crisis

[7] (*Remarks of I. W. Abel at the Basic Steel Contract Briefing Conference,* Sept. 29-30 and Oct. 1, 1971, pp. 5-8).

of capitalism.

The solution to the problem is not national isolation.

To find the solution one must pinpoint the cause.

The root of the problem is in capitalism. The enemy is not the workers of other lands. The enemy is the monopoly corporations. The attack must be directed against this class enemy.

The argument that the corporations' profits are not high enough, that the rate of productivity is not high enough is absolute hogwash.

The "buy American" campaign will be used to cut wages and speedup production—but it is not going to affect trade because the very corporations that use it to cut wages here are also the "foreign competitors." They have it both ways—they make profits by importing materials from their foreign plants, and they make profits from the speedup and wage cuts here. They do not even have to carry on the campaign. The Abels do it for them.

What is the solution?

The question is not whether there is a better solution than the "buy American" approach, because it is not even a poor solution. It is no solution to the new problems of the working class. Whenever anyone who is supposed to represent the interests of the working class begins to worry about the profits of the corporations, they close all doors to finding solutions to working-class problems. And so the answer to this and all problems must start with a militant nonnegotiable attitude of struggle against the corporations. The answers must be found in an attitude of class unity with the workers of other lands and especially with workers of other lands who are exploited by the same U.S. corporations. This class unity can include support for the organizations of trade unions and for their struggles. It should include a joint struggle for the nationalization of the United States-owned factories. It should include a campaign for loans from the United States—loans without political strings, long term loans on the basis of very minimum interest rates. The working-class movement must combine the struggle for its own class interests with a struggle against imperialism. This is in the class and people's interest at home and abroad. All other approaches that appear as if they are solutions are traps set out by monopoly capitalism.

From the viewpoint of the workers the "buy American" approach is fakery—it is a trap. The "buy American" campaign creates the atmosphere and leads to the campaign for increased speedup and wage cuts. That is the meaning of the phrase, "Our industry must be competitive." They never say the corporations or the corporation executives must take a cut in their billion dollar profits, or that their wages which total in the millions of dollars, must be cut so their industries can be competitive. In their class vernacular the phrase: "The high cost of profits or executives' salaries makes our products non-competitive," never appears. Theirs is a variation of one theme—"the high cost of labor." And the bootlicking trade union leaders chime in, "They're playing our song."

1971

7

IMPERIALISM, THE GROTESQUE PHASE OF CAPITALISM

The Rise of the Conglomerates

Imperialism is the final stage of capitalist development. It is the beginning of the end for capitalism. The decay is a process. This process takes place while capitalism still has periods of growth. The ebb and flow continues but the distortions become more grotesque. The periods of flow become less productive and the ebbs last longer. Capitalism fights against the effects of old age. The "innovations" become attempts to overcome crises. Each "innovation" may relieve one crisis situation only to give rise to processes that will lead to a new crisis. Remedies that used to give relief now tend to aggravate matters. The general decay of capitalism has reached a point where it cannot stay afloat without massive economic pump priming. What would happen to the economy if the 80 billion dollar war budget were to be cancelled? What would happen to the railroads, the airline corporations, such as Lockheed, Boeing, and Penn Central if the billions of dollars in government subsidies were to be terminated? They would collapse. Such is the state of affairs with the "free enterprise system." As capitalism decays the amount of outside pump priming must be increased. Like a narcotic addict, the dosage must be increased.

Only about 75 per cent of the total production plant capacity is now used. But there is a drive to increase the rate of labor productivity which only further cuts back on the percentage of the total plant that is in use. The idle capacity increases but the government pays for new plant construction and for the equipment through tax write-offs. This will also add to the non-used industrial capacity.

U.S. capitalism has increasingly faced the problem of accumulation of unused capital. There are no new continents and the shift in the world balance of forces has become a growing obstacle to opening up new areas of capital investment. The intense pressures built up by this condition have generated a kind of irrationality in the system; its channels for investment restricted, capitalism turns upon itself and devours its own. It is turning to conglomerates—capitalist cannibalism to the "nth" degree. This is a development fraught with significant political and social consequences.

In this new stage in the monopolization of the economy, the United States and other industrially developed countries are in the throes of a frenzy of corporate mergers. In the past, big fish have always swallowed smaller fish in the capitalist process, but the present wave of mergers is characterized by three new elements: first, the mergers have become uncontrollable; second, giants are being merged into super giants; finally, monopoly formations are giving rise to "conglomerates."

Mergers and acquisitions were usually distinguished as either "horizontal" or "vertical." Horizontal mergers are those between corporations in the same industrial classifications such as mergers within the tool making industry. Vertical mergers are those between corporations that are related to one another as actual or potential buyer and seller such as corporations publishing newspapers and corporations in the pulp and paper industry. The new conglomerate mergers are those for which there is no technological, production or market rationale. They are reaching the outer limits of capitalist anarchy. And this movement has spread over the entire economy; it has become the predominant trend, in contrast to horizontal or vertical merging.

The conglomerates introduce a new element of instability into capitalist relationships. Only the most profitable enterprises will be kept. Enterprises will be sacrificed to keep others operating. The conglomerates create new tax loopholes. They solve some problems but they set the stage for bigger bankruptcies. They give the monopoly corporations new leverage against the working class and the trade unions.

The conglomerates have a stranglehold on prices in wide sectors of the economy.

The very pinnacle of this lunacy is reached when these conglomerates become irrational aggregates in a galaxy of conglomerates, all financially owned and controlled by a giant bank. The rise of these hybrids is by no means limited to the domestic scene; it is becoming a structure for imperialist acquisitions. Increasingly, the imperialist bank has become the means of control by developing foreign conglomerates. For this purpose the United States has become the world's largest exporter of banks that are becoming the main controlling centers of U.S. imperialist holdings and conglomerates. For example, the Chase Manhattan Bank, a Rockefeller bank, now has over 1,600 overseas banking facilities of its own, plus hundreds of additional foreign banks under its control. Chase Manhattan is thus a private imperialist world empire, as well as one of the big controlling stockholders in U.S. war industries. It coordinates its profits from war industries with the Pentagon and its worldwide network of banks. To Vietnam it has exported napalm and banks, loans and bombs.

Thus, with the banks in control of industrial conglomerates, the United States has added a new link to its imperialist chain of domination of industries and governments through the banks. The forces of anti-imperialism must adjust their own tactics to this changing reality.

The rise of the conglomerates adds a new dimension to the anarchistic nature of capitalist production. They add a new dimension to its instability, to the parasitic character of capitalism. They sharpen the class contradiction as well as the relationship between the different sections of monopoly capital. They add a new quality to state-monopoly capitalism. They are new nails in the coffin of imperialism.

The new stage in the process of monopoly mergers and the rise of the irrational conglomerates deeply affects social and class relationships, accelerating the polarization of capitalist society. The gap between the parasitic top layer and the people has become a chasm; the process of alienation goes on apace; illusions as to the establishment fall before the exposure of its anti-humanist character. Concomitantly, it is giving rise to new problems for the class struggle. The conglomerates are in a position to use their control of one industry to fight the workers in another; they are in a position to liquidate whole industries. Under these circumstances the unity of workers in one industry is not enough; central trade union centers will be forced to become centers for coordinating and leading struggles.

The new stage in monopoly development demands a new perspective on the importance of anti-monopoly movements. We must take into account that the conglomerate stage of monopoly is closely related to the developments of state-monopoly capitalism. The system of superhawks directly controlling galaxies of conglomerates dominates government policy more directly than ever. In the United States it has made a mockery of anti-trust laws. Nevertheless, it is a development that does not result in the strengthening of capitalism, even while it does give rise to new dangers of war and fascism.

While capitalism develops along this irrational path, the forces of socialism continue to grow stronger.

The people of the world have two world systems on the stage —capitalism in crisis and unstable, socialism stable and developing without crises.

1971

8

IMPERIALISM AND RACISM

Twin Instruments of Oppresion

The voices of imperialism have never openly stated, "We are oppressing and exploiting the people of other nations in order to make extra private profits." Each has developed its special line of deception to cover up the profit motive. In the earlier years they were in the "humanitarian" business of "bringing religion and civilization to the backward peoples." This line of deception became the foundation for an ideology of great power chauvinism. When this line wore thin, they added a new line. Now they are "exporting democracy" and the "benefits of industry."

Because most of the countries of imperialism have been populated by people having white skin, while most of the people in the countries oppressed by imperialism have been people of other races, people having darker skins, this has always been a racist ideological tool of imperialism. Racism has become the main ingredient of great power chauvinism. Thus the main pillar of imperialist ideology is racist great power chauvinism. The world fountainhead for racist great power chauvinism is U.S. imperialism. This is so because U.S. imperialism is the center of world imperialism. But there is another reason. Racist great power chauvinism has deeper roots here than in any other country of the world.

Racism was an ideological pillar of U.S. capitalism long before it became an imperialist power. Racism was the poisonous fog covering the hijacking of Black slaves from Africa to the United States. Racism was the ideological foundation for the system of slave plantations in the South. From the very beginning of

U.S. capitalist development, racism has been the basis for the system of discrimination against Black Americans in industry. It is the basis for the system of segregation in housing, in schools, in businesses, in churches and in the trade unions. The weapon of chauvinism is used against Mexican-Americans, Puerto Ricans and Indian Americans. Anti-Semitism has deep roots in the United States.

For U.S. imperialism the propagation of great power chauvinism was an extension and enlargement of its racist ideology. Because of this history, from the very beginning the ideological essence of U.S. imperialism has been racist great power chauvinism. In most parts of the imperialist world, but especially in the United States, this ideology surfaces as white chauvinism—the concept of white supremacy. It is the most persistent and penetrating of all ideological concepts. It is the moving force behind actions all the way from a sickening paternalism to the actions of the lynch mob. The struggle against racist great power chauvinism is a special responsibility for us in the United States because it is an imperialist tool for both domestic and foreign policies.

The special systems of racist oppression against some 25 million Black Americans, five million Chicanos, two million Puerto Ricans, and against the American Indians are systems of special profits for the capitalist class. Because all of the profits from all of the sources go into the same corporation bank accounts, it is difficult to separate them.

The system of special oppression in the United States is without precedent. It is institutionalized in government, in industry, in all areas of social, cultural and political affairs. There is a class relationship between the special oppression of different groups. But the system of oppression and racism that feeds the others is the policies and practices of racism against Black Americans.

The nature and the end economic results of racism are clear in the following facts taken from reports put out by the U.S. government.

1. Median income of white households   (dollars) $8,756
2. Median income of Black households   (dollars) $5,291
3. Difference between the two   (dollars) $3,465
4. Number of Black households   (thousands)   6,053

5. Total extra profits from super-exploitation of Black people	(billion dollars)	21.0
6. On the same basis: Total extra profits from super-exploitation of Chicano, Puerto Rican, Indian people	(billion dols.)	7.0
7. Total super-profits from super-exploitation of oppressed peoples in the United States	(billion dols.)	28.0

NOTE: Calculations based on employed workers and wage differentials come out almost exactly the same.

The purpose of the racist great power chauvinism—of white chauvinism—is to cover up and to uphold this special exploitation, this racist system that results in these extra profits.

But even the above figures do not give the full story. Racist ideology is geared to divide the oppressed. Capitalism uses these divisions to cut into the share of the white workers. They pay for their racism by lower wages. These are also extra profits for capitalism.

Although the two kinds of racist oppression—colonial oppression and the special system of oppression within the nation—seem distinct, the links between the policies of U.S. imperialist oppression of other peoples and the system of special oppression at home are many. Both serve the purpose of extra profits. Both are continued under the fog of a racist ideology.

It is important to see the relationships between the two forms of oppression. But it is a disservice, as well as wrong, to say they are one and the same thing. To view the Black community as a colony leads to tactics that are self defeating. What is most decisive is that Afro-Americans by and large consider such concepts unrealistic.

The struggle against world imperialism coincides with the struggle against racist oppression in the United States. The struggle against racist oppression at home is an important contribution to the struggle against United States imperialism in the world. The enemy is the same.

Winds of social change that have gathered tremendous momentum are battering down the 300-year-old walls of racist oppression. The new level of political and social consciousness of some 25 million Black Americans has generated wave upon wave of militant mass protest. The struggle has broken the carefully woven curtain of promises and platitudes that has endured for generations. And there, for the whole world to see, in the heart of the land that boasted of "equality for all," is the most inhuman kind of oppression of 25 millions of its people. If many in the nation had always known it was there, many more had closed their eyes to it.

U.S. capitalism had refined and adapted the system, the practice, and the mentality of racial discrimination—the exploitation of a minority within the system of class exploitation. More than a 100 years after the Emancipation Proclamation racism cannot be described as the aftermath of slavery, but more accurately as a deliberate strategy in the maneuvering for super-profits.

The United States found itself in the sixties facing a serious political and social crisis—not a crisis of Black Americans but a crisis of national existence, a challenge to our vaunted democracy and morality. Large sections of white Americans responded to this moment of history, especially the youth. The ranks of the civil rights movement took on mass proportions and turned into one of the most meaningful struggles for liberation. The awakening of millions to the harsh fact of servitude existing within its own borders became a factor that raised the mass political consciousness of large sections of our people to a new level.

The struggle since the Montgomery bus strike has had many important victories. These can be viewed in two ways. If they are seen as substantive solutions, their significance is grievously limited. Like the assassins in Mississippi waiting to ambush freedom fighters, Jim Crow is always waiting for the opportune moment to counterattack. If they are seen as initial steps in preparation for a decisive change, then they become truly revolutionary in their implications.

Racism has always been one of the most deadly weapons of imperialist ideology. The color of a man's skin has generated more examples of man's inhumanity to man than almost any other atrocity. Imperialism has refined it and given racism a global character. Its influence has been the most serious obstacle to the development of class consciousness in the ranks of the workers and to anti-imperialist struggles.

U.S. imperialism is an extension abroad of its racism at home. Throughout the world, it directly exploits millions of wage workers extracting billions in profits each year. In addition, U.S. capitalism derives tens of billions in the super-profits it nets from the special system of racial and national oppression practiced against some 40 million of its own citizens. These policies and practices can continue only because so many Americans, brainwashed into racism, permit it to go on.

Nothing packs such dynamite as an issue that the processes of social development have placed on the agenda of history. Its resolution can no more be prevented than can the rising of the sun.

In 1776, such an issue was independence for the colonies, and independence was won. In 1863, it was freedom for the slaves, and slavery was abolished. The victories in each of these momentous conflicts were assured by the fact that great numbers of Americans, even though all did not fully grasp the significance of the issue, were nevertheless compelled by their own self-interest to join in the battle.

In our day, a central world issue that has come up for decision is the ending of imperialist oppression of peoples and nations. And the world system of colonialism is well on its way out. In our own country the key issue for resolution *now* is the eradication of the system of segregation and discrimination practiced against some 25 million Black Americans. Just as the United States could not have moved forward without its people resolving in their day the questions of independence and emancipation, so we cannot move ahead today without putting an end to a system that keeps 1/10 of our citizens half-slave and half-free.

The destruction of this system is of crucial significance to the majority of our people—crucial to the preservation and extension of democracy and to the working class in its economic struggles. It is a question that influences decisively the relations of the United States with the rest of the world. The technical standards of all Americans are at issue, for no people can tolerate the national oppression of a large section of its citizens without the weakening and corruption of the moral fiber of all its citizens.

Since the Supreme Court declared school segregation unconstitutional, millions of Black Americans and many whites—including tens of thousands of the clergy and hundreds of thousands of youth—have marched, sat-in, demonstrated and picketed, gone to jail, suffered beatings and the thrust of the cattle prods in the struggle for human decency and equality. Men, women and children have died as heroes and victims in this campaign.

But after all the militant actions, how do we evaluate the results? There have been positive gains—not to see this would be a disservice to the struggle. Some of the solid walls of segregation and discrimination have been broken down. There has been some progress in every area, but it has been painfully slow and limited. To fail to see how stubbornly the establishment resists the full resolution of the issue would also be a disservice. Disproportionate joblessness, wretched housing and a degrading ghetto existence are still the fate of the great majority of the Black people, as it is, in one degree or another, of the Puerto Ricans and the Chicanos.

Therefore, the people of the United States must ask again and again, what are the forces that so stubbornly resist and obstruct the nonviolent resolution of this shameful heritage of ours? What are the roots of its persistence? Who are the main perpetrators?

The affliction flows from the system of discrimination against Black Americans that is imbedded in the very fabric of U.S. capitalism. Racism has been and is still the policy of every major corporation in America; racism is inherent in the creation of big business. It is a method of squeezing maximum profits from the labor of all who toil. It is an instrument for maintaining in the halls of Congress and in state and city legislative bodies reactionary blocs of anti-democratic, anti-labor, and anti-Black politicians. It is an effective device for keeping the working class divided against itself. White supremacy, the ideological foundation of the system of discrimination and segregation, is a central pillar in the ideology of U.S. imperialism. It is this that explains the stubborn persistence of racism and bigotry.

At stake in the resolution of the civil rights issue are all the past gains made by our people. The stubborn resistance by the forces of reaction to its democratic resolution unifies and strengthens the ultra-right coalition. The nuclear-war maniacs, the rabid anti-labor crowds, the anti-democratic, pro-fascist gangs, the professional anti-Semites, the anti-Communist racketeers—all are now gravitating towards a unity with the Southern racists, the KKK and similar groups. This is indeed a crystallization of reaction, an alliance that can open the gates to fascism. And open racism flows through all their veins.

They emerged as the organizers and the shock troops of Alabama's Governor Wallace; most of the Wallace-appointed electors were members of the Birch Society. The anti-labor corporations financed the campaign, the Nazi groups financed the goon squads, and Wallace furnished unsurpassed demagogy. Each group made its special contribution to the evil alliance whose ultimate aim is the destruction of democracy in our country, and the use of nuclear weapons in the crusade to plant the iron heel of U.S. imperialism on all mankind.

The big business ideology of bigotry is like a poison gas designed to incapacitate the people, to distort reality and to bring on a state of confusion. We read stories of witchcraft in New England at an early period in our history, but is not the witchcraft of racism more fantastic, taking possession of the minds of millions of otherwise sane Americans?

U.S. capitalism took over the ideology of white supremacy from the slavemasters and upholders of slavery. Corporate capitalism has refined and further developed it, made it more subtle so that it penetrates into every layer of American life. In order to imbue the masses of white America with the illusion of superiority it was necessary to make sure that its Black fellow-citizens be deprived of equal educational, social and economic opportunities. Thus, unwittingly, millions of white people became instruments of the oppression of their brothers and sisters.

Under the influence of the deadly virus of racism, their own lives of toil, debt and hardship, in comparison with the lot of their Black neighbors, have been transformed into a myth of superior existence. While they rant against the Black, Puerto Rican and Chicano workers, they temporarily forget their own empty cupboards and lack of security. Thus it becomes more and more difficult for them to focus on their real oppressor—big business—which exploits both black and white.

If the roots of the system of discrimination and segregation are deep within the profit system, is it possible to eliminate Jim

Crow before capitalism is discarded as the outmoded system that it is? As militant resistance to this evil increases, this question is asked more and more often. It seems obvious that it will not be possible to dig out all of the poisoned roots while our present system exists, because the inherent nature of capitalism constantly generates new pressures for its revival. But it is possible to sever many of the roots and to destroy many offshoots and branches even while capitalism still stands. Victories in the fight for freedom are on the agenda right now, and many are being won. The Black liberation struggle has moved into the realm of economic and political equality, which means jobs, promotions, access to the professions and to business. In the political arena it means the extension of registration and voting opportunities to all and the election of Black public officials on every level.

The demands now go into areas that big business considers its very special private preserve, on which the monopolists have placed a "No Trespassing" sign—the prerogative of making profits. And as the struggle develops in these areas, its nature changes; there are new alliances, new support as well as more insidious and subtle resistance. For it is a law of capitalism that big business has never relinquished one cent of its profit or one ounce of its political power until it is up against an irresistible force.

At this stage, the civil rights movement comes up against the workings of the state-monopoly conspiracy. In some cases, the government runs interference for the monopolists; in others, the government expresses support by silently condoning abuses. In the South, the conspiracy more frequently comes out into the open; the government compounds terror and vigilante movements; it grants immunity to open murder. But in other parts of the country as well, militant leaders of the Black people are harassed, jailed, driven into exile and murdered.

The path to victory for both civil rights and peace—and they have become more and more interdependent—lies only in the direction in which the working class, Black and white together, confronting the same foe, coordinates its economic and political struggles. A labor-Black people's alliance is not a new concept, but it has a new and imperative meaning today. The state-monopoly conspiracy and the problems arising from automation are pressing hard against all working men and women, and new relationships must be molded by these realities since it gives rise to a new political consciousness.

To the indignation of the press and certain elements among our fellow citizens, Black leaders have been calling for a buildup of political power bases on local levels where Black voters are a sizable block or constitute the majority. Suddenly there are people (often liberals who were labor supporters of the freedom movement, who never had difficulty in accommodating to the ancient practice of white domination and exclusiveness) professing alarm and shock when Black leaders assert that the time has come for securing majority rule where *Blacks* are the majority in the political subdivisions, the counties, the cities, the towns, the congressional and senatorial and state assembly districts. Why is a majority rule democratic only when the majority is white?

Speaking directly to those white Americans who are raising the question of Black political power today in the most alarmist manner, as if it were a woeful dilemma, we say that the Black people in the United States must be allowed to secure full participation in governmental and community bodies, reflecting their just role in public office and leadership.

A further word about integration may be in order: formal integration does not necessarily mean equality; it can in fact substitute tokenism for real equality. The new stage of struggle is not so much concerned with the appearance of change as it is with the essence. For example, the continuing terror in the South shows how constitutionally granted rights can fail to correspond to reality. In the interests of democracy for all, the American people must put pressure on the federal government to enforce the laws and end the reign of terror. When the government refuses to enforce the laws, it is quite understandable why some have been compelled to seek protection by self-defense.

The labor-Black people's alliance will only be as real as the underlying unity of the working class. Such unity in the struggle against all forms of discrimination must start with the elimination of all bars to membership and leadership in the labor unions.

There are other minority groups whose size and importance have greatly grown in the past few decades. There are millions of Chicanos, Puerto Ricans and other Spanish-speaking peoples who suffer the indignities of discrimination, are crowded into the worst slums, and are given the lowest-paying jobs. The Chicanos make up a large part of the most severely exploited section of the working class—the agricultural workers. Large numbers of them work in unorganized industries, live in unspeakable slums, and are, like the Black people, the object of police brutality.

There is another group of Americans—indeed the original Americans—whose oppression is in some ways the worst of all—the American Indians. Confined to reservations, denied many of the rights of U.S. citizens, robbed of their birthright by broken treaties, they have moved onto the stage with strong protests against their exploiters.

The struggle for the rights of all these millions of Americans is essential to the fight for a united working class. A factor of special importance is the organization of unorganized laborers. Some breakthroughs have taken place, particularly among the Chicano agricultural workers of California. Class unity, beginning with Black-white unity and extending to embrace all oppressed minorities, starts at the level of self-interests. With the rise of a new political consciousness, it should develop from an alliance of convenience to a true brotherhood of mutual respect and equality.

The history of the Black people is one of struggle, bloodshed, heroism and sacrifice, of tremendous obstacles overcome, of survival against heavy odds. These struggles against their enslavement by the white rulers of the United States have left a proud legacy inherited by each succeeding generation as a guide in its own efforts to carry forward the resistance to tyranny. With working class unity we can hope to reach a point where class oppression and exploitation, as well as national subjugation and oppression, will be memories, relics in the museums of an advancing world whose peoples live in peace and happiness under socialism.

The winning of a life wherein all of our people will have full equality arises at a time in the history of mankind when the development of science and technology has made a world without want a realistic possibility. The material base for such a world can also be the basis for a world without wars, without bigotry or prejudice, without oppression of individuals, peoples or nations —a world where the practice of man's inhumanity to man becomes unthinkable.

The obstacle to the realization of this goal, a goal within the grasp of humanity, is capitalism. Big business, in its greed for maximum profits, is the one great hurdle civilization must scale before it can proceed to the "real history of humanity." The new social order that has discarded the profit motive includes one-third of the world's people, and this is a decisive factor for achieving socialism in the rest of the world.

1970

9

THE IDEOLOGICAL OFFENSIVE
AGAINST U.S. IMPERIALISM

U.S. imperialism is not only the arsenal of world imperialism, it has also become its ideological headquarters. There are hundreds of institutions, governmental and private, spending billions of dollars on this front, producing extensive cadres, thousands of books, magazines and newspapers each year as well as tens of thousands of ideologically oriented television and radio programs. Each of the armed forces has its own ideological department. The Defense Department, the CIA and the State Department have their own ideological sectors. Most of the large universities have specially financed ideological departments. Most of them operate behind some academic front. One of U.S. imperialism's special gimmicks, of course, is the demagogic veneer of "democracy" that goes so far as to pretend it is anti-imperialist, and that it gives support to "revolutions." They speak about "accepting" verdicts of history "if it is the popular will."

The ferocity of its aggression in Indochina has opened big gaps in this demagogic cover; shocking revelations about the work of its subversive arm, the CIA, have further exposed the true nature of its operations, while the mounting militancy of Black citizens has exposed to the world its anti-democratic and racist practices at home and abroad. U.S. imperialism "accepts" a verdict of history only when there is nothing it can do about it.

The Bay of Pigs fiasco, the shameless invasion of the Dominican Republic, the support of reactionary regimes in countries like Spain, Greece and Taiwan, the exposés about CIA penetration and control of "democratic" cultural, political and trade union organizations throughout the capitalist world—all these have resulted in an erosion of the demagogic veneer so carefully built up through the years. All this has opened up new possibilities for an ideological offensive against U.S. imperialism. It was the anti-fascist ideological offensive against German imperialism that was the foundation for the mass character of the world struggle against the imperialist axis powers of Berlin, Rome and Tokyo. Anti-fascism of the millions became the ideological ingredient that bound together a solid world front against the aggression of German, Italian and Japanese imperialism.

There may be many differences among progressive groups but there can be no question over the need to carry on constant ideological exposure and vigilance against imperialism. There are no shortcuts if we are to free ourselves of the all-pervasive menace of imperialism.

The setbacks suffered by U.S. imperialism have resulted in some corrosion of its ideological front. There is a growing sense of fear in the ideological hatching places of U.S. capitalism. They are no longer as complacent, as self-confident as they once were, in view of the revolution in the patterns of thought and attitudes of the American people. In the early stages of the present upsurge, the spokesmen of capitalism could invent rubber stamps like the "generation gap" and interpret it as a passing phase like mini skirts, beards and four-letter words. Actually, they saw only some of the surface manifestations, some of the symptoms of the real explosion. These were only the preliminary tremors for the political and ideological earthquake that was to shake the very foundations of the old social order.

There is now a growing realization in ruling circles that they are facing a new phenomenon. The old devices of flag-waving patriotism and politicians' promises are no longer relevant. Therefore the spokesmen for U.S. capitalism now speak about a "mass breakdown of moral and ethical standards," a "growing lack of respect for authority, government, parents, and schools," an "alarming decline of patriotism," "a tendency to destroy the power of our presidents." They now prate solemnly about "alienation," "new sets of priorities", "radicalization."

There is a new well financed campaign against "a new isolationism." Even the discredited ex-President Johnson is hauled out to warn against the "new isolationism." When the people refuse to support the policies of United States imperialist aggression, this is called the "new isolationism."

But it is imperialism that has become isolated. U.S. imperialism can end its isolation in the world only to the extent that it ends its policies of imperialist aggression. The imperialists attempt to deal with political and ideological phenomena as if they were psychological quirks, and the gimmicks they suggest as remedies are of a piece with the false premises. There is a kind of mass hypnosis induced by the endless rhetoric of empty platitudes.

All of this only further demonstrates the bankruptcy of capitalist ideology that finds itself increasingly impotent in face of the unprecedented change in the thought patterns of masses who are in motion.

Millions of our people are leaving old orbits of thought, rejecting outworn concepts; unprecedented numbers are probing and questioning all the areas of capitalist environment—and they are acting. That which was taken for granted yesterday is discarded today; old hollow pretensions are rejected; the trend is away from narrow nationalism. Capitalist intrenched institutions, the infallibility of the religious hierarchy, the ivory towers of the academic community are no longer sacrosanct.

What the ideologists of the old order try to cover up is that the upheavals, the alienation, the revolution in thinking and in world outlook by the masses are the tremors of a world passing from one social system to another. They are incapable of recognizing the most basic reality of today's historic transition. It is an explosive movement but it is predictable and even orderly, propelled by discernible forces and guided by social laws. The mass rejection of the status quo is basically progressive, signaling an advancing civilization. It is updating the social order to make it correspond to the potential of the breakthroughs in science and technology; it is life's way of reaching what was once unreachable, attaining what was unattainable in the old order of things, and it shatters the limits of the old status quo.

Since the United States is the very heart and center of world imperialism, the strongest bastion of the decaying world order of capitalism, it is understandable why the political, economic and ideological tremors resulting from the crisis of the old system should be felt so powerfully here. It is important to bear in mind that the transition is not just a simple change from one social organization to another; it is the beginning of a new concept in human relations. The transition to socialism aims to put an end to social systems based on man exploiting man. To put an end to man's exploitation of man is to put an end to capitalism—to imperialism. Although this concept is understood by many only on a rudimentary level, it is very much present in the new outlook of millions especially in the outlook of the younger generation.

Public opinion polls have become a nightmare for the myth-makers of U.S. capitalism. In spite of their imperfections, they cannot wholly conceal the shift in mass thought patterns. A recent issue of *Fortune*, the organ of U.S. monopoly capital, ran a poll asking people to react to a number of assertions often made in criticizing capitalism. Possible answers ranged from "strongly agreeing" to "partly agreeing." The reactions of the youth—workers, students, professionals—were most interesting. To the statement: "Business is overly concerned with profits and not with public responsibilities," 92 percent of the youth said "Yes." Fifty-one percent said they "strongly agreed" with the statement. To the statement: "Basically, we are a racist nation," 74 percent of the youth said, "Yes." And to the statement: "Economic well-being in this country is unjustly and unfairly distributed," 75 percent answered "Yes." Further, to the statement: "Morally and

spiritually our country has lost its way," 62 percent said "Yes."
And 60 percent thought, "Today's American society is characterized by injustice, insensitivity, lack of candor and inhumanity";
while 77 percent said "Yes" to, "Our foreign policy is based on
our narrow economic and power interests," and 56 percent of
the youth said "Yes" in answer to "The Vietnam war is pure
imperialism." To the statement "The individual in today's society
is isolated and cut off from meaningful relationships," 56 percent
gave a positive answer.

While such opinion polls are never fully scientific, they do
indicate trends. The questions did not test what percentage of
American youth think of socialism as the answer to their assessment of capitalism, nor what percentage believe in a reform of
capitalism as the answer. The poll does, however, indicate a
shift from past patterns and a definitely critical attitude toward
capitalism. There is a strong anti-imperialist trend in these
answers.

The *Fortune* poll was taken in 1969. In the two years since,
the thought patterns have continued to change. Now all polls
indicate that some 75 percent of the people are for the immediate
withdrawal of all U.S. armed forces—no matter what happens
in Vietnam. In some polls 51 percent now believe the war is immoral and unjust. And 31 percent believe the U.S. leaders responsible for the war could be tried as war criminals under the legal
and moral precedent set by the Nuremberg trials. This is the
most significant shift in mass thought patterns in our history. It
shows an unprecedented high level of conscious anti-imperialism.
This high level of anti-imperialist consciousness is reflected in
the rebellions of the armed forces. For the first time in our country's history the drafted armed forces have become an unreliable
military force. The extent of this rebellion is carefully covered
up. The high level of addiction to drugs in the armed forces is
only an expression of the dissatisfaction and a sense of frustration in the ranks of the troops.

The drug problem has now emerged as a serious problem because it has backfired. In the past the army brass has either
facilitated or closed its eyes to the distribution of cheap drugs
because it helped them to control the reluctant and rebellious

troops. Now, it has become a serious disabling factor.

The administration has taken some steps only because the youth who have returned to civilian life, while addicted to drugs, have become a political time-bomb.

There is no question but that the main source for the cheap drugs in Vietnam has been the puppet Saigon government with the connivance of the U.S. military brass.

There can be no doubt that there is alienation, that there is rejection of the old order of priorities. There is wide discussion of new values and new priorities associated with the shift in ideological and political concepts.

It is not a rejection of all values. It is a rejection of the sense of values and the order of priorities dictated by monopoly capitalism, an alienation from the inhumanity dictated by the military-industrial complex. It is a disenchantment with a "dog-eat-dog" life of imperialism. They are rejecting a culture built on the acceptance of "rich and poor," "workers and bosses," "haves and have-nots," and slums and ghettos in the midst of affluence. They recognize the new realities that have become possible because of the breakthroughs in technology and science. It is a mass rejection of the priorities dictated by policies of imperialism.

Youth rebels against racism because it is unjust and immoral, because it poisons the bloodstream of our nation. But they also reject racism because they see it as an instrument of profits. The Afro-American rebellion of the past ten years is destroying the roots of more than 300 years of racism. Tokenism is not acceptable to the 25 million of our Black fellow-Americans. This rebellion strikes fear to the hearts of monopoly capitalists, because in thought and action the Blacks place the responsibility for racism where it belongs, on capitalism, and they move toward rejecting the idea that the system holds the hope of eliminating racism.

The tens of millions of Americans who have taken part in the large mass peace actions in the history of our country are a measure of this new level of ideology, especially when one considers that these millions go into action against the most massive governmental pressure. Actions take place in the face of governmental violence, of fascist vigilantes, of the forces of jingoism, nationalism and right-wing hysteria. It is a movement that has to overcome provocation, slander and vilification. These mass actions take place against one's own government. A movement of this scope and of so many years' duration can be sustained only by a new level of thought and consciousness. Reflecting the opinion of the majority of our people, it is without precedent.

There are many, of course, who oppose the Vietnam aggression because they hate war and abhor bloodshed. But what is it that explains the difference in the reactions of our people to this war as compared to other wars? In World War II, for example, the masses identified the war with the self-interest of the nation. Fascism was a threat to the independence of all nations. In this war, there is a growing awareness of the relationship of policies of U.S. aggression, of U.S. military involvement and the policies of exploitation of other peoples by U.S. monopoly capital. Thus, a new anti-imperialist sense of values has begun to emerge.

The mass trends in the ranks of the working class are moving away from the class-collaborationist concept and toward a more conscious class outlook. This is clearly indicated in confrontations on the economic front, the movement toward independent political action and the official actions of a number of rank-and-file union members in support of the anti-war protests. The process is not an even one; there are detours and dead-ends; there are setbacks and frustrations and there are misdirected alienations. Thus, many, especially in the ranks of the youth, seek solutions in "dropping out," in ideas like "stopping the world and getting off." This has resulted in the setting up of isolated enclaves, desperately trying to separate themselves from the corrupt, profit-hungry debasing environment around them. This sometimes takes the form of setting up "communes," resembling the old utopian socialist communes that grew up in the United States before the turn of the nineteenth century. The attempt to escape reality results in the setting up of "counter-universities." It has created the concept of a counter-community, and many escape the contradictions of life in the illusory world of drugs. The ideologists, no matter how they groan about this, are not as alarmed as they might be at these particular diversionary developments because, at least momentarily, these diversions take these youth away from the path of mass action, of struggle. And in their frustration, some become easy victims to anarchist ideas and to police provocations. To be sure, these influences affect only small sectors of the people in the process of radicalization. But they do serve as a base for petty bourgeois radical concepts and for anarchistic and Trotsky-ite diversionary and divisive efforts. As a result, some become permanent "drop-outs" from struggle and from the revolutionary movement.

The main point, however, remains that there is a mass shift in outlook that not only reflects the historic world transition from capitalism to socialism but is also an important feature of a period of sharp domestic confrontation. The aggressive reac-tionary policies of the Nixon administration are a feature of this confrontation and polarization. The public mobilization of 50,000 armed troops in Washington, D.C., during the November 15, 1969, anti-war peace demonstration and the mass arrests during the 1971 Washington demonstration are symbolic of the Pentagon's contribution to the new confrontation. The new, fascist-like attacks on Black and youth militants, Vice President Agnew's Goebbels-like demand that the mass media conform fully to the class dictates of the ruling circles—these are all part of this new confrontation.

The fears and panic in the councils of monopoly capital reflect the advances of the progressive forces, but they also present some new problems and dangers.

In referring to the two forms of capitalist rule, Lenin said:

As a matter of fact, in every country the bourgeoisie inevitably devises two methods of fighting for its interests and of maintaining its domination, and these methods at times succeed each other and at times are interwoven in various combinations. The first of these is the method which rejects all concessions to the labor movement, the method of supporting all the old and obsolete institutions, the method of irreconcilably rejecting reforms. . . . The second is the method of "liberalism," of steps towards the development of political rights, towards reforms, concessions and so forth.

The bourgeoisie passes from one method to the other not because of the malicious intent of individuals, and not accidentally, but owing to the fundamentally contradictory nature of its own position.[1]

If it is possible for the ruling class to govern with the help

[1] V. I. Lenin, *Collected Works*, Vol. 16 (Moscow: Foreign Languages Publishing House, 1963), p. 350.

of demagogy, promises and some concessions, they will do so. But when the old remedies of demagogy fail, when the promises turn into empty myths and when the concessions dry up the monopoly circles turn to violence and open oppression. Thus the ugly spectre of fascism has again raised its ugly snout.

Because there is fear and grave concern in the ranks of the ruling class about the new patterns of mass thought, there is also the danger of reactionary oppression. There are elements present of the two forms "interwoven in various combinations." The Nixon administration is laying the basis and taking the steps to move toward what Lenin called "the method of force." When demagogic devices fail, capitalism always moves to rule by force. The "strict constructionist" majority in the Supreme Court is a reactionary ultra-right majority.

The danger of fascism is closely related to the policies of imperialist aggression. It is a way of forcing the people to accept policies that are against their own best self-interests. Therefore as the policies of aggression meet resistance the danger of fascism grows.

But on the other hand the possibility of defeating the attempts to establish fascist rule are related to the mass upsurge against the policies of imperialist aggression. Thus the policies of aggression bring on both the danger of fascism and the forces that can prevent it.

We must see both possibilities in this perspective. The new level of anti-imperialist consciousness is a solid base on which the conscious anti-fascist movement can be built.

Imperialism has escalated its ideological campaign. But it is meeting a strong resistance because of the new patterns of mass thought.

1971

10

THE MIDEAST CRISIS

The crisis of the Mideast has emerged at the center of the stage. It remains a grave danger to world peace. There is confusion; the facts, the basic truth is hidden behind a whipped up hysteria. What follows are thoughts that have been expressed before and during Israel's war of aggression in reply to a communication I received from the "Israeli Peace Movement."

AN OPEN LETTER TO THE "ISRAELI PEACE MOVEMENT"

I received your memorandum entitled "The Six-Day War Was on the Part of the People of Israel a Defensive War for Israel's Very Existence." In that sentence lies the root of our fundamental disagreement. No matter how often it is repeated, an aggression does not become a defensive war. It was, after all, the armed forces of Israel that attacked Egypt, Syria and Jordan; it is the armed forces of Israel that still occupy large sections of three Arab countries; it is the government of Israel that has taken steps to incorporate these sectors as parts of Israel. Public statements by Israeli government spokesmen, by leading religious and political leaders, openly declare Israel's intentions to continue the aggression. It was and is an illegal, unjust, immoral act of aggression—of imperialist expansion.

Indeed, there is not one fact showing that the armed forces of the Arab countries attacked or crossed the borders of Israel. You recite a long list of quotations showing the aggressive intentions of the Arab leaders. The refusal of Arab countries to accept and to recognize the existence of Israel is shortsighted and wrong; the speeches and editorials reflecting these policies must be condemned. But they do not justify Israel's armed aggression against the Arab peoples or governments. In the total justification you make for Israel's aggression you see the whole world through the blinders of Israeli nationalism. And to us it is apparent that the aggression was not really triggered by the anti-Israel speeches in Cairo and Damascus.

The root of the crisis in the Middle East is oil. The governments of the Arab countries have increasingly insisted on a greater share of the wealth extracted from their soil. The U.S. and British oil corporations have been increasingly unhappy with this development; the U.S. and British governments, with the skilled machinations of the CIA, have been very busy making one attempt after another to overthrow these Arab governments. They were successful in Iran. This crisis over oil became an opportunity for the expansionist forces in Israel. While for the oil corporations and the governments of the U.S. and Britain, the expansionist forces of Israel became an instrument to remove the Arab forces who stood in the way of maximum colonial profits from oil. Without U.S. and British support Israel would never have had either the material-military means or the confidence to carry out the aggression. U.S. and British spokesmen have demagogically blocked all effective action by the U.N.

It is difficult to avoid the conclusion that Israel's aggression was planned by a combination of varied forces whose different interests temporarily came together in the armed attack.

We note that you attempt to persuade the fighters against U.S. aggression in Vietnam that there is no parallel to be drawn between the two wars, stating that "there is no room for any comparison between the situation in the Middle East and that in Vietnam: the Americans in Vietnam are foreign invaders." Indeed they are, but what then are the armed forces of Israel in Egypt, Jordan and Syria? Angels of Mercy? As if this were not enough, you point out that the situation is different because "the final solution of the Vietnam problem lies in eliminating the Americans from there." You do not see the armed forces of Israel on Arab land as "foreign invaders" and you do not see the solution of the Mideast crisis in "eliminating the forces of Israel from there." Obviously you have accepted the Israel government position that their forces of aggression are going to stay in the occupied territories.

You further state: "Up to the last moment the Israel Peace Movement called for non-use of force, for honoring the armistice agreements, seeking for peaceful solutions." But by the words "up to the last moment" you seem to mean up to the moment Israel was victorious, because in the same bulletin you declare: "The six-day war smashed to smithereens the whole set of the Armistice Agreements of 1949—which no longer exist." This appears to be utter hypocrisy. Your fanatical nationalism blinds you to reality. Your statement "smash to smithereens" is your hypocrisy and demagogy.

Before Israel was victorious in its aggression, you say you fought to honor the agreements, but after the aggression succeeded you hail the "smashing to smithereens" of the "agreements" you fought to honor. Now you say, "they do not exist"! You stand naked as supporters of imperialist aggression.

It is now clear that you were for the Arabs honoring the agreement, but that you hailed the moment when the armed forces of Israel smashed them. You are guided by narrow bourgeois nationalism, it seems, and peace is a mere fig leaf for your nationalism. Your support for imperialist aggression, your defense of its brutalities is outrageous—but in addition your demagogy in trying to cover all this under progressive terms is contemptible and odious.

You speak about negotiations "including settlement of territorial problems." What territorial problems? You are obviously talking about retaining some of the Arab land the armed forces of Israel are now occupying. What other territory is involved? There are no Arab armies on the soil of Israel. It is clear that behind the phrase "including the settlement of territorial problems" you are hiding your support for Israel's annexation of Arab lands.

As other apologists for aggression have done, you cover up the atrocities committed by the Israeli forces. Some leading newspapers in Israel have called for a halt to these atrocities, and you pass this off by saying, "There were some hardships, as is usual in wartime." What wretchedness! Yes, there were indeed hardships, but these were widespread, brutal and inexcusable and they had nothing to do with military operations. They were cold-blooded mass killings. And they are still going on. Until the responsible leaders of Israel publicly expose and condemn these acts, it will erode the moral fiber and pollute the political life of your country and your people. They are pogroms against Arab peoples.

Proof of the fact that your statement does not represent the outlook of all the intellectuals of Israel is found in your last sentence. You say it was adopted by the majority; I have no doubt that the day is not far off when your position will be rejected by the majority, not only of the members of the Israel Peace Movement but by the majority of the people of Israel.

To support the aggression by Israel is not to support Israel. Progressive mankind supports the right of Israel to exist as a state, but they do not support its aggression. It is an axiom of unprincipled alliances that the weakest partner will take it on the chin when the alliance becomes a burden on the stronger partners. Israel cannot forever exist by doing the bidding of the imperialist powers, because imperialist objectives are against the best interests of its Arabs neighbors. Such policies will sharpen the relations between Israel and her neighbors. It is a path that can lead to Israel's destruction.

In the Middle East the dynamic social and political force is anti-imperialism, and it is this that will determine the course of events and mold the future of all countries. In the end, it is the only force that can resolve the Middle East crisis; the only force that can bring peace and harmony to the area. The future of Israel can only be assured if it lines up with the forces of anti-imperialism. A pro-imperialist policy leads to a dead-end.

Israel's real fight must start with a recognition that its present policy and acts of aggression are wrong, are unjust. Like all states, Israel has a right to defend herself, but aggression is not defense. One's convictions get their severest test when they lead to a struggle against the wrong policies of one's own government. The people of the United States have an honorable record in their struggle against their government's policies of aggression in Vietnam. Even when military and government leaders call it a defensive war, our people, by and large, have refused to join the bandwagon of false nationalism. As a people we will be judged by our actions against imperialist aggression. And as a people you also will be judged by how you fight against the unjust policies of your government. At the moment it may not be clear to all, but your struggles against the present policies of Israel would also be in the best interests of Israel and its people.

GUS HALL

In the United States the developments in the Mideast cannot be viewed as a "foreign affair." The councils of the imperialist syndicate have made the aggression in the Mideast an instrument of support for all of its reactionary policies—foreign and domestic. It is having a special effect on the Jewish communities. Jewish nationalism has become a serious mass influence. It has struck new deep roots. Because it is mobilized in support of an unjust, immoral, reactionary war of aggression, it generally moves more and more in a reactionary direction. The mobilization is under the leadership of the most reactionary sections of the Jewish bourgeois elements.

The rise of nationalism and the confusion has given the reactionary policies of Zionism a new lease on life. It now hides behind the demagogy—an attack on the reactionary policy of Zionism is an attack on all Jews—on all feelings of Jewish nationalism. Large sections of Jewish Americans reject these contentions. They do not go along with the reactionary policies now dominating Jewish nationalism. But they are not organized, they have very few public spokesmen.

The rise of a storm trooper-like movement cannot be separated from this reactionary ideological mobilization. The Jewish Defense League has made secret agreements with other ultra-right and fascist groups, and because of the support they get from within the police departments and the FBI, have become a force of reaction and fascism. This wing of Jewish nationalism is openly and viciously racist and chauvinist. The tactics of open terror are different, but the ideological roots are the same—it is reactionary bourgeois nationalism. It is an illusion to think that it is possible to be against the terror gangs, while defending or being silent about the ideology and policies that give rise to these groups.

This development has its reflection on the whole political spectrum. It has created a general mass base for reaction. It has become the broadest active mass base for anti-socialism and for anti-Sovietism. As it was for Hitler Germany, the big lie of anti-Sovietism is the big lie for U.S. imperialism. Thus the active anti-Sovietism in the Jewish community supports the policies of U.S. imperialism. The anti-Sovietism is related to the role of the Soviet Union in the Mideast. This only confirms that the mobilization of Jewish nationalism takes place as support for Israel's policy of aggression.

What are the truths?

The Soviet Union is the world bastion against imperialism. It is the most consistent supporter of the forces fighting imperialism the world over.

The Soviet Union carries out this policy at a great sacrifice. It is a policy based on the Leninist policy of proletarian internationalism. To speak about "Soviet imperialism" or about "Soviet expansion in the Mideast" is the big lie. It is the big lie to cover up the real imperialism—the U.S.-Israel imperialism. There are no private corporations in the socialist countries. The Soviet Union supports Egypt, Syria and the anti-imperialist forces in other countries because they are fighting against being dominated by oil imperialism. The policy of the Soviet Union is not anti-Israel, anti-Jewish—it is anti-imperialist.

The policies of the United States and Israel are the opposite of this. U.S. oil corporations are out to get the oil of the Arab lands as cheaply as possibly. Our Government's policies are geared to serve this purpose. The leaders of Israel have molded their policies of aggression and expansion in line with the U.S. and British policies of imperialist oppression and exploitation.

These policies come into sharp conflict with the anti-imperialist policies of the Soviet Union. This is the reason for and the purpose of the anti-Soviet mobilization in the Jewish community. The real issue is not whether you support the Soviet Union or not—the issue is whether you support or whether you fight the unjust, immoral policies and actions of imperialist aggression—no matter where they take place.

Apologists for imperialist aggression tailor their apologies to fit the audience. Some cover up the aggression by speaking about the "two world powers fighting to dominate the Mideast." If you can point the finger at "two big powers," this, of course, diverts the attention from the aggression by Israel, supported by the United States. But it is also a cover for U.S. imperialism because to speak about the "two powers" hides the fact that one of the powers, namely U.S. imperialism, is the aggressor. It is one of those unavoidable truths. The Soviet Union is not after one inch of the Mideast land or anyone else's land, it is not after even one barrel of oil from the Arab lands.

The other unalterable truth is that the U.S. private corporations have been trying, and in the future are going to try, to get hold of as much of the riches, the land and the oil for as little as possible, and by any means they can—intervention, subversion and aggression. This is the very essence of imperialism. To support Israel's aggression is to be a tool of U.S. imperialism.

The issue in the Mideast is oil. It is basically a struggle between the imperialist thieves who want to steal the oil and the Arab people who want to get the benefits of the riches that are there.

In this struggle, the government of Israel has lined up with the thieves, in the vain hope that she will be able to grab some of the stolen loot for herself.

The Soviet Union has lined up against the thieves in support of the just fight of the Arab peoples.

The assistance of the Soviet Union has made it possible for the Arab nations to fight for their liberation. They are able to fight the Israel-U.S. sponsored aggression.

The extreme and hysterical campaign to spread anti-Sovietism in the Jewish communities is directly related to this struggle. The charge of anti-Semitism in the Soviet Union is another fraud. This fraud derives from the frustration of not winning the support of the Jewish masses on the issue of Israel's aggression against the Arab nations.

The imperialist world headquarters in Washington pushes the anti-Soviet line because the Soviet Union stands as the most formidable obstacle to its policies of oppression, aggression and exploitation.

The leaders of Israel push the anti-Soviet line because the Soviet Union makes it possible for the Arab nations to fight against Israel's policies of expansion and aggression.

This anti-Soviet propaganda is based on the big lie of "Soviet imperialism" and "anti-Semitism in the Soviet Union."

Hitler's big lie of anti-Communism was geared to take advantage of mass ideological currents, including the bitterness over military defeats suffered by German armies. The present propaganda drive in the Jewish communities is also geared to take advantage of ideological currents. The Israeli and U.S. ideologists are fully aware of these currents. They know that generations of anti-Semitism, the crimes of the pogroms, and the memory of the nightmare of six million murdered by German fascism has left a deep imprint on the Jewish masses the world over. The masses view the emergence of Israel as a historic step that will put an end to the horrors of the past. The apologists know this has given rise to a deep sense of national pride. This pride is very understandable. There is nothing wrong with it. What is wrong is that with premeditated malice the rulers of Israel and the ideologists of U.S. imperialism have turned this national pride into an instrument in support of imperialist aggression, into support for Israel's aggression and expansion.

There is an inner logic to all human events. There are different reactionary groups, each fed by specific frauds, such as racism, jingoism and anti-Communism. The inner logic is that because they are all of a reactionary breed they tend to coalesce. And when there is some movement such as there is around the campaign for Israel, opportunist elements, like the Socialist Party and its youth sect join in. This tends to expand the reactionary base. Reactionary political candidates who respond to the campaign get support from people who otherwise would not vote for ultra-right candidates.

Because of this big lie the anti-Soviet campaign based in the Jewish communities affects the whole political spectrum.

People on the Left are not immune to the ideological blitzkrieg. Some also become victims and sink into the swamp of opportunism and bourgeois nationalism. As a rule, the trek to the swamp starts with some tactical accommodation to national chauvinism. But here, as in all matters, there is an inner logic of development. One can defend a tactic of struggle but it is difficult to defend an accommodation to wrong ideological concepts. And so, one accommodation can be seemingly defended only by another step of accommodation. That is the classical road of opportunism, to capitulation. When an accommodation cannot be defended as a tactic, it is turned into a principle. There is a point of no return on this path. Such has been the path of some on the Jewish Left, in the name of tactics. They started the slide with an accommodation to bourgeois nationalism. They have arrived in the swamp; they must now defend and advocate their position. Those who have refused to go into the swamp are called "nihilists." The opportunists defend bourgeois nationalism in the name of fighting nihilism.

There is a basic difference between enjoying and defending the rich culture of the Jewish people and feeling a deep sense of national pride in the contributions of the Jewish people, and defending a reactionary bourgeois nationalism that supports policies of imperialist aggression.

There is one other ideological matter that has further complicated the situation. It is the matter of Zionism. Zionism is a reactionary pro-imperialist ideology and political current based on Jewish bourgeois nationalism. Both from some circles within the Jewish movements, and from non-Jewish ultra-right groups, there is a drive to make Zionism, bourgeois nationalism, national pride and the Jewish religion one thing. For the ultra-right it is an instrument of anti-Semitism.

Within the Jewish movement it is a method of stopping any criticism of wrong policies. Any criticism of Israel or the reactionary policies of the Zionist movement are labeled anti-Semitic.

These are all important questions. They cannot be discussed within the concept of a "Jewish question." Criticism to be effective must be directed against specific policies and against organizations. To speak of Zionism as if it is the same as the Israeli people is a form of anti-Semitism. To speak of bourgeois nationalism as if it is the same as national pride or the culture of a people, is demagogy.

As in all political matters, there is a class approach to the "Jewish question." There is a working-class sector, and there is a capitalist sector. They are both a part of their respective classes of American society. A working-class attitude sees Israel as a historic reality, that must be accepted by all. But without any "ifs", "ands", or "buts", it rejects and condemns Israel's policies of aggression and expansion. It understands and accepts a sense of national pride, but it rejects bourgeois nationalism, chauvinism in all its forms. It rejects and condemns all concepts of imperialism and anti-Sovietism. It is for an end to imperialist aggression by the United States and Israel. The spokesmen for U.S. big business now talk as if they were always for Israel. When they thought they could continue getting the Mideast oil better without an Israel, they were against her. In 1948 *The New York Times* said editorially: "Many of us have long had doubts . . . concerning the wisdom of erecting a political state on a basis of religious faith." The editorial writer wrote about "religious faith," but the real concern was about oil. The tactics of U.S. imperialism have changed, but the concern about oil has not.

When Israel will not fit into the plans of U.S. imperialism, the "doubts" about Israel's existence will emerge anew. That is in the nature of imperialism.

1968

II

CZECHOSLOVAKIA

A Defeat for Imperialism

What follows were reactions to the Czechoslovak events within days after they exploded onto the world scene. The Czechoslovak events are an important milestone in the struggle against imperialism. What came to a head there was the most ambitious effort by imperialism to fulfill Dulles' policy of rolling back the borders of socialism.

One must not have illusions about the nature of imperialism— about its aggressive nature, about the scope of its efforts, about the resources at its command. United States imperialism has never —not for a moment—given up on its central obsession, on its self-proclaimed historic mission, the destruction of world socialism. This is not a contingency plan. This is an active policy. The destruction of socialism in Czechoslovakia was only one battle in the war plans to defeat world socialism. This is the framework; these are some of the fundamental premises on which we must judge these and all such events.

The entrance of the troops of five socialist countries into the territory of Czechoslovakia was an action which had far-reaching consequences for the future of socialism and the unity of the socialist world. In a very immediate and historic sense the events in Czechoslovakia became a crucial factor in the struggle between the two world systems. It is to be regretted that matters had come to such a pass that military action was considered necessary. However, subsequent events have fully confirmed the correctness of that decision.

The central issue was the defense of socialism against the threat of counterrevolution. In the course of a process of vital democratic reforms there was within Czechoslovakia an upsurge of anti-socialist elements, supported by the forces of subversion of U.S. and West German imperialism. At the same time, because of divisions and weaknesses within the leadership of the Communist Party of Czechoslovakia, a paralysis had developed that gravely increased the danger of an anti-socialist take-over. The paralyzed leadership retreated while the right-wing and anti-socialist forces advanced.

Imperialism never gives up its struggle for domination. Wherever it is not prepared for immediate military confrontation, it works by every means at its command to infiltrate, undermine and soften up those countries that are the objects of its attacks in order to lay the groundwork for military intervention at a later date. Ideological penetration has been placed high on the list of imperialist priorities. If it succeeds, military intervention is not necessary.

There are ideological departments, but there are also special departments, with carefully planned provocations, forgeries, planting of fake evidence, plans for assassinations, for acts of terror. There are specialists trained in the art of creating splits and liaisons.

In his work *War or Peace*, John F. Dulles stated the objectives of U.S. imperialism as follows: "The West can create in Central Europe an *advanced* strategic bridgehead which will undermine the military and political positions of Soviet Communism in Poland, Czechoslovakia, Hungary."

The crisis in Czechoslovakia was a product of both the weaknesses of the old leadership and the mistakes of the new in its process of trying to correct these weaknesses. Many of the new mistakes resulted from the failure to thoroughly understand the nature of the old shortcomings. For example, it has now become obvious that there are and have been serious ideological weaknesses in the work of the Czechoslovakian Party, in the mass organizations and among the youth. This must be laid at the doorstep of the old leadership. A bureaucratic administrative approach to problems was a contributing factor, as was the fact that the ideological life of the Party and the mass organizations had become dehydrated. Had the new leadership properly assessed the seriousness of the situation, it could have avoided many of its worst errors. The Dubcek leadership admitted "that they were surprised; that they were caught off guard at the speed of the emergence of the anti-Socialist upsurge," but instead of taking steps to head off the counterrevolution, they kept talking about how the people of Czechoslovakia were loyal to socialism. I am sure they were right in the main. There was a loyalty to the ideal of socialism, but loyalty without leadership and loyalty that is not organized to fight anti-socialist elements creates no assurance for the defense of socialism. Loyalty, after all, is only a feeling— it must be organized and mobilized before it becomes a political power.

During the years of expansion, the bureaucratic ways of the leadership did not come under sharp attack. At the moment of crisis all the pent-up grievances came to the fore. The new leadership should have opened up the path for a planned, orderly transition in economic and democratic reforms. Instead the Dubcek leadership opened up the floodgates to a tide that created anarchy, that swept in with it the forces of counterrevolution.

The leadership then faced the task of trying to solve the problems. But it was divided. The center forces joined with right-wing elements in a struggle against the Left. In this process the right-wing elements moved up into positions of leadership, and under this pressure the policies of the Party moved to the Right. The Party had its guard up against danger from the Left, but it became paralyzed in its struggle against the Right. Each new concession to the Right elements only opened the door further to anti-socialist forces.

The situation created confusion and demoralization in the ranks of the workers and the Party, while the leadership continued to make further concessions to the Right. With each concession, the Right elements became bolder, and without leadership the revolutionary elements became confused and demoralized. This situation continued for seven months, during which Parties of the other socialist countries had many discussions with Czechoslovakian leaders. At each stage the Dubcek leadership agreed to do something about the worsening situation, but nothing came of it. The leadership was dominated by right opportunist elements. Concessions and capitulation to anti-socialist elements always lead down a path to counterrevolution.

Today, because of the power of the socialist countries and because the imperialists know that the socialist states will not allow open counterrevolution the forces of imperialism have been working more cunningly. At this stage they support "progressive" movements, while they conduct terror campaigns and discredit and slander those who work to maintain Marxist-Leninist concepts. In the books of imperialism the "progressives" are the capitulators, the revisionist and the hidden anti-socialist elements. After they succeed in eliminating Marxists-Leninists from leadership bodies in trade unions and other people's organizations, then the problem of fighting counterrevolution becomes much more serious and difficult. Even the labeling of right opportunists and anti-socialist elements as "progressive" and Marxist-Leninists as "conservative" is geared to mislead and confuse people with a socialist consciousness.

In Czechoslovakia a number of organizations came to life out of thin air. In this connection it is interesting to note that the ex-CIA head of the division supervising the softening-up of socialist and newly independent countries stressed that in socialist countries, wherever possible, counterrevolutionary operations should proceed through established organizations that have mass support, that have a "legitimate reason to exist." In Czechoslovakia, organizations that had been in mothballs for years were revived, the Czechoslovakian Anti-Fascist Federation, for example. Obviously there was a time when it must have played a progressive role; many of the government leaders had once been members of it. Under these new circumstances it was reorganized. Its bulletin stated that it was now "an action organization," "a political organization," and that its task was the "persistent elimination of all elements of deformation as well as those who have caused it." This was a plan of terror against Communists. It became the base for trying to organize the veterans into an antisocialist formation. They set a date for a central "political action" when they would all converge on Prague.

There was a reorganization of the Slovak Democratic Party that openly called for elections in Czechoslovakia "to be supervised by the U.S., Britain and France"; they called for the return of collectivized farms to former owners by October 1st, and for banning the Communist Party and press.

The old Sokol (sports organization) and the boy and girl scouts were organized for the struggle. These forces could have been nipped in the bud, but again, as in Hungary, the Communist Party was paralyzed by factional in-fighting. The top leadership of the Czechoslovakian military cadre was also demoralized by factional struggles; the security forces were confused and demoralized; the border guards did not know what policies had been decided upon. Communist Party members received no leadership and they received no protection in spite of increasing attacks. The pathway to counterrevolution was wide open.

In this growing confusion, anti-socialist elements took over the leadership of local government bodies and organizations and, most important, of the press, radio and television. For some time no voices of resistance, of opposition to this direction of developments were heard in Czechoslovakia, and the open anti-socialist forces became bolder. The forces of counterrevolution captured much of the mass media.

The week before the military action by the Warsaw Pact countries, there were ten to twelve thousand West Germans in Czechoslovakia. Many CIA operators in the United States, especially those with a liberal or socialist coloration, had left for Prague during those weeks. They disappeared from their usual haunts. The lead story in the *People's World,* picked up from a San Jose paper, said that the state chairman of the Young Americans for Freedom in California declared that he had just returned from Czechoslovakia "organizing students against communism." These were the foreign shock troops of counterrevolution. The situation was heading for a confrontation.

The Bratislava Agreement could have been helpful, but the leadership did not fight for it. Instead the Dubcek leadership went on TV and lifted their fingers in a V-for-victory sign. This inaction was another victory for counterrevolution. It created more confusion and the leadership was rapidly losing the support of honest people, who were ready to defend socialism and the achievements of the Czechoslovak revolution.

Particularly alarming was the publication on June 27 of a "2,000-Word Statement" issued by 70 intellectuals carried in a number of newspapers and on radio and TV. This article was a platform of counterrevolution; under cover of liberalization, it aimed to wipe out the gains made since 1948; it sought to discredit the Communist Party and its guiding role and to undermine the fraternal relations of Czechoslovakia with its socialist allies. It proposed that the people make their own decisions, employing such methods as demonstrations, strikes and boycotts in order to get rid of Party cadres and personalities devoted to the socialist cause. They demanded "the establishment of our own civil committees and commissions"—in short, the take-over of power. They pledged to act with aims in support of the leadership that they would select—a direct appeal for an armed counterrevolution. The appeal contained much demagogic verbiage, such as the need for Communists in the government, but Communists of a particular kind. It became the rallying point for all anti-socialist forces.

All this was not just words—it became the real action program. With demagogy, with terror, they were forcing honest people out of leadership positions in government and in trade unions. The "2,000 Words" became the legal and political structure for counter-revolution.

Only after pressure from the other socialist countries did the leadership denounce the statement; however, in a subsequent reply to the Five-Party Letter, it again played down the threat, stating that things were under control.

After Bratislava, the activists of the counterrevolutionary forces did not cease in their campaign. Indeed, they became more aggressive. Public meetings and a slandering of the leadership grew; demonstrations increased; campaigns in the factories against those sympathetic to the Bratislava agreement grew; the signers of a letter to the Soviet Union in behalf of the Five-Party Letter were called traitors and were persecuted. Petitions were being circulated for the abolition of the People's Militia. The Presidium of the Central Committee criticized these actions but did nothing more. The press, radio and television forces were not taken in hand. What was developing in Czechoslovakia was a creeping paralysis of leadership and an insidious counterrevolution. The right-wing dominated leadership had shown itself too weak, too indecisive in a situation demanding resolute action to protect the gains of the past. This was the nub of the matter. The choice was clear—either to take actions to defend Czechoslovakian socialism or to accept counterrevolution and the return of Czechoslovakia to reactionary capitalism.

In the course of time, many more facts came out. Illegal arms were found in the basement of ministries including thousands of automatic weapons of West German and U.S. make. Powerful mobile radio broadcasting stations, made in West Germany, and never bought by the Czech government, turned up. They were secretly sent across the border. There were secret printing shops and full-scale gallows in town squares. (For practice, the right-wing elements hanged Communist leaders in effigy.) Among the counterrevolutionary cadre that marched to Prague was Leo Cherne, a professional anti-socialist organizer of the International Rescue Committee, widely believed to be a CIA agency connected with Radio Free Europe. Sacha Volman, a Rumanian emigre, was on the scene, too. He was director of the Institute of International Labor Research, a CIA-funded agency. It was Volman who organized trips to the Dominican Republic in 1966 to give approval to their elections. The forces across the border were set; a special force of especially trained Czechoslovak refugees and special CIA-trained group leaders had already crossed the borders from West Germany. Checkpoints were eliminated on the German border, all in the name of liberalization.

It was clear—the situation was headed for an explosion.

For seven months there were conferences between the parties of the socialist countries and the Communist Party of Czechoslovakia. The five socialist countries asked Czechoslovakia to control its borders with West Germany and to take up the fight against the anti-socialist forces. The Czechoslovak borders with West Germany were socialist borders with world imperialism.

The time and alternatives ran out. The open options narrowed.

If a wide open struggle had erupted, the sacrifices would have been much greater. As it was, Soviet soldiers were killed, but the report is that not one of the five-power military forces shot a bullet at any person in Czechoslovakia. Those who advise to wait until blood is shed are not serious defenders of socialism.

It is important to remember that when imperialism does not feel it is ready for a military confrontation in a given area, this does not automatically end the danger. That, in fact, is exactly when it places a greater emphasis on the softening-up process, multiplying its efforts at subversion and infiltration. Let there be no illusions. U.S. and West German imperialism had trained personnel on the spot ready to move—openly or secretly—whenever the softening-up process had reached the point where there was enough confusion and internal weakness to move. There are such forces ready and in action for every socialist country in the world. U.S. imperialism has a special active plan and a special contingency plan for every socialist country. It is clear that Czechoslovakia was high on the priority list of West German and U.S. imperialism.

The question arises in this connection about the right of the five parties of the socialist governments to cross the borders of another state in defense of socialism, especially since Communists stand for the self-determination of nations. But they never have viewed this right *unconditionally and in all circumstances,* because the achievement of the full self-determination of nations will only be solved by world socialism. The criterion in this situation, as in all Communist concerns, is: Does it serve the interests of the working class of all countries and of socialism, or does it hurt them? Marx opposed self-determination where it might hurt democracy and socialism.

Self-determination was an issue but not in the manner some of the critics charge. There is no one who denies that the great majority of the people of Czechoslovakia are for socialism. This is a fundamental issue of their self-determination. The action of the Warsaw pact states was in no way contrary to this determination. It was an act of support for the basic interests of the great majority.

Some have raised questions about violation of Czechoslovak sovereignty. Sovereignty is also not an abstract question. Let us put the shoe on the other foot. What would have happened to Czechoslovak sovereignty if her system of socialism had been destroyed? Would the CIA and West German-supported forces have honored her sovereignty? In a very basic sense the action of her socialist neighbors was a defense of Czechoslovak sovereignty.

Some Communist Parties have ignored the facts of the crisis and hidden behind one statement: "The action of the five Warsaw powers was a violation of the autonomy of the Communist Party of Czechoslovakia." In real life one very seldom has the choice between that which is totally good or totally bad, correct and incorrect. Often one is forced to accept the best possible. In the realm of political questions it is even less so. Even without having all of the facts, it is clear the assistance given by the five socialist states was in keeping with the will of the great majority of Czechoslovak Communists. The appeals for assistance came from Communist workers, from an important section of the leadership. The issue of "autonomy" is a fig leaf. It is easy to stand for some abstract principle when you are not asked to solve the concrete problems of the class struggle. It is demagogy to stand behind such "principles" while refusing to accept irrefutable facts about the dangers to socialism in Czechoslovakia, while refusing to project ideas on how the counterrevolution could have been avoided—without the action of the Warsaw Pact countries.

In fact, it is not the "principle of autonomy" that bothers some Communist leaders. It is an opportunistic and false use of the "principle of autonomy" in an attempt to "prove" their own Party's autonomy. Some continue to repeat the cliche about the autonomy of each Communist Party as if it were constantly threatened. There are no such dangers. Some use the autonomy issue as a shield to avoid criticisms of opportunistic practices by fellow Communists; for others it is an opportunistic way of trying to prove that the slander that there is a monolithic world Communist movement is in fact a slander. It would seem the repetition of such cliches does not disprove any slander. On the contrary, such repetition adds credence to the falsehood.

In reality there are two sides to the question of the autonomy of each Communist Party. There is no world organization of Communist Parties. There is not the dominance of any one Party. That's now an old established fact. There is no need to insert it after every paragraph.

The revolutionary process is a world process, the class struggle is a world struggle, the working class is a world class—and the struggle against imperialism is a world struggle.

The world Communist movement reflects this world reality. Marxism-Leninism is a world revolutionary science. It is the foundation for the work of all Communist Parties. There are constant exchanges of experiences between Communist Parties. We are a world revolutionary movement.

In the eyes of millions of non-Communists, especially in the eyes of million of militant, radical youth, this side of reality— these world relationships—have more meaning than the cliche about autonomy.

In Czechoslovakia there had been violations of democratic procedure within the Party, and there had also been violations of legality with regard to persons, organizations, and institutions. These were attributable to bureaucratic methods of work, a tendency of the Party to replace the state organization and an unwillingness of the leadership to correct these abuses of power.

But in the correction of these policies the Dubcek leadership went to the other extreme and forgot that the rights of free speech, press, etc. do not mean the right to undermine the leading role of the Party or to undermine socialism. To give rights to counter-revolution is to destroy the rights of the great majority. It can indeed only lead to undermining of democracy for the majority of the people; it can only lead to the restoration of capitalist democracy, that is, democracy for the monopolists, the capitalists. Capitalism in Czechoslovakia could only have been fascism.

As to the Czechoslovakian press, the new leadership also went to the other extreme and abolished Party political and ideological controls. The newspapers were making policy according to their editors' views. The *Student Magazine* carried an anti-socialist interview with Radio Free Europe—an outright CIA-financed fascist organization.

Referring to objections that the Party should not apply controls to literature, which requires special treatment, Lenin wrote:

> Calm yourselves, gentlemen! First of all, we are discussing party literature and its subordination to party control. Everyone is free to write and say whatever he likes without restrictions. But every volun-tary association (including a party) is free to expel members who use the name of the party to advocate antiparty views. Freedom of speech must be complete. But then freedom of association must be complete, too. I am bound to accord you, in the name of freedom of speech, the full right to shout, lie and write to your heart's content, but you are bound to grant me in the name of freedom of association to enter into, or withdraw from, association with people advocating this or that view. The Party is a voluntary organization which would inevitably break up, first ideologically and physically, if it did not cleanse itself of people advocating antiparty views.[1]

It is necessary to see these developments in their true setting. The central world contradiction is between capitalism and social-ism; the power balance between these two systems has reached a historic turning point. The very heart of the socialist base of power is the Soviet Union and the Warsaw Pact countries. The unity of this base is the very essence of this moment in history. The balance of power hinges on this unity. History would never

[1] V. I. Lenin, "Party Organization and Party Literature," *Collected Works*, Vol. 10 (Moscow: Progress Publishers, 1964), p. 47.

forgive Communists who would have permitted this base to be weakened or disrupted.

There has been some erosion of this base. In a crisis or in a period of offensive struggles, could the socialist world depend on all its sectors? This was by no means certain. Should not the development in specific socialist countries be the concern of the rest of the socialist world? I don't see how it can be otherwise. This in no way violates the real essence of autonomy. Working-class internationalism and the autonomy of Parties are not opposites.

As the crisis subsides, as life returns to normal in Czechoslovakia, as the Communist Party again assumes its role of leadership, as it surely will, a number of new facts will emerge to sustain the correctness of the actions taken by the five Warsaw Pact nations. That the situation deteriorated to the point where military action had to be taken to be sure was a setback for the revolutionary movement. This kind of relationship among socialist countries has not been, nor will it become, the rule. It was an exception brought on by an unusual set of circumstances, including the location of Czechoslovakia in the very heart of the socialist world, and sharing a border with West Germany—the very heart of the imperialist world in Europe. The socialist countries simply could not permit the emergence of a counterrevolutionary, imperialist controlled Czechoslovakia in their very center.

We do not deny that there were some momentary contradictions in the Czechoslovakian situation, but for a partisan of socialism, the choice had to be in support of the defense of the world revolution which meant support for Czechoslovak socialism. Such is a class approach to struggle. Life does not always give one only a good choice and a bad choice; there are times when it forces one to take the necessary choice, times when there are no good choices available.

To close our eyes to this aspect of struggle is to close our eyes to reality. We must see things as they are and then react to them as we see them. That's Marxism-Leninism.

At a moment when the forces of imperialism were desperately grasping at every possible scrap of material from "Communist sources" to use in their attempt to convince the masses of the culpability of the Soviet Union, Communists had a special responsbility not to play their dirty game. During the 1956 Hungarian events, the Socialists of Italy broke ranks and joined the reactionary crusade against the Soviet Union. General Secretary Togliatti said at that time: ". . . the place of the working man, the place of the man of the people who has a sense of revolutionary reality, is on the side of revolution and not on the side of reaction." To this he added, "And then when the battle is won (when the crisis is over) we will continue to debate about mistakes and how to correct them—but above all—we must not lose the conception of the place of those who fight for socialism and for peace."

Addendum

In 1970 the leadership of the Communist Party of Czechoslovakia adopted its own assessment of the crisis. They, of course, are in the best position to know all of the facts. They have made a searching self-critical Leninist-like study of all the factors. They have honestly placed the weaknesses on the table. They have set a good example. The study and the conclusions are published in a pamphlet, *Czechoslovakia: Lessons of the Crisis*. It is issued by the Central Committee of their Party. In the context of "autonomy of parties" it is obvious that in a basic judgment and assessment of development in the affairs of Czechoslovakia, one must above all else accept the opinion of the Communist Party of Czechoslovakia. The whole document is of historic importance, as can be seen from the following few lines:

The plenary session of the CC CPCz of October 1967, on the position and the role of the Party, became an important stage. A great role in the preparation of this session was played by a broad, representative survey of the attitudes of the Party public, in which around 600 basic Party organizations expressed their views on topical questions of Party work. The results of this survey contained grave warnings, drawing attention to contradictions between proclaimed aims and achieved results, to manifestations of bureaucracy, to the suppression of inner-Party democracy, to the low level of discipline and growing passivity of communists, to the insufficient contact of the leading bodies with basic organizations, to the inconsistent solution of economic problems. . . . They were an open and sharp criticism of the Party leadership, but at the same time the expression of the will and determination of the Party to overcome the accumulated difficulties. . . .

The tenacity with which A. Novotny defended his personal position resulted in the fact that the forces and the attention of the Central Committee concentrated primarily on the solution of the question of Party leadership. This resulted, inter alia, in the fact that the plenum did not expose in time the platform of those members of the Central Committee who in the discussion and assessing the situation and the further course of the Party proceeded essentially from anti-Party, revisionist positions (O. Sik, V. Slavik, Γ. Vodslon, J. Smrkovsky and others). . . .

The new Party leadership was faced by the enormously serious task and historic responsibility before its own Party, the people and the international communist movement:

—to utilize and transform the spontaneous agreement of the Party and the people with the solution of the January plenum for developing a broad activity aimed at overcoming the obstacles obstructing the further development of socialism in the CSSR;

—not to permit any abuse of the efforts of the Party to rectify shortcomings, and to wage an offensive ideological and political struggle against opportunist, revisionist and anti-socialist views, tendencies and forces. This principled orientation was all the more urgent as there existed the threat that the overcoming of the grave shortcomings of the Novotny leadership—unless accompanied by a resolute struggle against revisionism—would lead to a growth of the rightist danger which had already made itself noticeable in certain speeches at the January plenum;

—to strengthen even further our ties with the socialist countries, especially with the Soviet Union, so that Czechoslovakia may be a firm and reliable link of the world socialist system. . . .

After January 1968, it became, however, evident that the new Party leadership, headed by A. Dubcek, was in view of its heterogeneity, political disunity and overall weakness incapable of fulfilling this task. . . . A. Dubcek did not have the prerequisites for grasping the complicated character of the situation and the risk connected with the change in the leadership under political and economic conditions existing at that time in the Party and society.

His indecision and hesistance resulted in the fact that the Party leadership did not rely on the confidence of the overwhelming majority of members of the CC CPCz and on the support of the majority of communists, and did not put itself at the head of the Marxist-Leninist forces which had been striving already for many years for an improvement in the work of the Party. . . .

The Party did not have a clear line and an explicit directive for its further course in the decisive spheres. . . .

The right wing took advantage of A. Novotny's great unpopularity. . . .

Around the factional core of the revisionist rightist forces within the Party, there rallied an opposition current which gadually penetrated into an ever greater number of organizations and was creating its own political platform and oganizational structure. The right-wing gradually occupied important positions at all levels by placing there its own people or those who, for various reasons, went over to it and capitulated before it. It skillfully applied combined pressure from above—from the leading bodies of the Party and the State—and from below by means of the mass media, by organizing meetings, various resolutions, signature campaigns and so on, which were passed off as the working people, although they were often inspired by small groups or individuals. The failure of the Party leadership to give directions to Party bodies resulted in the fact that part of the functionaries did not fully discern the intentions of the rightists, while another part was withdrawing from the battle. This enabled the right wing, during the second stage of the district conferences, to penetrate by means of gross violation of the Party Rules into important positions of the district link of the Party. In view of the fact that the forces faithful to Marxism-Leninism did not get support from the leading bodies of the Party and, with a few exceptions, did not even have the possibility of stating their views in public, they gradually found themselves on the defensive and in isolation. . . .

The logic of political struggle induced the right wing to make even more aggressive efforts to recruit as its ally against the Party those political forces from among the ranks of the former petty-bourgeoisie which had been until then balancing on the fringe of socialist society, and even openly anti-communist forces. This resulted in the creation of a bloc of rightist revisionist and anti-socialist forces. Its individual components actually differed in their ideology and tactics, but they united in the decisive fight against the Party and the alliance with the Soviet Union.

Imperialism was in this way given the opportunity to realize in the CSSR, in the spirit of its global strategy and tactics, the aims which it had been elaborating over a long period against the socialist countries. This is why this bloc, under whose general onslaught the managing structure of the Party, the socialist State and society began to gradually disintegrate, found all-round political, moral and material support from the imperialist forces. . . .

The open and co-ordinated onslaught of the reactionary forces found its expression in the publication of the counter-revolutionary platform of 2,000 words, which was a forthright instigation to violent actions and to the destruction of the socialist system. This counter-revolutionary appeal went at the same time farthest in stirring up hatred against the Soviet Union, and even expressed a public threat against our allies with armed conflict. . . .

The fight for power became also a fight for a change in the foreign-political orientation of the CSSR. The rightist opportunist and anti-socialist bloc made efforts to liquidate the basic guarantees of the national and State existence of socialist Czechoslovakia, which lie in the alliance and friendship with the Soviet Union and other socialist countries. This should have created external conditions for the liquidation of socialism in Czechoslovakia.

These and many other facts document the connection between the events in Czechoslovakia and the fight of international imperialism against the socialist community. The strategists in the centres of world anti-communism had their direct assistants in socialist Czechoslovakia. One of them, I. Svitak, became the spokesman of extreme reactionary forces which were aligning themselves in such organisations as K 231 and the Club of Committed Non-Party Members (KAN). . . . The centre of K 231 was headed by K. Nigrin, J. Brodsky, V. Palecek, O. Rambousek and others who were mostly direct agents of western intelligence services. The founders of KAN were in addition to I. Svitak, the writer V. Havel and Professor V. Corny, who had close contacts with the post-February emigration. KAN and K 231 were tightly linked with western intelligence services and were given not only political but also material support. . . .

An important role in anti-communist plans based on the demagogy with so-called democratic socialism was held by the re-emerging Social Democratic Party. This Party was preparing to appear as an independent political force, playing upon the social-democratic survivals in the thinking of a part of members of the CPCz whom it wanted to bring over to its side. It was calculated that the Social Democratic Party, "unburdened with the period of the construction of socialism," would be attractive for the disoriented and politically unfirm part of society. With the agreement and the support of rightist functionaries of the CPCz, F. Kriegel, J. Smrkovsky, Z. Mlynar, J. Litera, L. Lis and others, an illegal preparatory central committee was created, whose members were, inter alia, Z. Bechyne, J. Munzar, O. Janyr, F. Supka. . . . These activities, which were developed in close co-operation with leaders of the Socialist International, had the task of achieving a political split among the working class. . . .

An important role in the anti-socialist game involving the fate of Czechoslovakia fell to the reactionary representatives of the Catholic clergy who were amply supported by the Catholic emigration living abroad.

The combined actions of foreign and internal reactionary forces were deepening the inner-political crisis which was ever more reflected in the relations with our closest allies.

The fraternal parties, especially the CPSU, endeavoured with great patience to eliminate the tension in mutual relations and to convince the leadership of our Party that it is necessary to resist the counter-revolutionary threat in the CSSR. To this end they made use of all possibilities provided by official and personal contacts. At the meetings in Dresden, Sofia and Moscow, in the first half of 1968, their representatives showed A. Dubcek on the basis of concrete facts that the situation in the CSSR was developing in a dangerous direction which, at the same time, endangered the common interests of the socialist camp. A. Dubcek's assurances that the leadership of the CPCz was also aware of the gravity of the situation and that it itself felt the need to redress the situation were, however, at home suppressed, evaded and not fulfilled. The minutes of the talks with Comrade L. I Brezhnev, Comrade J. Kadar and other comrades, as well as a whole series of letters which the General Secretary of the CPSU and the First Secretaries of other fraternal parties sent to A. Dubcek and to the leadership of our Party, just as the telephone talks, show quite clearly how sincerely and deeply the parties and the people of the fraternal socialist countries were agitated by the difficulties in our inner-political life and the danger which was developing into a threat to the existence of socalism in Czechoslovakia. They offered comradely support and assistance for coping with the situation and exhausted all political means which came into consideration in order to rouse A. Dubcek and his followers to adopting a responsible communist course. . . .

The designs and aims of the counter-revolution in Czechoslovakia were the same as in Hungary in 1956, merely the tactics were different in view of the different conditions and time. The anti-socialist forces in our country, which acted in harmony with the designs of contemporary imperialism, oriented themselves primarily upon using methods of political, ideological and power destruction and on a more gradual period of time than was the case in Hungary. . . .

Communists as well as non-communists, who were aware of the mortal danger threatening our socialist system, were demanding that the leadership of the Party and the State resolutely resist the counter-revolutionary forces and stand up in defense of the achievements of socialism. These urgent appeals were contained in many resolutions and letters to the CC, CPCz, but they remained without answer. At the time when the counter-revolutionary forces in Prague and at other places were going over into open attack in an effort to seize power, the rightist representatives in the leadership of the Party assured the public that 'everything is in order' and that 'the process of revival and democratization is successfully developing.'

Thousands of communists, individual citizens and entire collectives of working people, representatives of all strata of the population and various organizations, including members of the Central Committee of the Communist Party of Czechoslovakia and the Central Committee of the Communist Party of Slovakia, as well as members of the Government of the CSSR and deputies of the National Assembly and of the Slovak National Council, being aware of their class, national and international responsibility for the fate of socialism in Czechoslovakia, were persistently seeking a way out of the difficult, critical situation. In view of the fact that the rightist part of the Party leadership did not want to adopt any measures which would have led to thwarting the counter-revolutionary coup and to averting civil war, they began to turn to the leadership of the fraternal parties and to the governments of our allies with the request that at this historically serious moment they should grant internationalist assistance to the Czechoslovak people in the defense of socialism. They did so in the deep conviction that their class brethren would not leave Czechoslovakia at the mercy of counter-revolution which threatened with bloodshed, and that they would prevent our country from being torn out of the socialist community. . . .

The CC CPCz rejects the abstract concept of the sovereignty of a socialist State, which is being disseminated by bourgeois propaganda in the interest of deceiving the masses, and stands on positions which correspond also in the question of sovereignty to the class and internationalist character of the socialist State. It therefore regards the entry of the allied troops into the CSSR as fraternal internationalist assistance to the Czechoslovak people.

1969

12

U.S. IMPERIALISM IN AFRICA

Goals Remain, Only Tactics Change

The goals of imperialism never change. Only how they expect to reach their objective changes. In a basic sense there are no Republican or Democratic Party foreign policies. There is a policy of imperialist expansion that is inherent in the system of capitalism, that represents the interests of the dominant monopoly corporations, that is carried out by both parties of capitalism. Variations in carrying out the overall policies are reflections of differences within monopoly's closed circle.

The tactical line of an imperialist power is based on how these monopoly groups see the relationship of forces, both on a world scale and as they are reflected in specific areas of the world.

Whether it is military aggression, economic penetration, neo-colonialism or subversion—the goal is the same: super-profits for the corporations.

Africa is the last of the continents that has become the target of imperialist penetration. United States imperialism now leads the pack. The current scientific and technological revolution, especially the new technology developed in the war industries, needs the rare and difficult-to-get minerals found in Africa. In the United States there are no known deposits of manganese, cobalt, chromium, diamonds, lithium, beryllium, germanium or bauxite. Africa is the source of all the U.S. imports of lithium. Seventy percent of chromates, 50-60 percent of manganese ores, 50-60 percent of cobalt, over 50 per cent of industrial diamonds, etc. Zinc and lead comes from Morocco, titanium and zirconium ores come from Sierra Leone.

The crime of imperialism is not that corporations want to bring minerals from other countries. The crime is their policies of aggression, domination, subjugation, and enslavement in order to get these riches for a few pennies. The crime is to keep the people of these lands in poverty, in political and economic bondage. The crime is in robbing these people of the fruits of their labor and the riches of nature found on their land. United States imperialism now takes off in Africa where the early slave traders left off.

After the Second World War U.S. policy of aggression in Africa was geared to take full advantage of the breakup of the old colonial empires. There was nothing it could do about the disintegration of the old empires so it carefully set into motion the plans for building its own. There was little it could do about the African nations' winning political independence so it set out to build its influence within the newly liberated countries. It set out to build its empire on the basis of racism. It concentrated on influencing the least politically conscious elements, the armed forces, the police and the business elements. The CIA became an important factor in the internal affairs of many of the countries in Africa. Israel became the center through which huge sums of payoff money passed through. Lovestone's so-called International Department of the AFL-CIO made Africa its main point of concentration. It recruited a special brigade of agents, made up of people who had left or radical images—Blacks with some image in the civil rights struggle—trade unionists with a left or socialist image.

Reactionary trade union leaders in the other capitalist countries became willing tools of this operation.

Many of the leaders of the national liberation movements and governments did not have working-class backgrounds, the working-class parties were new and inexperienced, the governments did not draw in the people—and so became isolated. This set the stage for imperialist penetration. This situation was ready-made for United States imperialist operations.

For years after the Second World War United States imperialism used the cover of being against colonialism and racism. This was a convenient cover for the period when it was establishing its beachheads in Africa. It was especially a convenient cover in countries where Black Africans were in political power.

But once the beachheads were established the tactics also changed.

The new tactics are more openly racist, especially in countries where the white colonialists are in power.

Acts of open aggression replaced the anti-colonial rhetoric. The joint acts of military aggression with the forces of Belgium against the progressive forces in the Congo signaled the new tactics.

Nixon has taken these openly racist policies of aggression further.

The open policies of aggression have resulted in new alliances with the racist colonial governments of South Africa and Rhodesia.

This open support, these new alliances with South Africa, Rhodesia, Portugal and all of the most reactionary racist forces in Africa is the essence of the "new Nixon doctrine" for Africa.

As the patterns of aggression have shifted, the investments of U.S. banks in Africa have climbed. Between 1950 and 1959 direct U.S. investments grew by 556 million dollars. In the following nine year period they climbed to 1.830 billion dollars or 3.3

times as much, to a total of 2.674 billion dollars by 1968.

They have continued to soar. In 1968 the gross profits from these investments reached 679 million dollars.

It is a fact. United States imperialism has been able to slow down the national liberation movement sweeping Africa. The establishment of reactionary military governments in a number of the newly liberated countries are serious setbacks. It has successfully used the weapon of anti-Communism to disorient a number of the movements. It has established a number of military bases in Africa. The CIA is a serious factor in the internal affairs of a number of the countries.

But these are temporary victories for imperialism. The more basic factor in Africa is the continued growth of the national liberation movements. A number of the newly liberated countries are laying the base for socialism. There is a growing revolutionary military force.

The patriotic forces of the countries under Portuguese colonial rule, of South Africa and Rhodesia are building a powerful people's military force. A new wave of national liberation, and a new level of the class struggle are bringing with them a new stage in the struggle for social progress.

The new patterns of U.S. imperialist aggression cannot halt the inevitable march of history. They will only lead to sharper confrontations, to greater struggles and in the end to victories, and to the defeat of imperialism in Africa.

1969

13

"WHY PUERTO RICO IS THE MOST PROFITABLE ADDRESS IN THE U.S.A."

The above title is not mine. It is the title of a booklet put out to encourage U.S. corporations to invest in Puerto Rico. Because it is the most profitable address for U.S. corporations it is the address for indescribable squalor, hunger, indignities and oppression. Puerto Rico, an island of four million people, of which over a million have been forced to emigrate, stands as irrefutable proof of the brutal, ravaging, plundering oppression that is U.S. imperialism. After returning from Puerto Rico I tried to find the words to describe the unbelievable slums, especially in San Juan, the capital. Then I reread William Z. Foster's report about the same slums made 23 years ago. If anything, the slums have become even more indescribable. Only now there are more of the big tourist hotels that pour their raw sewage into the lagoons on which the slums are perched. Foster described a slum called El Fanguito. It has been replaced by others. Foster then said:

I went into this most wretched of slums with its immense population and talked to many of its miserable inhabitants. And I saw sights and heard stories of extreme poverty that will stay with me until my dying day. I burned with shame that such outrageous conditions exist on Puerto Rico and are caused by us. . . . A modern Dante, seeking to write a new *Inferno,* need go no further than El Fanguito.

El Fanguito is sprawled out over mosquito-infested, marsh-tide flats. The squatters' houses are thrown together of any material that comes to hand, and the shacks are incredibly over-crowded. Most of the places are unfit for hogs, much less for human beings. The houses have no toilet facilities, and there is no garbage collection. . . . Whole areas are completely dark at night, having no street lights,

and many of the people are too poor even to buy kerosene lamps
or candles. . . . There are not even streets in the horrible slum,
except where the people themselves have carted in soil and rubbish
to build up roadways of a sort.

The whole place is an indescribable litter of garbage, tin cans,
and other refuse. . . . Crazy foot bridges lead from one hovel to
another.

Children, mostly naked, with no toys and with no place to play,
wade about in the filthy water. At one place we visited, a big city
sewer belched its foul contents into an open canal, whence the stinking
flood was from time to time swept back into the squatters' village
by the rising tide. . . .

And sickness, too, flourished—tuberculosis, hookworm, malaria,
bilharzia, and many other diseases bred of poverty, filth, and under-
nourishment. The most terrible sickness hazard of all, so the people
told us, came from their naked children playing in the germ-laden
sewage water that periodically overflows the slum area.[1]

Earlier Rexford Tugwell, a former United States Governor of
Puerto Rico, had written, "the shacks were in rows . . . which let
some open space for filth to accumulate, and the tide lifted the piles
of garbage and deposited them again in the same place, twice
daily."

Now 25-35 years later the same ocean tide twice daily still
accumulates and redeposits the garbage amongst the slum shacks
that have no real floors, doors, windows, toilets or light. The 3
or 4 foot layer of floating garbage is the front and the back yard.
It is the children's playground. It is the 24-hour world for the
women and children.

Who lives in these slums? The unemployed! During these years
of industrial expansion the unemployment rate ranges from 12 to
25 percent. Who lives there? The people who have been driven
from the land. People who work as laborers and service workers
but do not make enough to be able to live in better housing live
there. The slums are the same, but much has changed in the past
25 years. There are changes but the colonial oppression is the
same. Puerto Rico has shifted from a country with a backward
agriculture to an oppressed industrial-agricultural country. Puerto
Rico has been turned into a U.S. military base. The slums of
Puerto Rico are a show case of imperialist oppression.

[1] William Z. Foster, pp. 5-6, *The Crime of El Fanguito.*

For U.S. corporations Puerto Rico has become an area for a "fast buck." They are given a 10 to 17 year tax-free ride. They pay no taxes to Puerto Rico. Besides, there are special zones where new materials enter free of customs charges and the finished products leave without duty. It is profits without any social responsibilities. The Pentagon has expropriated 15 percent of the land that can be farmed.

The United States has turned Puerto Rico into an imperialist military staging area. This was the launching area for the expeditionary forces to Cuba, Guatemala and Santo Domingo. This is the base for the nuclear strike force posed to strike any area in the Americas. The United States has refused to sign any nuclear-free zone treaties that would include Puerto Rico.

It is the clandestine training area for most of the special forces, for example the Green Berets, and the special sections of the Peace Corps. It is the center for the counter-insurgency forces. The CIA and the FBI operate in Puerto Rico as if it was a protectorate under their special jurisdiction. The National Guard has permanent hammocks in all of the important cities and villages. There are bases for atomic submarines and offensive missiles. The U.S. military has forced the residents of whole islands to move as they moved in. They use other islands as target ranges. The people have put up an extended militant struggle against this practice at Culebra.

The U.S. government agencies control all political, economic and social activities. The U.S. Congress exercises exclusive jurisdiction over foreign relations, citizenship, travel, armed forces, military recruitment, foreign commerce, customs, transportation, exchange notes, post offices, radio, TV, bankruptcy proceedings, patents, quarantine laws and the administration of courts. Congress decides how many acres of sugar the Puerto Ricans can plant and how much of it they can refine and what they can export. These U.S.-appointed agencies can prohibit the entry of any product into Puerto Rico. This includes the exclusion of books, newspapers, magazines. They regulate sea and air transportation. They control freight rates. All sea traffic must be in U.S.-owned ships.

Federal judges are appointed by the President of the United States. The language of the people of Puerto Rico is Spanish.

But it is not permitted in these courts.

The victims of these courts are sent to prisons in the United States where they can have very few visitors. There are Puerto Rican political prisoners in most of the federal prisons. I met a number in Leavenworth prison, doing life sentences for the "crime" of fighting for Puerto Rican independence. When we do not actively campaign for their freedom we objectively become responsible for their imprisonment.

The U.S. government holds the power of expropriation. With this imperialist power, without ceremony they evict people from land they expropriate.

Puerto Rico has become a country with an industrial base. But the U.S. corporations that own the industries have no concern for the land or the people. With the military they have destroyed the base of the old agriculture. They have driven the peasants into the slums or into migration. Puerto Rico has a foreign controlled industry that is oriented towards foreign markets. Thus the foreign commerce dominates the home market. The people of Puerto Rico are in the vise of getting low wages, producing goods for export, and paying inflationary prices for imports—which includes imported foods and agricultural products. They are victims of imperialist production and imperialist controlled commerce. Puerto Rico has an economy that is in a permanent crisis. In 1925 U.S. corporations took out about 25 million in profits. By 1968 this loot had reached over 300 million dollars annually. Private U.S. corporations control most of the industry, all of banking commerce and all of the service industries.

The 75 years of colonial oppression and exploitation by the United States has been devastating. Over one-third of the population has been forced to migrate. But this is also profitable for U.S. imperialism. When the people of Puerto Rico travel to the United States they become victims of another special system of discrimination and oppression. Very often the same corporations that exploit the people in Puerto Rico, are a part of the special system of oppression here. Whether in San Juan or New York most of the people of Puerto Rico remain victims of the colonial system that has oppressed Puerto Rico for 75 years.

U.S. laws that would benefit people in any way do not apply

in Puerto Rico. Laws that benefit big business do apply. Tax loopholes apply but the minimum wage law does not. All social security laws have special escape clauses for Puerto Rico.

In 1969 the average hourly wages received by industrial workers, was $1.71 compared with $3.19 in the United States. In the apparel industry the average weekly wage was $55.30 compared with $82.93 in the United States. The wages are low but the cost of living is higher than in the United States. Agricultural workers work for 45 and 50 cents an hour.

The U.S.-dominated business community keeps the drums rolling for more business. They list the advantages of doing business in an oppressed country:

ADVANTAGE NO. 1

"No taxation without representation" rings true in Puerto Rico. The island is outside the federal electoral and income tax systems. You pay no federal taxes, personal or corporate, on your manufacturing operations in Puerto Rico.

ADVANTAGE NO. 2

Liberal exemptions from Commonwealth taxes are extended to qualified manufacturers. Depending upon the location of your plant, exemption periods range from 10, 15 or 17 years—after which time, you *continue to save* through Puerto Rico's system of flexible depreciation.

ADVANTAGE NO. 3

Tremendous manpower is available from an ever-growing force of adept, willing workers. Many have specific skills that would be useful to your operation. You may expect from 4 to 10 *screened* applicants for every job opening. . . .

ADVANTAGE NO. 6

Excellent educational facilities exist in Puerto Rico, where considerable emphasis is placed on vocational training. Vocational high schools serve every area of the island with academic, basic trade and specialized training curricula.

The island has four colleges and universities, plus a full-time technical training center.

Government scholarships are granted for advanced engineering, management and specialized skills. And professional organizations sponsor management courses via television, inplant lectures and seminars.

ADVANTAGE NO. 7

Unusually high efficiency characterizes the Puerto Rican labor force. Precision, manual dexterity and adaptability to factory routine are all proven answers. Absenteeism and turnover are low. A regular factory job is a coveted position, a status symbol in the island communities.

A shoe manufacturer says: "Puerto Ricans make excellent workers . . . their eagerness becomes transformed into quick efficiency. For us that means high productivity."

The president of an electronics firm reports that "the most intricate wiring circuit doesn't confuse our workers—while our productivity continues to expand, our reject rate stays very low."

ADVANTAGE NO. 8

Reasonable wages keep your labor costs low. Unlike the U.S., Puerto Rico has set minimum wages for each industry—and the *minimum rate is maintained* within 10 to 12 percent. As of October, 1969 the average hourly industrial wage was $1.62. . . .

ADVANTAGE NO. 17

Duty-free trade offers several advantages for manufacturers whose operations involve foreign materials. If you locate your plant in Puerto Rico's *Foreign Trade Zone,* near the port city of Mayaguez—you do not have to pay U.S. customs duties upon the arrival of foreign raw materials.

You pay no U.S. customs duties on products exported to foreign countries. On those finished goods entered into U.S. territory, you may elect to pay duty based on the foreign raw material content or on the finished product—whichever represents a lower cost to you. . . .

ADVANTAGE NO. 21

Protecting the Dollar—when you locate your plant in Puerto Rico, your investment stays in the U.S. dollar area . . . you'll stem the dollar drain and reduce the balance of payments deficit.

And then they give the "clincher." "In Puerto Rico manufacturers average 30 percent on their investment."

And then in an unguarded moment *News Front,* a management newsletter, states:

Yes, there are the *arrabales,* slums of almost unimaginable dreariness. And there are untold numbers of citizens who have not advanced beyond that 1940 per capita (income) rate, and there is a great deal of grubbing around for mere existence, and there is a very serious drug problem, and some class resentment, and more prostitution than the Catholic Church is comfortable with. But Puerto Rico, for all its industry and its population density and its Americanization and its modernization, is still a place in which to live, to breathe; a place to move around in.

One can "live, breathe and move around" if one represents the foreign corporations. It is another matter for the great majority of the people of Puerto Rico. The people in the slums can move around when the garbage is at low tide.

The crimes of U.S. imperialism are not only measured by the statistics of its robberies of the natural wealth and exploitation of the people, as serious as they are. On the scale must be added the crime that appears in the atmosphere of frustration and hopelessness, the indignities practiced against each individual, the family and the nation. The crime is measured in the high rate of deaths per thousand, the thousands of innocent men and women in prisons and jails. The crime is in the imprisonment of a nation, the enslavement of a people, the crushing of a national pride, the crushing of a culture.

The colonial oppression is manifold. It is present in the special "sweetheart agreements" between U.S. corporations operating in Puerto Rico and the reactionary U.S. trade union leaders. These "sweetheart agreements" are bad enough between employer and trade union leaders of one country. They are unforgivable crimes when they are between trade union leaders and corporations of an imperialist country directed against oppressed people. Such agreements are present between outfits like the Hilton Hotels and the leaders of the International Longshoremen's Association (ILA). These "sweetheart agreements" are instruments of colonialism and obstacles to trade union organization. They bend the workers to imperialist slavery.

The "sweetheart" agreements between imperialism and class-collaborationist trade union leaders lock the workers of an oppressed country into a colonial vise. Such trade union contracts are instruments of oppression and exploitation. The workers' dues are checked off. If they start to organize their own unions they are fired. There are no laws to protect them. Such arrangements are part of the imperialist conspiracy. If workers and trade unionists in the United States want to help the workers of Puerto Rico they can do this by helping them to organize their own unions, by getting into the struggle to put an end to the United States' oppression of Puerto Rico.

Last year when the workers of Puerto Rico started a drive to apply the minimum wage law to their condition, the employers brought in Lane Kirkland, the Secretary-Treasurer of the AFL-CIO. He did his class-collaborationist "thing." He said the AFL-CIO would be "flexible" and would take "the island's interest" into account. As these trade union leaders have done for the past 75 years, he stabbed the Puerto Rican workers in the back. They are "flexible" about the slave conditions of the workers. The "island interests" are the imperialist interests of U.S. corporations.

Puerto Rico is a colony of U.S. imperialism in a very special sense. The 2,800,000 people living in Puerto Rico and the 1,300,-000 Puerto Ricans in the United States are victims of a special kind of imperialist operation. It is colonialism that reaches across the Atlantic into the barrios, the urban and agricultural slums where Puerto Ricans are forced to live in the United States. They are locked within a special system of oppression, whether living in Puerto Rico or being shuttled between the United States and San Juan. The same U.S. corporations oppress and exploit them in both lands. It is the colonial conditions in Puerto Rico that force the people into the barrios and slums of U.S. cities and farm areas. The Puerto Rican people in the United States, together with Black Americans and Chicanos are the backbone of a 40,000,000 community, victims of special oppression and exploitation.

The starvation on land and the indescribable slums of Puerto Rico are the conditions that make of Puerto Rico a special reservoir from which U.S. corporations draw a labor force into the specially oppressed areas. It is the same U.S. corporations that reap extra profits from both the oppression of Puerto Ricans in Puerto Rico and the Puerto Ricans living in the United States.

There are only a few experiences that one can say are beyond description. Visiting a Nazi concentration camp with its crematoria where millions of human beings perished is such an experience. A stay in a prison cell block where all of the prisoners are "lifers," ghosts of men, most already having served the greater part of their lives, is such an experience. A visit to the slums of Puerto Rico is another of these experiences beyond description. What heinous crimes human beings commit against their fellow human beings are beyond description. What U.S. imperialism does to the oppressed peoples of Puerto Rico and other colonial lands is beyond description.

In comparison to the United States, everything that is beneficial to Puerto Ricans reaches about 50 percent and everything that is negative and detrimental is always double or more. The negatives are doubled, the benefits cut in half. Unemployment is double that of U.S. figures. Unemployment insurance rates are about one-half. Child mortality rates are double. Wages are from one-third to one-half of U.S. wages. Cost of living is much higher. Social security benefits are about one-half. All of the anti-labor laws are applied in Puerto Rico, but the labor protection laws do not apply there.

For ten years U.S. corporations have moved into Puerto Rico because they were able to operate tax-free and with wages below one-half of U.S. wages. But now the rush is over and unemployment is reaching disastrous proportions.

Like thieves they make a fast buck and leave. New corporations come in to take advantage of the tax-free status. When the time is up they leave. Nothing is left in Puerto Rico. There is very little capital accumulation. The values produced by the workers are shipped out of the country either as the 30 percent profit or as exports to other lands. Tourism is promoted as a stop-gap measure.

As if the people of Puerto Rico did not have enough burdens, a new one has been added. Now they have been saddled with some 35,000 Cuban refugees. They were the hangers-on of the fascist gangster, U.S.-puppet-Batista government in Cuba before the revolution. Many of these declassed elements are willing tools of reaction in Puerto Rico. For this service the U.S. government has been very liberal in financing them. They have taken over the service industries, prostitution and shops. For many, this was their profession in Cuba before they were driven out. They have become a new base for the FBI and the CIA.

Writing about this new invasion, the *New York Post* columnist Jose Torres states:

Small businesses in Puerto Rico are almost entirely controlled by Cubans. Advertising agencies are almost completely dominated by

Cubans. The sports editors of every Spanish-language newspaper are Cuban. You hear a baseball broadcast and the announcer is Cuban. You go across the street for a newspaper and the store owner is Cuban. The drugstore is owned by Cubans. And a lot of jewelry stores are being run by Cubans.[2]

Many things stand out in Puerto Rico, the beauty of the land, where it has *not* been ravaged by imperialism. The modesty and beauty of its people. But the most striking fact is the unquenchable desire for independence. It is a volcano that will erupt.

The drive for independence from U.S. imperialism is the one single thought that dominates all discussions. It breaks through the papers, television, all meetings, picketlines. This urge for independence is all-inclusive. The only exception to this driving urge is a thin crust of office holders, the handful associated with the management of U.S. corporations, sections of the police force and the 35,000 Cuban refugees whom everybody refers to as "gusanos" (worms). Because of their reactionary position, U.S. imperialism has made arrangements whereby these Cuban refugees will all be able to vote in the coming 1972 elections.

The mood for independence has greatly escalated in the past years. There are various organizations fighting for independence. The reactionary forces are forced to maneuver with concepts of "Commonwealth" and "statehood." But the maneuvers will fail. There is a growing determination and a growing unity. With each new generation the demand for independence has grown louder.

Their struggle is not against the people of the United States. Their struggle is against the same corporations that exploit the workers of the United States. The friendship between our two peoples can flower—if we destroy the imperialist monster that oppresses us both. We, the people of the United States must accept our responsibility in this struggle.

Hubert Humphrey, the imperialist "butter and egg" man from Minnesota, called Puerto Rico the "miracle of the Caribbean." It is a "miracle" for the profiteers.

Call it the "Commonwealth," "protectorate," "statehood," "the emerald of the Carribean," call it by any other name, but Puerto Rico is a colony of U.S. imperialism. It is oppressed, enslaved and

[2] *New York Post,* January 23, 1971.

exploited by the monopoly corporations of the United States. The struggle for Puerto Rican independence is a just struggle. The freedom of Puerto Rico is a precondition for our own freedom. We the people of the United States, must become active partisans and participants in this struggle.

1971

14

U.S. IMPERIALISM AND THE CUBAN REVOLUTION

The Cuban revolution, and now the building of socialism so close to the shores of the United States has been and remains a bitter pill for monopoly capital to swallow.

The U.S. policy of aggression, the policy of economic blockade remains in full force, The naval base at Guantanamo is a base of U.S. aggression. It is a force of illegal occupation.

The Cuban revolution opened a new stage in the struggles of the revolutionary movement in South America. It opened a new chapter in the world struggle against U.S. imperialism.

All developments in the countries of South America have been and are deeply influenced by the Cuban revolution. The Cuban events have a deep effect on the radicalized masses in the United States. Thousands have joined the brigades which have gone to Cuba to help in the sugar harvest. Cuban independence, Cuban socialism is a monument to the revolutionary heroism of the Cuban people, to the leadership of Fidel Castro and his comrades, to the new level in the balance of world forces and to the rising tide against world imperialism.

The Cuban revolution has experienced a number of crisis points such as the victory against the Batista forces and the Bay of Pigs invasion. One of the most critical was the crisis created by the Kennedy Administration over the installation of defensive missiles.

It is necessary to see these crises in the context of the overall policy of U.S. aggression against Cuba. The aim of the policy was and remains the destruction of socialist Cuba.

Kennedy created the 1962 missile crisis as a means of testing how far the United States could go in implementing that basic policy. In looking back one should not forget what has been exposed, including the fact that the Kennedy Administration was seriously discussing the possibilities of assassinating Fidel Castro.

What follows is from a letter I wrote a day or two after the crisis was over.

It was the inherently aggressive nature of U.S. imperialism that motivated the armed blockade of Cuba, that pushed the world to the brink of a nuclear disaster. The central factor leading to the crisis was the U.S. policy to crush the Cuban revolution. If not for this policy of imperialism there would never have been the missile crisis. But there were many other factors that entered into this tense moment when the world came so close to war. There had been a growing sense of frustration in imperialist ranks because of the inability of U.S. capitalism to continue to expand and surmount all of its contradictions and problems, as it had been able to do during the earlier postwar years. There was a stubborn refusal to accept the new problems as typical of capital-alism during the later stages of its development and to see the earlier postwar years as having been extraordinary and far from "normal." Crises and decay characterize the present stage of capitalist development.

The bogged-down rate of economic growth the sharpening and growing challenge from all quarters to its dominant world position, the huge growing national debt, the increasingly burdensome tax load, a subterranean current undermining the rate of profits along with the continuing drain on gold reserves, the growing refusal of the working class to accept the burdens of the cold war, the heroic efforts of Black Americans and other North Americans to reject oppression, the upheavals among the new generation—these were only some of the problems that created the desperation in the ranks of the ruling circles of our land. As a result there had been a growing movement of ultra-right, monopolist and fascist elements who played on these frustrations and pushed for an even more sharply aggressive military policy, not even stopping at nuclear destruction.

During moments of crisis the mentally unbalanced can, and sometimes do, become a dominant influence. Concerning Cuba, the policy of the ultra-right and of powerful forces in the Pentagon was at the time for an outright, full-scale invasion and an attempt at re-enslavement of Cuba. The pressures for this policy were very great, and it is now clear that for some days the United States was within a hair's-breadth of an open invasion—with all its disastrous consequences for Cuba, for the United States and for world peace.

The world outlook of the ultra-right, militarist and fascist coalition, was for the preventive war; they argued that in a year or two it would be too late. The saner elements among the ruling circles saw the self-interests of U.S. imperialism in cold-war pressures and maneuvers, but could also see the necessity to avoid a world armed conflict. And this sanity did not come from any "enlightened" concern for the world's welfare but rather from a more realistic estimate of the balance of world forces.

When the crisis over the missiles broke, the issue of invasion had not yet been settled. The pressures for an armed attack, for a massive bombing of Cuba came from many quarters.

We will not attempt here to give an overall analysis of the developments that centered on the Cuban missile crisis and the threat of war that developed around the blockade of Cuba, but it is in order, perhaps, to express some general thoughts on the subjects. Whether the method and placement of specific types of defense weapons was correct procedure tactically is not at issue. Rather the basic question is that the Republic of Cuba was threatened by one of the world's most aggressive imperialist nuclear powers, that it had been the victim of an open military aggression—the Bay of Pigs invasion—and the attacks continued.

Under these circumstances, Cuba had the absolute right and the necessity of preparing a total means of defense. That the Soviet Union responded to Cuba's request with arms and defensive missiles was a historic act of proletarian internationalism. Maintaining Cuba's independence and the socialist system the people of Cuba were building has become one issue.

Most partisans of peace or of socialism, and all anti-imperialists, can but honor the Soviet Union for coming to the aid of Cuba. Without this aid, both military and economic, Cuba could not have withstood the strangulation and the military pressures of U.S. imperialism. This does not in the slightest detract from the glorious achievements and sacrifices of the Cuban people. They have proven themselves staunch fighters indeed against the implacable enemy 90 miles from their shores. The united militant response to the Bay of Pigs invasion by the leaders and people of Cuba has given imperialism some second thoughts. I am sorry to say, we in the United States could not have organized an opposition strong enough to halt the invasion.

Those few days when the world teetered on the brink of war or peace were a supreme test for the policy of peaceful coexistence. The central, foremost task before *all* was to prevent the invasion and re-enslavement of Cuba by U.S. imperialism, and to prevent that one act that would have triggered a world nuclear war.

It was, therefore, a historic victory for the policy of peaceful coexistence. The Soviet Union and the young Cuban Republic gave leadership in the best Leninist fashion during the crucial and frightening days. Workers in the shops and the people on the streets of our cities were heard to say, "Thank God for the Soviet Union and People's Cuba." In the thoughts of tens of millions the big reality was simply that the world was saved from a nuclear war. To millions the preservation of Cuban socialism was of historic significance. To the Soviet Union, but especially to Cuba, the withdrawal of missiles was a price for these important victories. Furthermore, it was a historic setback for the aggressive plans of U.S. imperialism. Cuban socialism stands proud and invincible, 90 miles from the barrels of the guns of U.S. imperialism. That is a historic victory.

In spite of tremendous efforts, the forces of aggression in the United States were not able to drum up any significant actions of mass support. The ultra-right, "war-now" forces have stepped up their drive for further aggressive actions, but the peace forces are now more united; they have drawn new sections of our people into the struggle.

The world is now reacting to the settlement of what is now called the "missile crisis." The reactions coming from Peking are difficult to follow. They are odd because People's China is a socialist country. In a sense they covered all bases. For them the placing of the missiles was "adventurism," the removal of the missiles was "appeasement," "Munich," "selling out to U.S. imperialism." And to top it off they took a position of neutrality—"the whole world sees that we neither requested the introduction of nuclear weapons into Cuba nor obstructed the withdrawal of the 'offensive weapons' from that country." And then the leaders of People's China made their assessment of what was to follow the settlement.

"The so-called assurances given by the United States that it will not invade Cuba are nothing but a hoax," "in fact the danger of invasion is greater," "the invasion is imminent." These quotations are all taken from the *Peking Review*.

Of course, if the original assessment that the agreement to remove the missiles was a "sellout" and "another Munich agreement," then the fears that the "danger of invasions is greater now" would have had some basis. Of course life is going to give us the answer to the question—whether the agreement was a "hoax"—or more accurately, life and struggle will give us the answer.

But the question persists. What is the explanation for this Chinese position? The only thing that fits is that the Chinese leadership was interested in a Soviet Union-United States nuclear confrontation. Anything short of that was "Munich appeasement." A defense of socialist Cuba does not seem to have any meaning for them.

For the record the facts should be clear. (1) The plan of United States imperialism was to attack and destroy socialist Cuba. (2) Cuba asked for the missiles because they knew about the planned attack on Cuba. (3) The Soviet Union as an act of working-class internationalism agreed to install the missiles. (4) This presented U.S. imperialism with a dilemma. Many in high places began to have second thoughts and there were divisions in the ranks of the Kennedy Administration. The problem was bigger than the missiles. The missiles were symbolic of the support the

Soviet Union was giving the people of Cuba. The missiles were symbolic of the determination of the Cuban people to fight in defense of their country. (5) The agreement was a setback for those who were pushing for a total attack on Cuba. (6) It was a victory for socialist Cuba—it was a victory for the world revolutionary process. (7) It is not the end of the struggle. U.S. imperialism will continue its aggression. But Cuba will continue to build socialism. Its standing will grow in South America, in the United States and in the rest of the world and the balance of world forces will continue to tip in favor of socialism. This will make it increasingly more difficult for U.S. imperialism to attack Cuba. It seems to me this is a more realistic estimate of the possibilities.

There is real historic substance to the fears of the ultra-right forces. With each passing year the possibilities of victories against the forces of socialism become more remote. Their pessimism is well-founded. It is a backhanded acceptance of the changing balance of world forces. The victories against imperialism will never be without struggle.

There is a shift in the economic and military arenas. It sets the stage for a shift in the political and ideological arenas. Victories in these areas are most crucial.

It seems to us that no matter how strong the socialist world becomes, this military strength cannot replace the need to give the maximum effort to the task of winning over the democratic, peace-minded elements of the capitalist countries—often anti-Communist and confused but entirely capable of seeing and opposing naked imperialist interference wherever the people rise up against their oppressors.

During the Caribbean crisis the government of our country made a decision to gamble on the use of thermonuclear weapons. The Kennedy administration took a calculated risk. It decided to see how far it could go—with its policy of aggression against people's Cuba. This was only one phase of the overall policy of imperialist aggression. We can never forget that the United States was the only country ever to drop an atom bomb. During the Korean war, threats were made to use it, but the voice of protest was so strong that it did not happen. During the missile crisis, our government once again made such a decision—with the knowledge that it might well plunge the world into a nuclear holocaust. But though it is important to note that they made the decision to gamble, it is even more important that they were again deterred from carrying it out.

At the same time our government made the startling public declaration that it had the right to lie to the American people and to the world if it decided that the national security was involved. Thus, the morality of the ruling class came publicly to embrace, in the name of "managed news," the resort to managed falsehood—the big lie. But even with the resort to outright fabrication, they were unable to carry out their decision to gamble.

By great effort and by sheer persistence, the world forces fighting for peace, progress and socialism were able to inch the world away from the brink of its suicidal plunge. This achievement must be viewed as an important victory. The interlude has presented mankind with one more opportunity to reverse the gears before it reaches the nuclear point of no return. The danger will continue to be with us; the madmen of U.S. imperialism will continue to have the power to press the nuclear button. But we must see it in the framework of the growing movement of anti-imperialism and the growing power of socialism, remembering that the socialist forces also have nuclear weapons to give the Pentagon pause. Socialism, together with the mass struggles for freedom from imperialism the world over, remains the most formidable force for peace, for national liberation, and for human progress. The socialist beacon, 90 miles from the shores of imperialism, remains bright.

1965

15

A NEW DAY

A Revolutionary Day in South America

A time bomb exploded in Panama. It had been ticking for 60 years. Sixty years of aggression and oppression, of violation against the national sovereignty and elementary rights of a small nation finally produced the explosion that shook Washington.

We Americans have many things to be proud of, but also not a few things to be ashamed of. One of the worst is the story of the Panama Canal and our government's role in Panama.

Panama was until a little more than 60 years ago a part of Colombia, a country in the northwestern corner of South America. The government of President Theodore Roosevelt demanded that Colombia give up 30,000 square miles of its territory in the region known as Panama so that the United States could build a canal there. The Colombian government refused to surrender the land that had been hers for generations.

The U.S. government cooked up a "revolution" in November 1903, set up a puppet government that broke Panama away from Colombia. Conveniently U.S. warships were on hand to prevent Colombia from landing troops to put down the rebellion.

In the very center of this conquered land the U.S. government set up a "master" race system of caste; Panamanians were hired at slave wages and paid with a spceial "scrip" instead of money. A system of segregation and discrimination was established, patterned after our southern plantation system. And the so-called independent government of Panama was given chicken feed as rent for the Canal Zone.

This is imperialism, this is U.S. imperialism, this is monopolistic big business and its reactionary policy. The aggression was wrong 60 years ago. It is wrong today. The people of Panama want a correction of 60 years of wrong. They want an end to 60 years of aggression.

When all these crimes exploded in their faces, U.S. government spokesmen went on TV and pointed the finger at Cuba. Assistant Secretary of Defense Vance brazenly lied that ten Cuban-trained Communists were arrested among the protesting demonstrators in Panama. Panama denied the whole story as false.

To the justified demands of Panama, the U.S. government says: "We will not pledge to negotiate a new treaty." Goldwater says: "We must not retreat, it is as much our territory as New York City." Richard Nixon stated. "If the United States retreats one inch in this respect we will have raised serious doubts about our bases throughout the world." *Business Week* in an editorial warns: "It's time we stopped such appeasement. Any breakdown in Panama would not only weaken our rights in the canal, but would have a chain reaction around the world."

Such are the voices and defenders of imperialism, of U.S. imperialism. They want to continue the policy of aggression, of political and economic domination. They don't want to give up the super-profits that the big U.S. corporations take out of the oppressed underdeveloped countries.

Each of the spokesmen fears the possible "chain reaction." From their imperialist viewpoint this is a very justified fear, because the conditions that brought to a boiling point the actions of the people of Panama are similar in the whole area of Central and South America. It was the conditions that brought on the revolution of Cuba.

The upheaval in Panama is a part of the worldwide revolution against colonialism, against imperialist slavery. The people of Central and South America have now joined this historic uprising of the colonial peoples everywhere.

The eruption in Panama is an omen, a clear forecast that the Andean mountain range and the land area of the Americas has now become the most explosive volcanic political terrain in the world.

Because of this, the political and social contours of this hemisphere are now shifting fast.

It is now an indisputable fact that one way or another there is going to take place a fundamental change in the economic, social, and political landscape of the Americas. This change is not going to wait, it is going to take place now. It is therefore the most urgent question for all of us who live in this area of the world.

What are the factors that are propelling this change? Why is this social explosion going to take place now?

In every other part of the world the national colonial liberation revolution is moving forward and being won. In this hemisphere it is the Wall Street corporations that are the imperialist slave-masters. And it is U.S. imperialism that remains the most arrogant, obstinate and bigoted. U.S. imperialism continues to operate under the illusion that it is so strong and so clever that it can withstand the tides of history.

More than anything else, the political, military and economic aggression against the Republic of Cuba exposes the real attitude that the U.S. monopolies have towards the nations and peoples fighting for freedom and independence. The reaction to the new developments in Panama is only a continuation of this same policy.

The economic and political upheaval in Central and South America is a revolution against foreign economic slavery. Largely because of this foreign economic slavery—the policies practiced by U.S. corporations—it is the only continent left where the standard of living continues to decline. In large areas the decline is from semi-starvation to death from starvation. Eighty percent of the people of this area are slowly starving. Most "development" income is from export of agricultural products, raw materials and fuels. The prices of these materials are at the mercy of U.S. corporations. They have continued to decline—it is the only world area left where the ratio of foreign capital over domestic capital continues to become even more lopsided.

In Venezuela the concessions of oil lands are distributed as follows: U.S. corporations have 73.9 percent, the British and Dutch have 25.4 percent and the domestic Venezuelan company has 0.7 percent. Rockefeller's Standard Oil Company of New Jersey is the dominant company. In some Latin American countries

Rockefeller owns 100 percent of the oil resources and the production of oil products. U.S. corporations like Standard Oil and United Fruit hold the South American continent as a private raw material preserve.

It is the only world area left where foreign capital is the foundation on which rests a plantation system of agriculture that practices actual slavery. In wide areas buying and selling of young boys and girls into life-time slavery is a common practice. The parents have the choice of either selling their children into slavery or to watch them starve to death.

Fifty-five percent of the people of Latin America are engaged in agriculture. Eighty percent of these people on the land never see or use money of any kind. They live in a slave system of barter.

It is the only continent where such slave conditions are on the increase.

Thanks to these conditions, Latin American food production per inhabitant in the past six years has sunk below the pre-war level.

It is the only continent where the exports to the outside world have stagnated. During the last 12 years world exports have increased by 88 percent. The exports from Asia have increased by 94 percent, from the Middle East by 125 percent—while the exports from Latin America during this period rose by 4 percent (this excluded oil exports of Venezuela).

There is no mystery as to why the countries of Central and South America are getting poorer. They are being robbed by foreign corporations, mainly U.S. corporations. These corporations take out from Latin America five times the rate of profits they get from their investments in Western Europe. In 1960 U.S. corporations invested 267 million dollars in Latin America. But during the same year they took out 641 million dollars. The oil sold at the port of export in Venezuela is worth over three billion dollars each year. Venezuela gets 800 million in oil tax, and this is more than most countries get. This is imperialist robbery—U.S. imperialist robbery.

Added to this economic plunder are the military burdens foisted on Latin America by the U.S. government as part of its own cold war policies. The 19 Latin American countries (excluding Cuba) have a total of 650,000 men under arms. This costs nearly one and a half billion dollars a year, which is 400 million dollars more than the so-called U.S. aid through the Alliance for Progress. Arms supplied by the United States and soldiers trained by U.S. military missions are used to suppress the people (this is what Batista did in Cuba) and to overthrow governments that try to introduce even small reforms (as was the case in 1965 in the Dominican Republic and Honduras).

Not long ago the now-defunct *N.Y. Herald-Tribune* stated that the Alliance for Progress was contributing to reviving militarism in Latin America. When the militarists overthrew the legal governments of Honduras, Alliance for Progress signs were seen on the army trucks. The soldiers carried U.S. machine guns and wore U.S. camouflage uniforms given them when they received their training at the U.S. anti-guerrilla school in Panama. Alliance for Progress? To Latin America's hungry millions it has proved in more ways than one to be an Alliance for Reaction.

The Andes volcano will explode because the rate of economic exploitation of its resources and people is the highest in the world.

It is going to explode because it is the only way that the people of Latin America are going to get their liberation. It is going to explode because the policies of U.S. imperialism are not immune to the laws of social progress, and because this is the point in history when humanity is going to hurl imperialism off its back.

We the people of these United States are not the exploiters or those who benefit from the slave policies pursued by the U.S. corporations. But we do have a responsibility and a stake in the outcome of this struggle. Our government, our name, the prestige of our nation and hundreds of millions of dollars of our tax money are used to make it possible for the big corporations to conduct their piracy beyond our borders. Our tax dollars are used to prop up and keep in power corrupt governments of the rich, in most cases they are reactionary military dictatorships. In the eyes of the world, silence or neutrality by our people is taken as support for the evil policies of U.S. corporations in foreign lands. We have the task of demonstrating that Standard Oil's policies are not our policies, that Nixon and the *Business Week* do not speak for us. In meeting our responsibility we must face some hard facts of life. We must recognize this simple and honest truth that the struggles of our neighboring peoples are *just* struggles. There are no legal, political, historical, moral, or ethical factors that can excuse or justify imperialist enslavement. No country can be independent or free if its economic life depends on what some foreign corporation is going to pay for its raw material. In this age a nation to be independent must build an independent industrial base.

How are the countries of Central and South America going to do this? To build an industrial base requires investment capital. The countries of Latin America now face the same problem as did our forefathers before 1776. The very money that could be used as investment for capital goods to build industry is taken to a foreign land. As long as the profits of industry and trade went to Great Britain the colonies had no capital with which to establish an industrial base. This became possible only after the war of independence was won. The countries of Latin America are never going to be able to build an industry of their own as long as the profits from their present production and raw materials are filtered into the bank accounts of the U.S. corporations on Wall Street.

The governments of Latin America have only one realistic choice, one path that leads to independence and economic well-being. The first step along this path is to nationalize the foreign-owned corporations. If we are for the independence of under-developed countries we must support the forces that are for nationalization of foreign-owned assets. The present U.S. policy, including the Alliance for Progress, is to place every possible obstacle to block this path.

In most of the countries of Central and South America the governments are corrupt and in the control of a small group of bigoted families who are the instruments through which the U.S. monopolies dictate their policies of slavery.

Here is how a former Secretary of State, Henry L. Stimson, placed the question:

Irrespective of the policy of Washington, and the personalities of

statesmen, the operations of such enterprises as the United Fruit Co.
of the U.S. and oil companies create independent political interests
in the territories subject to their economic operations which supple-
ment and often determine official policy both in Washngton and in
the various Latin American capitals.

The people of Latin America face the task of winning their
independence from U.S. imperialism. But they cannot gain this
victory without removing from positions of power the corrupt
families who in most cases are the spokesmen for U.S. imperialism.

How the people of Latin America are going to proceed is for
them to decide. In all likelihood they will travel many different
paths. In some countries the democratic institutions will be the
vehicle. Where this path will be closed, explosions will follow as
night follows day. We can only be sure of one fact; that in one
way or another the people of Latin America are going to get rid
of both U.S. imperialism and the corrupt domestic regimes that
speak for it.

The latest Defense Department guide book states: "Although
it is not the center of the world's news interests, the area South
of the border is extremely important to the U.S. The supply of
new materials from South of the border is vital to us in peace
and war." To the spokesmen of imperialism, it is a private preserve, a "South of the border area." It is not nations, peoples,
governments. It is a vital area of raw materials. It does not even
occur to these spokesmen that because a neighbor has something
"vital," this does not justify your murdering him in order to steal it.

The continuation of the policy of aggression by U.S. imperialism
against the countries of Central and South America, including the
aggressive policy against Cuba, carry within them the seeds of
worldwide war. The people are going to force through their just
struggle for freedom and bread. They have a right to appeal for
help, for protection to their neighbors, to governments and peoples
of the world. To ignore this new reality is to be blind to facts
of life.

We can expect to earn the right of friendship with our neighboring peoples only to the extent that we help make it possible
for them to determine for themselves what kind of a society they
want to build and live in. We can be good neighbors only to

the extent that we fight for a policy that will help them build their own industries and a healthful economic life that will end hunger and oppression.

The Americas are a wonderful part of our earth. The one obstacle that prevents all of the people from enjoying its benefits is U.S. capitalism-imperialism for which the interests and the happiness of people has no meaning.

In the United States alone some 25 million Negro Americans are kept half slave because it adds to the profits of big business. U.S. corporations enslave a continent because there are super-profits from it. Workers are laid off, shops are closed because automation means millions more in profits. Rents go up because it means more profits. Not profits for the people, but for a small group of big business. This is capitalism. This is U.S. capitalism.

The heart of the problem for all of our people in the Americas is big monopoly capitalism with its home base in Wall Street. A unity of the peoples of the Americas in a common struggle can make this the most wonderful part of our globe.

1970

16

THE DOMINICAN REPUBLIC

The Ghosts of Past Realities

U.S. imperialism uses the tactics of neo-colonialism when these tactics achieve results. But when they get into difficulties they quickly shift to the use of military force.

In the Dominican Republic the C.I.A. helped to overthrow the first democratically elected government in over 30 years. When it appeared that the people were going to elect a new government that was not to the exact specifications of subservience, laid down by U.S. corporations, the Johnson administration sent in the Marines. The cover for the action has become an example of imperialist hypocrisy. The excuse was that there were "58 Communists there." Because of these 58 Communists, Johnson sent in 35,000 armed Marines. Shortly afterwards President Johnson spoke to the problem at a meeting of the O.A.S.—"The American nation cannot, must not, and will not permit the establishment of another Communist government in the Western Hemisphere." Two things should be said about that remark: One, the government that was overthrown in the Dominican Republic had no Communists in it and, two, history will most likely record them amongst the "famous last words before the event" stories.

Not to be outdone, and after a number of high-sounding speeches about the "inherent right of all peoples to determine their own destinies"—some went ever further and called it a "God-given right"—the U.S. Congress passed the following resolution:

Resolved that it is the sense of the House of Representatives that (1) Any such subversive domination or threat of which violates the principles of the Monroe Doctrine, . . . and (2) In any such situation any one or more of the high contracting parties to the Inter-American Treaty of Reciprocal Assistance may, in the exercise of individual or collective self-defense . . . take steps to forestall or combat intervention, domination, control and colonization in whatever form, by the subversive forces known as "international communism" and its agents in the Western Hemisphere.

These will go down in history as the famous last words of an imperialist government.

It was a declaration that the United States will permit governments only to its liking.

Such declarations expose the intentions of U.S. imperialism—but they are based on a myth long since gone, the myth of eternal domination by U.S. imperialism over all of Latin America.

1967

17

"PASSING THE WORD"—WHOSE WORD?

When asinine and fraudulent statements are made by public figures, it is necessary to place for the record a rejection. Joe Curran's column in *The Pilot* calls for such treatment. Joe Curran is the president of the National Maritime Union.

The only truthful word in the whole piece is the title "Passing the Word." The CIA's propaganda department has a large stable of professional falsifiers who for cash grind out filthy red-baiting fiction by the ton. In the trade union movement this malodorous bilge is pumped for publications by a Lovestone who holds down a CIA desk in the front office of the AFL-CIO. This drivel is published in the trade union press under the name of any official who can be convinced, paid off or forced into the use of his name.

Red-baiting has always been a camouflage for the crimes and misdeeds of demagogues and scoundrels of all types. It took a lot of red-baiting to cover the crimes of Hitler and Mussolini. Senator McCarthy's redbaiting was the cover for the crimes of the Korean War and the attempt to discredit the democratic institutions, including our trade union movement. And in retrospect one must say that the damage to the trade union movement was inestimable. It takes a lot of red-baiting to cover for the crimes of the U.S. aggression against Vietnam. And it took a wave of fanatical red-baiting for the Meany-Lovestone-Dubinsky clique to put over an endorsement of these crimes of the Johnson Administration at the recent AFL-CIO convention.

Curran's column entitled "The War in Vietnam—Part of America's Defensive Freedom" and his asinine red-baiting speeches at the convention are also a part of this red-baiting camouflage.

The column by Curran is a rehashing of the fraudulent red-baiting filth that has been peddled by every anti-labor, anti-demagogue from Hitler to Hoover, from Eastland to Robert Welch of the Birch Society. In fact the same stable must have shoveled out the swill for the administration spokesmen at the AFL-CIO convention, because it is difficult to say where Rusk's speech ended and Curran's began. The ugly imperialist aggression against Vietnam, aggression that is more unanimously condemned by the world than any in history, is defended by Curran. The demagogy he uses is that this is a continuation of the struggle against fascism. This will fool no one. U.S. imperialism is doing today what German imperialism did under Hitler. The forces who fought fascism are today fighting U.S. imperialism. The forces who defended fascism are today defending U.S. imperialism. Curran tries to cover up for this brutal aggression of imperialism by saying, "All Communist countries act as if there were no such things as national boundaries." Such idiocy cannot cover up the undeniable facts that it is U.S. imperialism that has crossed the boundaries in Vietnam, the Dominican Republic, Taiwan and was instrumental in the crossing of the boundaries of Egypt, Jordan, and Syria.

Curran's column talks about the danger of "Communist global take-over." Hitler's Minister of Propaganda coined the phrase, German fascism used it as a cover to murder some 40 million people. Joe McCarthy adopted it—it has been the cover for every United States imperialist operation—and now when others are ashamed to use it Joe Curran picks it up. This is a threadbare defense of the greatest "take-over" in world history. U.S. imperialism is now the largest colonial power in history. It exploits more human beings than any power in history. It has more war bases around the world than any government in history. U.S. capitalism controls more industries, banks and utilities overseas than any class in history. All the red-baiting in the world will not cover up this banditry.

Curran says, "Our hopes of worldwide solidarity of workers through the World Federation of Trade Unions were torpedoed by the Communists." It is too late for this big lie. Since the public exposure of some of the operations of the CIA, no one will buy this hogwash. It is now common knowledge based on exposure and open confessions that it was U.S. big business through the CIA, through Lovestone, Meany and Dubinsky that set out to split the trade union movement. It is now common knowledge that they spent huge sums running into hundreds of millions to bribe and otherwise corrupt trade union officials around the world in order to use them to split the trade unions of the world. The very latest of these exposes and confessions by labor leaders comes from Finland where trade union leaders admitted being on the CIA payroll for the specific purpose of splitting the trade unions of Finland.

No amount of red-baiting bilge is going to cover up the fact that because of its subservience to big business, the AFL-CIO leadership has become more isolated from the trade unions of the world than at any time in history. The trade union movement of the world has rejected the very red-baiting filth that Curran now peddles.

In this column Curran trots out all of the old ultra-right fascist garbage, including the charge of "Moscow gold," subversion, etc.

It takes a lot to cover up an ugly unjust war of imperialist aggression. The Lovestone stables pulled out all stops so Curran could say, "In Vietnam it requires full scale war," and, in his speech at the Convention, to add "a call for and a prediction of an armed U.S. aggression against the Republic of Cuba."

The red-baiting at the AFL-CIO convention became the cover for the reactionary policies of its top leadership. But in spite of this, it took five members of the President's Cabinet, army brass and dozens of other government officials and the prepared red-baiting trash to keep down the voices of revolt within a convention whose delegates were largely hand picked.

Curran is not "passing the word" of the seamen. They will blush with anger and shame because the name of this great union is being used as an instrument of the most reactionary anti-labor forces in the world. Curran is "passing the word" of the CIA, of big business. He has become an instrument of a new wave of McCarthyism. But he is an instrument of a lost cause. Americans and American workers will draw lessons gained in the struggle against McCarthyism of the fifties. Why Curran has fallen for this ultra-right swill is not the most important question. That he has is important and it cannot be denied or ignored.

All the red-baiting in the world is not going to solve the problems of the seamen. Crawling on one's belly never won anything. All the endorsements of the crimes of the administration is not going to make it easier to organize the men in the ships of the U.S. foreign runaways.

The war of aggression is going to take an increasingly bigger slice from the worker's loaf of bread. The rank and file of the unions are not going to be sidetracked by the red-baiting of the leadership. The rank and file of the trade unions are not supporting the war of aggression in Indochina.

1966

18

ANTI-COMMUNISM IN ALGERIA

There is a growing uneasiness about some developments in Algeria. Increasingly I am asked the question: What about Algeria? This concern is shown and the questions are asked by those who are supporters and partisans of the Algerian Revolution.

There is good reason for this concern. Algeria remains one of the cardinal bases in the struggle against world imperialism. What happens there greatly affects the balance of world forces in the struggle. The victorious struggle of the Algerian people against French colonial rule was one of the great historic events that sent revolutionary shock waves around the world. Since the victory for political independence, progressive and socialist partisans throughout the world have hailed every forward step including the nationalization of industries and other actions that have cleared the path for a socialist direction in Algeria.

Now, however, there are some developments that are disturbing, to say the least. They are disturbing because these developments threaten to reverse the course Algeria has been following.

The internal affairs of each country are for the people to determine. The internal affairs of Algeria belong to the Algerians. This, of course, does not mean that friends should remain silent. Serious friends will applaud victories and honestly express concern when they see weaknesses.

We feel the need to express some thought about Algeria for three reasons:

(1) We are partisans of the struggle for socialism.

(2) We are partisans in the struggle against imperialism; and

(3) We are convinced that U.S. imperialism is deeply involved in and has reactionary plans for Algeria.

What are the developments that are disturbing? Within Algeria there has emerged a strong reactionary right-wing force. It has become very active—both openly and beneath the surface. It is well organized. It has a small storm-trooper-like force that leads a campaign of terror against Communists and other left and progressive forces. It is a campaign against the staunchest supporters of the Algerian revolution. It also operates from posts within the Boumedienne government. It is not, however, the dominant force in the government.

These right-wing elements have an influence beyond their numbers because other sections of the leadership make concessions and close their eyes to the acts of terror. This is the source of the deep concern.

These right-wing forces are conducting a brutal campaign of terror without authority. During the past weeks the arrests, illegal kidnapping and systematic torture of political prisoners and the general harassment has greatly escalated. It is common knowledge that for more than two months Khaled Benmouffok, the General Secretary of the Leather Workers Union, Belmadani and Lakhdar Cherfaoui, all of them very active trade unionists, have been detained and still are in the hands of the torturers. In fact, torture has become a rule practiced against members of the Communist Party and other left and progressive people who are arrested.

The right-wing campaign has lately expanded to include a McCarthyite inquisition and hunt for suspected Communists in the government apparatus, in trade unions and other mass organizations. The weapon is anti-Communism but the target includes the Left, the progressives and other advanced revolutionary forces.

What is the aim of these reactionary forces? Their right-wing drive is related to both domestic and foreign developments. The aim is to reverse the course of the Algerian revolution. Internally they want to halt the government policy of nationalization. The truth is that they have already successfully stopped the implementation of the Boumedienne program of agricultural reform. In this they have the support of the big landlords of Algeria.

Algeria is in a sharp struggle against the French oil monopolies that still operate in Algeria. In this they have the support of U.S. imperialist interests. U.S. imperialism expects to repeat history. As it took over from French imperialism in Indochina, it expects to take over the French interests in Algeria.

U.S. imperialism is interested in the oil and gas deposits, but it is not interested as an ordinary buyer. It is seeking for a political and ideological beachhead to be used in the robbing of these riches.

That Algeria wants to negotiate the best possible deal in selling its national riches is just and deserves the support of all anti-imperialist forces. But U.S. imperialism wants more than oil and gas. It wants what the the right-wing reactionary forces in Algeria want. It wants to reverse the course of the Algerian revolution.

The CIA is deeply involved in Algerian affairs. It is the instrument for the securing of the beachheads.

It is not accidental that the campaign of terror conducted by the right-wing forces closely follows the ups and downs of the negotiations with U.S. oil corporations. Just a few weeks ago the contracts were ready for the signatures but at the last minute the State Department stepped in and postponed the signing. This was not a concession to French oil interests. It was clearly an act designed to further influence the political developments within Algeria. It was an act of political extortion.

The negotiations involve billions of dollars. The U.S. corporation directly involved in these negotiations is the El Paso Gas Corporation. Incidently, this is the corporation that has the monopoly with the U.S. Atomic Energy Commission in the use of nuclear explosions in extracting oil and gas. El Paso is directly involved but those associated with it in the Algerian deal constitute a list of "who's who" in the top U.S. imperialist monopoly circles.

On the board of directors of El Paso are representatives of the Mellon banks and the United Bank in California. Connected in the deal are Columbia Gas, a Morgan corporation; Consolidated Gas, Rockefeller; and, of course, the Rockefellers' Standard Oil of New Jersey. Besides these negotiations, U.S. imperialism has also other avenues of penetration. The State Department has approved a $250 million loan to Algeria for a gas liquefication plant. It has also approved a large loan for the buying of U.S. jet airliners.

All this would still have no special significance if they were deals on the basis of trade with no political strings attached. They would have no significance if they were not related to the escalation of a campaign of terror against the most consistent and strongest supporters of the Algerian revolution.

The danger is in fact that this reactionary drive of terror by right-wing elements is carried on as a concession, as an accommodation, to the policies of U.S. imperialism. It is an attempt to show U.S. imperialism that Algeria is a safe area of investment. This type of opportunism is a dangerous path for any country.

There is also a further development in the right-wing campaign. There has surfaced an open anti-Communist campaign by some leading Algerian government figures. This has appeared in the speeches of people like Kaid Aheed, a leader of the National Liberation Front; Ahmed Taled, the Minister of Education, and in the speeches of M. Kassim and C. Mekki, who are specializing in anti-Soviet slanders.

These developments are in contradiction to the direction of the Algerian revolution. They present a serious challenge to all progressive forces, including the people around President Boumedienne.

U.S. imperialism is the most brutal and cunning imperialism in all of history. It has perfected the tactic of political, ideological and economic penetration into a fine art. It is the master at using division and fissures in the ranks of its opponents. It is the master of the art of seepage of ideological concepts. To in any way accommodate policies to its skillful line of extortion is the most deadly of all errors. Anti-Communism is its most successful weapon. To buy "favors" from U.S. imperialism by taking part in its anti-Communist campaign is opening the gates to its ideological penetration and economic domination.

Anti-Communism is an instrument of imperialism. Revolutionary forces which, for whatever reason, join in this slanderous campaign, sooner or later become themselves instruments of imperialism. Anti-imperialism cannot solidify a front if it accepts an ideological instrument of imperialism.

The aim of imperialism's anti-Communism—anti-Sovietism—is to confuse, to disarm and to divide the masses. This is preparatory to further steps of penetration and aggression.

One must draw lessons from the experiences of others. When the Truman cold war started, U.S. monopoly capital had to destroy the resistance to its foreign policies at home. The aggressive policies in world affairs were therefore accompanied by an anti-Communist campaign at home. Many liberal, left and progressive forces accommodated themselves or remained silent when these attacks took place. Many joined the ranks of the red-baiters. It was not too long thereafter that the trade unions and other mass organizations retreated in confusion and defeat.

The purpose of the anti-Communist campaign is to confuse and to destroy the resistance of a people and the attempt is to move them along a reactionary path. The noose of anti-Communism is designed for all who support the Algerian revolution. By their silence the broader democratic and revolutionary forces inadvertently are readying the noose for their own necks. A revolution can move forward only on the basis of organized, politically conscious people. To permit right-wing elements to carry on their reactionary activities of division and confusion is to court disaster.

Like racism, the imperialist ideological poison of anti-Communism will be with us as long as there will be capitalism. Like racism it will penetrate wherever there is the slightest weakness or opening. If not actively fought it takes over. It must be fought in all its variations, in all its forms. It cannot be successfully fought by taking a stand against it in one form while making concessions to it in other forms.

This is a critical question for all revolutionary movements, as it is a critical question for us in the United States, It is a critical question for the countries that have won their political independence and are now struggling to build economic independence and, of course, it is a critical question for all countries that are moving towards socialism.

U.S. imperialism is a cunning foe but it is suffering defeats in many parts of the world. We are confident the revolutionary forces of Algeria are not going to permit the penetration of its influence into their arena of struggle.

We are confident the people of Algeria will fully deal with these right-wing groups and will give their full support to the revolutionary policies of nationalization, of agricultural reforms and for the steps that will clear the path to socialism.

Algeria will find the necessary strength and aid in close and equal relations with the socialist countries of the world. We are concerned but we are also confident.

1968

19

NOT ALL PEACE TALK IS TALK FOR PEACE

Vietnam and the Vatican

Pope John XXIII charted a new course for the Catholic Church. His celebrated encyclical *Pacem in Terris* was hailed by all progressive forces in the world. He opened a path of dialogue between Catholics and other forces of social progress. He set into motion forces of progress within the Catholic Church—a historic struggle that continues today. The forces fighting for progressive policies within the Catholic Church have made impressive gains. But it is not easy to change centuries-old encrusted policies and deeply imbedded bureaucratic hierarchies.

Pope Paul VI has not given the same kind of leadership for the realization of these policies. He often uses the same words as Pope John but very often they do not have the same meaning. For Pope John's words and messages were meant to carry the idea of activity, of movement as instruments of change. Pope Paul's messages convey the idea of inaction, and the defense of the status quo—especially the reactionary status quo.

This difference is clearly demonstrated in his December 15, 1969 call for "A Day of Peace." Even more than a call for inaction, Pope Paul cynically condemns the forces who do act for peace. In the message there appears the following paragraph:

> Accordingly, in conclusion, it is to be hoped that the exaltation of the ideal of peace may not favor the cowardice of those who fear it may be their duty to give their life for the service of their country and of their own brothers, when these are engaged in the defense of justice and liberty, and who seek only a flight from their responsibility, from the risks that are necessarily involved in the accomplishment of great duties and generous exploits.

This is said at a moment when the mass resistance to the dirty war is growing. At a time when increasing numbers of youth are saying: "We will not go!" The Pope's words come at a time when greater numbers of Catholics are joining the peace ranks. It is a message of comfort to the forces of imperialism. It is an effort to discourage and label millions who are fighting an unjust and immoral war of aggression.

In essence Pope Paul says: Think of peace but don't do anything about it. Go right ahead and fight and die for imperialism. If you refuse to take part in this dirty war, it is because you are a "coward."

The label of cowardice does not belong on the foreheads of the young Americans who are putting up a heroic struggle against the dirty war in Vietnam. It should be placed at the doorstep of those who do not have the courage to resist.

Rather, I want to discuss the word in relation to the Vatican position on the Vietnamese situation.

To deliver a sermon "Thou shalt not steal" equally to a thief and the victim while the robbery is going on is in fact to side with the thief.

To declare "Thou shalt not kill" equally to the victim and the murderer while the murder is going on is to side with the murderer.

To issue abstract statements about "the blessings of peace" directed to both sides while an aggression is going on is to side with the aggressor. Not to condemn the aggressor and not to call for actions against the aggression is to side with the aggressor.

And further, to slander those who fight for peace as "cowards" is to become an accessory in the crime of imperialist aggression.

The Vatican's one-sidedness regarding the Vietnamese situation has appeared at other crucial moments. Each Vatican statement about "the dangers of the war spreading" has been issued at moments when there were statements about the Vietnamese getting some new weapons with which to fight for their independence. Such statements have not come from the Vatican when U.S. imperialism has escalated its aggression.

Frankly, the sincerity of all general statements about peace must be measured by the actions against the aggressor. Calls for peace without differentiating between the forces of aggression and the forces fighting a just war for the right of self-determination objectively become a cover for aggression. In fact the Johnson administration has used such calls to say, "See, the Vietnamese have not responded," while the United States has escalated the aggression.

Even these general professions for peace come under further suspicion when Cardinal Spellman, speaking in Vietnam, said: "War in fact has brought out the noblest instincts and the best traits of human courage and endurance in the annals of history." This blatant glorification of the war of aggression by a leading Catholic spokesman was not objected to from any Vatican quarter. The silence can be interpreted as acquiescence.

When social struggles sharpen, the fence of neutrality becomes uncomfortable. Generalities and platitudes turn into demagogy which objectively sides with the forces of reaction.

To give comfort to an aggressor by placing the aggressor in the same position as the victim is not neutrality—it is supporting the aggression.

Such conduct is not even pacifism. As a rule pacifism refuses to support wars of aggressions. In this sense Pope Paul's position is not neutrality or pacifism.

Pope John gave the Catholic Church a new direction. The blessing of wars or slandering the young men who refuse to support an ugly imperialist aggression is not in keeping with the spirit or the meaning of that path. And it is contrary to the thought and actions of the progressive forces within the Catholic Church.

1970

20

A FEW IMPERIALIST EXCURSIONS AND INCURSIONS

Mr. Imperialism Visits Rumania and Yugoslavia

We see nothing wrong in a spokesman of a capitalist country being invited and received by leaders of a socialist country; and, of course, there is nothing wrong in having discussions on matters affecting the relations between the two countries, or, in fact, reaching agreements on these matters, provided that these agreements in no way weaken the struggle against world imperialism. These are features of diplomatic relations of peaceful coexistence between countries with different social systems.

Therefore it was not Nixon's visit to Rumania per se that concerned me. It was, rather, the hero's welcome this most reactionary spokesman of a relentlessly aggressive imperialism received— the kind of welcome that has nothing in common with policies of peaceful coexistence.

As a matter of fact this was Nixon's second "triumphant visit" to Rumania. Nixon had visited the Philippines, India, Indonesia, Pakistan, Thailand. In these countries, he received a "diplomatic" welcome, but there were also mass protests by the forces of anti-imperialism. Only in Rumania did he receive a "warm, enthusiastic" welcome. From all accounts it seems hundreds of thousands turned out to greet him. The majority of Rumanians, of course, did not turn out, and some did come out of curiosity, but for those who did cheer and wave flags, what was the cheering about? What was the dancing arm in arm of Nixon and the Rumanian leaders about?

If it was in friendship to the American people, it was misplaced. Nixon represents the class that is the root cause of all the problems and difficulties facing the nation and our people. Friendship is not an abstract matter. It has something to do with a willingness to help solve the problems of one's fellow man. Friendship with the American people is related to the concern about the racist oppression of 25 million Black Americans; it is related to forcing an end to the U.S. aggression against Vietnam; it is related to the working-class struggle against the most cold-blooded class of exploiters in all history. It is related to our struggle against reaction and fascism.

Nixon is the face of the class enemy; a show of warm welcome to him is the opposite of friendship and concern with the people of the United States. To cheer him is to cheer the man in whose hands rests the power to continue or to call a halt to the mass murder of Vietnamese men, women and children; we all know that he has chosen to continue and to expand the carnage. He is the leading spokesman for the gang of multibillionaires who enslave and exploit the millions of people in Asia, Africa and South America. Only recently ten people in South America sacrificed their lives in blocking a welcome for Nixon's partner-in-crime, Rockefeller. To cheer Nixon is to cheer monopoly capitalism. To cheer Nixon is to cheer policies of imperialist aggression. There is nothing about Nixon or what he represents that calls for cheers. To dance on the street with Nixon is an insult to our people.

While in Rumania Nixon said: "The United States believes that the rights of all nations must be equal." Coming from a spokesman of a class that exploits more people and enslaves more nations than all the rest of the capitalist world put together, this is the absolute limit of hypocrisy. He also spoke about being ready to accept the real world of different social systems—this from the leader of the foremost world force in the struggle against world socialism. This from the world spokesman for counterrevolution. But Rumania provided a convenient platform for this outrageous demagogy.

And, who in Rumania challenged these demagogic falsehoods publicly? No one. In the struggle against imperialism what was said privately has absolutely no real significance. One should have no illusions of how U.S. imperialism and Nixon viewed the trip. The forces he represents in American life are incapable of friendship; theirs is the friendship of the wolf pack. Their very existence is a record of oppression and exploitation of people. And the new balance of world forces is the main obstacle to U.S. imperialist dreams of dominating the world. U.S. imperialism views the Soviet Union as the chief obstacle to its plans of conquest, because it is the one world power that can challenge it in economic, scientific and military power. Because of the might of the Soviet Union, U.S. imperialism cannot meet the forces of world socialism head on and because of this reality is forced to maneuver.

All its maneuvers are related to overcoming this central core of world reality. Its ideological crusades, its diplomatic forays, its splitting tactics, including the president's visits, are all geared to overcoming the central obstacle to its plans of aggression. To this end, they are maneuvering to divide the socialist world; to this end, they are willing even to make temporary concessions to some countries. Their bridgeheads however are bridgeheads of aggression, not friendship.

This is the hard core of present-day reality for the forces of world socialism, who must never be trapped into any illusions that Nixon and U.S. imperialism can be friends with one or two socialist countries, while they are sharpening their spearheads against the world socialist system. Proletarian internationalism means vigilance against being "used," even inadvertently, by imperialism. The use imperialism makes of such bridgeheads is to create splits in the socialist sector, and to create illusions amongst the masses. The most widespread picture of the trip was the head of the Rumanian Communist Party dancing on the street arm in arm with Nixon.

"Let us turn out tomorrow and greet the respected guest, his wife and his aides." This was the call issued by the Socialist Alliance of the Working People of Yugoslavia. Again the guest was none other than Richard Nixon. President Tito did not go to pay his last respects to the President of Egypt, Gamal Abdel Nasser, so that he could be with the "respected guest." And the crowds in Yugoslavia did turn out to yell "Viva Nixon"!

Again the questions are not about diplomatic relations or about having trade relations or about an American president visiting a country; the questions are about mobilizing the people to give him a mass welcome, about the cheers, the kisses and hugs. The questions also are about what is *not* said or done.

Why did no one say, "Nixon, get the forces of U.S. imperialism out of Indochina now"? On numerous occasions the leaders of the Soviet Union, Hungary, Bulgaria, German Democratic Republic have said this is the obstacle to better relations.

And why was he received as a respected guest? It cannot be because he is the commander-in-chief of the forces continuing to murder thousands of men, women and children in Vietnam, Laos and Cambodia. It cannot be because he comes from the headquarters of the counter-revolutionary forces of the world, or that he is the dispenser of the arms, the napalm for all the reactionary forces of the world.

It cannot be because he has just decided to arm the fascist forces of a government that is Yugoslavia's neighbor, Greece; nor because he has taken the lead in the policies that are escalating racism and genocide against Black Americans; nor because at the very hour that he departed for Yugoslavia, he announced an increase in U.S. imperialist military forces in the Mediterranean Sea.

Or can it be because he symbolizes and represents the imperialist forces who are conducting a military aggression against the Arab lands that Nasser represented? Or is it because just before he left he met with the "invisible government" on how to overthrow the results of the Chilean popular electoral victory?

But these are all compelling reasons why a socialist country should *not* stage a hero's welcome for Nixon. What does Yugoslavia hope to get for these "cheers." At most, if his past trips are a criteria, Yugoslavia will get some small favorable trade concessions. To cheer Nixon for a few crumbs of trade is crass opportunism.

And what is it that U.S. imperialism is after? Some say it is good for Nixon's electoral hopes. They are right. To be received as a respected guest in a socialist country tends to hide the naked reactionary policies of the administration. Some say it also fits into the central U.S. imperialist struggle against the socialist countries and especially into the anti-Soviet policies of U.S. monopoly. Some say it is an attempt to make U.S. imperialism appear democratic and peaceful. Others say it is an attempt to split the world anti-imperialist forces. All of these hypotheses happen to be correct. That is exactly what U.S. imperialism expects from Nixon's visits.

Perhaps the intentions of the leaders of Yugoslavia in this instance are not important, in comparison with the fact that giving Nixon the respected guest treatment was a plus for U.S. imperialism and did help to create the smokescreen it wants. The roots of these actions lie in the policies of the Tito leadership—in the policie of "nonalignment." Nonalignment is another word for oppor nism. The worldwide struggle between the working class and the capitalist class is an indisputable reality. Whatever action any ountry takes, it affects this struggle. When such a country d s not give its full support to the working-class side, it is a plus for capitalism. For a socialist country to become nonaligned is to withdraw from the class struggle.

Nonalignment is opportunism because such a course is followed only in the expectation of getting some concessions from the class adversary. And indeed imperialism is ready and willing to distribute some crumbs. But politics based on opportunism make gains that have a very short life span. To continue its payments, imperialism expects continued performance.

And it is important to stress that these over-friendly welcomes have nothing in common with policies of peaceful coexistence, which are policies of struggle and not such as to play into the hands of imperialism.

Indeed Tito's speech about the big powers is very much in line with the policies of opportunistic nonalignment. It is in fact a classical example of the classlessness of nonalignment. To speak of the socialist Soviet Union and the imperialist, capitalist United States as if basic class differences do not exist is crass opportunism. It is the kind of defense and cover-up that U.S. imperialism appreciates very much indeed, while at the same time being the kind of anti-Soviet slander that the Nixons value greatly. Nixon does not mind if the host says he is concerned about the welfare of the Vietnamese people as long as no one points the accusing finger at U.S. imperialism. Diplomacy and opportunism are not the same thing. There is working-class socialist diplomacy and there is the diplomacy of nonalignment, classless opportunism. To view the narrow short-ranged benefits of one's own nation, even if it is detrimental to the struggle against imperialism and to the unity of the socialist sector is opportunism; it is nationalism; it is a form of betrayal.

The policy of nonalignment is ideological, political and military. For a socialist power it is retreat from the class struggle. Private talks and negotiations with the spokesmen of the principal imperialist power can have meaning only if the spokesmen of imperialism knew they are dealing with the united power of the socialist and other anti-imperialist forces. They are not going to retreat when confronted with policies of nonalignment, which are policies of weakness and division.

In the framework of the real world there is no nonalignment. U.S. imperialism would like nothing better than to get all the socialist countries to take the path of not being aligned. Then it could deal with each of them separately, and it could combine its aggressions and exploitation unhindered the world over. The policy of nonalignment for some socialist countries is possible only because the other socialist countries have refused to follow such a course. Thus opportunist policies are possible only because of the non-opportunist policy of others. The opposite of these opportunist policies is commitment—commitment to the working-class struggles on a world scale, commitment to the worldwide anti-imperialist struggle.

Policies of nonalignment lead to disunity, to divisions, to the weakening of the progressive forces, while commitment leads to unity, to the growing strength of the forces against capitalism. To the world forces following the policies of total commitment to the struggle against imperialism, Nixon is not a "respected guest." We extend a hand to the millions of Yugoslav and Rumanian people who did not turn out to welcome Nixon but said, instead: "Who wants Nixon? What do we need him for?"

The head of the U.S. government, is in a sense the leading spokesman for world imperialism. Such a spokesman cannot be treated as a "respected guest." Nixon is a respected guest to the forces of world imperialism.

The existence of the two world systems is a hard reality. It cannot be ignored. The socialist states cannot isolate themselves from the rest of the world. It is this reality that has given rise to policies of peaceful coexistence between states with different social systems. They are policies of struggle, not capitulation.

After the victory of the Soviet revolution Lenin spent a great amount of time molding a policy of relations with the capitalist world surrounding the Soviet Union. He rejected Bukharin's idea that there can be no peaceful coexistence between the Soviet Republic and "international capital." "After capturing state power the proletariat does not thereby cease its class struggle, but continues it in a different form and by different means," wrote Lenin. Now the struggle is being waged in the international sphere; this is struggle on a different plane, the struggle of the proletarian state surrounded by capitalist states. This situation is an entirely novel and difficult one. "The question of selecting correct forms of struggle is all the more important because in the sphere of foreign policy the victorious proletariat comes up against a particularly strong, experienced and crafty enemy—world imperialism. . . . And one must know how to fight him," Lenin stressed. And further, Lenin said, the socialist revolution in other states ". . . must be helped. And we have to know how to help it."

It was on this foundation that Lenin developed the policy of diplomatic, trade and cultural relations with the capitalist world.

In these relationships there must not be even the appearance of ideological coexistence. The struggle against imperialism requires ideological convictions. The struggle against world imperialism requires a struggle against its central force, U.S. imperialism.

What is the effect of such acts of welcome and embracing of "warm friends" on the masses? In Rumania and Yugoslavia they must increase the illusions. In the United States, it creates confusion about the nature of the struggle between the two systems. Proper diplomatic relationships do not demand "warm welcomes."

The "warm welcomes," of course, are symbolic reflection of much deeper problems. They reflect weaknesses on the very question Lenin spoke about: "After capturing state power the proletariat does not thereby cease its class struggle." Any weakness towards giving up the class struggle is opportunism.

1970

21

ON VIETNAM

1. Nixon's Troop Withdrawal

During the past year (1969-70) the position of U.S. imperialism in Vietnam has become more vulnerable and the Nixon policy is headed for a new explosive crisis. The scheduled token withdrawal of U.S. troops at this point is significant only as a symbol of the U.S. dilemma in Vietnam and as a device to halt the popular protest. The present policies cannot win and they also cannot drag on indefinitely.

But how to retreat without giving up the objective of the aggression is the U.S. dilemma. The Nixon objective is no different than was the Eisenhower objective with the reactionary Diem regime. What Eisenhower and Kennedy tried to do through Diem,

Nixon is trying to do through Thieu. It is to maintain a reactionary puppet regime. The Nixon plan envisions a cutthroat South Vietnamese armed force with the U.S. armed forces staying for a long time in fortified centers and in air fields with their bomber fleets. This is the essence of the so-called "Vietnamization of the war." Nixon's troop withdrawals are based on the expectation of such an end.

That is why U.S. imperialism has scuttled the Paris peace negotiations, as Dulles did with the Geneva agreement in 1954. The Paris talks would involve political questions. The representatives of the Democratic Republic of Vietnam and the Provisional Revolutionary Government of South Vietnam are not going to accept and they are not even going to discuss a defeat they have not suffered on the battlefield. Thus the Nixon-Agnew plan is a fraud. It is, in fact, continued aggression advancing behind words of "withdrawal" and "troop withdrawals" based on conditions that will never become a reality.

Their plan is headed for a crisis. Because of popular pressures Nixon will continue the token troop withdrawals. He will do this as long as it does not affect the military situation in Vietnam. He will postpone the inevitable crisis as long as possible by dragging out the troop withdrawals—but there will come a point when the troop withdrawals cannot continue without affecting the military balance. This will come at a time when the military, diplomatic and political strength of the Vietnamese national liberation forces will be greater, when the puppet forces will be weaker. At this point the milions of Americans who now believe Nixon is trying to end the U.S. aggression will become disillusioned.

Such are the ingredients of the new crisis-point of the Vietnamese aggression. It is to this reality we and the broad forces opposing this ugly U.S. aggression must gear our activities. The removal of the Thieu-Ky puppets and the recognition of a people's representative government becomes a key demand. With fraudulent maneuvers Nixon has changed the scenery on the stage, but the plot remains the same. The shift in scenery has had a temporary blunting effect on the peace movement. But we would make a mistake if we did not foresee that the Vietnam policy is headed for a new crisis and that disillusionment and heightened anger by the American people are inevitable.

So on the balance sheet the position of U.S. imperialism in Vietnam has become weaker and more vulnerable. And as a result the forces of world imperialism are also weaker.

2. Moment Ripe For Peace Push

(Speech delivered May 1, 1972 in New York City)

This is one of those rare moments when the people have the magical power to change the course of human events.

The moment is ripe for a radical change of direction. This is the Moment!

This is the Moment! When the dirty U.S. war of aggression in Indochina can be ended.

This is the Moment! When the killing—the slaughter of men, women and children can be stopped!

This is the Moment! When the people of Vietnam can win the right to determine their own destiny.

This is the Moment! When the U.S. troops can all be brought back home.

This is the Moment! When the policies of "Vietnamization," "Cambodianization," "Laosization" are going up in smoke!

This is also the Moment! We can put an end to "Nixonization" of America!

This is the Moment! When imperialism—imperialist aggression —racism—can be given a fatal blow!

This is the Moment! When the forces of national liberation can win historic victories—the world over!

This is that critical—that crucial Moment! When the forces of progress—the invincible forces propelling the world revolutionary process can win decisive victories.

This is the Moment! When imperialism is on the ropes. It can be forced to retreat to its corner.

The Moment is NOT next November, not next year. The Moment is NOW.

Life does not present victories on a silver platter. It presents opportunity. It creates possibilities for victories.

Life has now presented such an opportunity! It's up to us to determine what we want to do with it. We can turn it into historic victories—or into missed opportunities.

This critical moment has emerged because the forces of national liberation in Vietnam—in a matter of days—have blown Nixon's plans sky high. They have exposed to the world Tricky Dick's lies. Forced Nixon's fraudulent hand.

Nixon never intended to end aggression.

The plan was to use puppet troops and massive air power. This was Nixon's Asia plan.

Puppet troops looked good on the parade grounds. Under fire they either turned and ran or turned their tanks and guns around and fought for liberation. The foundation of Nixon's "Vietnamization" plan melted in the battlefield.

The escalation of the bombing has exposed Nixon's fraud further.

Bombings are acts of desperation. But they are more—a planned new approach to imperialist aggression.

The new plans of aggression are based on genocide.

Open military aggression has failed.

Para-military tactics—have failed.

Destruction of bridges, churches, hospitals, dams—have failed.

Now they use the tactic of genocide. This is Nixon's "secret plan" promised during the last election.

The "secret plan" is a war of genocide!

American military scientists have developed a new system of weapons called anti-personnel weapons. Not intended to destroy bridges, tanks, buildings, bunkers. Designed only to penetrate—to tear human flesh.

Old bombs loaded with steel-pointed nails strike any living thing in an area bigger than this Union Square. Hospital X-rays could detect these steel nails. Some scientists thought of how to overcome this. Now they use plastic nails in these bombs.

B-52s drop converted anti-personnel bombs—15,000 lb. bombs —100,000 plastic pellets. Bombs—size of a half dollar camouflaged to look like a piece of rag leaf. Dropped by millions in populated areas.

This is a new kind of war—a new kind of aggression. In brutality it surpasses Hitler.

We witnessed the bombing of Hanoi—Haiphong.

Nixon, Laird, Abrams, Rogers are unmitigated liars when they say they are hitting military targets. These are terror bombs, bombs of genocide.

They seek out places where people are. Women, children, parks, markets, streets, playgrounds.

No President in all of our history has so completely lived on total lies as Nixon!

He lied when he said he had a "secret plan for peace." It was a plan of aggression.

He lied when he said he was going to end the war.

He lies when he says the air attacks are on military targets.

He lies when he talks about an "invasion from the North."

He lies about the need to escalate to protect U.S. troops. The best way to protect them is to get them the hell out of Vienam!

The new escalation is not just an escalation in bomb tonnage. It is an escalation in barbarism, cannibalism, cold-blooded automated mass murder.

In North Vietnam, U.S. bombers have totally destroyed 490 Catholic churches, 385 Buddhist temples.

At the moments when Nixon and Billy Graham are giving their phony religious services, U.S. bombers are destroying churches.

They destroyed 1,040 hospitals and medical centers, 640 dams. Are these military targets?

These also failed. Now the new weapons—designed only to tear human flesh!

We have witnessed the bombing of Hanoi—Haiphong. The work of the insane butcher.

We have seen the criminal insanity of imperialism.

But—we have also seen a people, heroic, totally dedicated to national liberation.

We have seen the unity of socialist forces—the help of the Soviet Union.

The people of Vietnam say, "We have no choice. We must fight on."

No force on this earth can defeat them.

The people of Vietnam say: This is the Moment!

They are ready to fight for a military conclusion. But they are ready to negotiate a political settlement.

The issue is simple, clear. The right to determine their own affairs.

There are two obstacles on this path: The U.S. armed forces, and the U.S.-controlled and paid-for puppet gangsters.

The solution is simple.

1. Set a date for total withdrawal.

2. Set up an interim government composed of all forces.

3. Agree on elections.

This is the Moment because the options for U.S. imperialism are closed.

"Vietnamization" is closed. It was a fraud, an illusion. It exploded just as the B-52s did when hit by missiles. In South Vietnam the national liberation forces have the upper hand. Also in Cambodia and Laos the national liberation forces have the upper hand.

What are Nixon's options? Re-escalation—using ground troops. A nuclear attack.

Nixon has disavowed these options.

What is left open?

Set the date!

An interim government!

As soon as U.S. imperialism gives up its aggression the war is over. It makes no difference if the negotiations are open or secret.

This is the Moment! We the people must speak.

An end to this criminal, dirty war.

It is in our best self-interest.

Continuation of war is only to the best interests of the monopoly corporations.

In the scrap yards of Hanoi are planes, tanks, guns, poison gas canisters, cans for defoliage chemicals. The labels—General Motors, Ford, Honeywell, Budd, IBM, ITT—the profiteers from Death.

This criminal war is a national shame! The war pictures constitute a gallery of national shame.

At this Moment—

Silence adds to our guilt!

Our self-respect demands we end this slaughter!

Human decency demands we stop the genocidal killing of children!

It is impossible to appeal to Nixon, Kissinger, General Motors, Honeywell on humanitarian grounds. They have no sense of conscience, shame, national honor! The self-interest of our people means nothing to them. They are cold-blooded seekers of private profit. They can only be moved by force. By the force of the people of Vietnam, the political force of our own people, the force of world opinion.

This is a Moment to speak out!

To be silent is to acquiesce to a crime. Silence is taken as approval.

This is a Moment when imperialism is on the ropes!

This is a Moment to strike blows against wars of aggression, against racism, against Nixonomics.

This is the Moment to free Angela Davis.

This is a Moment when mass action can make history.

This is the time to turn the 1972 election campaign into a drive to end the war—to end the policies of racism and reaction.

This is the Moment to discard Wallace and his racism.

This is the Moment to end Nixon's political life.

This is no time to just change names.

There is no difference between a Richard Millhous and a Hubert Horatio. They are a perfect pair—of nothing. Never a more perfect tweedledum and tweedledee.

There never was a new Nixon. There is no new Humphrey. They remain the cold war twins. Both are advocates of imperialist aggression.

They remain two puppets of monopoly capital.

This is a moment for a new breed of "political cats." This is the moment to dump all of the tweedledums and tweedledees.

If you want to move the whole political spectrum to the Left—

If you want to help create a force—a movement to unite the Left. A force that will help mold a broad people's movement. If you want to strike a solid blow against racism, wars, inflation, taxes. If you want to bring the working class into play.

You can do this only by joining the campaign to elect Communist candidates.

This is the Moment for all of us to unite for action!

3. *Speech To The People Of Vietnam*

(Delivered April 1972, in Hanoi)

There is no greater honor nor a moment of deeper meaning for a citizen of the United States and especially as an American Communist, than to be standing here hearing your words of comradeship and concern.

What could be more symbolic of your profound working-class internationalism—your unyielding anti-imperialism, your deep humanity, than that a day after the new criminal and barbaric attacks on your beautiful cities of Hanoi and Haiphong, we are gathered here to express your solidarity with the people of the United States, who are struggling against U.S. imperialism, its policy of aggressive wars, racism, oppression and genocide.

Only the poets will be able to express the beauty, the full meaning of this gathering.

Because we have shared with you an air-raid shelter, because our hearts like yours, have beaten faster because of these criminal air attacks, because we have experienced your resoluteness, your calm confidence, we will never again rest for one second until we have put the imperialist maniacs of Washington in straitjackets.

Nixon thought he was going to get away with his "Vietnamization" fraud. He thought he could fool enough Americans with his four years of troop withdrawals to get re-elected—while continuing to get the Presidency again—while continuing the aggression through terror and destruction by massive air power, while maintaining puppet governments in office. He thought he could create the illusion of a man seeking "peace for generations." The historic offensive of the forces of Vietnam's Liberation Front against the escalation of the bombing has blasted the fraud to smithereens. Nixon stands naked, exposed for what he is—a cruel, cunning faker, a desperate imperialist maniac, trying to forestall the inevitable—a total withdrawal from all of Vietnam.

You have added another page to the glorious history of the Vietnamese people. You have added yet another contribution to the destruction of world imperialism.

The struggle of the American people against the imperialist aggression is without precedent in our country's history.

It is a struggle in the best self interests of our people. It is an expression of our anti-imperialist consciousness. It is an act of proletarian internationalism.

We are proud of these contributions. But we are keenly aware that as long as imperialism is able to use our soil, our youth, our resources, to oppress, to attack, to kill any place in the world we have not fully met our responsibility.

We have fought, we will continue to fight, but until we are able to smash the power of monopoly capitalism, until we will force the closing of all U.S. mliitary bases in foreign lands, until we will padlock the Pentagon, until we hogtie U.S. imperialism, we the people of the United States cannot fully escape from the national shame these crimes have saddled us with. We cannot escape our responsibility.

U.S. imperialism is guilty of mass murders. Until we stop its killings we as a people cannot completely wipe off the blood of the millions of victims of an imperialism that operates from our shores.

This terrible war has created some very special bonds of friendship between our people. They are sacred bonds, unshatterable by any force. It is nurtured by our common hatred for imperialism. It is fed by our common understanding that every nation and all peoples must have the right to freely determine their own destiny. It is rooted in the deep human desire to live and progress in peace with one's neighbors.

On this historic occasion and from this august podium in Hanoi, from Vietnam, where the struggle against U.S. imperialism is the fiercest, permit me to say to the people of the United States, to the revolutionary and working-class movements the world over, this is a moment of serious dangers—but it is a moment that can be turned into historic defeats for imperialism. As no other time in history, this moment calls for unity and united action.

From this podium I can only pledge to you, our dear comrades of Vietnam, the following vow: For every step of Nixon's escalation of the war we will do our very best to escalate the struggle against the policies of imperialist aggression. We shall not rest, we shall not lose a day or an hour, in taking every step that will mean an end to this infinitely brutal war, and until we help you bring the peace into being that our peoples yearn for.

We mean a peace that will safeguard your nation and your children forever, the seven point program that embraces the goal of ending the war and achieving your full and eternal freedom and independence. We have studied Ho Chi Minh's words and life and we share the light and inspiration that he has given his people and the world.

4. Padlock the Pentagon To Keep Peace!

(Speech delivered on May 22, 1972 at Peace Demonstration in Washington, D.C.)

Having just returned from Hanoi, I have the honor to extend to you the warm greetings of the people of Vietnam, Laos and Cambodia.

Having just returned from the field of battle I can tell you —Nixon's hoax of Vietnamization, the crime of pacification, are deader than dead.

Having just returned from the harbor of Haiphong I can tell you—the mining of the harbors of Vietnam, while presenting a new danger of a world war, is not going to stop the flow of materials needed by the Vietnamese.

Having just returned from Hanoi after meetings with the leaders of the Democratic Republic of Vietnam, the leaders of the national liberation forces of South Vietnam, Laos and Cambodia, I can tell you the escalation of the genocidal bombings of the populated centers, while brutal and barbaric, is not going to affect the will, the determination of the people of Vietnam to win their right to determine their own affairs.

Having just been a guest of the people of Vietnam I can tell you, the people of Vietnam want peace. They want an end to the killing. They love life. But more than peace, more than life itself they want independence.

They want peace and independence now—but make no mistake about it—they want peace and independence now, but if need be they will fight another 2,000 years for it!

The very meaning of their lives is expressed in the most often quoted statement of Comrade Ho Chi Minh. "The most precious thing in life is independence and freedom."

Having just returned from the air raid shelters I can tell you there is no force on this earth that will ever prevent the people of Vietnam from reaching their goal of independence!

Having also just returned from Moscow and Warsaw I can tell you, on the highest of authority, that the continued all-out support of the Soviet Union and the other socialist countries to the just struggle of the people of Indochina will not be up for discussion or negotiations when Tricky Dick visits those cities. Whatever the Vietnamese want they will get. Their all-out support to all struggles for national liberation has not been and will not be negotiable. Their support has been and is an unalterable fact of life. Anyone who says different is an unmitigated liar.

Having just returned from Hanoi, Haiphong and Moscow I can tell you—no mining of harbors, no amount of bombing, no visit, nothing—absolutely nothing—is going to save U.S. imperialism from its ignominious defeat in this barbaric, ugly, dirty war!

We need not worry about whether the Vietnamese will continue the struggle.

We need not worry about whether their allies and friends will continue to give and deliver all the military equipment they need.

What we need to worry about is whether we, the people of the United States, can corral and retire the mad bomber from the White House!

What we need to worry about is whether we can mold a coalition of forces that will prevent the desperate men—the hyenas of reaction who screech for more escalation, for more blood—whether we can prevent the vultures of the monopoly corporations, the bloodhounds of the military-industrial complex from forcing a nuclear confrontation!

What we need to worry about is whether we will be able to forge a coalition of forces, based on the working people, the Black, Chicano, Puerto Rican, Indian and Asian peoples, in time —and strong enough to be able to smash the power of the Presidential-military-corporate monopoly dictatorship, before it develops into fascist dictatorship!

What we need to worry about are acts of provocation by enemy agents—and some possible dupe who can be misled into thinking washrooms are seats of power!

There is much talk in Washington about the need for gun control laws. The most effective gun control must start by padlocking the Pentagon.

There is much talk about cutting the 80-billion-dollar military budget. The only meaningful cutting is *to cut it out*!

There is much talk about problems of mental health. The most meaningful step to improve the mental health of the land is a massive use of straitjackets here in Washington, D.C. (including the Mad Bomber)!

There is much talk about priority. The only meaningful list of priorities is the one headed by the historic task of ending this criminal, ugly war. This national shame!

There is much talk about "turning the country around"—about "a new beginning." The new beginning can begin when we close all military bases, including in Puerto Rico—and Guantanamo.

Padlock the Pentagon!

Close the books on all military appropriations!

Declare racism a crime—when we free Angela Davis!

Scrap all anti-labor laws, including all phases of Nixon's economic slavery!

We can have a new beginning when we are united enough to make the welfare of every citizen the number one priority item.

This is a moment of crisis. But it is also a moment when a historic progressive leap is possible, when imperialism can be dealt a crushing blow.

It is a moment when we must apply maximum pressure.

It is a moment when we must all walk that extra mile!

Having just returned from Vietnam I want to appeal to all Americans, in the best interests of the people of Indochiina, in our own best self interests as Americans, in the interest of all that lives and grows:

WE MUST NOT, WE DARE NOT, WE WILL NOT fail in our responsibilities!

WE WILL put an end to this butchery, to this gravest crime in all of history.

WE WILL—So we can live in peace with our neighbors—but even more important—*we will* so we can live in peace with ourselves.

1972

PART THREE

The Struggle Against Opportunism

I

BEWARE OF OPPORTUNISM

Marxism-Leninism and the world and class outlook of the Communist movement have largely been molded in the struggle against the influence of opportunism.

Before the First World War Lenin observed: "War is often useful in exposing what is rotten and in discarding conventionalities."[1]

This is true for all moments of crisis. The basic contradictions stand in sharp relief. Differences are forced to the surface. The central focus is on the key links that can move the whole chain.

The First World War was a war between imperialist powers. It was a war between the private corporations of the imperialist powers. The issue of imperialism appeared on two levels. How to assess the overall development of imperialism was a more general question. But the real test was—what is your attitude towards the imperialism of your own country? This was for the socialist parties of the world the real test. The war "exposed what was rotten."

The acid of opportunism, unseen and unnoticed, had weakened the ideological fibers within the revolutionary movement. It had finally destroyed many powerful working-class parties of socialism. The acid had done its harm. It is of current importance that the crisis came in the struggle against imperialism. When the test came the professed internationalism of the different working-class parties vanished. The unity between parties first was diluted to a formal unity. But very quickly, even the formal ties became obstacles to carrying out opportunist policies. World and class ties between parties became an embarrassment.

[1] V. I. Lenin, "Opportunism and the Collapse of the Second International," *Collected Works*, Vol. 22 (Moscow: Progress Publishers, 1964), p. 115.

Each party stated its internationalism would be expressed through effective work, each within each of the national entities.

The leaders of these socialist parties very quickly made "new" discoveries. They decided Marx was wrong. There were no laws of capitalist development that applied universally. There were no worldwide concepts of the class struggle. In each country they discovered "fundamental" national pecularities that overshadowed international similarities. The working-class interests were watered down to where they did not appear in contradiction with the interests of the ruling class.

The class struggle became purely a "people's struggle." Class concepts became national concepts. No party openly condemned internationalism, they just put it on the shelf for "the duration."

Many of the parties became large mass parties. This was good. But what was not good, was that they became broad popular parties by going along with popular concepts of nationalism and classlessness. They became mass parties by giving up their advanced working-class positions. Their growth was fed by opportunism.

Only Lenin saw the nature of the acid. Only Lenin saw its creeping insidious nature.

Much has happened since then. Much has changed. But the need to be on guard against the acid of opportunism has not. The acid is the same. It still eats at the fibers of internationalism. It still erodes class concepts. It feeds on and itself feeds nationalism. It still leads to an accommodation to the pressures of the enemy.

The relationship of forces is different. The pressures are different. There are different kinds of opportunism. But as long as there will be a struggle between the two classes there is a need for a struggle against opportunism.

Until the emergence of the first working-class state power the class struggle took the form of a struggle within each capitalist country. All political and ideological currents were reflections of that reality.

With the emergence of the Soviet Union a new decisive factor was added. For now the working class had a state power on its side. Now one-third of the world's people are building socialism. The capitalist class has lost state power, and the working class has won state power in this third of the world. This has added a new quality, a new dimension to the class struggle. It has added a new dimension to the central contradiction of our times. This is the new reality. Thus all present political and ideological elements are reflections of this reality. The class struggle in each of the capitalist countries is a part of this new world scene.

Before the emergence of working-class state power opportunism was a reflection of the class struggle in each country. This is still so—but now opportunism has a new dimension reflecting the new dimension of the class struggle. Of opportunism Lenin said: "It is quite ripe for an open, frequently vulgar, alliance with the bourgeoisie. . . ."[2]

That is still true except it is now reflected on the backdrop of the new dimension in the class struggle. The vulgar alliances take place on the issues that have an effect on the world struggle between the two world social and economic systems. Opportunism leads to "vulgar alliances" with capitalism in this world struggle. Frederick Engels once said about opportunism, " 'honest' opportunists were the greatest dangers."

This is still true. But again the opportunists operate within the new dimensions in the class struggle.

What position one takes on the fundamental issues affecting the class struggle as it is represented by the two world systems is the new yardstick by which the revolutionary forces must measure the influences of opportunism within its ranks. Opportunism is capitulation and accommodation to the class enemy. It is an avoidance of struggle. It is a policy of non-confrontation. On many levels it is a betrayal of the interests of the working class. On the level of the new dimension in the class struggle it is capitulation, accommodation, a policy of non-confrontation and a betrayal of working-class interests on the issues as they are reflected in the world confrontation.

The revolutionary movement in each country is a reflection of the class struggle in their respective countries. But to argue that it is possible for such movements to ignore the issues of the class struggle as they appear in the confrontation of the two world

[2] V. I. Lenin, "Opportunism and the Collapse of the Second International," *Collected Works,* Vol. 22 (Moscow: Progress Publishers, 1964), p. 113.

systems is fakery and opportunism. To proclaim one's neutrality in the class struggle on a world scale is fakery and opportunism. It is a way of siding with the class enemy. U.S. imperialism because it is the center of world imperialism is a proper target for all anti-imperialist forces the world over. It is an important test for all forces. But to be against U.S. imperialism, is not yet the final test for the revolutionary movements in other imperialist countries. It is possible to be against U.S. imperialism and have an opportunist position towards the imperialism of one's own country. The strongest position against U.S. imperialism in these countries is to combine it with a struggle against the imperialism of one's own country.

Now that there is a world revolutionary process and a world revolutionary force, policies of disunity also take on an added significance. The Maoist policies of driving wedges into the ranks of the socialist countries, creating divisions between the socialist countries and the movements for national liberation, the efforts at disrupting the unity within the world Communist movement is a historic service to world imperialism.

What is the tactic of *imperialism* in the context of today's world? It is to disrupt the unity between the socialist countries and the national liberation movements and in the first place to isolate them from the Soviet Union.

The socialist states and the growing unity between them and the national liberation movements is the main roadblock to imperialism. It is an unalterable fact that U.S. imperialism can succeed in its aggression in Asia, Africa and South America only to the extent that it can create divisions between the forces of national liberation and the socialist countries. U.S. imperialism carefully weighs its acts of aggression taking into account to what extent the socialist countries can present a united front against it. It must deal with the forces in each of the countries it penetrates— but even this is determined by their relations to the world forces. So in the final analysis the key to victory or defeat against imperialism rests on whether the forces of socialism and national liberation can unite their forces, and to the extent the socialist powers are united.

All forces, all trends and processes are moving towards a

united worldwide front propelling a worldwide revolutionary process against imperialism. The potential of this force is more powerful than any social force assembled in all of human history. It has propelled a historic push forward. In its path the old imperialist empires crumbled. Eighty-odd countries won political independence.

But in all candor one must say this new force has not reached its full potential. Why not is an important question. The answer to this question must start with a study of the influence of opportunism. There are new problems including a need for new concepts, new relationships and new structures within the revolutionary movements. But these were not and are not available. These problems became obstacles only because opportunism had penetrated sections of the revolutionary forces.

Nationalism began to show its negative side. Most of the forces have travelled the path of unity and internationalism. Most have remained loyal in the anti-imperialist struggle. There are some important exceptions. The exceptions have been able to plan an opportunistic game of accommodation with imperialism only because the others have not.

It is these weaknesses of opportunism and nationalism that have provided the entering wedges for imperialism. They have created divisions, they have provided imperialism with the ideological instrument. Some have covered their opportunism with left phrases, others with right phrases. In most cases the opportunism is an accommodation to imperialism's anti-Sovietism. In this opportunistic swing Mao Tse-tung and the leading group around him in the Communist Party of China have distinguished themselves. They have reached into the very lowest depths of the swamp.

For the last 50 or so years the central imperialist world point of reference has been U.S. imperialism. It also provides the most reliable check-point for anti-imperialism. U.S. imperialism and anti-imperialism are counter points. Of course, there are exceptions to this as there are to all generalities.

The Maoist leadership of the Communist Party of China has bitterly denounced U.S. imperialism in words but during the last years its position on specific world developments has been in the same orbit with U.S. imperialism.

Starting with the present and going back, the record is as follows:

Both the United States and the Chinese delegates together with delegates of South Africa and Portugal did not vote for the resolution demanding that Israel withdraw from the Arab lands. United States and China abstained. South Africa and Portugal were absent.

Both the United States and China called the people of Bangla Desh "rebels" and voted against the motion to permit their representatives to speak. Both supported the reactionary military regime of Yahya Khan of Pakistan. Both provided him with arms with which to slaughter the people of Bangla Desh. Both voted against and condemned the Indian government for giving the people of Bangla Desh military assistance. Both sneered at the concept of the right of self-determination for the people of Bangla Desh.

To see the full meaning of the United States-China policy one has to ask: What would have been the practical results if their policy had won out? The military operations would have ended. The troops would have retreated to the frontiers. The butchery in East Pakistan would have continued and the ten million refugees would have continued dying in the refugee camps. The reactionary military dictatorship in Pakistan would have continued to rule and continued the policies of genocide in both parts of Pakistan.

In the UN the General Assembly adopted reports dealing with territories under Portuguese administration and the question of Southern Rhodesia. The resolution on the Portuguese-administered territories condemned Portugal, called on all states to discontinue any form of aid to Portugal and, on the other hand, to aid the African peoples struggling for self-determination.

It was adopted in the Fourth Committee on December 3 by a vote of 99 to 6 with 6 abstentions. Opposing it, along with Portugal, Brazil, South Africa, Spain and the United Kingdom, was the United States. The Assembly adopted it by a vote of 195 to 8 with 5 abstentions. Opposing it were the United States, Portugal, Brazil, Spain, United Kingdom, France and South Africa. China was absent.

This was the resolution that cut the clearest line between those who are ready to be counted against imperialism and the countries who are either for imperialism or playing the opportunistic game of accommodation with imperialism. China's calculated "absence" is an act of accommodation.

The pattern has become crystal clear. At the UN the Chinese delegation is following the Maoist line to the letter. It is using the UN platform for slandering the Soviet Union and opportunistically either voting with the United States or when the issue is too hot, opportunistically staying away. This is opportunism. This is playing footsy with imperialism. This is the stuff unprincipled alliances with imperialism are made of. The few weeks following the admittance of People's China into the UN has done much to expose the raw nature of opportunism, the depth of the unscrupulousness of the Maoist policies.

Both the Maoist leadership and the United States took the same position in their reactions to the events in Czechoslovakia. They ignored the dangers to socialism and the counterrevolutionary nature of the internal and external forces that gathered around Czechoslovakia. They both called the placement of defensive missiles in Cuba provocative. After the missiles were withdrawn China called it a "sellout" by the Soviet Union. On November 1, 1956 the first Chinese statement on the Hungarian events was in support of the counter-revolution. Two days later they shifted their position.

What is the basis for this similarity in positions? How is it possible that the position of a socialist nation so closely parallels that of an imperialist nation on so many areas? There is no deep mystery about what motivates U.S. imperialism. Its position on all matters is dictated by the drive of the private corporations for profits. But there are no such private interests in China. In its foreign policies, in its relations with other socialist countries and in so many of its domestic affairs China veers off the socialist path. It remains a socialist power but with deformation. The basic roots of a socialist concept lie in a class approach to all problems. It is working-class power. In countries where the working class is numerically weak its influence comes through the Communist Party. This has been the basic issue of contention within the leadership of the Communist Party of China. This was the basic issue in the turmoil of the "cultural revolution." Throughout its history Mao Tse-tung has been a spokesman for the non-working-class policies in the leadership of the Communist Party of China. He has always been the spokesman for the policies of petty-bour-geois nationalism. When this trend could not ruin the struggle within the Party, they created a diversion and by terror and con-fusion they destroyed the Communist Party, the Young Communist League and the trade unions. These were the working class in-struments.

In place of working class concepts the Mao leadership brought in policies of national chauvinism. The Mao cult is fed by illusions of grandeur. What came together were concepts of Chinese great power chauvinism and the illusions of revolutionary grandeur. Thus the dreams of China's great power would be realized through a situation where the Communist Party of China—or more ac-curately Mao Tse-tung—would become the one dominating world Communist leader. The petty-bourgeois distortion of the revolution became the dominating influence on the Mao policies. Those who resisted these policies, even within China or in the world, became the enemy. It is understandable why the struggle developed within the world Communist movement. This is where the Mao policies met the challenge. In his warped concepts Mao has not given up the struggle against capitalism. In his scheme of things that will come after he has established his leadership over the world Com-munist movement. When he could not win a Communist Party, he publicly attacked it. When that did not work, he has worked to set up Chinese-dominated groups the world over. The Soviet Union and the other socialist powers became obstacles to his plans. They became the enemy. In October of 1971 Lin Pao said: "The resto-ration of capitalism in the Soviet Union and certain other socialist countries, is the most important lesson to be drawn from the last fifty years of the history of the international Communist movement."

When the socialist countries did not bow to the dictates of Mao they became "capitalist." When the Communist Parties around the world refused to accept his petty-bourgeois radicalism —they became "capitalist oriented." Once the Maoist distortion reached this point, their policies and the policies of U.S. imperialism began to travel along parallel lines.

The Maoist concept is a conjured-up mirage of self-deception, fed by national chauvinism and illusions of grandeur. It is a distortion of Marxism. It veers away from policies of socialism.

U.S. Imperialism Is Looking For "Dividends"

"Now, if that just happens to irritate one or the other, that just happens to be a dividend." That remark was made by the U.S. Secretary of State Rogers on British television. By the words "one or the other" he, of course, meant the Soviet Union and the People's Republic of China. The "dividend" he was referring to is the benefits U.S. imperialism expects to get from the maneuvers that it is carrying on in its relationships with the People's Republic of China.

The steps taken by the U.S. Government are very small. They are tactical. They have the element of trial balloons, but they are of significance because they are surface manifestations of the more basic processes. They are a crack in the U.S. policy of blockading and isolating People's China. They are reflections of the bankruptcy of this policy. They are reflections of the fact that the world has rejected these policies. They are of significance, but they do not yet, however, indicate any change in basic policy. A meaningful change in U.S. position would come with the removal of the Seventh Fleet, that is an aggressive force both against China and Indochina. It would come with an end to occupation of Taiwan, a removal of trade restrictions against all of the socialist countries and an end to the blockade against Cuba and a policy of total withdrawal of all military forces from Indochina. Such a change in policy would come with the establisment of diplomatic relations on the basis of equality. These would be meaningful steps. Anything short of these steps is in the framework of the policy of continued active aggression. The present maneuvers do not indicate any such change in the basic U.S. policy. Such changes will come only when United States imperialism has no other options open. As long as imperialism expects to get "dividends" from its maneuvers, it will not retreat from its basic positions. It will retreat only when its options for "dividends" are closed.

Diplomatic maneuvers are not abstract niceties. They are reflections of political and economic policies. They are reflections of ruling-class interests. One should never have illusions of the fact that U.S. policies are geared to advance only the monopoly corporate interests.

The maneuvers of U.S. imperialism in its relations with People's China must be seen in the overall mirror. Such moves cannot be separated from the policies that each government involved pursues. These maneuvers must be placed in the overall framework of the main world contradiction, how they affect the class struggle as it is reflected in the struggle between the two world systems. They must be seen in the context of the struggle against colonialism. It is in these areas that U.S. imperialism is looking for "dividends." It is in these areas where the options must be closed for imperialism.

How to close off the options, how to cut off the flow of political and financial "dividends," how to destroy even the illusion or the hope of imperialism making any gains from its maneuvers has emerged as a most crucial question for all forces who oppose the policy of U.S. imperialism. As options are closed, imperialism is forced to retreat. The closing of the options expresses the present stage in the struggle against world imperialism.

What, specifically, is U.S. imperialism after? Maximum corporate profits, of course, but it is seeking political "dividends" as well that then become the basis for the gathering or the profitable financial harvest.

The long-range political "dividends" that U.S. imperialism seeks from all of its policies and maneuvers are divisions, confusion and disorientation in the ranks of all those who oppose its policies. Basically, it is an extension of its class policies of divide-and-rule at home.

What, then, is it that closes the options, that cuts off the expected imperialist "dividends"? It is the expressed and unbreakable unity of the forces of anti-imperialism, behind an active policy of struggle. Unity of forces in struggle has always been an important factor for the working class. It has been the ingredient that made the difference between victory or defeat for the working class in moments when they were up against a more powerful class foe. But, on a world scale, the element of unity has acquired a new significance. It is determining how the balance of world forces tips as world imperialism has lost its ability to determine the course of human affairs. As it has lost its unchallenged military and economic might, the importance of creating confusion and disunity in the ranks of its opposition has become a central weapon in its arsenal. Because of this, imperialism has assigned new priorities for the ideological front to subversion and efforts at creating confusion and corruption. The task of sowing the seeds of disunity has a very high priority in the tactic of neo-colonialism.

What are the specific "dividends" U.S. imperialism is expecting from all of its maneuvers, but especially from its relations with the socialist and newly-liberated countries. These are:

(a) For a continuation of the split between People's China and the rest of the socialist world.

(b) For a division between the socialist countries and the countries which have recently won political independence. The unity between the socialist countries and the newly-independent countries is a major stumbling block on the path of non-capitalist development within these countries.

(c) To continue the split in the ranks of the world trade union movement.

(d) To fire-up the differences and the divisions in the world Communist movement.

(e) Because the Soviet Union is the most formidable world military-economic bastion of anti-imperialism, anti-Sovietism has the highest priority in the arsenal of U.S. imperialism. It is the most formidable obstacle to the gathering of "dividends" for imperialism.

These are the political "dividends" U.S. imperialism is seeking. In one way or another, every diplomatic and political and military move is related to these aims of U.S. imperialism.

What are the main instruments of division and confusion? They are the thousand and one varieties of anti-Communism. They are the rehashing of all old anti-working-class concepts. They are in the never-ending varieties of racism and chauvinism. They are in the use of nationalism and national pride, in the buying-off and corruption of government officials. It is carried on by the distribution of economic crumbs to the countries trying to rise from the low levels of industrial development that imperialism condemned them to. U.S. bankers, like gangster loansharks, travel the world entrapping unsuspecting countries into large loans and debts and then threatening to close the mortgage unless they kneel under.

The overall goal, of course, is to keep the anti-imperialist forces confused and divided so imperialism can continue its policies of aggression, exploitation and oppression. Leaders and countries who follow policies of unity and militant anti-imperialism cannot be used in the maneuvers of imperialism. The easiest victims are those who have the illusion that they can somehow use the maneuvers of imperialism to further some narrow national interests. Countries and leaders who think they can use the maneuvers of U.S. imperialism to squeeze the Soviet Union will end up only in being squeezed themselves, from which imperialism will gather its "dividends." Invariably, they become the source for imperialist "dividends."

So, the yardstick of whether U.S. imperialism gains "dividends" from its tactical maneuvers is not how the countries react to the specific maneuvers.

That People's China will get its rightful place in the United Nations, that there will be trade and diplomatic relations between People's China and the United States, or that there will be exchanges of people and correspondents between the two countries are not "dividends" for U.S. imperialism. These would be setbacks for the bankrupt policies of imperialism. An attitude toward these steps does not determine whether U.S. imperialism is going to make any gains. How Parties and countries react to the basic goals and to the political "dividends" U.S. imperialism expects to achieve with the maneuvers is the test of all anti-imperialism. How the Parties and countries react to the U.S. imperialist goal of creating disunity in the ranks of anti-imperialism is the test. How the Parties and countries react to the imperialist propaganda of anti-Communism and anti-Sovietism is the test. How the Parties and countries reject policies dictated and influenced by short-range and narrow nationalist interests is the test. How the revolutionary working class Parties maintain their positions of internationalism and reject the concept of disunity promoted by U.S. imperialism is the test. How the revolutionary Parties of the working class fight against and reject the concepts of racism and chauvinism is the test. These are the tests that will determine whether U.S. imperialism gathers political "dividends" from its maneuvers.

The argument that unity in the world working-class movement can be based on each Party and country "doing its own thing" and doing it in its own way opens the gates for "dividends" for imperialism. Such disunity and dispersal does not correspond to the revolutionary tasks of this moment. It is a framework in which U.S. imperialism can deal with the working class of each country, with each socialist country, with each neutral, independent country one at a time on its own terms. It is a framework for getting "crumbs." Unity is the only framework in which imperialism is forced to deal on the basis of quality. The hook of imperialism is always out to entrap "strays."

These are most important questions for the present state in the balance of world forces. These are most timely and live questions, affecting the relationships and policies of peaceful coexistence between countries with differing economic and social systems. These are decisive questions, relating to the present level of the class struggle on a world scale.

The unavoidable yardstick is how you react to what are the instruments and goals of imperialism.

We are in a special moment when the question of unity is the most critical of all questions. The U.S. aggression against the peoples of Indochina is at its most critical juncture. The crisis is reflected in the escalation of the domestic political crisis in the country. The great majority of the American people now demand an immediate withdrawal from Indochina. The rising angry mood is uniting the people against the Nixon Administration. The political crisis is reflected in the crisis of the cities. It is reflected in the militancy in the unprecedented size of the anti-war demonstrations. It is reflected in the unprecented actions of the returning veterans from Vietnam. It is reflected in the new militancy of the working class, the forces of Black and Chicano liberation and the new movements amongst the students.

In a sense, U.S. imperialism is seeking for its political "dividends" at a moment when it is on the "ropes." It is obviously why the question of unity of the anti-imperialist forces, both at home and on the world scale, is crucial.

Whether the tactical maneuvers of U.S. imperialism in its relationships with People's China will result in "dividends" for U.S. imperialism to a large extent depends upon the leadership of the Communist Party of People's China. This will be determined not by how they react to the maneuvers. The test is how they will react to the goals and the instruments of the U.S. imperialist ideological and political offensive. It is impossible to separate the imperialist maneuvers from the policies that the leadership of the Communist Party of China are following. Their policies of disruption, their attempts to split the world working class socialist and anti-imperialist movements have been, for some time, "dividends" for U.S. imperialism. Their slanderous campaign of anti-Sovietism has been and remains a "dividend" for U.S. imperialism.

When the United States and its South Vietnamese puppets invaded Laos, it became a critical moment for the forces of anti-imperialism. The leaders of the other socialist countries, as they have done at every critical moment, again called on the leaders of the Communist Party of China to join in a united effort of all of the anti-imperialist forces of the world to turn back the new aggression. After four weeks of silence, the rejection, that has now become standard, was sent. As always, the rejection for united effort was accompanied by a vitriolic, slanderous attack on the socialist countries. This was a big "dividend" for U.S. imperialism.

The joint editorial in all of the leading Chinese papers, appearing days before the 24th Congress of the Communist Party of the Soviet Union and after the new aggression in Laos, continued the most vulgar, slanderous campaign against the Soviet Union. These editorials were a "dividend" for U.S. imperialism.

As long as these policies continue, U.S. imperialism will continue to collect "dividends." From all this, it is clear that if the maneuvers of U.S. imperialism are not going to result in "dividends," the leaders of the Communist Party of China will have to change their policies.

For the leaders of the Communist Party of China to continue to speak as if the Soviet Union and the United States are the same, is a welcome "dividend" for U.S. imperialism.

These are the hard facts. They are realities one cannot evade. To close one's eyes and act as if they do not exist would be opportunism. No socialist country, for any reason, under any circumstances, can join hands with imperialism if, in any way, it undermines the unity and the power of the camp of world socialism and anti-imperialism. This has nothing in common with policies of peaceful coexistence between countries having different social and economic systems. While we welcome the cracks in the U.S. imperialist policy of trying to isolate People's China, we cannot close our eyes to the overall framework in which they take place.

When it comes to the issues in the class struggle, we are not neutrals. We are totally partisan. That is the only revolutionary position.

Opportunism vs. Internationalism

There are two opposite approaches to the question of relationships between internationalism and national interests. Whenever these are monetary differences between international responsibility and some specific national interests, opportunism will in all cases lead to discarding of internationalism. Opportunism leads to an emphasis on the differences and on nationalism. A working class revolutionary concept will lead to a search for the points of unity between national interests and one's international responsibilities. Opportunism will seek to widen the points of difference. Revolutionary concepts leads to the elimination of the differences. The struggle for concepts of internationalism is a struggle against opportunism.

Theories of disunity are also not new in the history of the revolutionary movement. They always appear in opposition to working-class internationalism.

In the parties of the Second International, internationalism was never condemned. It was dispensed with as an obstacle to unity. Their scuttling of internationalism was covered by the numerous theories of disunity.

We are for the rejection of all excuses and theories supporting disunity.

We rejected the Maoist theory that constant splitting is as

natural for the revolutionary movement as it is in nature. It is an open theory of disunity. It is also a distortion of the dialectics of nature. It is an attempt to justify splitting tactics of opportunism. We reject the theories that attempt to bring about class unity but in fact only bring disunity.

We also reject the concept that silence can disperse ideological differences and thus create the basis for unity. Opportunism feeds on silence. Some cover their silence behind the statement, "We will not interfere in the internal affairs of other parties or countries." Such a concept is totally foreign to working class internationalism.

How imperialism uses the opportunism of some leaders of some socialist countries or Communist Parties is not a matter of signed agreements or contracts.

The same end is accomplished by giving the massive imperialist propaganda networks the material with which to vilify and slander the Soviet Union, socialism and the Communist Parties of the world. The imperialist networks are much more anxious to spread slander coming from a socialist source than slander from its own barn of ideological fabricators.

U.S. imperialism has a specific, worked-out plan of action for the ideological penetration of every socialist country, for every newly liberated country, for every political party throughout the world.

No world power has ever had an active policy of penetration, of subversion, of corruption, of buying off, of terror and murder on the massive scale as is the case with U.S. imperialism.

But the pivot around which these plans revolve is the plan against the Soviet Union.

Any accommodation to the ideological pressure that arises from this reality weakens the forces of anti-imperialism. No amount of ideological tip-toeing or sidestepping is going to change this hard rock of reality.

It is true that the Soviet Union does not ask for nor does it need the kind of defense the first young socialist republic did. But even then the significance of the worldwide campaign was far more than the defense of the Soviet Union per se. It was an important ideological campaign for working-class and socialist consciousness. In fact this was its central purpose.

For this same reason the statement of Soviet self-sufficiency while correct cannot be a cover for not taking up the ideological challenge of the anti-Soviet campaign. Silence for whatever reason has political and ideological consequences—not in the Soviet Union, but to the masses in the rest of the world. Herein lies the importance of replying to the slander no matter where it comes from.

Opportunism expresses itself in attitudes to specific developments. It must be fought around these specific issues and events. The struggle against the influence of opportunism has always been a matter of decisive importance. The new dimension in the class struggle has added a new dimension in the struggle against opportunism.

Slogan of "Superpowers" is Super-Opportunism

The world is not divided between "superpowers" and "nonsuperpowers." The central contradiction, the struggle in the world, is not between "superpowers" and "non-superpowers."

The basic division of society is between two classes—the working class and the capitalist class. The basic division between social systems as they represent these classes is between the working-class system of socialism and the capitalist-class system of capitalism. The basic division in the world is between socialist nations and capitalist nations. The basic struggle in the world is the class struggle as represented in the struggle between the two systems.

This basic class division determines the interests and the world position for each country.

In countries where the working class is in power, in a fundamental sense the class interests and the national interests merge. This is true in domestic affairs as it is true in world relationships. The task of a revolutionary party is to find this path of merging interests.

To speak about "superpowers" in general terms is to forget the basic class essence of all phenomena. To speak about "superpowers" in the abstract is to forget the class struggle. To speak about "superpowers" is an opportunistic evasion of the class struggle.

We in the United States have for a long time had experience with such phrases. The most reactionary anti-working-class big business forces in the United States speak about the twin evils of "big business" and "big trade unions." Any worker knows such forces and such slogans are not against big business. The "big business—big trade union" slogan is a cover for an attack on the trade unions, on the working class. It is a class slogan of monopoly capital. It is the "superpower" slogan for the domestic scene.

The "superpower" concept, no less than the "big business—big trade union" concept is a slogan put out by monopoly capitalism, by imperialism.

On the domestic scene the "big business—big trade union" slogan blunts and confuses the anti-monopoly movement. On the world scene the "superpower" concept confuses and blunts the anti-imperialist sentiments. That is why U.S. imperialism, above all, pushes the classless "superpower" concept.

It is demagogy to speak about a struggle against the most powerful imperialist world force, and also to speak about the evils of "superpowers."

To speak about "superpowers" in the abstract is to confuse the issue. It is a way of running interference for the dominant imperialist power. It is a cover for imperialist aggression.

It is in this sense that the remarks of Premier Chou En-lai of the People's Republic of China, as quoted in the June 9 issue of *The New York Times,* do a disservice to the struggle against imperialism and to the class struggle on a world scale.

Premier Chou En-lai spoke about "the evils of power politics of superpowers." There are no classless power politics. There is the power politics of imperialism, headed by U.S. imperialism, which is the reactionary evil force in the world. There is a growing power of the socialist world, in alliance with other anti-imperialist forces, which is the progressive force in the world. In the very center of this force is the socialist Soviet Union.

The power of Soviet politics is totally committed to the struggle against imperialism. The power of U.S. imperialist politics is totally committed to oppression, to exploitation, to the enslavement of people.

Can one speak in the abstract about "superpower politics" in Indochina? Is the role of U.S. imperialism and the Soviet Union the same in the Mideast, in Africa, in Latin America? They are at the opposite dialectical poles. One is the main force of oppression and exploitation, the other the main outside force of support to the force of liberation and freedom. To speak about them in general terms as "superpowers" is a service to U.S. imperialism.

We in the United States, who have the historic responsibility of fighting against the most ferocious and most evil imperialism in the world, reject any concept that any socialist power, in any way, is similar to this reactionary force. We reject any concept that dilutes, camouflages or confuses the basic nature of this beast. To compare a socialist country to U.S. imperialism, in any sense, is a service to U.S. imperialism.

Years ago, during the U.S. aggression against Korea, the movement against U.S. imperialist policies when it was in its initial stages employed the slogan of "a plague on both your houses." Our Party never accepted that because it was opportunism. We do not accept it in the struggles and movements of our people and we do not accept it as a legitimate concept in the world revolutionary movement. We call down a "plague" only on the forces of imperialism. We say: "A plague on imperialism, on capitalism."

We are for the closest unity of all forces in the world in the struggle against imperialism, in general, and against U.S. imperialism in particular. We are against any concept that in any way blurs over this class approach to all problems. We are against any concept that provides a way out, a cover for U.S. imperialism.

1971

2

SOME PROBLEMS OF ANTI-IMPERIALIST UNITY

The struggle against imperialism is global in scope. It is one of the initial tests of one's ideological commitments. To go on record, or even to repeat the vow does not meet the test. The malignancy of opportunism is covered up by statements of anti-imperialism. General statements are not enough because the struggle is specific, around concrete issues.

Proclaiming one's anti-imperialism, while refusing to unite with other forces in a common fight is not meeting the test. Being against imperialism in general but refusing to take a stand against the specific and real U.S. imperialist aggression in the Mideast is also not meeting the test. To speak in terms of nonalignment, or "a third force" between two equally guilty parties is far from meeting the test. When a government or a political party softens its attack on specific policies of imperialism in order to gain some temporary trade concessions, it is nowhere near meeting the test.

These are all policies of opportunism.

It is in this context that one must react to anti-Sovietism. The question is not whether one defends the Soviet Union. It is not even a question whether one agrees or disagrees with the Soviet Union.

The real question is whether one rejects or supports or is neutral toward a central ideological pillar of U.S. imperialism, that is, the big lie of anti-Communism. The big lie about anti-Communism is no different than it was as practiced by Hitler fascism. Fascism took power in Germany "because of the danger of Soviet aggression." German and Italian fascism helped fascism come to power in Spain, "because of danger of Soviet aggression." German imperialism trampled on Austria, on Czechoslovakia—because of the danger of Soviet aggression. Anti-Communism was fascism's main ideological weapon. Now U.S. imperialism has built 3,500 military bases around the world "because of the danger of Communist aggression." U.S. imperialism has conducted a most brutal massacre in Vietnam, Laos and Cambodia "because of the danger of Communist aggression." The United States sent 35,000 troops into the Dominican Republic "because of the danger of Communist aggression." The CIA organized and armed a gang of cutthroats that overthrew elected governments in Guatemala, in Iran—again "because of the danger of Communist aggression." In the name of fighting the "danger of Soviet aggression" the U.S. government has given over 100 billion dollars in arms to every possible reactionary fascist group and government in every corner of the world. This fraud of "possible Soviet aggression" is the centerpiece in the big lie of anti-Communism. How one reacts to this fraud is an important question in the struggle against imperialism. It is a critical test of the influence of opportunism. Most forces understand and reject the effort as a form of the big lie—anti-Communism. But there are some who try to play with or who skirt the issue. Of course, it is never done openly. Opportunism always covers its tracks. Some speak about the "evils of the two big powers." Some proclaim their "nonalignment." These are statements of neutrality. But neutrality toward what issues and what forces is the question. What are the basic issues, the basic contradictions between the United States and the Soviet Union? Is it not the contradiction between the two classes, the working class and the capitalist class? Is it not the contradiction between the two world social systems, socialism and capitalism? Is it not the issues between imperialism and anti-imperialism— between policies of war and aggression and policies of peace and liberation, between policies of racism and policies of fighting racism, between progress and reaction? Does this struggle not result from the fact that one is a leading force within the world revolutionary process and the other is the fountainhead, the center of world imperialism   To hide this central fact of today's reality is the sole aim of U.S. imperialism's campaign of big lie anti

Communism. These issues cannot be separated from the forces that give them reality.

To be "nonaligned" is to be nonaligned from these issues and these forces. But, in fact, it is not nonalignment. In view of the basic issues involved, how is it possible to speak about the "evils of the two big powers"?

It is not possible if one is to remain a factor in the struggle against imperialism. To conciliate in the struggle against imperialism is opportunism. To be nonaligned or neutral is to make a concession to imperialism. To be nonaligned is to withdraw from and to weaken the forces fighting imperialism. To speak of the third world as being a force between two evil forces is also a form of opportunism. It is also a concession to imperialism.

To speak of the Soviet Union as being "social imperialist"— as the Mao group in the leadership of the Communist Party of China does—cannot be described only as concessions to imperialism. It is that, but it is opportunism and bourgeois nationalism at a level where it acccepts the imperialist big lie slander and adopts it as its own. Finally, there is the opportunism of some who try to establish their image of "independence" by accepting and using small doses of the big lie. This is also a concession to imperialism. The real issue all forces of the world revolutionary process must face is how do you react to a central pillar of imperialism's ideological attack. That is the test. Do you accommodate to it, do you opportunistically try to go around it or do you meet it forthrightly?

The struggle against imperialism is a daily test of all concepts and policies. It is difficult for anyone to sit on the fence for very long periods. Because the struggle is fought around concrete issues, affecting the daily lives of masses, even sitting on a fence is an opportunistic concession.

It is one thing when dealing with issues and struggles within the boundaries of one's own country. A new dimension is added when the struggle crosses national borders. The struggle against imperialism presents the problems of this additional dimension. One of these is how to fit in the struggles around issues of national interest with a working-class approach to internationalism.

There are two approaches to the question of relationships between internationalism and national interests. Whenever there are differences between one's class's international responsibility and some specific national interest, opportunism will in all cases lead to discounting of internationalism. Opportunism leads to an emphasis on differences and on seeming contradictions, by emphasizing nationalism.

A working-class, revolutionary concept of internationalism seeks out the points of identity and syntheses between the two. Opportunism is not a reflection of contradictions between the working class of one's own country and the workers of some other land. Rather it reflects the contradiction in the capitalist class of one's own country and the class interests of workers of other lands and in some cases, with the interests of the capitalist class of other lands.

It is one thing to take note of and examine differences and momentary contradictions within the world socialist sector. But it is another matter to use this as the basis for a theory of disunity that in essence says, "That's how things are and that is how they will be. This is progress. This is great. Let's have more diversity and disunity." They say therefore we must accept and hail this, as a fact of reality and any attempt to find a path of unity is based on an illusion. This theory goes further—it condemns those who seek unity, because in the struggle for unity it is necessary to discuss the issues and attitudes that have created the disunity.

We dare not lose sight of the fact that U.S. imperialism has never for a moment given up its drive to chip away at the unity of the socialist world. For capitalism, the focus of the class struggle on the world scale is the Soviet Union, the political and military power base of the world's working class. It views the Soviet Union as the main roadblock to its plans of world conquest. This remains the pivot of its policies.

Thus its main ideological attack is on the Soviet Union. U.S. capitalism is ready to make significant short-range concessions to any group, party or state if these concessions fit into the tactical or strategic plans of U.S. imperialism against the Soviet Union, into its plans of dividing the socialist sector from the other forces of anti-imperialism.

For example, for years there has been a well-organized, high-powered political group composed of some of the most reactionary imperialist forces, called "the China Lobby." Rightfully it should be called the Anti-China Lobby. It has been the organization and ideological center for U.S. policies of aggression in the Far East. This most reactionary force of U.S. imperialism has now undertaken a drive, both in the open and behind the scenes, to bring about a working relationship between the United States and the People's Republic of China. This is a well-financed drive, supported by some of the most aggressive monopoly forces in the heartland of world imperialism. Needless to say, they are not interested in U.S.-Chinese friendship; their main interests are not even trade with Communist China. Their aim is to use the split in the socialist world; to try to use China in their anti-Soviet plans; it is to open the doors of China for political penetration. One cannot blame China for what U.S. imperialism does, but one cannot ignore policies that have led imperialism to believe China could be used in its schemes. The use of such negative policies are not necessarily a matter of agreements or contracts with imperialism; the same ends can be accomplished by giving the far-flung imperialist communications networks the material with which to vilify and slander the revolutionary movement. The imperialist network is much more anxious to spread slander coming from such a source than to use similar material from its own stable of ideological fabricators. U.S. imperialism has a specific plan of action worked out for every socialist country, for every newly liberated country, and for every political party throughout the world. What the progressive forces of the world must understand is that no world power has ever had an active policy of penetration, of subversion, of corruption, bribery by terror and murder on such a massive scope as the United States. The policy is worldwide but the pivot around which these plans revolve is the plan against the Soviet Union.

Any accommodation to the ideological pressures arising from this reality weakens the forces of anti-imperialism. No amount of ideological tiptoeing or sidestepping is going to change the hard rock of reality. Any attempt by one socialist country or one Communist Party to gain favors by being silent or by any other form of accommodation to U.S. imperialism can only lead to capitulation and defeat.

It is true that the Soviet Union does not ask for nor does it need the kind of political defense it received when it was the first young socialist republic. But the fact of Soviet self-sufficiency cannot be a cover for not taking up the challenge of the ideological anti-Soviet campaign. In essence it is an attack on concepts of socialism, on Marxism-Leninism, on the working class. Silence, for whatever reason, has political and ideological consequences for the masses in the rest of the world. Anti-Sovietism is a special ideological instrument in the imperialist drive to create dissension in the socialist world and to mislead the anti-imperialist movement.

The best possible solution for any dissension that may arise between Communist parties is comradely and democratic discussion. There is a long history of the efforts of most Communist Parties to try to find a basis for a dialogue with the present leading group in the Communist Party of China. There have been periods of private exchanges, public discussions, periods of no public or private retorts to vituperative attacks from Peking. Silence in the face of injustice and slanders is support for the injustice, the slanders, and that is how it is utilized by the imperialist network.

The main thrust of the Maoist ideological attack is anti-Soviet as is that of the attack by U.S. imperialism. In this there is an identity of ideological positions between the Mao group and U.S. imperialism. The Maoist policy, far from confronting the forces of imperialism, moves in the direction of a sharper confrontation with the forces of socialism. The real question is how to reverse the present direction of the Maoist policy and to bring the Chinese people and nation back into the stream of anti-imperialism and into the world Communist and socialist movements.

The divergence of the policies of China from the orbit of Marxism is of serious concern to all fighters for social progress; it remains a divisive force in the ranks of the world system of socialist states and damages the movement for world socialism. The policies of Mao have followed nationalist lines, and nationalism replaces working class ideology and especially internationalism.

Possibly the greatest confusion is centered around the question: Is peaceful coexistence compatible with Marxian concepts of class struggle, with the struggle against imperialism, with the concept that socialism will be the next stage of history throughout the world? When we speak of policies of peaceful coexistence we are not speaking about peace between the working class and the capitalist class, we are not speaking about peace between imperialism and the oppressed peoples. We are speaking about countries of socialism living in the same planet with countries of capitalism. We are speaking about an approach for resolving the problems between them without resorting to war. This does not mean the socialist countries are going to be neutral about the class struggles. The concept of peaceful coexistence is closely related to the concept that it is impossible to export revolutions.

There is no question some create a caricature image of peaceful coexistence and then attack the caricature. Some have used these policies to cover up their own opportunistic practices with capitalist countries. But because of the distortions or because of the misuse, the revolutionary movement should not discard this weapon. We believe that the policy of peaceful coexistence is compatible with and facilitates the class struggle, the struggle for an end to colonialism and the emergence of world socialism. Such concepts do not negate or nullify these objectives they have nothing in common with maintaining the status quo. The world is not going to stand still; in fact, struggles, upheavals and mass movements are trademarks of this age of transition and change. Moreover "peaceful coexistence" does not apply to internal relations between classes and groups. It is only a dogmatic caricature of the concept that tries to give the impression that it means a moratorium on such struggles. Indeed the policies of peaceful coexistence are policies of class struggle in the context of the new epoch.

Thus peaceful coexistence does not mean class peace. As long as private productive property exists which, therefore, exploits the labor of the non-owners, all talk of class peace is an illusion. Communists are not pacifists. We naturally favor, however, the peaceful path of socialism through the advance of a mighty people's anti-monopoly coalition. We believe the Communist Party will play a decisive role in this coalition.

The state machine—the police, armed forces, CIA, FBI, and other agents of repression—will have to be dismantled and controlled by the forces that represent real democracy. This presents problems for peaceful transition since no exploitative ruling class gives up power voluntarily. After World War II, however, amidst the deepening general crisis of capitalism and advance of the world revolutionary process, a number of countries in Eastern Europe took state power peacefully and arrived at the socialist stage despite the intentions of the former ruling bourgeois and feudal classes. The peaceful advance to socialism is possible depending on the specific situation in each country.

1970

3

ANTI-COMMUNISM

Imperialism's Spurious Alibi

In the preceding chapter, we discussed the ideological Trojan horse of our times—the device of anti-Communism to justify imperialist aggression, no matter how flagrant its crimes against humanity. Hitler fascism murdered 40 to 50 million people under the cover of fighting the specter of Communism. The late Senator Joseph McCarthy used it when he said, "I hold in my hand a list" —and then called for the nullification of the Bill of Rights. Senator McCarthy was not an isolated nut in the wilderness. He was financed and politically supported by powerful corporate interests. He was a spokesman for a section of the capitalist class. The presence of "58 Communists" in the Dominican Republic was righteously flaunted as enough reason for president Johnson to send in 35,000 U.S. marines. Even gangsters like Al Capone and Anastasia made bids for understanding and respectability because, they said, "After all, we are anti-Communists." The historian Arthur Schlesinger justified his own admitted use of a deliberate anti-Communist lie when the facts would not convince the American people that the Bay of Pigs invasion of Cuba made sense. In the hysterical climate during the McCarthyite witch-hunts, Congress passed laws like the McCarran Act that completely subverted the Constitution. The U.S. Congress knowingly and cynically used total and complete falsehoods as an excuse to pass these laws.

Without the big lie of anti-Communism Nixon would be a political zero. As Hitler did in Germany, Nixon has used the falsehood as his main ladder to power. The Congress of Industrial Organizations cut a new path for the trade union movement. The path led to militant class-struggle trade unionism. The capitalist class was determined to divert the process. The instrument was the big lie of anti-Communism. The conservative elements in the leadership joined the crusade, immediately closely followed by the leaders with a liberal and social democratic image like Walter Reuther, Sidney Hillman and Philip Murray. David Dubinsky was a dispenser of the big lie most of his life. This big business offensive was successful. Communists who had influenced the CIO towards class struggle policies, towards a struggle against racism, towards positions of anti-imperialism, and towards labor's independence in politics were expelled. Non-Communist militants were either expelled or silenced. The corporations moved against militants in the shops, while Congress passed crippling anti-labor laws. The FBI, the press, radio and television joined with McCarthy in creating an atmosphere of hysteria. Tens of thousands of militant workers were fired. The big lie of anti-Communism had done its work. The CIO was diverted from the path of class-struggle trade unionism.

This demagogic appeal to baseless fears has become *the ideological narcotic of our day*. It is dangerous because under its influence anything goes, it has become the prime weapon against everything progressive. It is utilized by all anti-democratic, anti-labor, anti-Black, anti-intellectual forces within our land. The years of repression under McCarthy's shameful domination amply proved how it could silence and intimidate all but the most dedicated men and women. People who in their own minds know better repeat the slander so they will not be charged with being "soft on Communism."

The character of the "artillery of words" about Communism is in itself an indictment of the state of our social science and the corruption of an intellectual community. The fusillade of clichés is in great part a random operation. It is not devoted to a rational, objective examination of the subject; it has no concern with the facts; it does not engage in dialogue nor does it challenge the concepts of Communism. Its purpose is to confuse, to divert, to cover up facts, to distort the truth. It is, rather, like sticking pins in a straw effigy, as it goes on about "foreign agents," "cloak-and-dagger conspiracies," "violence and subversion," "a world-wide plot against God, country and motherhood."

It is not a discussion about Communist ideas, about the program of the Communist Party. It is not a dialogue about socialism as it is being built. Its main purpose is to hide the truth, to distort the facts, to rewrite history.

And, of course, it has become the principal rationale for the war of aggression in Vietnam. If this poisonous fog increasingly envelops our country and the rest of the capitalist world, the stage will be set for an unthinkable nuclear disaster. Thus, the responsibility of clearing the air, of rejecting the poison is a task not for Communists alone, but for all who advocate peace, freedom and democracy throughout the world. The question is not whether one agrees or disagrees with the positions of Communists. The issue is truth.

Hitler's anti-Communism, we must remember, after inflicting its horrors upon the world, ultimately led the German nation to catastrophe. Now the anti-Communism of U.S. corporate power visits tragedy upon other peoples, but its ultimate victim, if it is not checked, will inevitably be the people of the United States.

There are many school districts that have compulsory courses in the big lie of anti-Communism; in the state of Louisana one cannot leave high school without a six-week course and a certificate in "anti-Communism." There are similar courses in the schools of Boston, Chicago, Indiana and Pennsylvania. One outline speaks of "The ruthless accomplishments of Communism." And then it lists the following accomplishments of the USSR:

It has made great progress in heavy industry through successive five-year plans. It has built up the biggest military machine in the world, has built up a navy comparable to that of the United States, has an air force comparable to that of the United States, has made development of atomic, hydrogen and guided missiles comparable to those of the United States, has stressed scientific progress probably more than the United States, has built up a propaganda apparatus—Cominform —to spread worldwide Communism [this, by the way, does not exist], has probably wiped out illiteracy. . . .

These are the "ruthless achievements" of Communism!

The same outline lists important Americans who have made contributions to the heritage of American history including Benjamin Franklin, George Washington, Thomas Jefferson, Abraham Lincoln, Eli Whitney, Woodrow Wilson, Franklin D. Roosevelt, Thomas Edison, Walt Whitman, Ralph Waldo Emerson. No. 21 among great Americans listed was J. Edgar Hoover! The reactionary bigot, with his police-state mentality was passed off as a great American. This servant of monopoly capitalism who has made a lifetime career of oppression, distortion and hounding of anyone with progressive thought was listed as a "great American!"

Anti-Communism corrodes all our democratic processes. For example, when Byron White became a Justice of the Supreme Court, the first day after he took his oath he had to sign an affidavit stating he was not now and never had been a member of the Communist Party. This violated the First Amendment and the very Constitution he is supposed to protect.

And not so very long ago, Dixiecrat Senator Eastland charged that the Supreme Court had rendered "40 votes for Communism." If this were true then we Communists would be up there discussing the immediate reorganization of American society along socialist lines. The accusation is, of course, sheer absurdity; the court's decisions were concerned with constitutional liberties, the ending of racism, the rights of labor, questions of peace and democracy. It is, of course, true there are issues on which the Communist Party has strong positions, but they are not "votes for Communsm." But Eastland and his racist colleagues from states whose racist electoral systems have permitted them to remain in Congress with the votes of less than ten percent of the population, spew forth their hatred because of the Court's redistricting decision that opened the way for more democratic elections. We Communists are in agreement with many of the decisions that extend the rights of the people, but to say they are "votes for Communism" again exposes how this big lie is used against all progressive forces.

Anti-Communism is calculated to play upon the two of the most sensitive mass emotional reactions—national pride and patriotism and the inherent desire of all peoples for a democratic way of life. Thus the demagogues hammer away at the charges that Communists are foreign agents and that Communism is basically and fundamentally anti-democratic. Of course, if one speaks about "foreign imports," then one must start with capitalism as a system. It was imported from Europe into the colonies.

We must at all times differentiate between the ultra-right type of anti-Communism described above and the opinions of those who honestly disagree with the Communist viewpoint. I believe that if the honest dissenters were to be shown the dangers involved in the use of anti-Communism, if the trade union leaders, liberals, progressives and socialist leaders are shown the nature of anti-Communism as a reactionary, big business, Hitlerite weapon, they would realize the grave danger of using it themselves. The passage of the concentration camp section of the McCarran Act stands as a grim reminder of the intimidation and the collapse of those liberals who in the 1950s endorsed the McCarran Act and were ready to see the Bill of Rights destroyed in order to get immunity from reactionary attack. They sold out but they did not get immunity for long. The most fascist-like section of the McCarran Act was proposed by Hubert Humphrey who likes to pose as a liberal.

Anti-Communism has not developed to the level where it cannot be defeated. Most Americans will join forces on common issues affecting them. They will argue with Communists, debate with them, but if they understand the nature of the big business, ultra-right use of anti-Communism to defeat democratic movements, they will repudiate this fraud in their own interests.

It has always been a tactic of reactionary movements to utilize seeming neutrality as a cover for their attacks on progress. Unfortunately, there are many honest people who have fallen victim to this line of even-handedly blaming both Right and Left.

Let me quote a few lines from the letter of an obviously honest progressive. This was written at a time when reaction was trying to use the assassination of President Kennedy to whip up a hysteria against Communists and the left generally.

Neither accusation accomplishes anything for tolerance, wisdom or understanding. On the contrary, both only contribute to the atmosphere that can unhinge any unstable mind of any political belief. If there is any good to come out of this awful violence, it is a cessation of accusations, recriminations, insults and threats *from both sides.*

On the surface, this sounds reasonable and balanced enough. But when it is applied to the realities of life, its import is the very opposite. For it still ignores the most pertinent question: Who is and who is not guilty of the crime? It condemns without asking or getting an answer to this question; therefore, even if inadvertently, this approach provides a cover for ultra-right forces. It is a form of running for cover. It is opportunistic capitulation to reaction.

There is nothing in Marxism or in the policies of the Communist Party that in any way promotes or encourages individual acts of terror or violence. The very essence of the Communist movement—its understanding of the role of classes in society, of the need to win over the majority of the people through their experiences in mass struggles and education—is in fact the strongest possible counterforce against any such acts. Individual acts of violence and terror are a product of dead-end frustrations. The Communist theories and viewpoint do not lead to such conclusions; on the contrary, they seek to indicate a path through which solutions of society's ills can be sought through mass movements and actions.

On the other hand, a William Buckley (a leader and ideologist of the ultra-right) has said publicly: "The point has come (if Welch is right) to leave the typewriters, the lectern and the radio microphone and look instead to one's rifle." And Buckley has never said that Welch is wrong. This is the ultra-right advocacy of violence.

The historical truth is that Marxism and the policies of the Comm nist Party have their genesis as much in the struggle against all concepts of individual acts of terror and violence as in the struggle against capitulation or surrender to the mercy of capitalism. Marxism-Leninism has given the working class the understanding that it is the people who are the makers of history; that individual acts of terror are weapons used against it by a class that cannot rely on the people because history is forcing it off the stage of life. Communism points out that in history acts of individual terror are the weapons of the provocateur who commits acts the enemy can falsely use against the working class. This was true in the cases of Mooney-Billings, the Chicago Haymarket martyrs, Haywood and dozens of others.

It is interesting to note that there are no laws against the ultra-right and no prosecutions. Hence, under the guise of even-handedness, the attack in reality is directed against the Left. Even Hitler rose to power by using the trap of struggle against "democracy, bureaucracy and Communism," and it was this that blocked the path to united struggle against fascism which was able to march to power through the division this created in the ranks of those who opposed fascism.

The same misguided logic is extended to equating the crimes of the racist dynamiters of small children with the actions of Black Americans struggling for equality, on the grounds that "both are extremists." Clearly, to protest and to organize the fight against 300 years of slavery is not fanning the flames of bigotry. Nor can one designate as "accusations, recriminations and insults" the protests and struggles of workers who are tossed on the discard pile by automation, or to equate them with the conspiracy of the reactionary forces who have thrown them there and who are using the products of science for their own selfish ends. It is not sowing hatred to condemn the warmongers and racists. On the contrary, to call for nonparticipation and "neutrality" where there is cruel oppression, bigotry and racism, is to support the bigots and racists.

Thus we cannot permit the just struggle for peace, equality and socialism to be tarred by the brush of "you are both guilty." We will join with all Americans in working for an end to bigotry, to hatred, to racism, and we will do so by fighting together with them to end exploitation, discrimination, segregation and warmongering.

The basic method of big lie anti-Communism is to create a

caricature image of Communists, of Marxism-Leninism and of socialism and then attack the caricature. This bag provides something for everyone. There are some left as well as right covered goods.

One that has increasingly come into vogue is a concept that Marxism-Leninism is a "dogma", it is a "religion." And because it is a "dogma" it is "one-sided," it is hostile to "objective reality" or to facts. Thus they conclude one who is a participant in struggle, or who is a partisan cannot be objective about reality. Therefore, Communists, because they are participants in the class struggle cannot be expected to be objective. Only the liberals can see both sides. This, of course, is not only total nonsense, it is an effort to blur the vision of the masses. It is running ideological interference for the forces of reaction. It is a form of ideological neutrality. Only those who understand the class nature of imperialism and participate in the struggle against it can have a clear image of today's objective reality. Only people who see racism as a class instrument of exploitation and fight against it have a clear vision about objective reality. There are two sides, but one is wrong and one is right, one is just and the other unjust. One is progressive and the other reactionary. There are no abstract concepts unrelated to the struggle for human progress. There is no objective reality that is unrelated to this process. The slander that Marxism-Leninism and, therefore, Communists are "dogmatic" and cannot relate to what is new and developing is also fakery. It is the opposite of what is the truth. Marxism-Leninism is a science. It is a reflection of a continuously changing reality.

One does not have to agree with the Communist viewpoint to fight for civil liberties. But one cannot properly wage that fight by accepting the anti-Communist lies and in effect joining the forces of reaction, because it is on this cornerstone that the forces arrayed against civil liberties stand. To join in the slander, for whatever reason, is to chip away at some of the smaller branches of the tree of reaction while watering and fertilizing its roots. The "both are extremists" approach is giving comfort and indirect support to reaction.

In searching our souls as Americans, here are some of the questions that arise. What can be the moral or ethical atmosphere in a nation which, as a matter of policy, holds some 25 millions of its citizens half-slave, keeps them in the status of economic untouchables, forces them into ghettos and slums, segregates and discriminates against them from the day of their birth not only to the grave but even in the grave? And all the while the official oratory continues to spout equality and the rights of man, justice and the dignity of the individual.

What kind of an atmosphere and standards of ethics can a nation build when its lawmakers and law-enforcement agencies live by a big hoax of anti-Communism. The head of the government law enforcement agency has made a lifetime profession of promoting, inflating and daily expounding this lie.

The lesson to be learned from Hitler Germany has been strikingly expressed by the Reverend Martin Niemoeller, who was imprisoned by the Nazis:

> In Germany, they first came for the Communists, and I didn't speak up because I wasn't a Communist. Then they came for the trade unionists, and I didn't speak up because I wasn't a trade unionist. Then they came for the Catholics, and I didn't speak up because I was a Protestant. Then they came for me—and by that time no one was left to speak up.

The ideological weapon of anti-Communism cannot be separated from imperialism, because it is its main weapon. To support anti-Communism is to support imperialism. It is impossible to fight imperialism without taking a stand against its main ideological weapon of anti-Communism.

Anti-Sovietism

Ideological struggles are not exercises in abstract, "pass-the-time-of-day" dialogues. The struggle is for the "mass mind." Its aim is to win mass support for a partisan view in a struggle. Ideology cannot be neutral. It is on one side or the other in a battle.

In the main the history of organized human societies has been a history of class contradictions and class struggle—the struggle between the exploited and the exploiters. It is this struggle that has basically determined the nature and the issues in the field of ideology. This is true for philosophy, history and theories of economics.

In our time the central contradiction is between the two main classes—the capitalist class and the working class. Again, it is the contradiction between the exploited and the exploiters. The present ideological concepts serve one or the other in this class battle. Capitalist ideology tries to justify the exploitation. When this is impossible its task is to hide it. In our times its assignment is to cover up and defend the operations of imperialism.

The class struggle started when the first worker said, "I produce ten pairs of candles but you give me only the value of one pair in return." The struggle moved one step higher when the workers of one shop collectively asked for a bigger share of the value they produced. When this did not bring results the workers joined forces on an industry-wide basis. This was followed by the organization of nationwide unions.

At each step the ideologist of capitalism developed new arguments. In this process there also developed an ideology that justified and defended the positions of the working class.

As the struggle developed the need for an overall theory, the need for a science that explained the basic nature of the struggle became a historic necessity. Many contributed to this process. But it was two men, Karl Marx and Frederick Engels who put it all together into a developed science.

For the last 100 years the main task of capitalist ideologists has been to try to refute the science of Marxism.

It was one thing to defend capitalism at a stage when only the exploiters had state power.

But the nature of the class struggle took a sharp turn when the workers of one-sixth of the world took state power into their own hands. That is why the ten days of the Soviet revolution shook the world.

Now there were not only two classes but there were two social and economc systems representing the two classes—socialism and capitalism. This gave the class contradiction a new dimension. The basic class contradiction on a world scale was now focused on the two world systems. The new dimension of the class struggle became the new dimension in the ideological struggle as well.

For capitalism the birth of the Soviet Union was the establishment of a working class beachhead. This was also the birth of anti-Sovietism as the main pillar of capitalism's ideological struggle against the working class. As the power of the Soviet Union has grown the attack on it has grown. The Soviet Union as a working-class socialist state has become the main obstacle to the plans of world imperialism. To weaken, to isolate, to remove this central obstacle remains the central aim of imperialism It is the central aim of capitalist ideology. This is the hard core of today's reality.

As the Soviet people build socialism it emerges, in ever sharper focus, as the example of socialism to the people of the world. In their struggle against socialism, imperialism is forced to try to destroy the image of socialism as it is being built in the socialist countries. Thus anti-Communism also takes the form of anti-Sovietism. Whether knowingly or unknowingly people who lend a hand to anti-Sovietism are in fact lending a hand in destroying the image of socialism.

As the contradiction between the two world systems sharpens, as capitalism decays and sinks into internal crises and as the countries of socialism build the society without insoluble crises, the ideological struggle will sharpen.

Anti-Communism will appear in ever new forms, in new disguises. It is an effort to distort and to deny a changing objective reality, because it is an effort to deny the law governing the nature of history and progress. The laws governing the march of progress have condemned imperialism to history's garbage heap.

1968

4

THE STRUGGLE FOR LENINIST CONCEPTS OF PROLETARIAN INTERNATIONALISM

Working class internationalism is an essential weapon in the struggle against imperialism. In its basic essence the struggle for internationalism in the revolutionary movement is a struggle against opportunism. How one reacts to and identifies with the problems of one's own class is a measurement of class consciousness. How one reacts to these same problems in some other country, or when they affect the lives and struggles on a world scale is a measure of the depth of one's internationalism.

Internationalism is class consciousness that reaches beyond national boundaries. Internationalism correctly sees the oneness of the national self interests of one's class, and the worldwide nature of the class struggle. Proletarian internationalism is not a slogan, or a cute phrase that one trots out on some ceremonial occasion. It is an ideological concept that must lead to a line of actions. It is an outlook that must influence a line of tactics. It is a world outlook of a class. It is a weapon of struggle. The concept has its roots in the hard necessities of the class struggle. It reflects the realities of the working class. Capitalism is worldwide. Class exploitation is worldwide. Monopoly corporations cross state boundaries. The world nature of capitalist exploitation is further developed in the rise of the multi-national corporations. More than ever the class enemy is international. Without the concept of internationalism the working class cannot rise above the limits set by narrow nationalism. Without the concept of internationalism the working class cannot fulfill its historic assignment of leading civilization along the path of social progress. Without it the working class cannot be the revolutionary class. Without internationalism the working class cannot successfully challenge and defeat capitalism which operates and coordinates its own activities on a world scale. Imperialism is a worldwide network. Without the concept of internationalism, imperialism cannot be crushed. The concept of internationalism is a working-class response to imperialism

Proletarian internationalism is an integral feature of Marxism-Leninism. The concept has grown with the development of Marxism. Proletarian internationalism is inseparable from the basic concept of the nature and role of the working class, the only class in society whose self interests are not in contradiction with the forces and direction of social progress. Working-class self-interests coincide with the direction of history—towards a civilization, a social order that will eliminate the curse of classes forever. In proletarian internationalism the working class introduces a kernel of an outlook, the ideological makeup of the future, more advanced civilization. It presents a kernel of the one-worldness of future relationships. It presents the kernel of the new morality, the ethics of a society not torn apart by a greedy drive for profits. It is an effective weapon of struggle because it contains the seeds of classless tomorrows.

The working class of each country faces two responsibilities—national and international. How to unite these tasks has always been a challenge to the revolutionary movements. Many have floundered on this issue. The main weapon of the enemy is a skillful use of chauvinism, nationalism and a false use of patriotism.

A sense of national pride or a love of one's country is not necessarily good or bad, positive or negative, in the abstract. The real issue is to what use it is put. What class content does it express? Is it used to advance or to retard social progress? Is it a weapon in the hands of the capitalist class or the working class? Does it weaken or strengthen the working class? In a capitalist society the best self interests of the people is represented by the working class. To monopoly capitalism, the people and the nation are objects of exploitation, and nationalism and patriotism are instruments of oppression. National pride with a working-class content, fused with the concept of proletarian internationalism, is a progressive force.

Nationalism

Nationalism has its origin in the need to protect the property of the ruling class. It was a method of getting masses to identify their interests with the propertied interests of the ruling class.

A main carrier of nationalism as an ideological concept in a capitalist society is the middle class. The petty-bourgeois elements of society cannot fully identify their interests either with the working class or with the class of big business. So they tend to see the solution and protection of their self-interests in nationalism, that seemingly covers both classes.

In the imperialist countries this nationalism is turned into great power chauvinism. It becomes the ideological instrument of reaction and imperialism. Under fascism it becomes the basis for the "master race" concepts. It is always the basis for racism.

Great power chauvinism in its totality is a reactionary outlook. It is the vehicle for the ultra-right and fascism. It is a weapon of oppression. It tends to infect all sections of the population. It is used to brainwash, to confuse and to mobilize masses for the most reactionary, anti-democratic policies. In the United States, great power chauvinism has grown as a counterpart to and an instrument in the expansion of U.S. imperialism to a world power. One of the most vicious and deep-seated manifestations of this in the United States is expressed in white chauvinism. It is a deep-seated corrosion, a blind hatred that takes on many forms, from open terror to a condescending, patronizing attitude that betrays an ideology of "superiority." It is monopoly capitalism's most effective tool in its policy of divide, rule and exploit.

In the oppressed colonial countries, nationalism is a basis of unity in the struggle for independence. Here it is a progressive vehicle. It is an anti-imperialist force. When liberation is won, the role of nationalism changes. The reactionary elements use it to mobilize the masses for policies of capitalism and for neo-colonialism. Progressive movements use it to appeal to the masses for policies that would continue the struggle for national liberation to complete independence and move towards socialism. In these cases there is already a difference. The nationalist appeal already has a mixture of working-class internationalism included.

Internationalism has always been one of the acid tests of the revolutionary movements. It has always been a yardstick by which it has been possible to measure the influence of opportunism and bourgeois nationalism within these movements.

Lenin resurrected the Marxist concepts of internationalism. He returned internationalism back to the class rails. He reinserted a working-class content into internationalism. Thus he moulded it into an effective instrument in the struggle against imperialism and national chauvinism.

Internationalism is not a material thing. It is not something you can weigh on a scale, or measure by yards.

It is not a matter of one's emotions. It is not limited to abstract ethical or moral concepts, although internationalism gives working-class morals, working-class humanism a unique quality.

It is an ideological concept. And like all things related to ideology it can be measured only by how one reacts to specific events and specific forces. A repetition of the phrase or to proclaim one's adherence to internationalism does not measure up, it does not meet the test. As a body of thought working-class internationalism has a tremendous world significance. It is an essential feature of a revolutionary social science and movement.

But what is a Leninist concept of internationalism?

It is a class concept. That is why it is correctly called working-class or proletarian internationalism. It rests on the unity of self-interests of all workers of all lands. It rests on the Marxist-Leninist concept that there is a basic class self-interest that is worldwide.

It is a working-class weapon against the global nature of capitalism and the class struggle.

The Leninist concept of internationalism is deeply humanistic. It gives meaning to the phrase, "We are our class brothers' keepers." It is an instrument of the class struggle—but it will flower into full bloom when there will be no classes or national divisions. Thus it will have its greatest meaning in classlessness, in a period when human society reaches that classless plateau. And so, in the conditions of today's class struggle it already contains the essence of the future relations and the humaneness of all future human societies.

The sharpest test of our internationalism today is how we react to the U.S. aggression in Vietnam. Not so much what we say about the aggression, but what we do about it in organizing masses to resist this criminal policy. Without a constant struggle against the aggression that is conducted in our name, internationalism would be an empty phrase.

National chauvinism and racism are the ideological opposites of working-class internationalism. Therefore the struggle for internationalism is a rejection and a struggle against all forms of racism and national chauvinism. We can not develop working-class internationalism amongst white workers as long as they are influenced by racism in their attitude toward Black Americans. The struggle for internationalism and the struggle against racism are closely intertwined and inseparable. In a sense the struggles of the recent years are a proof of this fact. We have made some headway against the influence of racism during our struggle against U.S. aggression in Vietnam.

The imperialist aggression against the peoples of Indochina has been a source of racism. The struggle against it has strengthened the struggle against racism.

Here are two separate statements by Lenin on internationalism:

> Petty-bourgeois nationalism proclaims as internationalism the mere recognition of the equality of nations, and nothing more. Quite apart from the fact that this recognition is purely verbal, petty-bourgeois nationalism preserves national self-interest intact, whereas proletarian internationalism demands, first that the interests of the proletarian struggle in any one country should be subordinated to the interests of that struggle on a world-wide scale. . . .[1]

And on another occasion he said the following in "Tasks of the Proletariat in our Revolution":

> There is one, and only one, kind of real internationalism, and that is—working whole-heartedly for the development of the revolutionary movement and the revolutionary struggle in *one's own* country, and supporting (by propaganda, sympathy, and material aid) this, *and*

[1] Lenin, *Selected Works,* Vol. 3, (New York: International Publishers, 1967) pp. 425-6.

only this line, in *every* other country without exception.[2]

Do these two concepts contradict? Not at all. They are very often misused when they are quoted separately in order to create a one sided emphasis. In fact these two concepts are like two guideposts on two sides of a principled path of struggle. Beyond the guideposts on both sides there are the swamps of opportunism. These two Leninist concepts mark the area where the unity of the national and international tasks of the working class must be worked out. When one realizes that the task is to find a path of unity between the national interests of a working class and its international tasks, then the two concepts of Lenin become a guide to action rather than a contradiction.

It is an axiom of human affairs that things often get more complicated before the solution appears. In Karl Marx's time the problem of unity between the national self-interests of the working class and the international class tasks was rather simple. One's internationalism was reflected in the attitude one had towards the struggles of the workers in other countries. Today the question is more complicated. It is not the concept of internationalism that has become more complicated. Imperialism has added new wrinkles to the class struggle. Export of capital, neo-colonialism, the rise of multi-national conglomerates have all added new dimensions to the class struggle. While they have created new problems, they have also given a new meaning to proletarian internationalism. The advent of socialism as a reality has also added some complications. Now the workers of over a dozen countries are in power. Their class self-interests and the interests of the people of their nations are now one. Now the question of internationalism involves unity of national people's interests and international class interests, unity of the national interests of each socialist country and the interests of the community of socialist countries as it is related to the global interests of the socialist sector, and the interests of the newly liberated countries and national liberation struggles in general. These are new complications resulting from victories in struggle.

[2] Lenin, *Selected Works,* Vol. 2, (New York: International Publishers, 1967) pp. 38-9

From these developments some have drawn erroneous conclusions. The expressions of the error vary but they all move in the direction of weakening or discarding internationalism. To one extent or another they take a position against world working-class unity. They are against world Communist unity. They argue that meaningful internationalism is either not possible or that it is not necessary. They all gravitate towards nationalism. Some argue that the essence of internationalism is for everyone to do their own thing. One cannot argue against each doing their own but by itself it does not add to internationalism. The opportunism of the leadership around Mao Tse-tung is more open, so their cover is more open.

The *Peking Review* speaks of two kinds of nationalism, "progressive nationalism," and "reactionary nationalism." This attempt to invent two kinds of nationalism is not a Marxist-Leninist concept. That nationalism can be used and can serve both reactionary as well as progressive causes and movements, is a fact. But nationalism is nationalism. Yes, Marxists must make an assessment and have a position depending on what purpose nationalism is being used for in a specific situation, but this does not change the basic concept as to what nationalism is. The invention of "two kinds of nationalism" opens the gates to replacing proletarian internationalism with "progressive nationalism." The invention of "two kinds of nationalism" is a cover for the penetration of bourgeois nationalism into the outlook of parties. Instead of inventing "excuses" for bourgeois nationalism, the Marxist point of view is that the ideological concept of proletarian internationalism must be dominant and finally will replace all other concepts.

In Marxist parties petty-bourgeois nationalism must be viewed as a non-working-class, petty-bourgeois influence. It is a harmful influence.

It is one thing to have national pride and socialist patriotism. It is another thing to permit nationalism to influence the overall policies and outlook of a party of the working class.

The concept of proletarian internationalism must always remain dominant in a working-class Marxist party.

In People's China "progressive nationalism" has led the Communist leadership into a swamp of opportunism. They have become the most divisive and disruptive force in the world socialist and anti-imperialist movements. On one issue after another they have joined with the forces of imperialism. There is nothing progressive about Mao's "progressive nationalism."

Because the Leninist concept of internationalism is a weapon in the class struggle it is always related to the main contradiction of our times. It is related to the relationships and the status of the world forces on the two sides of this main contradiction. The main contradiction is the class contradiction. The main social process is the class struggle. There has taken place a quantitative shift in the overall balance of the two class forces representing the two sides of this main contradiction.

The Leninist concept of internationalism has been moulded in the fires of the struggles that have raged around this main contradiction. The issues around the First World War were a test of the internationalism of the revolutionary parties of its day. With a few exceptions they did not measure up. They were engulfed in the waves of nationalism that swept each capitalist country. The internationalism of most social democratic parties turned out to be but empty shells. They had been ideologically corroded by national chauvinism. They continued to talk about internationalism but they were guided by bourgeois nationalism. Opportunism had destroyed their ideological fibers. From this point on the struggle for Lenin's concept of internationalism and the struggle against the influence of opportunism in general became very closely intertwined. In fact, they merged. The First World War was followed by the greatest of all social explosions. The working class came to power in one-sixth of the world. This gave birth to a new reality. This explosion created a new wrinkle in the main contradiction of our times. For now the working class had a beachhead. The working class was a state power. This gave the class struggle on a world scale a new meaning.

World capitalism fully understood the meaning of the establishment of this working-class beachhead. They turned all their guns toward this working-class breakthrough. The onslaught was physical, political, ideological. Thus the imperialist concept of anti-Sovietism was born. The birth of the Soviet Union, a working-class state, and the world capitalist all-out struggle against it became the new world reality. It added a new quality to the class struggle on a world scale. This new reality became the test of one's internationalism. Now the working-class parties had to react in defense of their international class interests by defending a nation—a socialist nation—because the working class had come to power in that nation. In this new class confrontation, in this new test of class loyalties again most of the world's social democratic parties, all of the Trotskyite groups and most of the liberals, caved in. Their "internationalism" turned into national chauvinism. They joined the forces on the other side of the class contradiction. They caved in under the capitalist onslaught. They joined the camp of anti-socialism. For 50 years they have covered their treachery to the working class under left phrases.

The opportunism of the social-democratic parties and the Trotskyite organization has led them into an odd corner for organizations that say they are for socialism. They are for socialism, but they are against socialism wherever socialism is being built. The Trotskyites are "against" the war in Vietnam, but they are not for a victory of the forces who are fighting against United States aggression "because it would be a Communist victory."

The Communist Parties of the world stood by their international tasks. They defended the new working-class state. They condemned the opportunistic capitulation of the social-democrats and Trotskyites. This became the ideological base for the fraudulent charge that Communists are foreign agents. The foreign agent charge is based on the fact that the Communist Parties did not cave in and took a firm stand of internationalism, as it was reflected in the new realities.

World imperialism continues to use this big lie. It remains a key element in the ideological struggle between the two forces of the main contradiction. It is a critical factor in the test of one's internationalism. Not all Communist Parties at all times meet the test.

The next new reality that tested everyone's internationalism was the struggle against fascism. The internationalism of the world Communist movement met the test in Spain and in the worldwide struggle against fascism. Again the social-democratic and Trotskyite groups caved in and became disruptive and divisive forces.

They rejected the concept of a united front against fascism.

The Second World War resulted in the next big shift in the balance of world relations. The world confrontation of the forces on the two sides of the main contradiction now took on a new turn. On one side of the alignment was the new world community of socialist states, the historic growth of working class movements in all of the capitalist countries and an explosion of colonial liberation revolutions. Together they formed the new revolutionary force of a world revolutionary process. The class forces were sharply drawn between the two worlds, the capitalist world and the socialist world. On the other side of the contradiction are the greatly weakened forces of world capitalism in an alliance of imperialism centered on the United States. How to react to this new reality has become the acid test of today's internationalism. The struggle against U.S. aggression in Vietnam is a key feature of this larger framework. How we support the struggles against U.S. imperialism in South America, Asia, Africa is the acid test of our internationalism.

Within this new reality there are some new factors that test one's internationalism. The developments in the Mideast present such a test. To set the stage for this test, one must place the central question squarely. Where do the contending forces in the Mideast developments fit into the overall world alignment of forces? Where are they within the world revolutionary process? It is clear the Israel-U.S. oil alliance is an imperialist alliance, and is on the reactionary imperialist side of the world confrontation. On the other hand, the main forces of the Arab countries, the main direction of the progress within these countries are anti-imperialist.

Some ask: "What about some of the reactionary currents amongst the Arab forces? How can they be considered anti-imperialist?" The answer is that we are against such forces in the Arab countries. We condemn such reactionary currents, including the ugly reactionary currents of anti-Semitism. But this does not answer the central question. And, besides, the thrust of the Israel-U.S. aggression is not against these reactionary forces in the Arab countries. It is not directed against the reactionary forces of Saudi Arabia or Morocco. The act of military aggression was not to overthrow the reactionary governments. And again it does not answer the main question. One's position must be based on: what are the main forces and the main currents and how do they align themselves with the forces in the world struggle? This is a necessary feature of internationalism. It has always been true that one must choose between national chauvinism and internationalism. But when ethnic nationalism and working-class internationalism clash there can be no hesitation about one's choice.

The right of Israel to exist as a nation must be defended. Israel's policies of aggression are indefensible. For the Jewish people in the United States to defend the rights of Israel is understandable and correct. It is a just cause. But for the Jewish people to defend the unjust policies of Jewish aggression is blind nationalism. It is a violation of all concepts of internationalism.

Blind nationalism is the greatest source of weakness in the Arab countries. It is the most powerful instrument imperialism has within these countries. It is blind to the needs of the struggle against imperialism. It blinds the masses from seeing the need for anti-imperialist unity. It blinds the masses from seeing the true meaning of imperialist ideology, the dangers that lurk behind the anti-Communist, anti-working-class propaganda spread by imperialism.

Blind nationalism in the Arab countries is the weapon of the most reactionary sectors including the stooges of imperialism. Blind nationalism is the roadblock to a development along a non-capitalist path. It is an obstacle to a socialist development. Unless checked, blind nationalism can reverse the course of national liberation movements. As it is an essential element for all struggles, working-class internationalism is a necessary ingredient for all national liberation movements. Working-class internationalism is a foundation on which the Arab peoples and the people of Israel can build an anti-imperialist alliance. It can be the only basis for peace and friendship in the Middle East.

The central aim of imperialism and its national chauvinism is to divide and disorient the forces of the revolutionary process. Lenin's statement, "working-class internationalism demands first that the interests of the working-class struggles in any one country should be subordinated to the interests of that struggle on a world scale," must be transferred to the scales of today's reality. It is within this concept that one must assess the policies of all parties, of all countries, including the policies of Communist parties and socialist countries. In this sense the new diplomatic maneuvering taking place in the U.S.-China relations has a special significance. It is related to the main contradiction of our times and to concepts of proletarian internationalism.

There can never be any doubt about the intentions of U.S. imperialism. It is out to strengthen its world position by weakening all of the forces of world socialism. The main obstacle to U.S. policies of aggression is the power of the Soviet Union. Therefore its main aim is to try to isolate and weaken the Soviet Union. For the moment the anti-Soviet efforts of U.S. imperialism are geared to sharpen relations between the Soviet Union and China. In the pursuance of this goal U.S. imperialism is ready to make some concessions to China.

This is in the very center of every diplomatic move U.S. imperialism makes. The U.S.-Soviet relationship is the sharpest expression of the main class contradiction of our times on a world scale. There is absolutely no way a socialist country or a Communist Party or any other political or social force can avoid reacting to this central phenomenon to this basic challenge of this moment. The options are limited. Either one doggedly holds on to a firm revolutionary position of not adjusting, accommodationg, flirting with or opportunistically not "using" this central class contradiction, or one takes an opportunistic position of accommodation, of taking momentary advantage, or ingratiating onself to the class opposition by one's silence or acquiescence. This is opportunism. This is class collaboration. It is playing the game by rules laid down by imperialism. This is not working-class internationalism. It is an unavoidable challenge of our times. As the balance of world forces has shifted, this main contradiction has forced itself to the center of the stage more and more. There are some new developments between U.S. imperialism and People's China. As these U.S.-China relationships develop one is compelled to ask what is the essence of the motion on the part of the Chinese leadership. What do they expect to get from these developments? One has to take into account the nature of the Maoist line in foreign policy of the past years. In an important

sense it has been a Chinese nationalist line. It has not been propelled by proletarian internationalism. It has not been based on
working-class considerations. It has not shown any concern for
problems of worldwide class unity, for the unity of the anti-
imperialist or socialist forces. And, in a final sense it has not been
even a policy in the interests of Chinese socialism. It has been a
fanatical, nationalist binge. Within the world Communist movement, within the anti-imperialist movement, it has been ten years
of disruption, ten years of irresponsible slander, ten years of constant, provocative efforts to divide and confuse. It has been ten
years of trying to dominate the world revolutionary movement.
It has been for ten years the main support for every possible
factional, divisive, crackpot sect. It has been ten years of disruption within China.

There are no indications that the Mao leadership is moving
away from these policies. Therefore, one must assume these
policies will be continued within the context of the U.S.-China
maneuvers.

It is this erroneous policy of narrow egoistical nationalism that
has led it to a position of fanatical anti-Sovietism. This has been
its main preoccupation. Therefore, it seems clear that no matter
what anyone's intentions are, in the U.S.-China dialogue each one's
own brand of anti-Sovietism, each for its own purpose, will be
a factor. If it was not for the policies of the Mao leadership during
the past ten years there would be no questions about these developing relations. Then they would not and could not have an
adverse effect on the world struggle against imperialism.

It is the height of naivete and extremely dangerous and self-
defeating for the leaders of any socialist country to think they can
"use" an imperialist power as a counter-weight in settling dis-
agreements with other socialist countries. It is opportunism because
while it results in some temporary concessions, it takes place at
the expense of the working class and the rest of the socialist community. Such policies become a drag on the socialist countries and
an obstacle to winning relationships of equality with capitalist
countries. This is how we have to state the new test of one's
internationalism.

The new factor in the U.S.-People's China developments is

the agreed upon visit of Nixon to China. The announcement came as a lifesaver for U.S. imperialism. It came at a moment when Nixon's Indochina policy of aggression was in a serious crisis. It came at a time when the Vietnamese seven point proposal for peace, including the proposal to release all prisoners of war, as soon as Nixon would set a definite date of withdrawal, had created an untenable dilemma for the Nixon Administration. The announcement of the trip took the heat off. That was the obvious reason for the public announcement ten months before the trip was to take place. It has become evident the U.S. aggression against Vietnam was not considered an obstacle to a Mao-Nixon meeting. Chou En-lai said nothing and Kissinger said an end to the aggression was not a condition for the get-together.

It is also evident the Chinese participation in the meeting is based on narrow national interests. As long as the Mao leadership continues its present policies, U.S. imperialism is willing to make concessions to the narrow nationalist interests of the Chinese. Not to take up the U.S. policies of imperialist aggression is a concession to imperialism. In its relationship with other countries the leadership of the Communist Party of China has followed a narrow nationalist course. This was the basis for the Nixon visit.

This course led them to support the reactionary military dictatorship of Pakistan in their heinous and brutal campaign of mass murder against the Bengali people in East Pakistan

There was no voice of protest from the Chinese leaders when the C.I.A.-created provocation led to the murder of Communists and other revolutionary leaders in Sudan. The reasons for these actions is obvious. Policies of narrow nationalism are non-working class. They are not dictated by working-class interests. In such policies defense of working-class interests is not a factor. Policies based on narrow nationalism are not based on anti-imperialism. The Mao leadership of narrow Chinese nationalism agrees with anti-imperialism or with working-class struggles only if they serve narrow Chinese nationalism. Mao and Chou En-lai do not support working-class internationalism. Their policies have been a negative factor in the class struggle and in the anti-imperialist struggle.

We have always been and are for People's China getting its place in all world organizations. We have been and are for diplomatic relations with China. We are for trade based on equality. We are for all of these relationships—as long as they do not in any way strengthen U.S. imperialism or in any way weaken the socialist working-class and anti-imperialist forces of the world.

To prevent and to checkmate imperialism's use of differences between socialist countries, differences between Communist parties, differences between newly liberated countries—differences between any of the forces of anti-imperialism—has emerged as a most decisive question of our times. It is the acid test of one's ideological fiber. In today's world it is *the* test of one's working-class internationalism. To permit oneself to be an instrument of this tactic of world imperialism in any way, no matter how commendable one's intentions are, is opportunism. It is class collaboration. To be of service to imperialism, even in the slightest, is to be a servant of imperialism.

Lenin's concept of internationalism demands a constant struggle against opportunism. Some forces in the world revolutionary process, including some Communists, are having difficulties in finding the path of unity between national class interests and the demands of the working-class struggle on a world scale. It is understandable why this is especially a problem for Communist parties who, for obvious and historic reasons, must place a heavy emphasis on electoral struggles. Electoral appeals are made to the widest possible audiences. This is perfectly understandable. This appeal is made to people who are influenced by narrow national considerations. This is also understandable. The Party's struggle to create a broad popular base and image, and to win large votes for Communist candidates is an important phase of the class struggle.

But there is a tendency to assume that, in emphasis on electoral struggles, the responsibilities of these Parties and working-class movements to the world struggle—working-class internationalism—is unnecessarily sacrificed. When such an emphasis continues and when it becomes more than an electoral tactic it becomes opportunism. When this happens these Parties have a difficult time finding the area of unity between national interests of their working class and the international class responsibilities. With some parties working-class internationalism becomes an empty cliché and narrow nationalism becomes the practice.

The Czechoslovak events of 1968 were a test of internationalism. Large numbers of masses in capitalist countries were greatly confused. There were great pressures around the Czechoslovak events. There were pressures of national chauvinism, both internally and externally. Within this context some Parties again had difficulties in finding the path of unity between the two sides of the working-class struggle. It was necessary to again clearly keep in mind where the forces in that contest, both external and internal forces, fit into the struggles of the world revolutionary process. It is clear the actions of the Warsaw Pact socialist countries were actions in defense of socialism and against imperialism. This was a necessary basis for one's judgment of where one's internationalism must express itself. The issue was international support to the struggles against the anti-socialist and imperialist forces within and without Czechoslovakia. A few weeks after these events, one Communist leader, speaking to the world press, said:

We feel that we have once more provided *unquestionable proof* of our *complete autonomy* precisely in connection with the events in Czechoslovakia and in relation to an extremely important and meaningful moment in the international policy and action of the Soviet Union.

It was the wrong thing to say at the wrong time. It reflected an opportunist "use" of the maneuverings of imperialist anti-socialist forces. Such a reaction was not in fulfilment of one's internationalist tasks. It was rather a sacrifice of one's internationalism in the opportunistic quest for "unquestionable proof of our complete autonomy." It was too high a price to pay for such "proof." In a crisis internationalism demands emphasis on unity, not autonomy. Statements of solidarity and unity and not "proof of our autonomy" are called for.

In the United States in an overall sense the test of our internationalism is our struggle against the influences of great power chauvinism, white chauvinism and racism.

Working class internationalism arises from the demands of the class struggle. It is an essential feature of the revolutionary movement. The test is how we react to concrete events and forces as the world moves along its prescribed path toward world socialism.

1970

5

MARXISM-LENINISM AND ITS CONTRIBUTION TO ANTI-IMPERIALISM

Marxism-Leninism has added an important dimension to the science of social progress in its exploration of the relationship between cause and effect, particularly concerning the influence of economic laws on a nation's political, cultural and intellectual activities. It has lifted the study of economics from the narrow confines of statistics and abstract speculations, rescued philosophy from the unworthy task of making excuses for a dying social order, and lifted thought from its departmentalization and separation from reality. For culture and art the dialectical approach integral to Marxism has added meaningful purpose. And in the realm of ethics and morality it has engendered a sense of dedication to one's fellow human beings in all forms of social re-relationships, whether mental or physical.

Intellectual activity in the service of a dying way of life leads to warping and the eventual decay of the mind. Marxism-Leninism directs thought away from paths that lead to dead-end frustrations. It transfers intellectual activities away from the musty cloisters and meaningless ivory towers, and into the life-giving sunlight of meaningful activities and struggle. It rejects the concept of thought as the province of a neutral observer, and opens the way through which philosophers, economists, historians and cultural producers can escape from the confines of detachment and become active fighters for progress.

As capitalism in the United States moved on to the stage of imperialism it increased its efforts to imprison all progressive thought. In the economic field it illegalized trade unionism. Trade unions were declared conspiracies punishable by death. In the field of politics it declared illegal any organization that advocated socialism. In the field of thought it declared Marxism illegal and dangerous. Marxism was forbidden in the market-place of ideas. Marxism has not been permitted in our colleges or universities. Marxist books and teachers have been banned. Terror, imprisonment, denial of employment, ridicule, ostracism, torture and death have been meted out to those who espoused it in the face of all hazards. Sometimes the ostracism took the form of a conspiracy of total silence. To be sure, the ideological custodians of the reactionary establishment finally introduced the study of anti-Communism when they saw the revolutionary potential inherent in this new science of society. But in the 50's, they still taught that "dialectical materialism is more than a delusion—it is a sin." But their schemes have begun to backfire; too many are discovering the truth. The establishment apologists have shifted to more sophisticated methods. From the position of rejection and frontal attack they have moved to that of "properly interpreting Marx," or to modifying it, or to saying, "Marx was right in the past, but life has bypassed his ideas." Thus while the conspiracy of silence has been broken, the vulgarizations continue. Marxism-Leninism is the most formidable weapon against imperialism.

One vital phase of human existence is the construction of tools with which to extend man's own limited capabilities, to enable him to reach further, probe deeper, understand more and more complex phenomena. The systematized body of thought that makes for man's greater control of his environment is incorporated in the sciences.

The development of the sciences is an extension of human knowledge. Scientific socialism is such an extension, enlarging the scope of the human mind's ability to observe and understand itself and its world. Like other sciences, it gathers to itself experiences from all processes, itself developing further as it gathers and correlates these experiences. Like all sciences, it continually uses its improved tools to extend the power of the mind to cope more fully with the past, present and future of social development.

Through analysis and selection, after Marx and Lenin had passed from the scene this dialectical approach continued to take account of contemporary human conditions and changes. It has fought to reject the weeds that can choke healthy growth, pruned off false offshoots and superfluous branches that have attached themselves to Marxism. And thus far it has proved to be mankind's most effective instrument with which to probe the inner processes of society and to change the conditions that obstruct social progress.

This science is revolutionary because it is focused on reality in constant flux; because it rejects the separation of thought from action; because it extends vision making it possible to project and to recognize the forward movement of history. Those who see the path ahead are better able to act and provide leadership in the struggles of today. Theory does not reject experimentation, but it also does not engage in purposeless, random schemes, fantasies.

The need to defend itself against the bourgeois systems has kept the Marxist-Leninist instrument sharp in struggle. Lenin's life was devoted to the defense of the revolutionary content of Marxism in the very midst of his most crucial practical activities. His stand against the opportunism of the parties of the Second International was a tremendous contribution. He forced the membership of the Socialist parties to face the fact that the opportunism, chauvinism and nationalism was betraying the interests of the working class. He re-argued the question of proletarian internationalism and proved on the basis of the new realities that while there may be short-term crumbs for the people of a country following a course of narrow nationalism, it is both a betrayal of the world working-class interests and the betrayal of the longer-range interests of its own working class.

Thus the struggle against opportunism has been and remains a crucial question in the defense of Marxism and in its further development. Opportunism corrodes, distorts and denies Marxism. Opportunism is always hidden behind whatever at the moment is the most effective fig leaf. It is always present and if active and continuous battle is not waged against it, it will seep into an organization and swamp it.

The struggle for unity in the world Communist movement is in essence a struggle against the influence of opportunism. The fight for proletarian internationalism is a fight against it and simultaneously a fight for a working class world outlook. The tendency of parties to withdraw into their national shells results from the influences of opportunism. They are acts of retreating before difficulties.

Our own point of reference at this time is the U.S. aggression against the people of Vietnam. We are fully aware of the brutal nature of U.S. imperialism, but a realistic estimate of its weaknesses leads us to believe that the combined forces of anti-imperialism can force it to retreat. The United States is learning that aggression is a costly business not only in resources and in human lives but in many other ways. To be the gendarme of world imperialism when the world is in revolt against this kind of oppression, when the balance of world forces has shifted, calls for an unprecedented militarization of every phase of our life.

The cost reflects itself in the crisis of the dollar, the gold that flows outward in a steady stream from Fort Knox, the crisis of taxation and inflation and the deepening and widening of the enclaves of poverty. The cost is in the crisis of the cities and in the growing pressures for restrictive trade policies. Because the United States is the pivotal state in the capitalist world, it is also the place where the crisis factors of world imperialism are focused and magnified. This is the price our people pay for permitting the United States to be the reactionary military, financial, and ideological headquarters for a world system in crisis, in decline.

It is this sharp point in world reality that influences all developments.

1969

6

SOME THOUGHTS ON REVOLUTION: I

In an editorial in the April 1966 issue of *Monthly Review*, the following passage appears:

. . . In our opinion, the only kind of revolution that has any chance of succeeding in Latin America today is a socialist revolution. We were, we believe, among the first to say that the Cuban Revolution would be forced to advance rapidly to socialism. . . . in 1963 we stated our opinion in these pages that there is no such thing as feudalism in Latin America and that it therefore makes no sense to talk about a bourgeois revolution.

These sweeping conclusions are not made by the revolutionary movements and parties in South America who are directly involved and are answerable to their people, but by the editors of a magazine in the United States who are not directly involved and are not answerable to any organized group anywhere. This is not to say they have no right to state their opinion, but it is also necessary to know the relationship of what they say and how much of it reflects real experiences that come to those who participate in organized movements and struggles. It is difficult to imagine another paragraph containing more basic errors than the one quoted.

What is the meaning of the words, "the Cuban Revolution would be forced to advance rapidly to socialism?" If the Cuban Revolution had started as a socialist revolution, it would not have had "to advance rapidly to Socialism." The first stage of the Cuban Revolution was anti-imperialist. It was for national independence. The fascist Batista regime was a puppet of U.S. imperialism, it had to be overthrown, and this was correctly placed by the Cuban revolutionaries as the first task of the revolution. Only after this was successfully concluded could it "rapidly advance" to a socialist reorganization of society, and the people of Cuba did exactly that. So, if anything, this disproves the main contention of the editorial.

The error, I believe, is in the attempt to ignore the historic nature of the struggle against imperialism and to replace it arbitrarily with a socialist revolution. It sounds revolutionary but it is not. In practice, such a policy would not result in a successful struggle against imperialism, neither would it set the stage for a socialist revolution. Whenever imperialism is a factor, a mass struggle against imperialism for national liberation is a necessary part of the struggle for socialism. It therefore does make "sense to talk about a bourgeois revolution," because that is what it is.

Why are these concepts so important? Because the motive force of social revolutions is people. And people will fight for what has been placed on the order of the day by objective processes. Therefore if socialism is not on the order of the day in the sense of calling for it today, and the advanced forces nevertheless present it as if it were, it can only result in the isolation of the revolutionary forces. Under such circumstances, the leadership of the anti-imperialist struggles will be turned over to non-socialist and anti-socialist elements. The conscious organization and advocacy of advanced ideas, including socialism, are very important, but they can generate power only if they are related to the level of objective developments of the moment.

It is necessary to clearly define each juncture, and the forces involved at each stage of developments. It is possible to leap over such stages of development only if one is not concerned whether words are a reflection of reality or fantasy. There are no compulsory sets of factors that you have to deal with in the world of fantasy. Much of petty-bourgeois radical rhetoric is set in such a fantasy world.

But there is a third factor to the two elements—advanced ideas and the objective situation. It is the relationship between them. Therefore as important as it is to define the different junctures within the revolutionary process, it is as necessary to clearly understand the relationships between them—not only in theory, but as a factor that must be taken into consideration in the daily tactics of struggle. A revolutionary force must be an influence at all stages of the processes. The preparations of the forces that will propel the struggle to a new stage cannot be postponed for a later date, or left to chance. The preparation of the masses for the socialist revolution is on the order of the day at all times. In this sense the political, ideological preparations for socialism are always on the order of the day, at every stage of the struggle. Only in this way will the revolutionary forces become a conscious force, a factor that will give birth to a new stage of struggle.

The elements of a higher stage of struggle must be cultivated and nurtured in proceeding stages. Without this revolutionary essence, the struggle for reforms will cultivate reformism.

The editorial quoted states "there is no such thing as feudalism in Latin America and it therefore makes no sense to talk about a bourgeois revolution." The realities of Latin America, of course, deny any such assertion, for most Latin American societies are a mixture of capitalism and feudalism. The editorial is a flight to fantasy. But the dominant phenomenon facing most, if not all, Latin American countries is that they are all victims of imperialist oppression. To one degree or another the countries in South America face the struggle of freeing themselves from United States imperialism.

Thus, breaking the chains of U.S. imperialist domination is the present overriding task. This is closely related to the struggle against feudalism and capitalism. Masses who have had enough of colonial oppression, but who have not yet reached the level of political consciousness of deciding what kind of society they want to build, will join those who are convinced of the need for socialism in a united struggle against imperialism. The period between this hurdle and the struggle for socialism may be very brief, the two may overlap and often do. It may all take place in one sweep or it may last for years. And, of course, the existence of the socialist world has a direct influence on these struggles. But the two tasks cannot be confused. They each have a specific historical task, each propelled by a specific set of forces. Those with socialist convictions will be part of the anti-imperialist front and, while helping to lead and to organize it, will be working to convince all as to the advantages of the socialist path.

Eduardo Mora Valverde, member of the Secretariat of the People's Vanguard Party of Costa Rica, discussed these questions. Here are some of his thoughts:

Feudal survivals, too, still make themselves felt, or even predominate, in the countryside in most Latin American countries. In Peru, Ecuador, Paraguay, Guatemala, El Salvador and some other countries, precapitalist production relations are much more pronounced than in Argentina, Uruguay, Chile or Mexico. . . . But in all circumstances, in order to pave the way to economic progress it is essential to win freedom from imperialist domination.

Needless to say, our Party as well as the other Latin American Communist parties, unlike some 'ultra-revolutionary' groups . . . do not consider the winning of power by the working class and the full realization of the program of the socialist revolution to be the immediate task. . . .

Moreover, world-wide experience (and for us Latin Americans the experience of Cuba above all) shows that at the present time the victory of the anti-imperialist and anti-feudal revolution is, as a rule, a precondition and point of departure for the socialist path of development.[1]

To which we add:

We live in a revolutionary age that in scope and depth eclipses all prior ages of social upheaval and transformation. Today the revolutionary tide extends to all continents, penetrates into the most remote jungles of Africa, climbs the most inaccessible peaks of Asia and stalks the plantations and mines of Latin America, sweeping in its wake the overwhelming majority of mankind. Former revolutions ushered in the age of capitalism. Today's revolutions mark mankind's historic transition to socialism.

Contemporary revolutions bear two distinctive marks: they are socialist, they are anti-imperialist. More than a billion human beings are embarked on socialist revolution; a larger number is in varying stages of anti-colonial revolution. In the struggle

[1] See Eduardo Mora Valverde, "Economic Situation in Latin America and Development of the Revolution," *World Marxist Review*, August, 1965, p. 36.

for the overthrow of imperialist domination, feudal bondage and political tyranny, a broad national unity is attainable that will even include capitalist elements who chafe under the oppressive restrictions of foreign monopoly. The attainment of such aims, progressive and liberating as they are, is not yet socialism. There is, however, a close relation between the socialist and colonial revolutions in that imperialism is the common enemy of both; the speed and scope of the colonial liberation movement is made possible by the existence of the socialist world—by its revolutionary example, by its economic, diplomatic and military assistance, which greatly restricts imperialism's ability to suppress or strangle colonial revolutions.

Thus, to go back to the original passage from the article in the *Monthly Review*, it is apparent that it is based on an unrealistic assessment of the course of the revolution in Latin America and a failure to understand the existence of successive stages in the achievement of the people's liberation.

The error was not a one article detour. It is a basic line of many years standing. The *Monthly Review* is only one of the voices for this policy. Its application was not limited to the events in Cuba. Some began to apply it to the struggles in the United States. The Black liberation struggle became a struggle for socialism, the anti-monopoly struggle was "old hat" because it was not per se, an anti-capitalist struggle, the working class was a part of the "establishment" because they fought for economic demands and not for socialism.

It has been an erroneous guide resulting in serious defeats and setbacks. To many it has been a guide leading to isolation, frustration and inactivity. In this sense the *Monthly Review* line objectively served the enemy.

It has been an instrument of division and diversion in the ranks of leftward moving masses. It sets up its own world of fantasy. It then reacts to it with grandiose revolutionary-sounding rhetoric, that is possible only when you deal with a fantasy world. But this then becomes the yardstick for measuring and slandering revolutionary forces who refuse to be coerced to accept the tactics based on this unreality. This slander is also used by the forces of imperialism.

This petty-bourgeois radicalism conjures up its own imaginary "revolutionariness." It is used to judge what is revolutionary and what is not revolutionary. It has nothing to do with life, with struggle. It is presented as a "revolution within a revolution . . . Power from the end of a gun barrel."

These are attempts to replace a serious revolutionary policy with empty bombast. But it divides, disorientates, it confuses and misleads dedicated but inexperienced forces into the "valleys of death."

Honest, correct motives are, of course, very important, but they do not necessarily result in correct policies or tactics. Therefore the explanation of what gives rise to these incorrect policies may not be found to be in bad motives. Of course, the damage is no less because the motives were honest. We have to seek for the roots in deeper soil. They are to be found in basic assessments and judgments of objective laws and development of human society. Marxist-Leninist judgments of these objective factors lead to an understanding of the class nature of society, the class struggle, the role of classes and the special role of the working class. Marxist-Leninist concepts of struggle are based on such assessments. History is made by classes. In the present stage of human development it is the working class that makes revolutionary history.

Petty-bourgeois radicalism is a rejection of these basic concepts. Any concept that does not rest on the premise that the working class is the only class capable of sustained revolutionary action is a concept that cannot for long remain on the revolutionary rails of history.

The laws of capitalist development not only give rise to a working class, but they constantly create the objective conditions that mold it into a force capable of sustained revolutionary struggle. Only policies based on that reality can give sustained revolutionary leadership. The only winning policy is one that combines the conscious revolutionary force with the force that is created by objective processes. Lenin said:

Marxism differs from all other socialist theories in the remarkable way it combines complete scientific sobriety in the analysis of the objective state of affairs and the objective course of evolution with the most emphatic recognition of the importance of the revolutionary energy, revolutionary creative genius and revolutionary initiative of the masses—and also, of course, of individuals, groups, organizations, and parties that are able to discover and achieve contact with one or another class.[2]

Lenin correctly gives emphasis to the combination of the two. He gives importance only to groups or parties that are able to combine the two elements. Petty bourgeois radicalism goes off into a fantasy world because it does not accept the real world of classes, and the class struggle. This leads to idealistic judgments of forces and movements.

If one does not accept the materialist concept as a foundation for policy what is left is the idealist concept. Idealist concepts are what the fantasy world is made of. In it ideas do not necessarily have to be related to realities. If a class is not a basic formation on which policies are based, then the role of individuals becomes basic. Ideas unrelated to material reality and individuals unrelated to classes become the forces in a world of unreality. In this world it is not the workings of capitalism that create the conditions that result in a process of radicalization, but rather the "radical ideas." The logic of fantasy is that if a "radical idea" is of such importance then an "individual act" is even of greater significance. This is the foundation for anarchism, for individual acts of terror. Such policies lead to isolation because their theoretical roots are in isolation from the only force capable of sustained struggle.

Petty-bourgeois sectors of society are not as closely bound to the class realities of capitalism. Their radicalism tends to take the path of rejecting the path based on the class struggle.

Thus the error of petty-bourgeois radicalism has its roots in basic concepts of judgment. It is a rejection of historical materialism. Its assessment of anti-imperialist struggles is unrelated to reality. For Marxism-Leninism the character of a revolution is basically determined by what social contradictions it resolves, what socio-economic system it overthrows and what socio-economic system it establishes in its place. The power,

---

[2] V. I. Lenin, "Against Boycott," *Collected Works*, Vol. 13 (Moscow: Foreign Languages Publishing House, 1962), p. 36.

the motive forces that bring it about are the classes that bring in the victory.

The editors state, "In our opinion, the only kind of revolution that has any chance of succeeding in Latin America today is a socialist revolution."

When one gathers the editorial positions of the *Monthly Review* over a longer period of time what emerges is a collection of mish-mash, of subjective rhetoric. Not long after the quoted editorial appeared the editors had doubts about Cuba's socialism. One wonders what kind of socialism the editors do approve when some time later one of the editors, Paul Sweezey, approvingly quoted Lin Piao, the chief advocate of Mao's ideas as follows: "The restoration of capitalism in the Soviet Union and certain other socialist countries is the most important lesson to be drawn from the last fifty years of the history of the international communist movement."

Sweezey does not want to be totally negative. He does not want to appear as if he has closed the books against socialism, so from his armchair he leaves the door ajar. "This, of course, does not mean that there will never be socialism in the Soviet Union." Throughout the years Sweezey's basic flaw has been that he has been and is for "socialism" without the working class or without the class struggle. He has always been against working-class revolutionary parties. He has always accommodated himself to the imperialist pressure of anti-Sovietism. He consoles himself by saying, "I have not however found any which are specifically addressed to the question of the proletariat's ability or readiness to build a socialist society." So the picture is complete—the working class is not a revolutionary class, it is not a factor in overthrowing capitalism and is incapable of building socialism.

In speaking of the working class Marx and Engels said, "The regeneration of mankind lies in its hands."

1966

7

SOME THOUGHTS ON REVOLUTION: II

In this, the most profoundly revolutionary period of history, explosive mass upheavals continue to dominate the world scene. Militant mass movements have now become an irresistible force that propel and shape human events. They reflect a new sense of values, a new mass mood, a new level of expectations by the exploited and oppressed. There is rapidly increasing dissatisfaction, unrest and rebellion because of the deterioration of the lot of the people in the capitalist world.

Many factors contribute to the new mass mood—among them the people's awareness of the potential productivity of the new level of science and technology and their own stagnating or deteriorating conditions. The exploited are not willing to accept passively the existence of poverty and affluence as next door neighbors. There is a growing consciousness of the gap between what is possible and what is available to them. They are painfully aware of the way in which capitalism uses the technological leap of automation for its own profit and against their jobs.

The example of the world socialist system has a powerful impact, as has that of the newly liberated countries. Understanding and knowledge are heightened by the greatly expanded mass means of communication. Capitalism and imperialism and their institutions no longer appear all-powerful.

There was an interesting moment when President Johnson was trying to explain to reporters why he had withdrawn from the race for the presidency. He inadvertently raised the curtain of deception just long enough to express a thought that must increasingly haunt the control centers of monopoly capitalism. He said he withdrew from the race because he had a sense that his world was falling apart, because he saw "catastrophe all around him," because the world was "in turmoil and divided."

He is, in fact, referring to the world of U.S. imperialism and not his personal world, although his own political world could certainly have been said to be falling apart. But what he really was reflecting was the setbacks U.S. imperialism had suffered, and for that moment at least he closed the credibility gap.

The events that to the spokesman for capitalism appear as catastrophes are for the forces of progress the promise of a great new day. The once seeming solidity of the status quo is turning out to be nothing but a roadblock to progress. *Fortune*, the ordinarily silky, soothing voice of monopoly capital, in a recent issue reflects editorially, ". . . we are in the midst of a Time of Troubles —one of those periods in which the disintegrative forces in society seem at least temporarily more powerful than the integrative forces."

To capitalism, of course, the forces of social progress always appear as "disintegrative forces." The only disintegrative forces are those that stand in the way of the march of human progress —decaying monopoly capitalism and imperialism. Human society can fully enter the path of healthy integration only after capitalism has been abolished.

The sharpest expression of capitalism's crisis is that of its imperialist aggression in Vietnam, which has come up against the realities of this epoch in a dramatic encounter with a new balance of world forces—not only a sector of the forces of national liberation and those of world socialism, but those of its own working class and other forces of anti-imperialism and peace. And the crisis deepens as U.S. imperialism suffers one historic defeat after another. Its plans of conquest are floundering; its superiority over most countries in military hardware cannot overcome the disadvantages in the overall scales of history.

This was the handwriting on the wall that L.B.J. saw just before he threw in the towel. His abdication was symbolic of a historic moral and military defeat. And while such a defeat can and may result in acts of desperation that make imperialism even more dangerous in some respects, it can also mean that it will suffer defeats in other fields. French imperialism was forced out of Indochina; then, a few years later, out of Algeria. This moment can mean that U.S. imperialism will be forced out of Africa and Latin America, and it also spells heightened struggles and new victories elsewhere.

During these past few years it has been necessary to resist the petty-bourgeois theories of "hothouse" revolutions that have no relation to reality; it has also been necessary to reject anarchistic concepts of artificially "creating the conditions for a revolution from the outside." The mirages behind these concepts have damaged and weakened the world revolutionary processes, setting up obstacles to taking full advantage of objective forces, and destroying heroic cadres. They have disoriented and discouraged millions and set back revolutions the world over because they play into the hands of the enemy. These ideas continue to appear in new forms even after they have been exposed, so the struggle against them must go on.

1966

8

THE COMMUNIST INTERNATIONAL

One of the Finest Achievements of the World Revolutionary Movement

Fifty years ago, the leading revolutionary fighters and thinkers, representing the revolutionary Marxist-oriented working-class organizations, met in a founding convention of the Communist International.

This marked the opening of the historic stage of civilization passing from capitalism to socialism.

The gathering was deeply influenced, as was the working-class movement, by the fact that the first socialist state was a reality; the monolithic world structure of capitalism had been shattered by the birth of the Soviet Union.

The founding Congress of the Communist International was a reflection of the new world reality that the Communist movement was now a world reality. The birth of the Comintern embodied and symbolized the new meaning of proletarian internationalism. The struggle against world imperialism had risen to a new level.

The Communist International emerged as a center where the Communist Parties and other revolutionary forces exchanged experiences, worked out tactics, initiated worldwide struggles and further developed the theories of Marxism-Leninism.

The birth of the CI struck terror into the hearts of world capitalism. The vilifications, the attacks, the slanders, the provocations against the CI were never-ending. Revolutionary leaders in all parts of the world were "Comintern agents."

The dissolving of the CI did not stop the attacks, because, obviously, it was not the structure they were afraid of; they feared the ideas it represented.

For too long, the world revolutionary movement has permitted the attacks to go unanswered. For too long, the world has only heard about the weaknesses and about the mistakes. As a result, the history of the Comintern has become a victim of distortions. The contributions of the CI have become buried and distorted because of the influence of opportunism in the present movements.

The CI made mistakes, some even serious, but it remains one of the finest achievements of the world revolutionary movement.

With the advantage of new experiences, gathered from the dramatic unfolding of the world revolutionary process, the revolutionary forces of the world are beginning to take a new look at the historic contributions of the Communist International on this 50th anniversary of its memorable birth.

As the forces of the transition from capitalism to Communism gather new experiences, they are making a more positive and, because of this, a more balanced assessment of the CI's contributions. There is now a growing interest in the positive side of the

Comintern's work. There is great interest in the lessons of this greatest of all organized experiences in working class internationalism.

In many sectors of the world revolutionary movements, the new look into the history of the CI is coupled with a critical examination of some ideological and political weaknesses in the movements and Parties of today. This renewal of interest in the experiences of the CI is not emerging because anyone wants to resurrect the old structure. There is no need for a Comintern-type of world organization today. The new interest about experiences of the Comintern arise from a growing feeling that the world revolutionary movement needs to find new forms of relationships that reflect today's reality by which to continue the ideological, political and theoretical discussions and exchanges that were initiated and coordinated by the CI in its day.

The birth and the deliberations of the CI are one of the finest achievements of the revolutionary working class movement. It gave the revolutionary movement a world outlook. It was a vital instrument of the struggle from capitalism to Communism.

Its existence, its history are inseparably bound up with the development of Marxism-Leninism. Much of Lenin's thoughts were projected and developed around the political and ideological work of the CI.

The CI dealt with the problems of the revolutionary movement within the reality of its time. Both the form and the historic framework in which the questions arose have greatly changed. But most of the questions facing the revolutionary forces then are still present. They must be dealt with differently and in a different framework—but they cannot be ignored. To ignore ideological and political questions is to invite disaster.

The CI was born in the struggle against the opportunism that had engulfed the parties of the Second International. The birth of the CI was a response to the opportunism that had infested large sections of the revolutionary movement. In most social-democratic parties, the corruption of opportunism had developed beyond repair or correction. In the formative years of the CI, at its Second Congress, Lenin said, the opportunistic practices of the social-democrats "has shown that the active people in the working-class movement who adhere to the opportunist trend, are better defenders of the bourgeoisie than the bourgeoisie itself. Without their leadership of the workers, the bourgeoisie could not have remained in power." The social-democratic parties continue to give their historic service to capitalism. They are still the "interceptors" of masses who are moving along the path toward revolution.

It was clear that in many countries new revolutionary formations had to take the place of these infested groups. Thus, the struggle against opportunism in all parties resulted in the birth of new Communist and Marxist Parties in many parts of the world.

But the problems of opportunism within the working-class organizations did not disappear with the demise of the Second International. While born in the struggle against opportunism, the new revolutionary parties were not immune to its virus. The struggle against opportunism is a permanent feature of the class struggle. Under Lenin's leadership, the struggle continued against both "left" and "right" strains of the virus affecting the Communist-Marxist Parties. Lenin's brilliant book *"Left-Wing" Communism* was and remains an indispensable weapon in this battle. This raised the struggle against both manifestations of opportunism to a new level.

To its last days, the CI was a powerful bulwark in the struggle against opportunism.

In the fires of this struggle, it worked out guidelines as to what are correct relations between a revolutionary party and the masses; the relations between military and non-military methods of struggle; the correct relations between parliamentary and non-parliamentary forms of struggle. It fought against tailing behind radicalized masses, and it fought against anarchism and abstract radical-sounding programs that had no relations with mass movements. It molded and developed the science of revolution.

The struggle against opportunism on all levels is one of its historic contributions. A world organization reflecting the struggles of all continents was necessary in the struggle against the corruption of opportunism. The CPUSA disaffiliated from the CI some time before the International was discontinued. This "disaffiliation" was not only because of anti-Communist laws. It was motivated by the deep-seated opportunistic Browder revisionist trends that had already set in. The act of "disaffiliation" from a world organization only added fuel to the fires of opportunism and revisionism.

The setting has changed, but who can deny that the need to raise the struggle against the penetration of opportunistic influences is a most vital matter for the world revolutionary movement of today! Wherever there is not an open, continuous struggle against it, opportunism penetrates and takes over. Is it not a sad fact of today's reality that opportunism has engulfed some parties and groups?

Opportunism is a virus of accommodation. It is hidden behind right policies or left phrases, but it is accommodation. It is a form of capitulation. It is an attempt to bypass struggle. As a rule, it is justified as a tactical necessity. It is the most insidious of all ideological penetrations. Very often unnoticed, it eats at the revolutionary fabric of a working-class movement, and is not noticed until there is a critical moment. At such moments the class struggle needs its maximum strength; it needs concentration; it needs revolutionary will and determination. An organization that has become weakened by the virus of opportunistic accommodation cannot rise to meet the challenge of such critical moments.

World exchanges between parties, worldwide discussions and assessments are a necessity in the struggle against the influences of opportunism. The influences of opportunism are themselves obstacles for such relationships.

The CI was a most effective tribunal of proletarian internationalism. Its very existence was a buffer against the influence of divisive, narrow bourgeois and petty-bourgeois nationalism within the working-class movement. It was itself a product of the concept of proletarian internationalism. It was the wellspring of internationalism. It initiated world-wide movements of working-class solidarity.

Who can deny that the world revolutionary movement, including the Marxist sector, suffers from the negative influences of narrow nationalism? The CI recognized the role of nationalism as a factor in the struggle for social progress. It did not deny its role in struggles, but it did not forget its class base or its limitations. It stubbornly stuck to its concept of working-class internationalism. It viewed nationalism, and movements and struggles motivated by nationalism, within the framework of the class struggle and the role of classes.

The CI was a working-class instrument of struggle. It fought with working-class stubbornness and tenacity against all ideas of "classlessness." It firmly held on to the Marxist-Leninist concept that the class struggle is the pivot around which all the forces of social progress revolve. It fought against all illusions regarding the forces of capitalism. It recognized the irreconcilable contradictions between the two classes. The setting has changed but challenges to these ideas persist.

Are there not now illusions about "classless" paths to social progress? Are there not groups within the revolutionary spectrum that deliberately sidestep the class struggle? Are there not old theories in new dress that deny the revolutionary role of the working class? Are there not pseudo-revolutionary petty-bourgeois theories whereby the peasants are presented as the vanguard of the revolutionary process? Is not the concept of "third force" one of these "classless" concepts? In this connection, what Comrade Palmiro Togliatti said at a Cominform meeting in 1950 is instructive, both as to the need for international exchanges between Parties, as well as to the matter that he dealt with:

This ideology of the "Third Force" is, at the very first glance, a crude deception. What "Third Way" can there be for the sincere Socialist between the interests of the working class and toiling masses and the interests of monopoly capitalism and the privileged castes? It is impossible to stand "half-way" between the Soviet Union, pursuing a consistent peace policy, and the imperialists, who are poisoning the world by advocating and provoking a third world conflict.

The false theory of a "Third Force" is nothing more than an instrument utilized by the Right-wing Social Democrats for their foul work, who link the land of Socialism with the leading groups of imperialists and warmongers in the United States and Britain.

Doing their ignoble work, the apostles of the "Third Force" always make it possible to say that in each separate country they are "honest and loyal administrators" of the interests of the capitalist bourgeoisie and faithful servants of imperialism in international affairs. . . .

They substituted advocacy of the "neutral," so-called "Third Force" and blended it with the old opportunist, anti-Marxist and anti-scientific theory of the change from "national" capitalism to a super-capitalist organization, which should be modeled on, and led by, American monopoly capital. . . .

Proletarian, Socialist internationalism constitutes the basis for the solidarity of the working people and cooperation between the peoples in defending their independence from the machinations of imperialism, in defending peace.

This was a struggle for a working-class approach to questions. Are there not efforts today to speak of the "classless," "big powers"? Are there not efforts to break the ranks of the socialist world with talk against "blocks" and the need to "break up all blocks?"

Another example of how the CI fought for a correct class approach to struggle was its 1929 resolution on events in China. It was critical of some Chinese Communist leaders for advocating an alliance with the kulaks (the rich peasants) at a time when the issue of foreign aggression against China was nonexistent.

In the light of some present-day erroneous theories of the Mao leadership about the role of the peasantry, this early criticism is of special interest. It is of interest also because of some errors of the Communist Party of Indonesia in their attitude toward some feudal landlords. This weakness was a factor when the counter-revolutionary forces struck. The Party did not have the support of the victims of the feudal lords because they had not conducted the struggles against the feudal elements effectively enough.

The CI resolution said:

And it is at this point that we must deal, first of all, with the question of the attitude to the kulak, since it is in this respect that the Chinese comrades have permitted the most substantial errors. The question is not a new one for the Chinese Party. . . . They continued to count the Chinese kulak among the allies of the proletariat. . . .

The slogan of "alliance with the kulaks" advanced in a number of Chinese Party documents does not follow by any means from the Leninist formula. . . .

If it pursues the line of alliance with the kulak, or even if it only fails to intensify the struggle against the kulak, the Communist Party will be unable to take the lead in the class struggle of the village poor; it will dull the edge of their activities, to the benefit of the exploiting kulak strata in the Chinese village. . . .

This task should be undertaken without "side glances" at the kulaks, without the fear that he will "quit the revolution." Such fears are completely incomprehensible in the present situation, when the Kuomintang, not unsuccessfully, is using the kulaks to exert pressure on the peasant. . . .

The organization of the agricultural proletariat, and the uniting of the village poor, are essential to the struggle for the leading role of the proletariat in relation to the basic peasant masses in the bourgeois-democratic revolution. . . .

To end our letter, we would like to give warning against wholly incorrect and purely Trotskyist conclusions about the socialist character of the Chinese revolution. . . . In giving greater precision to the decision of the Sixth CCP congress on the attitude of the different social strata in the village, and in dropping the opportunist slogan "alliance with the kulak," we do not waver in our analysis of the character of the coming stage of the Chinese revolution as the bourgeois-democratic stage. . . .

At the same time, it must be pointed out that the uniting of the proletariat with the village poor and the consolidation of the leading role of the proletariat over the entire peasantry, which is already happening at the present stage of the liberation struggle, together with other circumstances, should in their turn have a favorable reaction on the speed with which the bourgeois-democratic stage develops into the socialist stage of the revolution.

The position and the advice of the Comintern was correct. The Chinese revolution did not skip the stage of the bourgeois-democratic revolution.

But the same ideas about "skipping" stages of struggle are very much alive today. The rejection of the Trotskyite concepts by the Comintern and by experience of life has not put an end to them. Some promising national liberation movements have failed because of this same error—the error of thinking that it is possible to "skip" stages, or that it is possible to "create" and "make" revolutionary situations without regard to objective factors keeps reappearing. Only a revolutionary movement that takes into account the objective reality can "make" revolutions.

If the CI had not accomplished another thing except its contribution in working out the "Thesis on the National and Colonial Qusetion," this would have fully justified its place of honor in the pages of history. In this memorable document, Lenin laid out the concept of the "world revolutionary process" that combined the dynamic of the socialist revolution with that of the national and colonial liberation revolution. This thesis was possible only because of the struggle against the influences of great power chauvinism and racism. It was a powerful blow against opportunism of all shades. There is the need for a continuous struggle for the concepts in this thesis. The need is to see the primacy of the class struggle, the primacy of the revolutionary transition to socialism and the inter-relationship and the dynamics that emerge when the anti-colonial, national liberation revolutions sweeping the world are seen as a part of this world revolutionary process. All attempts to downgrade the role of the working class and the attempts to drive a wedge between the forces of world socialism and the national liberation movements are attempts to deny the essence of the Leninist thesis contained in the CI "Thesis on the National and Colonial Question." The world has changed, but the inter-relationship of the forces for socialism and national liberation within the over-all revolutionary process remains a correct and vital concept.

It is difficult to see how the struggle against world fascism would have developed without the bold initiatives and organizing role of the CI. The Seventh Congress of the CI gathered all of the world's experiences and laid out the tactical and strategic plans for the struggle against fascism. The threat was worldwide. The CI plan was worldwide. It remains one of history's greatest contributions to human progress. The concept was bold and simple. It was to mold a unity of all forces whose interests were threatened by fascism. To unite all whose interests paralleled—no matter how momentary the parallel interests were. It was a tactic of broad unity but a unity in which the working class was the dominant factor.

To get a measure of this contribution one only needs to compare this with the betrayal of the social-democrats. Time after time they refused to join in united efforts against fascism. They hid behind their demagogy of advocating "class against class." They, who had given up the class struggle and betrayed it, now used the "class against class" slogan as a fig leaf. Even the conservative Socialist Party of the United States took up the cry "class against class." It was sheer demagogy. It was a left cover for their refusal to join in the struggle against fascism. It was a left cover for the old opportunism of the Socialist Party.

It can also be said that the CI's contribution in the revolutionary struggle against imperialist wars was historic. It was a major contribution for the advancement of mankind. In 1928 it stated, "War is inseparable from capitalism. The struggle against war above all calls for a clear insight into its nature, cause, etc." It prodded and criticized parties. "One of the principle defects in the work of parties against war is their excessively abstract, schematic and even shallow attitude to the question of war." They asked the Communist Parties to do more in exposing imperialism.

In 1936 before the onslaught of World War II, it prodded again:

The fact that fascism has begun to undertake a military offensive . . . the fact that the reactionary leaders of Social Democracy give support to fascism under the cover of hypocritical anxiety to "maintain peace," the fact that they cultivated the disunity of the proletariat, which leads to the interests of the international proletarian solidarity being sacrificed to the interest of the national bourgeoisie all urgently require the working class movements of all countries to carry out a united international policy of the working class in the interests of maintaining peace.

The CI was not only the depository of the worldwide revolutionary experiences. These experiences became the source material for the further development of the science of Marxism-Leninism. This was an invaluable service for the new, developing Marxist Parties.

The above are only indications of some of the areas where the CI made fundamental contributions to the development of the world revolutionary movement. These are areas where the framework, the specific set of circumstances have changed, but to one extent or the other, the questions, problems and weaknesses continue within the new reality of today.

These are also areas which need constant international airing. They are areas that respond to exchanges of experiences on a global scale.

Without question, there are many negative lessons one can draw from the existence of the CI. Even in the framework of its time it was structurally too centralized. Also, in many instances it did not carefully give consideration to the differences in the national scene in which the different parties functioned. At times it tended to push for uniform global tactical approaches. But these negative expressions in no way should lead to negative overall conclusions about the historic contribution of the Comintern.

The contributions of the Comintern argue for:

—new concepts of relationships between Communist-Marxist parties;

—the need for some method of exchanges and discussion between parties;

—the need for a continuous world-wide struggle against the influence of opportunism;

—collective estimates of trends and relationship of class forces;

—the need for some world initiatives in some areas of struggle. This is necessary especially in the struggle against imperialism and war;

—the need for continuous transmission of news and views about the class struggle on a world scale. Marxist newspapers need to have available news of the class battles throughout the world.

The problems have changed. The set of circumstances are different, but the need for closer relations, stronger bonds and firmer unity of the world Communist-Marxist movement remains an urgent task.

1965

9

POLITICAL-IDEOLOGICAL STORMS

The central ideological and political storms of our times swirl around the issues created by imperialism. These winds affect every one. There is no effective insulation against them. To pretend one is not affected is self delusion. Neutrality, non-involvement—being a noncombatant—are all small, slippery, transitory, very fragile pebbles from which one can slip in either direction at any time. Moreover, in the context of today's realities such positions are fraudulent.

In today's world it is impossible not to react to the central question of our times. Are you for or against imperialism? Are you enough against imperialism that you will get off the slippery rock of nonalignment and join those who are fighting imperialism?

In this struggle, the forces of imperialism are working to get two kinds of support. They want open support, but they are also working to draw forces from the ranks of the opposition to a position of "neutrality." It is a hard law of struggle. When forces who are in the ranks of the opposition to imperialism move to a position of nonalignment, it is a victory for imperialism. But when forces who support imperialism move to a position of "neutrality," that is a defeat for imperialism.

Imperialism cannot win any kind of mass support based on honesty or truth. Its policies are against the real self interests of the great majority of all people. Therefore it must resort to falsehood and demagogy. It must work to create a fog of confusion and misunderstanding. It is of necessity forced to use the technique of the big lie. This fact adds a unique element to the ideological and political struggles of our day.

Just And Unjust Wars

Most nations now accept the formula that all nations and peoples have a right to national independence, that all people have an inherent right to determine for themselves what they want to do with their lives, their national riches, their land and everything in it.

It is an accepted formula—in words—but it is not an accepted practice.

There is only one force that has trampled on this elementary right of nations. For imperialism it has been and is a way of life. National independence and imperialism are opposites.

If one accepts the formula of the right of nations to independence then it follows that the struggle against the forces that threaten such independence is a just struggle. It further follows that when such struggles lead to a military conflict it is a just war by the forces who are fighting for national liberation.

Because it is a right, it is a just struggle. Because it is just, peoples and nations have a right to fight for or defend it by any means available, including an armed struggle. A struggle for in-independence, a struggle to preserve independence is a just struggle. People fighting for independence do not ask others to make moral judgments of their right. They do ask the world to support them in their just cause. We Communists supported, we are supporting, and we will continue to support the struggles for national liberation. In one way or another this central question touches on all political and ideological questions.

Neo-Colonialism Is Imperialism

Because U.S. imperialism emerged on the world scene at a stage when the forces of anti-imperialism were already a developing factor, it was forced to develop the art of neo-colonialism. U.S. imperialism emerged at a moment when the world front of capitalism was shattered by the appearance of a revolutionary socialist power, the Soviet Union.

U.S. imperialism extended its tentacles of exploitation at a moment when cracks began to appear in the walls of the old imperialist empires. Its development did not follow the traditional path of empire building—of outright militarily oppressed colonies. That it did not follow this course everywhere did not stop it from such a course in Cuba, Philippine Islands, Puerto Rico, as well as in dozens of smaller island areas and peoples.

For years the apologists for U.S. imperialism used this fact to deny that the United States was an imperialist power, as they demagogically used the revolutionary traditions of the war of independence.

U.S. imperialism is the oldest practitioner of neo-colonialism.

Imperialism gives up old methods of aggression only when it is forced to do so; it may use new tactics, but it returns to the old methods whenever it can. In this sense, military aggression remains very much a part of the imperialist arsenal. It is manifest either by the open, direct aggression, as in Vietnam, or by the indirect, supportive aggression, as in the Middle East, where the main power behind the Israeli aggression against the Arab countries is U.S. imperialism.

Neo-colonialism is imperialism's new way of adjusting to the new power of anti-imperialism. It is an adaptation for this historic period when the balance of forces has shifted. It is a form of colonialism when imperialism has lost its direct political and military control over enslaved countries. It has become the dominant form of imperialist oppression and exploitation. The forces of world anti-imperialism must update their tactics to counteract this new phenomenon. Neo-colonialism is not just "soft" imperialism; its iron heel is just as brutal.

The newly liberated countries are not yet out of the imperialist woods. They remain objects of intensive exploitation. The profits the corporations of imperialist powers take out of these countries mean for them unbuilt factories, electric power stations, schools, hospitals, and houses. This exploitation continues to be the main cause for the extreme poverty and overall misery.

Most of the newly liberated countries are celebrating their 25th anniversaries. What has happened in this quarter century testifies to the tenacity of imperialism's grip. About two-thirds of the people in the non-socialist world live in these newly liberated countries, but even today they account for less than one-tenth of capitalist industrial production. The old imperialist powers still can boast of controlling more than 70 percent of the foreign trade of these lands. And the gap is becoming a gulf. The share of the developing countries in world trade has declined from 27 percent in 1953 to 19 percent in 1967.

This cannot be regarded as mere stagnation. Out of 350 million families who are engaged in farming in the capitalist world, 250 million live mainly in those areas where neo-colonialism holds sway. And they still use the hoe and wooden plough as their principal work tools. There are no profits to be made from building roads, schools or irrigation projects, and there are no imperialist private funds available for these social projects.

Neo-colonialism makes much noise about aid to developing countries, but this aid can propel these young nations down a pathway to bankruptcy. For 95 of such countries receiving aid in the form of loans and grants from imperialist powers, indebtness has increased five-fold since 1953. The annual interest payments on these mortgages runs to five billion dollars, and this sum increases from year to year! Increasingly the new loans go to pay the interest on the old loans. The economic gap between the imperialist countries and the underdeveloped countries continues to widen. The countries of Latin America, for example, suffered a trade loss of one billion dollars to U.S. imperialism in 1970. This is loot extracted from these countries that could otherwise use their accumulated capital for industrial development, for schools, housing, hospitals, and, of course, for higher wages.

Thus neo-colonialism moves to replace the old direct political control with economic and more indirect political manipulations, and places an even greater emphasis on ideological controls. Increasingly the structure and the priority of state monopoly capitalism are programmed to the aims and problems of the neo-colonial operations.

The foreign aid programs are totally geared into this operation. The same is true of all U.S. government subsidies and "gifts." This large network of special federal banks and financial institutions that use taxpayers' dollars to protect the foreign property and profits of the monopolists, are key links in this network.

A system of U.S. government and private officials handles special loans and subsidies throughout the capitalist world. The CIA pay-off system supplements the payoff men of the corporations. There are foreign "aid" government experts in every field—labor, culture, finance, agriculture. But, above all, they are experts in securing the upper hand for U.S. capitalism.

It is now an accepted practice to staff these departments of the state, with direct representatives of the corporations for whose benefit the government authority is utilized. As a rule, these staff members are appointed, and there is no public control over them. In most cases they are in closer touch with the monopoly combines than with the government. Where there are no special departments, there are special presidential "advisers." All of these make up the extra-legal "invisible government." The closer a government department or an "adviser" gets to the imperialist foreign policy operations, the more "invisible" they become. They are invisible only to the people. They are fully visible to the corporations and banks they serve. This invisible sector of the government continues to expand its operations at an alarming speed. The development of state monopoly capitalism—a phrase denoting the increased role of the state dominated by the monopoly corporations—is influenced by the tasks set for it by neo-colonialism.

In earlier periods imperialism ruled either by having the military forces present or by dealing with some despot-ruler representing corrupt feudal lords or through other puppets.

Since the end of the Second World War over 60 new countries have won political independence and the problem of imperialist domination has become more difficult.

Now in most cases imperialism must deal with national states. In most cases these new countries now fight for their national interests. Imperialism is also aware that these newly liberated countries do have another path if they so choose. The mere existence of the socialist world—like the existence of a union in a shop gives power to all workers—gives the newly liberated countries leverage. This has changed the odds. The new countries are more equal. In past periods the corporations went after immediate and direct profits. The task of neo-colonialism is more complicated. Because the new countries do have an alternate path available the imperialist countries are forced to deal with the overall question of which path will the newly freed countries travel.

In a sense the central task of neo-colonialism is to plant the seeds, to nurture the roots, to fortify the tendency of capitalist development in the newly independent countries. The aim is the same but they are forced to take a longer range viewpoint. In the interest of these longer ranged profits they put on the act of benevolence and even postpone taking all of the booty.

In the pursuit of nurturing the roots of capitalism the agents of neo-colonialism pay special attention to the rising capitalist class in these countries. In a very limited way, they even provide loans for the development of some industries—like the manufacture of parts of machinery. This is necessary for many reasons. It gives the imperialist a base of operation—it keeps the economy moving—it plants the roots of capitalist development, and besides, it is profitable. But in all of the numerous schemes of industrial development, there are built-in safeguards to keep such industries in a subordinate position to the imperialist corporations.

Because the monopolies are not ready to risk their investments the state takes the people's tax dollars, makes "loans" to the newly independent countries so they can buy machinery and equipment from U.S. monopolies and then to top it off the state acts as an insurance company for the whole project.

In addition, the growth of the state sector of the economy in the developing countries was always a bitter pill for the neo-colonialists to swallow. They now view it as a temporary evil. They hope to destroy that evil after the roots of capitalism are planted.

To one extent or another all of the liberated countries face a crisis of direction—whether to take the socialist or the capitalist path. It is a period when the struggle must move to a qualitatively higher level. If it does not the situation either stagnates or there will be retrogression. In some countries, the decision has been made, but in most countries it remains a grave dilemma. In some countries, the shift is a matter of days; for others it has become a moment of years' duration. The struggle is closely related to the development of the class struggle in these countries. This struggle is of deep concern to the neo-colonialists because these newly independent countries can be a source of profit for imperialism only if they can be kept in the world capitalist orbit. It is also a fact that they will remain in that orbit only if their economic development moves into the channels of world capitalism. To resolve this question in favor of capitalism has become a primary overall objective of neo-colonialism. It is a struggle over which path to follow.

The aid programs are specifically designed to act as stimuli toward a capitalist development. Special institutions have been set up to keep the independent countries within the capitalist orbit. For example, the Agency of International Development and the government-controlled foreign investment funds in the banks that handle most of the aid, are geared to force the newly liberated countries into the capitalist orbit.

This intensifies the dilemma of the newly liberated countries because 80 percent of the total influx of new capital now comes from the "aid" devices of imperialism. The string that is attached to all of them is: Remain in the capitalist orbit—or else.

Another neo-colonialist gimmick is to select repesentatives of business as junior partners in U.S. imperialist-controlled industrial enterprises.

Neo-colonialism is *not* nonviolent imperialism. In today's world use of the Marines is not always advisable; therefore, U.S. neo-colonialism has developed its own "invisible" military force— the counter-insurgency corps, which is, in fact, the counter-revolutionary insurgency corps of world imperialism.

This is government-sponsored and financially sustained gangsterism; it is a hydra-headed monster, consisting of the CIA, the Green Berets, the Army, the Air Force and the Marines, each with its own special sector! The instruments of these groups are murder, assassination, frameup, political and financial corruption and terror. It has now come to light that President Kennedy on a number of occasions seriously discussed the subject of whether and how Fidel Castro should be assassinated. This was at the very time that Kennedy was launching his much-touted Alliance for Progress programs.

The U.S. imperialist policy of counter-revolutionary insurgency also includes a bigger role for the police departments of the oppressed nations. In testimony before the Senate Subcommittee on American Republics Affairs, Professor David Burke of Indiana University stated:

> I think we have to face a reality. The reality is that when the insurgents appear, the government will call upon the army to eliminate the insurgents. But there comes a point—and this came in Cuba in 1957 and 1958 when Castro was in the Sierra Maestra—there can come a point when the army cannot handle this kind of situation because the military establishment tends to use too much force, tends to use the wrong techniques and tends therefore to polarize the population and gradually force the majority of those who are politically active to support the revolutionary or insurgent force. The troops are not trained—their orientation is not such that they are really competent to handle this kind of a problem. Whereas a civil police force —with the people all the time carrying on normal functions of control—therefore can move very quickly whenever an insurgent problem develops.

Thus, as a part of its neo-colonialist policies and the launching of the Alliance for Progress in 1962 under President Kennedy's direction, U.S. imperialism established the Inter-American Police Academy. As of February 1969, there were 3,000 students—60 percent from Latin-America—graduated for police work. In addition to these training programs in the United States, AID sends "Public Safety Advisors" to Latin America. In 1968 at least 91 such persons were employed by AID.

The End Is In Sight

The power behind the shift in economic relations is the shift in the political and ideological outlook of the people. This change in thought patterns determines the nature of political parties and alliances.

The old alliances in which the rich landowners and the capitalist elements were the dominant force have lost their mass base. Only the new alliances in which the working class, the Left and Communist forces are a factor measure up to the new levels of political and ideological outlook of the masses. It is the new alliances that are emerging as the new political and state power. This new revolutionary element in the political alliances influences the form of the struggle against imperialism. In many countries this fact is changing the essence and nature of state power. They are forced to pass anti-imperialist laws.

Three generations of Rockefellers have had their way in Venezuela. For three generations they have robbed and pillaged the people and riches of Venezuela. Now there is light at the end of the tunnel for the people of Venezuela. *The Wall Street Journal* of December 10, 1971, reports this fact:

Caracas—Four decades ago, Venezuelans were living under the harsh dictatorship of Gen. Juan Vicente Gomez, and U.S. oilmen couldn't have been happier. Americans holding leases to Venezuela's rich oil fields praised the country's petroleum laws as "the best in the world."

The U.S. executives, of course, may have been a bit prejudiced. After all, their companies' attorneys wrote most of the laws for Gen, Gomez. [Mainly attorneys on Rockefeller's payroll.—G.H.]

But times have changed drastically, nationalism is rampant, and oil and nationalism don't mix. Nowadays, oilmen rarely have anything good to say about Venezuela's petroleum laws, especially one decreeing that oil leases will revert to the government beginning in 1983.

Clearly, the surge of nationalism that is sweeping Latin America has caught hold in Venezuela. Nation after nation here is asserting its right to own and manage its natural resources: practically none will give out new oil claims except as joint ventures with state companies. Chile has seized the holdings of three large U.S. copper companies. Peru has taken over its biggest oil company and all mining claims. Bolivia has nationalized Gulf Oil Co.'s holdings and U.S. Steel Corp.'s lead and zinc mine. Guyana has expropriated bauxite mines.

To protect his massive oil interests in Latin America, Rockefeller, after returning from his mission on behalf of Nixon, included among his "Recommendations for Action" a continuation of the police training:

The United States should respond to requests for assistance of the police and security forces of the hemisphere nations by providing them with the essential tools to do the job. Accordingly, the United States should meet reasonable requests from other hemisphere governments for trucks, jeeps, helicopters and like equipment to provide mobility and logistical support for these forces—for radios and other command control equipment for proper communications among the forces—for small arms for security forces.

This is the worldwide program of "Vietnamization" for the counter-revolutionary insurgency of U.S. imperialism.

The growth of monopolies and the development of state monopoly capitalism are formations peculiar to the imperialist stage of capitalist development. These are influenced by the difficulties and roadblocks facing present-day imperialism. The state now has new assignments in carrying out the policies of imperialist aggressions, a new and heightened role in carrying out neo-colonial policies. The aid programs are state-sponsored, and the grants are state grants, while private imperialist investments are insured by the state against all losses. These grants and loans are, in fact, subsidies coming out of the people's tax dollars to augment the super-profits of private monopolies.

New problems have appeared, however, from the fact that neo-colonialism is forced to deal with national governments, with states that are supported by militant liberation movements. These new problems have been turned over to the imperialist state. The state gives aid grants only to governments who move in the capitalist orbit or promise to do so. To get the support of the governments of Australia, New Zealand, South Korea, Thailand and the Philippines for the Vietnamese aggression, the U.S. government paid out billions of dollars as "aid!" These huge sums have been kept secret from the people of the countries involved as well as from the people of the United States. The state also has assumed a new role in the imperialist operations because of its role as the enforcer of ever higher taxes at home in order to pay for the war and the "subsidies" incurred in the imperialist operations of oppression and exploitation.

But it is not only the state that has a dominant role in carrying out neo-colonialist policies. A trade union leader who supports capitalism's foreign adventures can become a very important cog in the wheels of neo-colonialism. The AFL-CIO leadership is a case in point; U.S. imperialism has assigned an expanded role in its operations to Meany, Lovestone and the cadres around them. The International Department of the AFL-CIO, headed by Lovestone, is to all intents and purposes a branch of the CIA. It is a department of U.S. imperialism. That is its only function. Its specific assignment is to keep the trade unions of the oppressed countries in the capitalist orbit. The AFL-CIO Foreign Affairs Department has increasingly become an instrument of imperialism and exploitation at a moment of history when economic and indirect methods must be used. This department was set up by using large sums of money provided by the monopolies and by the government for its ideological dirty work. Leaders of U.S. trade unions are used as funnels through which money is passed to corrupt trade union officials in the oppressed countries.

To be effective, neo-colonialism must try to hide its basic imperialist nature; it must hide behind facades like the "Alliance for Progress," "Good Neighbor Policy"; it must mouth words about "brotherhood and peace." As U.S. imperialism has been forced to turn to neo-colonialist practices, it has increased its use of cadres with social-democratic or Left "covers." It was the social-democrats who organized and ran the "trade-union schools" to train imperialist-orientated cadre for the trade unions of Latin America. A few years back, exposés revealed that these schools were financed and run by the CIA to train forces to control the trade union movements of Latin America. These schools had a "socialist" cover to train imperialist agents.

There is a very important lesson here. After the exposures, some leading personalities of the Socialist Party of America admitted they had been very much involved in these activities. In fact they organized and ran the schools. Some said they did not know the money for their "schools" came from the CIA. This confession only adds an additional dimension to the story. The reason they and their Trotskyite cohorts did not know where the money came from is that they were all in the same business—the business of anti-Communism. The anti-Communism of these people who speak of socialism, led them to an alliance with the forces of imperialism. U.S. imperialism wanted anti-Communist class-collaborationist trade union leaders in Latin America. The leaders of the Socialist Party set up and ran schools to train such leaders The CIA would have had some difficulties in organizing the school. But the fact is that they didn't have to. They were well pleased with the anti-Communist school run by "socialists." All they had to do was to finance it. This they did through one of its "foundations."

The role and power of the socialist countries is a reality imperialism cannot evade—it is the single most formidable roadblock in its path. Socialism has removed one-third of the world from the capitalist orbit. And, beyond that, the socialist world is an economic, political and military source of strength for all anti-imperialist forces. This fact of life has put an end for all time to imperialism's being able to say to its victims, "You have to bow to our demands because you have nowhere else to go."

The socialist world, therefore, is the decisive force in the struggle to determine which direction the liberated countries will take. It is the great magnet drawing them to the non-capitalist path, it is the only source of capital aid without strings for countries who choose a humanist future—the socialist way to progress.

Much is written about the diplomatic, political and economic activities between the socialist countries and the countries referred to as the "third world." What is not generally known is that this is not the ordinary activity between states. It is related to the struggle between the two world systems. It is a struggle over which of these paths the newly liberated countries will take. It is a feature of the world class struggle that this has emerged on a new plateau. The policy of the socialist countries is geared to make it possible for these countries to take the socialist path if they so desire. Because of its high level of development and because of the policy its leadership pursues, the Soviet Union is making a historic contribution in this fight against world imperialism.

These are some of the maneuvers of neo-colonialism. But as is the case with the best made plans of mice and men, life changes them. There is a growing contradiction between the national interests of the developing countries and the neo-colonialists. There is taking place a class differentiation within the developing countries. Countries tied in any form to the world capitalist structure are affected adversely by the crises in the major capitalist countries.

Neo-colonialism can slow down the world revolutionary process, but it can neither stop nor turn back the clock of history.

As the world revolutionary process keeps destroying the bases of imperialism it becomes more difficult for the forces of imperialism to hide their true aims.

Actions do speak louder than words. For years the imperialist powers led by the United States prevented the United Nations from setting up a Committee on Colonialism. Finally in 1961 the majority of the delegations made up of the delegates from the socialist countries, the newly liberated countries and others voted to set up such a Committee. After it was set up the United States and Britain became members. Now, ten years later, the United States and Britain have withdrawn from the Committee. What is the problem? The Committee on Colonialism did some things against colonialism. The UN sent delegations to investigate the inhuman, brutal conditions in colonial Africa. And the Committee on Colonialism drafted a resolution that was passed over the objections of the United States and Britain that stated: "All forms of colonialism are a crime against humanity and a violation of the UN Charter." The resignation of the U.S. and British delegates speaks louder than all of the hypocritical speeches they have made about colonialism.

For ten years they sabotaged the work of the Committee from the inside. When this was no longer possible, they walked out.

1972

10

REVISIONISM AND COUNTER-REVOLUTION

The events in Czechoslovakia served as a test tube for many ideological processes. Events moved swiftly—so the events there were to a political scientist what a fruit fly is to a biologist. One day some were "revising" Marxism and a few days later they were openly in the camp of counterrevolution.

In Czechoslovakia the affinity between revisionism and counter-revolution emerged in sharp focus. Revisionism prepares the soil for counter-revolution. Revisionism is the softening up process. It destroys revolutionary vigilance. It creates the confusion and the divisions that are necessary for counter-revolution.

As a witness let us call on one of the ideological fruit flies. This witness is interesting because since he wrote the words that we will use, he has come out openly as a defender and a proponent of the worst features of capitalism and imperialism. In fact, his conversion from a reviser of Marxism-Leninism to an open proponent of capitalism seemingly took only a few days—in fact, the few hours that it takes one to fly from Prague to New York City. The witness is Ivan Svitak, a leading "theoretician," an active figure in the 1968-69 Czechoslovakia. Today this Svitak is a leading figure in an educational institution sponsored by a U.S. counter-intelligence agency. He is an interesting witness because, among other things, he proves that the line between those who set out to destroy Marxism-Leninsm by revision and distortion and those who openly extol capitalism is a quite thin one.

Now let us see how he presented his revisionist views in Czecho-slovakia in 1967-68, this popular "Marxist intellectual" figure on Czechoslovakian television, radio, newspapers and magazines who espoused a "socialism with a humane face."

He started by saying "Lenin must be separated from Marx." In great haste he added the reasons for this dissection. "We must distinguish Marx's great thought about the liberating role of the working class from Lenin's specifically Russian thought about the leading role of the Communist Party."

Marx would have had some choice words for our witness had he heard himself described as "an earnest European with deep roots in the European culture based on antiquity, Christianity, the Renaissance and enlightenment. But his teachings were taken over in the East of Europe and in Asia where there was no enlighten-ment." In the hands of this vulgar revisionist, Marx's deep inter-nationalism and the profound international significance of Marxism is turned into "West European" chauvinism. Of course, such a caricature of Marx has nothing to do with the real revolutionary Marx. The caricature image of Lenin has nothing to do with his genius and leadership at the most crucial turning-point in history.

The aim of all revisionists is to downgrade the role of the Com-munist Party. It is an attempt to take the class essence, the class approach out of all questions. Once the working class is out of the way, once the leading role of the Communist Party is destroyed, the path is open for counter-revolution.

To the revisionists, capitalist and imperialist countries are "capitalist democracies" but the working-class rule in the socialist countries are "totalitarian dictatorships."

They are ready to accept the "mythology of Marx," if only Lenin had not used this "mythology" to develop and concretize the concepts of victorious working-class struggles and applied it to developing concepts of working-class power and the necessity to build a vanguard revolutionary political party.

Our vulgar witness draws the logical conclusions from his dis-tortions. "Marxism-Leninism is a functional ideological tool used by apparatuses to manipulate masses and not objective truthful and historical interpretations." To the vulgar revisionist the revo-lutionary party becomes "an apparatus." And leadership in struggle becomes "manipulation of masses." Marxism-Leninism becomes their "ideological tool." From this point the transition of Svitak to counter-revolution was a matter of days. On his first U.S. appearance he called on the United States to attack Czechoslovakia by military means.

We can now let the vulgar revisionist witness return to his present ideological home prepared for him by the most brutal, most warlike class of exploiters in all of man's history. Here he now defends the class that enslaves and exploits more people than any other in history. Here he defends the class that exploits 80,000,000 workers, holds some 40,000,000 of its people in special bondage by a system of racism. Here he can sing glory to the class that is killing hundreds of thousands of men, women and children in Vietnam. On this ideological dunghill Svitak still crows about "the freedom of man." This is the inevitable pattern of vulgar revisionism if it is permitted to go unchallenged.

Marxism-Leninism is one indivisible revolutionary social science. It cannot be separated in form or content.

It is a living science. It is a science of life. Like all sciences it gathers experiences. It goes through trial and error and the corrections of errors. It continually studies the past and probes the new, the future. And in this process it develops, it grows. The aim of revisionism is to stop this process, to direct it to dead-end pathways.

One can confidently say to all vulgar revisionists: your attempts are coming too late in history. Your efforts may cause a disruption here or there, but the very processes of life and the class struggle have condemned you to failure. Marxism-Leninism is the process of truth. It is indivisible, it is indestructible.

1970

11

NEO-COLONIALISM NEEDS A LABOR COVER

Jay Lovestone is an old renegade from the working-class movement. If he ever had any, he sold his soul and body to big business 40-50 years ago.

He has been a most obedient toadying flunky to monopoly capital ever since. He has been like the pet poodle to the Rockefellers and Du Ponts. He has made a lifetime career of manufacturing falsehoods, of fingering working-class leaders, perfecting the art of frameup and corruption. In the top councils of the AFL-CIO leadership his special task is to feed the more ignorant with the CIA, imperialist line. He writes the foreign policy sections of Meany's reports and speeches. He proposes the imperialist-supporting press releases that go out in Meany's name. While others in the service of imperialism have carried out assassinations —it is Lovestone who has been the fingerman.

This operation, in the name of labor, supporting the policies and actions of the United States has grown into a large secret underground network.

Lovestone heads the so-called AFL-CIO Department of International Affairs. When leaders of the AFL-CIO have had a falling out they have admitted that his "department" is nothing more than a cover for the work of the CIA and other departments of imperialism. It is a department of imperialist aggression specializing in the labor field. This is class collaboration in total. This is an operation paid for mainly by large corporations, used to enslave workers of other countries. It is an instrument for keeping the wages of these workers down. The lower wages in these countries are the source of higher profits. But it serves their purposes. The U.S. corporations use these areas for runaway shops. They use the threat of moving their factories to cut the wages here. So this "department" of the AFL-CIO is in the full sense of the word an anti-working-class department. Lovestone prepares the soil so it is profitable for U.S. corporations to transfer their operations to other parts of the world. U.S. corporations pay $15 to $20 per month to their workers in South Korea and Taiwan. But it is Lovestone's "department" with Meany's blessings that works to keep the unions there subservient and ineffective.

In keeping with its policy of supporting U.S. imperialism, the top leadership of the AFL-CIO have just issued another pamphlet. It is called "Who is the Imperialist?"

The introduction states:

"Imperialism" is a word often heard these days. At work, at meals, wherever people get together and talk about the sad state of the world, imperialism is blamed again and again.

If imperialism is causing so much of the world's trouble, then free men everywhere should know the facts.

What are the facts? What nations recklessly seek to extend their domination and control over a tense and nervous world?

Who is the Imperialist?

In his covering letter, Lovestone states:

By the presentation of clear statistics, facts and maps, the history of the last thirty years of Communist territorial expansion is contrasted with the efforts of the free world to implement the principles of self-determination and national independence.

Clarence Darrow, the noted militant people's attorney, who had to face countless stoolpigeon provocateurs and professional liars, used to say that the most difficult witness to handle is the psychopathic liar, because he puts forward a total falsehood and then it is easy for him to fit in the pieces.

Lovestone's total falsehood is Hitler's big lie. This is the essence of his pamphlet. The big lie, as it was for Hitler, has been the framework for the work of Lovestone and his AFL-CIO "department." As it was with Goebbels, so it is with Lovestone. The more U.S. imperialism is exposed, the bigger gets the big lie.

What is Lovestone's total falsehood? He takes the real world and turns it upside down. The world is in a period of transition from capitalism to socialism. This has accelerated the worldwide revolutionary process. It has unhinged the old order of things. People are not accepting the status quo of capitalist domination. Oppressed countries are rebelling. They want the right of self-determination. Others have moved to replace capitalism with socialism. Lovestone knows imperialism is a hated word. So in his pamphlet he labels all the victories *against imperialism*, as "imperialism."

The Soviet people were the first to abolish capitalism and to establish a socialist order of things—so in Lovestone's big lie all people who have since either established socialism or who have won national independence are victims of "Soviet imperialism." He lists them—"Cuba, Hungary, Poland, Czechoslovakia, North Korea, North Vietnam, East Germany, Bulgaria, Cambodia, Laos, Tibet, Albania, Estonia, Latvia, Lithuania."

Then Lovestone lists all of the nations that have won political independence since World War II with the following twist—"They have exercised self-determination. . . . They had been *dependencies* of Australia, Belgium, Denmark, Egypt, France, Great Britain, Italy, Japan, the Netherlands, New Zealand, Spain ana the United States." They had been "dependencies," *not oppressed* by imperialism. They had "exercised self-determination," not fought and won independence. This shallow game is an attempt to give the appearance that imperialism had, because of its benevolence and kind-hearted charitableness, granted the right of self-determination. Of course, any worker will ask: If this was so, how come these same countries robbed, murdered, pillaged and enslaved these people for over 100 years? On page 54, Lovestone states: "In 1954 after signing the Geneva Agreements Hanoi left thousands of its military and political cadres in South Vietnam to subvert the fledgling republican government."

The world by now knows that Dulles would not sign the same Geneva accords. The world knows from public documents that it was the United States that conspired to wreck the Geneva accords. In the secret Pentagon papers it is revealed that while the Geneva conference was in session, the National Security Council, chaired by Eisenhower, decided to destroy the agreements. The papers state "The American aim in Indochina is a military victory."

Dulles implemented this policy by drafting a resolution asking for Congressional approval to send troops to Indochina. The U.S.

Chiefs of Staff Committee wrote regarding self-determination through free elections that intelligence reports compel the Chiefs of Staff Committee to suppose that settlement of the conflict on the basis of free elections would almost certainly be accompanied by placing Vietnam, Laos and Cambodia under the control of Communists.

This is now common knowledge, but Lovestone keeps saying, "Hanoi wrecked the Geneva accords." These are the specific falsehoods that fill in the gaps of the big lie. This is a moment of transition. Imperialism has forever lost its position of dominance. It is forced to retreat. The day of its total demise is not too far off. All the vulgar falsehoods conjured up by the ideological psychopaths of imperialism are not going to change the course of history. History has already given its verdict.

1968

PART FOUR

An Historical Necessity

I

REVOLUTIONS ARE THE EXPLOSIONS OF HISTORICAL NECESSITIES

Revolutions are the explosions of historical necessities. The laws of capitalist development create the objective conditions that make radical solutions a necessity. This process gives rise to a social force, to a consciousness, to a class, to an organized movement that carries out the changes that have become historical necessities. Thus history places on the order of the day only the problems for which it has solutions.

Each step forward is prepared within the old order of things. The forward thrust is made possible and necessary. The old dominant class becomes a reactionary force, desperately holding on to the status quo. A new class, a new force emerges as the champion, as the propellant behind the forward thrust. The new impelling force develops new patterns of thought, a new consciousness, a new culture, new sense of values, new priorities. All this reflects the new potential for human progress. This process is continuous. But there are moments when the process turns into explosive leaps, moments of revolutionary transition. There are periods when social progress gathers great momentum. We are at one of those moments. The next thrust has been prepared. It has become an historic necessity. People are not satisfied with things as they are. Many do not have the solutions, but they are ready to seek radical solutions.

There is a new momentum in all processes. The new momentum in the field of science and technology tends to break it out of the patterns and limitations set by capitalist relationships.

It places on the table new contradictions. It opens up unlimited possibilities but they cannot be achieved under the capitalist mode of production. There is not only a revolution in technology, there is a revolution in the application of the new techniques. In the 18th century it took 100 years before a new scientific idea found application in industry. In the middle of the 19th century this was cut to 50 years. At the end of the past century it took about 30 years, and at the beginning of the present about 10-15 years. Now the time of application is about 3 years. This is a feature of the new momentum.

National boundaries also are no obstacle to technology. The time it takes for a new process to find its way across national boundaries has been greatly reduced. Eight years after the steel oxygen conversion started production in Austria it started production in Britain. In a few short years it has revolutionized the world's steel industry. It has made over-capacity a chronic condition in the steel industries of all capitalist countries.

The concept that capitalism comes to its end in stagnation and self-suffocation is an over-simplification of a very complex process. The process of decay leads to a sharpening of the inner contradictions, as can be seen with the emergence of the new technology. The new technology presents unprecedented possibilities. They can be achieved only on a new level and scope of planning, a new level in the division of labor, and new priorities. But these are beyond the capabilities of capitalism. It is in this sense that capitalism becomes an obstacle to human progress. We are at a moment when the new thrust in social progress is ready to move. Something must give because the new thrust has become an historic necessity. Capitalism has become a brake on social development. The world revolutionary process is the explosion. The socialist one-third sector of the world, the working class of the capitalist countries, and the broad national liberation movements together constitute the force that is carrying out the task the laws of capitalist development have made into a historical necessity.

Because this historical necessity must be resolved at a moment when U.S. imperialism has become the pivot around which world imperialism revolves, it places a special responsibility on the people of the United States. No matter how we try to avoid it, and whether we accept it or not, the special responsibility is ours. One cannot side step assignments of history. What we as a people have done about U.S. aggression in Indochina is an example of how we must accept our assignment. The struggle against the aggression in Vietnam is one of the finest pages in the history of our people.

We can fulfill our end of the responsibility only if we can mold an anti-imperialist unity. This unity must not be viewed as a movement separated from the concrete problems of our people. Imperialism is not an abstraction. There is nothing in our life that is unrelated to imperialism. State monopoly capitalism is a feature of the imperialist stage of capitalist development. Imperialism is evil because of specific actions and policies. Therefore, the anti-imperialist unity will encompass movements that rise in opposition to specific forms and actions of imperialist oppression. The anti-imperialism of workers must be related to speedup in the shops, to wages, taxes and prices. The anti-imperialism of Black Americans must be related to the struggle against racism.

Within the overall anti-imperialist unity there is a need for some organizations whose main task is the exposure of imperialism in all of its aspects, including its capitalist roots.

There are important forces who see their self-interests on the level of fighting against monopoly domination. These are forces who do not see the interlocking nature of monopoly capitalism's domestic and foreign policies. The scope of their present viewpoint often does not penetrate past the problems created by the corporations that are clear and present dangers to their lives. The anti-monopoly sentiment and movement is very closely related to the anti-imperialist sentiment. But there is enough of a difference to make it necessary to take it into account in formulating tactics on specific slogans for action.

Some say: "Since imperialism is capitalism, therefore it is not possible to eliminate imperialism without overthrowing capitalism." The point here is that abstract generalizations can be guides to action but they can also be guides for inaction. When it is said imperialism can be eliminated only when we overthrow capitalism, one can have two different things in mind.

If the intention is to emphasize the fact that imperialism is capitalism in its last stages of development and that the roots—the laws of capitalist development that gave rise to imperialism—will remain as long as capitalism exists then we have no quarrel. But if the intent is to indicate that the only real struggle against imperialism is a struggle to overthrow capitalism then we have a disagreement. Objectively, all struggles for reforms, all struggles against specific acts or policies of imperialism have, to one extent or another, an anti-capitalist content. They are an important phase of the struggle against capitalism. The broad movement against U.S. imperialist aggression in Indochina is directed against an act of imperialism. It is not per se a movement to overthrow U.S. capitalism. Should we who are for overthrowing capitalism either abandon this movement or insist that as a movement it must take a stand for overthrowing U.S. capitalism, if not, we will ignore or denounce it? Anyone serious about overthrowing capitalism would reject such a concept. Such a stand would isolate the revolutionary sectors from the very people they must lead and convince if they are to be a factor in overthrowing capitalism. Such tactics have isolated and destroyed many promising movements. One must see the dialectical relationship between different levels of mass consciousness. An historical necessity is not always seen from the same vantage point by all. An historical necessity must be seen both as it appears to the more advanced sectors, and as it appears on the level of self-interests of different groups. Struggle is a process of political and ideological development. As masses go through various stages and experiences of struggle and if, in the process, they have a leadership that understands the relationships between these struggles and the more basic revolutionary process leading to the destruction of capitalism, then the historical necessity will come into clearer focus to increasing millions.

In the present stage U.S. capitalism is state monopoly capitalism. The big corporations have a stranglehold on the economy, on banking, trade and the government. Small business, small farmers are being forced out. It has become almost impossible for anyone to start a meaningful new small business. The handfull of big corporations determine wages, taxes, prices, rents, insurance rates, land values, fares, medical costs, and even funeral costs. They control the two parties of capitalism and most of the politics in them. It is this iron grip of the big corporations that blocks social progress. The grip has become tighter. But the struggle against it is growing. The confrontation is getting sharper.

The workers in the industries are the most direct victims of the monopolies. Where trade union leaders play ball with the corporations the rank and file are taking things into their own hands. They are setting up their own rank and file forms of organization.

Black Americans who are the victims of a special system of racist oppression are in rebellion. Women are rebelling against their special form of discrimination.

The young people are keenly aware of the necessity of this historic moment. They are rejecting the priorities and values reflecting monopoly capitalism and its needs. The movements of Mexican-Americans, Puerto Ricans and Indian Americans are in motion against the policies of racism and discrimination.

There is rebellion and movement amongst the professionals, farmers, and small business people.

These are the victims of monopoly capitalism. This is the growing force behind the historic necessity.

These movements are building their own organizations. There is a growing unity of action between them. Within the old political structure people are forming the new political formations. The people's movement is toward political independence. These movements are already electing new kinds of people to public office. They are seeking political power. These movements will grow. They will give rise to a new people's anti-monopoly party.

The struggle against the grip the big corporations have on our country has become a historical necessity. The movement against monopoly will come from a thousand directions. It will coalesce, it will grow in consciousness, it will merge into a mighty irresistible stream.

The objective laws of capitalist development and the rising struggles and movements against the evils of capitalism are joining forces in placing the transition to socialism on the order of the day.

Of all the historic necessities the destruction of capitalism and the building of socialism is the most meaningful. It is creating the historic line of demarcation. Future history will be divided into periods before and after socialism. When human society puts an end to capitalism it is going to eliminate the one basic crime in all of human history—exploitation of the many to enrich the few.

1968

2

AN ASSESSMENT OF TODAY'S
EPOCH-MAKING WORLD CHANGES

As we have indicated, imperialism can no longer dominate world developments and indeed has lost its historical initiative. The overall direction of developments is now determined by the forces that propel the world revolutionary process. There is a new main thrust to world events, a new main direction.

Does this mean that we are living in a new era? Lenin said, "An era is called an era precisely because it encompasses the sum total of variegated phenomena." The debate, whether this moment in history should be designated as an era or epoch with its distinct characteristics facing specific historic tasks and propelled by a set of forces unique for this epoch is much more than of academic interest. The assessment sets the priorities, the tasks and immediate goals for the revolutionary movement. It is an appraisal of the class forces involved. This is obvious from the nature of the arguments of those who raise questions whether this moment in history is a unique era. Some are now saying it is an overstatement.

These are not questions about the words "a new epoch." The questions are whether we are not overstating the strength of the working class, overstating the strength of the national liberation movement, and whether we are not overstating the relative strength of the world socialist sector. These are questions about underestimating the strength of imperialism. It seems clear some have drawn overly negative conclusions from some of the setbacks suffered by some forces within the world revolutionary process. Their assessment is one-sided. They do not take into account the momentary nature of most of the defeats, and they do not give the proper weight to the weaknesses and setbacks suffered by world imperialism. They do not clearly enough see the longer range processes and their historic effects. For example, they raise specific questions about the annual economic growth rate statistics of the Soviet economy.

We may now ask ourselves: Did the birth of the Soviet Union change the relationship of forces and therefore bring on a new epoch? It was the explosive and monumental beginning of the process, but it did not yet tip the scales. And if we ask whether the concept of the new epoch should be tied to the industrial index of the Soviet Union, it can only be said that it is one of the key factors but the question is not determined by it alone. Whether Soviet production surpasses the U.S. industrial index in 1970 or 1973 does not by itself determine the nature of this epoch. That a socialist nation is going to overtake and surpass the highest developed capitalist country in the field of science and technology is, of course, of the greatest significance.

The unprecedented development of the Soviet Union is a crucial factor on the scales of history. In a short 50 years, it has emerged from almost total destruction and backwardness, and after two devastating wars, into a nation that in science, economic development, production, technology, medicine, culture and in military power equals and surpasses the best capitalism has been able to produce in some 250 years of effort. There would be no new epoch without this development.

Both the shift and the trend in the competition between the United States and the Soviet Union is unmistakable. Keep in mind capitalism in the United States had a 200-year head start, and without the direct involvement in three destructive wars. After the Second World War the Soviet Union was 39 years behind the United States in industrial production. In 1960 it was only 14 years behind. By 1967 the years were cut to six. Since 1967 the gap has narrowed down further. In such areas as expenditure on education, health, culture, social insurance the Soviet Union has surpassed the United States for a number of years. This is not a competition between two peoples—it is a competition between two socio-economic systems.

Among the many phenomena of this epoch, the world socialist system *is* basic, and it is in this context that its economic, scientific and military might takes on its full significance.

A year ago there was resistance to concretely assessing the damage that had resulted from the split in the world Communist movement caused by the differences between the world Communist movement and the Maoist leadership of the People's Republic of China. Some of our comrades did not want our Party to take a stand on the errors of the Maoist group. They did not understand the fundamental nature of this challenge to Marxism-Leninism. But, seemingly, this factor now emerges as so crucial that it should influence us into making a new assessment of the nature of the present epoch. There is no doubt, there has been a weakening of the unity of the anti-imperialist forces and of the world Communist movement because of the opportunist-nationalist excursion of the Mao leadership. But we maintain that it has not affected the relationship of forces in a fundamental way. It has not tipped the scales in favor of imperialism.

A second powerful factor that Lenin discusses is the national liberation movement and the revolutions arising from them. Do setbacks in the field of national liberation indicate that the sweep of these movements has now come to a halt or been reversed? Again the answer must be a ringing No!

There have been some setbacks. Some have been very serious. The developments in Ghana, Greece, Sudan are setbacks. Further, we would not be realistic if we would not assume there will be further defeats. But what is most important is that they take place in the overall context of victories, the continued growth of the forces of national liberation and the correction of the weaknesses that led to the setbacks.

Other factors affecting the nature of the epoch are, of course, the actions of the working class in all countries, including the fact that the majority of the working class in countries like Italy and France are socialist-oriented. That Cuba has thrown off capitalist controls and is building socialism is of key significance in assessing the forces of this epoch.

The key factor, the key propellant of this epoch is the many-sided world revolutionary process. But as is the case with all processes it is not an uninterrupted, evenly flowing stream. It has its ebbs and flows, and they are important and must be taken into account. But they must be seen in the context of a powerful water-way of history that relentlessly flows in one direction.

Even the setbacks and weaknesses that have developed in the unity of the international Communist movement can teach fundamental lessons. Some Parties have shifted their emphasis away from the self-interest issues of their people while trying to adopt untenable features that were tenable in other revolutionary movements and experiences. Some have shifted from a reliance upon the maximum mobilization of mass consciousness to a reliance on military groups, or to a reliance on generalized slogans. The general concept of anti-imperialism is not enough—the struggle must be related to and start with the self-interest issues as the masses see them. It must be related to oppression and exploitation in concrete terms. Deviations from this fundamental approach to struggle have led to self-isolation and to temporary defeats. In most areas these errors have been only momentary detours.

In studying the setbacks, for example, in Indonesia and Ghana, it is obvious that new levels of organization of mass political consciousness are needed; new dimensions are needed, too, in the content, methods and scope of political and ideological mobilization of the masses. One should not discuss lightly the serious difficulties that block the revolutionary path. But one also should not overlook the subjective weaknesses of leadership. Most of these weaknesses have one root—not understanding the critical nature of organizing and mobilizing masses.

One of the basic conclusions we draw from the new epoch concept is the fact that world wars are not now inevitable. In the epoch when imperialism was the dominant force, wars of conquest between imperialist powers for the redivision of the loot were inevitable. The shift in the world balance of forces has made a shift in the outlook for peace not only possible but crucial for mankind's survival. The danger of world war continues but its prevention has become a real possibility.

The struggle against world imperialism is a struggle against its ability to conduct wars of conquest. The struggle is to destroy it. The choice is not between peace or continued imperialist oppression and exploitation. The struggles against imperialism and for national liberation are not negotiable at any price. The relationship of world forces of this epoch makes possible the conclusion that imperialism can be corralled and destroyed before it destroys civilization.

Our conclusion is that the national liberation, anti-imperialist sweep has deep roots in the worldwide revolutionary process and that it will continue. In a moment like this, developments rarely take place in their pure form. When the Ben Bella government in Algeria was overthrown, many thought that this was per se a right-wing, counter-revolutionary coup. In Algeria, however, the struggle for a new political direction continues. The pressures of the times, including the new level of mass political consciousness, were factors that could not be ignored by the Algerian government and they tended to blunt the right-wing nature of developments.

Yes, there will be ebbs and flows, ups and downs, zigs and zags in this epoch of revolutions and great mass upheavals, but an overall shift is taking place in the forces propelling the world revolutionary process, and the general direction of the process takes place within the historic epoch of transition from capitalism to socialism.

The law of motion, the law of continuous change, applies to social systems as it does to all of nature. This concept is bitterly fought by those who want to credit capitalism with a perpetual mandate. Each economic system—primitive communalism, slavery, feudalism and capitalism—has had its day. They all served their historic purpose and then gave way to higher forms of relationship. Each reflected and served a specific level of human development. New social systems enter on to the stage of history as an answer to new social and technological developments.

In its time, capitalism was an important step, an answer to a specific level of human experience. Now new problems are pushing for solution. A technological and scientific revolution has taken place, a new social order is emerging.

If this analysis once seemed theoretical or merely philosophical, it has come alive—moving from the textbooks to the field of action. The process of change has reached the qualitative point of social explosion. Civilization is passing through its greatest moment of change. A distinct phase of this revolutionary process is the explosive breakup of the old capitalist-imperialist empires.

For those who are not convinced of the laws of change, this new reality is a shock. They cannot accept it as an inevitable development, sometimes attributing its manifestations to some kind of conspiracy, to infiltration by dangerous rebels, subverters of the status quo. It is difficult for some to adjust to the fact that civilization has now reached the stage where the people of each nation want freedom and independence. They demand the simple right to determine for themselves all matters within their national boundaries, and they want a place in the sun—and they want it NOW.

The people of the world insist on reaping the full benefits from their labor and from their national resources. What is new is that they have the power, they have the will, and are ready to fight for it. The cause of those fighting for independence in any corner of the world is as just as was our cause at Valley Forge.

And it has also become clear that socialism cannot be imported. Social revolutions cannot be made to order. Here, it will be an urgent, immediate question when the majority of Americans are convinced there is no other solution to their problems. At that point no power on earth can stop them. With all due respect to the experiences of the countries that have established socialism, socialism in the United States will not be patterned after any other model; it will be molded by the world experience and by our own experiences, by our own traditions as a people. It will follow the general path of world socialism with a distinct United States bent.

One very basic point of reference remains: capitalism as a system is on the way out and socialism as a system is on the way in. Already existing over one-third of the world it now appears as all mankind's bright horizon. The struggle against imperialism cannot be separated or isolated from this transition from one world socio-economic system to another. It is this transition that is molding and giving this epoch its unique character.

1968

3

EVENTS THAT DETERMINE AN EPOCH

When human history is in the process of one of its truly revolutionary changes, there is no way of precisely designating an epoch or an era on the calendar, despite the fact that we do celebrate certain great victories and remember defeats on specific dates. The processes and forces that propel us into a new era are in the process of development while the forces of the old still retain vitality and even the capacity for further growth. The processes that rise to the new, intermingle and overlap with the old.

The birth of the first socialist republic, the Soviet Union, shattered the shell of world capitalism and established a working-class beachhead on the mainland of world imperialism. The event shook capitalism to its foundations but it did not end capitalist power and relationships in the rest of the world. It did, however, pave the way for an unprecedented movement of the people of the world. It raised the world revolutionary process to a new level.

The nature of the new social system was soon demonstrated in the primary role played by the Soviet Union in crushing fascism. This historic victory marked the beginning of a new stage in the new epoch; a vastly augmented global revolutionary potential emerged as a powerful current. The socialist sector grew into a powerful economic, military and ideological community, while world capitalism was reaching its apex.

The contradictions between the two diametrically different systems projected them ever more sharply on the world scene. Powerful working-class movements in capitalist countries were set in motion; tidal waves of national liberation struggles swept most parts of the earth's surface. And it was clear that human society had indeed arrived at the most profound revolutionary turning-point in its history.

It is sometimes difficult to realize that this turning-point is neither ancient history nor on the distant horizon. It is here, and we are in the eye of the storm—mankind's most explosive qualitative leap. All processes of social progress, all movements, all the struggles of today are related to this leap, and they can be understood only if they are viewed in this dialectical relationship.

There are periods when the process does not produce a shift of state power in a specific country or countries. There are setbacks, frustrations, periods when the process levels off on a new plateau. There are explosive and violent transfers of class power and others that are not so violent.

This many-sided process of the unfolding of reality is based on the laws of social development. To one extent or another, all present-day phenomena are shaped by the revolutionary process whose motive power is generated by the laws of capitalist development. Those who have "updated" Marx by declaring these laws obsolete confuse form and content. What changes is the framework within which they operate. The rules of the game have changed but the predatory character of imperialism remains the same.

We are witnessing the prolonged demise of the last of a long line of social systems based on man's exploitation of man. The aggressive, angry beast of imperialism is now forced to seek its prey in circumstances where it is no longer the master of the forest. As a result, it has been forced to shift its tactics. With greater cunning and newly acquired skill it seeks to divide and insulate its intended victims. It cannot be tamed or petted; like any beast that is being cornered it is a dangerous foe.

The internal processes of each imperialist country as well as its external relationships are also basically governed by the laws of capitalist development, which themselves are being increasingly influenced by the shift in the balance of world forces. The tremors of these shifts are sharply felt at the heart of world imperialism.

There is some measure of crisis developing in every phase of our life—except one. The exception is the amount of monopoly profits. These two sentences express not only an assessment of the way things are, they are also a statement of *why* things are as they are. The root cause of all the manifestations of crisis is the unending, limitless drive by the capitalist class for maximum profits.

The multiplying war budgets of the 1960s—especially in the period of the Indochinese war—have made this a period of unprecedented profit expansion. At the same time, the rate of exploitation of labor in manufacturing has gone up some 30 per cent in the past ten years. And this despite the fact that the workers, in the past two or three years, have won the biggest money settlements ever.

The drive for profits results in a continuous polarization of our people into a richer rich and a poorer poor. Unheard-of profits are drawn from the exploitation of 80 million workers and from the unremitting racial and national oppression of 40 million of our people. Skyrocketing prices, inflation, and a staggering tax load burden us all while the crisis in education and housing deepens.

Today the economy does not simply move spontaneously in response to economic laws. It is also manipulated by giant monopolies and cartels and to a high degree regulated by the government acting on behalf of these monopolies. There are, of course, limits to what they can do; they cannot indefinitely ward off the operation of economic laws, nor escape the contradictions generated by the system itself. As the crisis deepens, their range of choice narrows, options disappear, particularly because the laws now operate in a more advanced state of capitalist development and in a world in which there are two social systems.

1970

4

THE STRUGGLE TO BREAK THE GRIP
OF MONOPOLY

Today struggles in any sector of life turn into a confrontation with monopoly capital. Search the surface anywhere and you touch some tentacle of monopoly corporate interests. The industrial worker meets the monster on the production line daily. This confrontation is direct and clean-cut. The small farmer confronts the beast in the form of banks, the agri-corporation and monopolies in the distribution of farm products. The small businessman is squeezed between the monopolies who control the economy. The Afro-Americans, Chicanos, Puerto Ricans, the American Indian peoples are the victims of the monopolies' special system of oppression and discrimination. The students face the fiend in monopoly-controlled college boards. Women face the monster of reaction-inspired male chauvinism.

In the United States one cannot escape the tentacles of monopoly capitalism. They have a choking grip on industry, banking, newspapers, radio, television, magazines, on retail trade. They control the two parties of capitalism. Monopoly capital has a controlling influence on the government on all levels. We have a state monopoly power.

How to unite the victims of monopoly oppression is a serious question for the working class, the victims of the special systems of oppression, the farm groups, professionals and people engaged in small business. To "turn the country around" is to turn it against monopoly capitalism. Any meaningful "new beginning" must be an anti-monopoly beginning. An anti-monopoly coalition is an inevitable political development, because the power of monopoly is an obstacle to any progressive development. It will give rise to a new political party. The struggle will lead to an anti-monopoly political power, to state power. This is an inevitable path of struggle. Because it is inevitable it is necessary to have a continuing dialog about the problems of building a broad anti-monopoly coalition. One must start with the fact that masses will identify with the anti-monopoly struggles who are not for the destruction of capitalism as a system. They are going to be for measures that restrict and cut back the power of monopoly. They are going to be for measures that put the burden of taxes on the monopolies. The anti-monopoly measures will include laws that support workers and small farmers. They will support laws that strike at racism. Inevitably the anti-monopoly direction will move to nationalization of banks and industries. It will move towards greater democratic controls in all areas of life—political, economic, cultural.

The question facing the revolutionary movement is not whether it should initiate an anti-monopoly movement. Monopoly domination gives rise to and feeds such a movement. The question still debated in many sectors is what should be the attitude to the anti-monopoly struggles and movements that exist. Should they be ignored as "diversions from the 'real' struggle against capitalism," or should people who are for the destruction of capitalism help organize and lead anti-monopoly movements and struggles? It depends on how one views the path leading to socialism. If one sees the path lined with bull-horns, and record players, repeating slogans and rhetoric of the need to overthrow capitalism then, of course, it is not necessary to consider such realities as monopoly domination, because "capitalism is monopoly and monopoly is capitalism." On the other hand, if one sees the path to socialism lined with people in struggle over the issues that pain them most, fighting and learning to recognize the real class enemy, becoming conscious of its own class power, and in the process being taught about socialism, then the anti-monopoly struggles become indispensable. In a country like the United States, to ignore the anti-monopoly movement and struggles is to ignore the most basic element of our reality. To disregard the anti-monopoly element is to overlook the most revolutionizing factor in present-day capitalism. It is the first stage in the understanding that the problems of the people are rooted in a social system dominated by monopoly corporations. The anti-monopoly struggle is an expression of masses who are radical, militant, but a step away from the level of a revolutionary struggle to overthrow capitalism and establish socialism. One could even say they are anti-capitalist but not yet for socialism. In the real sense there is no choice for serious revolutionaries. It is the same masses who are now and are going to be in the anti-monpooly struggles, who are going to overthrow capitalism and establish socialism in the United States. They are wetting their socialist feet in the struggle against monopoly domination. To turn the country towards socialism is to turn it to fight monopoly domination.

The anti-monopoly concept is a broad, flexible term reflecting the varied nature of the struggle. Anti-monopoly struggles take place in every sector of life, because monopolies dominate every sector of life. The anti-monopoly struggles are laying the bricks for an anti-monopoly coalition. The specific issues that give rise to anti-monopoly struggles are economic, political, anti-war, for civil rights, for democracy. The working class is forced to take an anti-monopoly position. The struggles in all sectors move toward a confrontation with monopoly corporations.

Because of the new role of the state, anti-monopoly struggles tend to become political struggles. The politics of the Democratic and Republican Parties are the politics of monopoly capitalism.

It is an illusion to think that anti-monopoly politics can ever establish a long term political base in these two old parties.

The basis for anti-monopoly politics is political independence from the twin parties of capitalism. There will be a period when the independent forces will use the two-party, one-class electoral apparatus which serves monopoly, but the struggle must be for the breaking of that political vise and the setting up of a new anti-monopoly party based on the working class.

The aim of the anti-monopoly struggles must be the creation of an anti-monopoly coalition strong enough to break the economic and political stranglehold of monopoly capital. This of necessity means a struggle for economic and political power. Economic and political power cannot evade the question of state power. It means anti-monopoly state power.

Economic and political power that breaks the grip of monopoly of necessity means the nationalization of monopoly-controlled industries. It may not start with nationalization but the logic of the confrontation will lead to nationalization.

In a country like the United States the advent of an anti-monopoly state power will be an explosive event. It will rock the class structure from top to bottom. Nationalization with democratic controls will change the balance of class power. The role of the state will change. The state will become a bigger factor in influencing and directly regulating economic developments. It will have to add the element of planning. Workers will be drawn into councils that will have power over economic relationships. It is clear these are also necessary steps moving the country toward socialism. As there is a relationship between the struggle for reforms and the struggle to overthrow capitalism, there is a dialectical relationship between the struggle against monopoly and the struggle for socialism. Within the overall framework of the class struggle there are struggles that take place on many levels around a multitude of issues.

1971

5

THE EVER-CHANGING BALANCE OF WORLD FORCES

In the balance of forces between imperialism and anti-imperialism nothing stands still. Reflecting the law of the uneven development of capitalism, the imperialist countries are subject to constantly changing relationships.

Imperialism develops new tactics and new ideological arguments to meet changing reality as do the forces of anti-imperialism.

Any idea that each sector of anti-imperialism can effectively deal with the shifting global challenge in a piecemeal fashion is a dangerous illusion. U.S. imperialism remains the most aggressive, warlike force in the world, continuing its bloody aggression against the people of Vietnam, its conspiracies against the people of Cuba, its military, political and economic aggression in Latin America, Asia and Africa. It remains the base of operation for the forces of imperialism everywhere in the futile attempt to halt the world revolutionary processes.

U.S. imperialism is in an ever deeper crisis and it can be defeated, but to underestimate the aggressiveness and the danger it presents would be the height of folly. For an effective struggle in any arena, one must know one's enemy. While maintaining that it wants to end war, imperialism prepares ever more lethal and insidious forms of aggression, arming the enemies of progress to the teeth in every part of the world.

Yes, U.S. imperialism is a powerful, dangerous foe, but it is in serious difficulties. In cash value, the annual price of its policy of aggression is reaching the $100 billion level. At home this is translated into runaway inflation, ever rising prices and rents. More than 50 percent of all workers' wages are now extracted in taxes and real wages are now declining. No people or nation has ever been in such debt, the total of individual, corporation and government debt has now reached more than one trillion dollars. We are the most mortgaged people in the world.

The U.S. financial-industrial complex with the powers of the state machinery at its service and with the new scientific breakthroughs at its command, organized and controlled through monopolies and conglomerates, has developed into history's most fiendishly efficient exploiter and devourer of resources, both nature's and man's. Geared to the extraction of maximum profits, it finds ever new methods for squeezing more. During the past ten years the rate of the exploitation of labor has been forced up by some 30 percent.

The uniquely inhuman nature of U.S. capitalism is shown in its oppression of national minorities. For more than 350 years it had maintained the special system of oppression that is still in force today against 25 million Afro-American citizens. And after the long years of militant and heroic struggles, even though some important victories have been won, the special system remains largely intact, continuing to maintain discrimination and inequality, segregation, and the ghettos, with all their degradation. Its results are appalling: an income less than two-thirds of the national level, an unemployment rate twice as high, a death rate that is triple (compared with a death rate twice as high in 1940), slum housing and chronic hunger and inferior education, work at the lowest-paid and most dangerous jobs and at the bottom of the seniority lists.

To the special oppression of Afro-Americans, U.S. capitalism has added special forms of oppression against five million Mexican Americans, two million Puerto Ricans and the segregation of those who survive among the Indians into reservations that are barren graveyards of hunger, social deprivation and inhuman wretchedness, while similar policies are inflicted upon the Eskimo people of Alaska.

Thus capitalism has created a monstrous structure, but it has also created a militant working class, the forces of mass revolt. It has generated a militant movement of Black Americans; it has set in motion a youth and student revolt of massive proportions. It has spurred a mass campaign for peace and against militarism that cuts across class lines and penetrates deeply into the very armed forces of U.S. imperialism.

Millions of women, who in many areas of struggle are more active and militant than men, have been stirred into action. And pervading the overall atmosphere of this land there is a national uneasiness, widespread dissatisfaction, distrust and contempt for the bourgeois establishment. In this process of radicalization, we pay special tribute to the heroism of soldiers and sailors who are challenging the autocratic military regimes, who are raising the banner of peace and equality in the barracks, in the mobilization and induction centers and at the military bases. Never before in the history of our country have so many members of the armed forces taken direct action against militarism; more than 53,000 desertions took place in the year ending June 30, 1968. There are more than 23,000 draft delinquents; thousands of them flee the United States for Canada or seek refuge in Sweden, France and other countries. There are underground and anti-war papers published by GI's on major military bases. No wonder the ruling class is exploring the possibility of abolishing the conscription system and raising military salaries so that it may build an arm of mercenary professional servants.

One of the most potent expressions of the new wave of radicalization is the rapid growth of organized rank-and-file movements in the shops and trade unions. The power of these movements can be seen in trade union elections in which old, encrusted trade union bureaucracies are being overthrown. The qualitative shift finds expression in the rank-and-file caucuses of Afro-American union members, now an active force in hundreds of shops and locals. The designation of "revolutionary workers' caucuses" is an accepted form among increasing sections of Black workers.

Motivating this upsurge are the new problems of the class struggle, the special problems of Black workers, the need to reshape and retool the trade union movement as an instrument of class struggle that can meet the problems of today. The demands of the students that higher education be recognized as an inherent right and a realistic possibility for all youth add up to more than just "letting off steam." They are demanding an end of the system in which the wealthy benevolently dole out college entrance permits, an end to the racist barriers and systems of tokenism in all institutions of higher learning, an end to the use of educational institutions as adjuncts to the military-industrial complex. They fight to bar the doors of our colleges and universities against recruiting for the military and the development of lethal gases and other instruments of mass death, and they want to abolish the elitist Reserve Officer Training Corps.

These demands go to the heart of the basic problems of capitalist society and form an integral part of the struggle against the aggressive war policies and astonomical military expenditures of imperialism.

Young workers in great numbers spark the rank-and-file movements for a revitalization of the trade union movement. They are a strong force in the struggle against racism because they are free of the ingrained prejudices of many of the older workers. Products of the radicalized generation, they are more open to new socialist ideas. On the basis of the upsurge in non-working-class sections of our people, many petty bourgeois theoreticians have developed "theories" about revolutions that will be made without the working class, without those who are involved in the production process. Not only are these "theories" erroneous but increasingly they are being rejected by the very same youth they were designed to deceive.

1972

CONCLUSION

At no time in history has life presented so much irrefutable evidence that capitalism as a socio-economic system is outmoded and therefore on the skids to extinction.

When the huge, prehistoric animals that foraged and roamed the earth could not keep up with the changing reality around them, they became incompatible, and thus were marked for extinction.

This law of nature is no less applicable to social structures. This is the last stage of capitalist development. Imperialism is in its period of decay. It is suffering from a crisis of incompatibility. It is an outmoded, crisis-ridden, bankrupt, petrified, obsolete old structure that is ready for the litter basket of history.

The explosive scientific-technological breakthrough has brought into the field of vision the potential of abundance for all human needs. Thus, human society needs a system for the distribution of abundance.

The new level of production based on the new technology demands computerized planning, socialized capital investments, a planned socialized system of distribution, a plan that synchronizes production and human needs, a worldwide division of labor, a plan creating abundance while safeguarding the environment. Technologically, abundance in most wordly needs is achievable *now*.

For this task capitalism is primitive. The anarchistic existence of each corporation in its own cave, interested only in how to increase its private loot, is incompatible with the needs and possibilities of today's reality.

Like the prehistoric animals, capitalism is losing the struggle for survival to a new social order, a society compatible with today's potential. It has been driven out of one-third of the world's feeding grounds. It is in difficulty everywhere. The new species taking the field is socialism.

Socialism is a system geared for the production and distribution of abundance. It is compatible with and in fact is programmed to the new level of technology. In today's reality to be with it is to be for socialism. The crisis of imperialism is a crisis of its extinction. It is dangerous because it would rather destroy civilization than accept the verdict of its extinction peacefully. It is dangerous because it has in its possession the means with which to destroy every living thing.

Basically, imperialism will never change. It will be the socioeconomic dinosaur to its last day. But there is nothing so unalterable as a verdict of history, and the verdict is: You have had it. Take your choice, depart peacefully or be kicked out!

The makers of history are people. Their instrument is struggle. Thus, there will be struggle. There are victims—like the imprisonment of Comrade Angela Davis. There will be sacrifices, and there will be setbacks, but most of all, the verdict of history will be carried out, and the victims of today will be the victors of tomorrow.

We in the United States carry a heavy responsibility in carrying out this verdict of history. We inhabit the nesting grounds of the dinosaur of world imperialism. This is its lair. This is the base of its arsenal. We carry a heavy responsibility but we are also presented with an historic opportunity. Because the United States is the pivotal center of world imperialism, every blow we strike for our own freedom from imperialism is a blow against world imperialism and every blow struck at world imperialism is a strike against U.S. imperialism.

Capitalism is marked for extinction because it has become an obstacle to social progress, the roadblock to a better life. That is the underlying process, the meaning of the present explosive epoch. In history and in daily events, we are in the midst of the surge of the tidal flow of the transition from capitalism to socialism.

As the poet said, "*Change* is nature's mighty law." And a mighty force it is on the world scene.

The shock waves of change have rocked and unglued the old structure and made significant qualitative changes in the world's political, social and economic landscape.

The most significant of all developments and most expressive of the essence of this moment is the coming apart of the postwar world capitalist house designed and built by U.S. imperialism.

Like mansions in the mud slides of Southern California, the postwar capitalist world structure shows cracks and has been pushed off its foundations. It is helpless before the mighty force of change.

The drive of U.S. imperialism to dominate, exploit and enslave the world, launched after the Second World War, has ignominiously bogged down.

Some call it "over-extension," others a "miscalculation," but no matter what one calls it, it is imperialist aggression, and it is those policies of aggression that have now suffered defeats. These are defeats for imperialism in general but they are serious defeats for U.S. imperialism in particular. The aggression has bogged down in the rice fields of Indochina, in the desert of North Africa, in the mountains of Chile and the sugar fields of Cuba. U.S. imperialism is forced to maneuver and retreat. It cannot stand on its old ground.

World imperialism has met its equal and superior social system. It is losing the most crucial battles. It has been driven out of the command post of human affairs.

The balance between imperialism and the galaxy of forces propelling the world revolutionary process has again significantly tipped against imperialism. As the scales tip against it, imperialism is forced to maneuver and to retreat.

As the balance of forces tips against it, the general crisis of capitalism deepens.

Thus the break-up of the postwar capitalist structure has ushered in a new qualititative point in the overall crisis of world capitalism.

It is a turning-point. It is a new point of reference in history.

Most important is that we understand the nature and significance of the moment and the tasks flowing from it. As is true with all new shifts this also brings with it new opportunities of struggle and victories as well as new dangers.

What are some of the factors that characterize this new level in the overall decaying process of capitalism?

In a basic sense the central factor is that there is a new qualitative shift in the overall world balance of forces. There has taken place a qualitative deterioration in the structure of world capitalism and there is a new level of consolidation, growth and stability in the socialist world. In a new qualitative sense capitalism has further lost its ability as a class to influence or intervene in world affairs, and the forces of the world revolutionary process, led by the forces of socialism, qualitatively in a new way determine the course of world developments. There is a new upswing in the struggles and victories of the peoples fighting against imperialism and against reactionary governments subservient to imperialism. There is a new upsurge in working-class struggles in the capitalist world.

The old postwar period of capitalist world stabilization was dependent on the stability of U.S. capitalism. It has become a source for instability. The new stage is reflected in numerous developments. It is reflected in the new level of contradictions and the sharpness of the relations between capitalist countries, especially between the United States and its imperialist rivals.

It is reflected in the breakup of the world imperialist pyramid based on and dominated by U.S. imperialism. U.S. domination created sharp contradictions within the capitalist world, but it has also served as the main source for its stability. The breakup of this structure brings with it an increase of instability.

It is reflected in the collapse of the dollar. Since the Second World War, the dollar has been the stable currency that served as a medium of exchange for the capitalist world. The refusal—or more accurately, the inability of the United States to back up the dollar with gold—has pulled the rug from under the dollar as a stable medium of exchange. The floating currencies in the capitalist world reflect the floating economic and political relationships in the capitalist world. There is a deep financial crisis. The capitalist world financial structure has disintegrated because there is a new level in the general crisis. The ruling circles have only come up with patchwork solutions. The inability of the capitalist world to come up with a more stable solution is reflective of the deeper crisis.

The new stage is reflected in the existence of a significant unused industrial capacity in all of the industrially developed capitalist countries. This raises new problems for capital investments, and presents a new problem for the multi-national corporations. The crisis is causing serious economic dislocation in all of the capitalist countries. That it may result in a capitalist worldwide economic crisis cannot be ruled out.

The new stage is reflected in the paralysis and in the disintegration of postwar military alliances. Outside of NATO, most other alliances are in one or another stage of disintegration. Even NATO reflects the growing sharpness in the relationships between the United States and the capitalist countries of Europe. The European Security Treaty initiated by the socialist countries and supported by the working class and popular forces of Europe has emerged as a political factor, and resulted in new relationships that no one can ignore. NATO is not now a passive instrument of U.S. imperialism.

The new stage is reflected in the absence of a single economic, military and political center of coordination for the capitalist world. World capitalist relationships are in flux. World imperialism has lost the position of initiative because it has lost the ability to unitedly determine the course of human events. The new stage is reflected in the inability of the capitalist world to follow a unified class position in their relations with the socialist world. The United States has not yet dropped its dollar curtain, but the policies of worldwide blockades, worldwide discriminatory tariffs, and the policies of boycotting socialist-operated ships are all under attack. As the organizer of these imperialist policies, the United States is now left holding the bag, full of plans rejected and discarded by a changing world.

The economic policies that sustained the Cold War are being discarded by most capitalist countries.

The new stage is reflected in the new level of anarchy, and the new contradictions brought on by the development of the multi-national corporations.

The new stage has its roots in the tipping of the world balance against imperialism. It is reflected in the new level of the building of socialism. The qualitative shift in the competition between the two world systems is dramatically illustrated by the fact that in 1971 the Soviet Union, a socialist state, became the world's No. 1 producer of steel.

Each step in the growth of the economic, political and military might of the socialist states narrows down the ability, and the area, in which imperialism can forage and maneuver. The new stage is reflected in the consolidation and growth of the national liberation movements. It is reflected in the new difficulties imperialism has in transferring the cost of its crises onto the backs of the working class and oppressed peoples of the world.

In this new stage, the capitalist class of each nation is seeking for itself a new place within a receding capitalist sun. Their rivalries have become sharper. The new stage is a new level of instability. The "law of nature" is reaping its harvest. That which does not change becomes incompatible, and that which becomes incompatible is marked for extinction. The new stage of the crisis is only further proof that life has marked capitalism for extinction and is making good on its promise.

That world capitalism has been marked for extinction and that world imperialism is in serious new difficulties are assessments of processes; this does not mean the processes have reached their end. U.S. imperialism will continue its policies of aggression. It will continue to seek for a new capitalist world structure. It will continue to be the arsenal for world reaction. What is important is that the struggle against its policies will take place in the context of the new balance of relationships, in the new stage of the crisis.

All countries of capitalism are affected by the crisis because the overall process is related to the decay of a socio-economic system. One of the unique features of the present stage of decay is that the most profound effects of the crisis are to be found in the very heart of world imperialism—in the United States.

To one extent or another, the policies of all countries are in difficulty, but it is above all the policies of U.S. imperialism that have bogged down. It is a crisis of the state monopoly capitalist structure.

In its world relationships, U.S. imperialism is forced to retreat and to maneuver, but in its basic world outlook, in its basic objective, it has not changed one iota. It continues to pursue its basic policy of aggression. It is violently racist, it is anti-labor, it is reactionary and anti-democratic.

The postwar world structure is being shattered, but U.S. imperialism remains the main power base, the main supplier of arms, the main base of political and economic support for every fascist, racist military dictatorship the world over.

The new stage in the crisis of world capitalism presents new dangers—but most important, it presents the possibilities for new victories against imperialism.

The new stage calls for new initiatives, new struggles. The new struggles call for a firmer worldwide unity. There is a need for new initiatives to bring about a new unity between the socialist nations. There is a need for new initiatives to bring about a new world working-class and trade union unity.

The new stage gives a new dimension to the conclusion stated in the basic document of the World Communist Conference of June 1969: "Imperialism can neither regain its lost historical initiative nor reverse world development. The main direction of mankind's development is determined by the world socialist system, the international working class, and all the revolutionary forces."

1972

INDEX

A

Abel, I. W. 134ff
Abrams, Gen. Creighton 239
Aden 13
AFL-CIO 189, 198, 217ff, 338, 344f
Africa 11, 13, 21, 54f, 70, 79, 88, 111, 142, 187ff, 229, 254, 269, 297, 311, 318, 340, 369, 374
Agnew, Spiro 37, 46, 111, 159, 236
Agency for International Development (AID) 334, 336
Aheed, Kaid 223
Albania 113, 346
Algeria 14, 220ff, 318, 360
Alliance for Progress 79, 212f, 335, 338
American Iron and Steel Institute 57
American Indians 34, 143, 151, 245, 355, 365, 370
Anastasia 277
Anti-Semitism 143, 147, 169, 297
Angola 11
Argentina 311
Asia 51, 53, 55, 65, 70, 79, 211, 229, 254, 297, 311, 369
Atlantic Richfield 53
Australia 18, 338, 346
Austria 271, 352

B

Bakunin, Mikhail 93f
Bangla Desh 256
Batista, Juan 199f, 212, 308
Bay of Pigs 153, 201, 204, 278
Bechyne, Z. 185
Belgium 18, 189, 346
Belmadani 221
Ben Bella 360
Benmouffok, Khaled 221
Bill of Rights 277, 281
Black Americans 11, 34f, 41, 45, 62, 71, 79, 98, 122, 125, 129, 143ff, 157, 159, 189, 198, 202, 215, 229, 231, 245, 283, 292, 353, 355, 365, 369ff
Black Liberation 106, 109, 263, 312
Boeing Aircraft 139
Bolivia 11, 337
Boumedienne, Houari 221ff
Brazil 11, 256
Brezhnev, L. I. 186
Britain 13f, 18, 38, 57, 73, 75, 80, 105, 108, 162, 174, 213, 256, 323, 340, 346, 352
Brodsky, J. 185
Browder, Earl 322
Buckley, William 282
Budd Corporation 240
Bukharin, Nikolai I. 234
Bulgaria 113, 231, 346
Bundy, McGeorge 116
Burger, Albert E. 34
Burke, David 335
Buxbaum, Dr. 42

C

Caltex 53
Cambodia 13, 231, 240, 244, 271, 346f

Canada 18, 53ff, 59, 131, 370
Canal Zone 208
Capone, Al 277
Caribbean 200, 206
Castro, Fidel 201f, 335
Catholic Church 185, 225ff
Celler-Kefauver Act 29
Cento 66
CENTO 66
Chase Manhattan Bank 140
Cherfaoul, Lakhdar 221
Cherne, Leo 176
Chicanos 34f, 98, 129, 143, 147f, 151, 198, 245, 263, 355, 365, 370
Chile 61, 311, 337, 374
China, People's Republic of 14, 76, 110, 113, 206, 256f, 259ff, 268, 274, 294, 299f, 302
China, Communist Party of 255, 258, 264, 272, 275, 301, 358
China Lobby 274, 301
Chou En-lai 268
Churchill, Winston 80ff
CIA 52, 70, 81, 88, 103, 111, 118f, 152f, 162, 174ff, 188, 190, 193, 199, 215, 217ff, 222, 271, 276, 301, 332, 335, 339, 344
CIO 278
Cities Service Co. 53
Civil War, U.S. 41, 62, 106, 125
Clay, Gen. Lucius 88
Cold War 78ff, 83, 86, 90, 376
Colombia 208
Common Market 79
Communist International 318ff
Congo 18, 20, 189, 376
Continental Oil Co. 53
Corny, V. 185
Costa Rica 311
Cuba 14, 193, 199ff, 209ff, 214, 219, 257, 259, 278, 308ff, 330, 335, 346, 358, 369, 374
Curran, Joe 217ff
Cyprus 14
Czechoslovakia 113, 170ff, 257, 271, 303, 341, 346

D

Darrow, Clarence 345
Davis, Angela 241, 246, 373
Day, Virgil B. 94
DeGaulle, Gen. Charles 100
Democratic Party 32, 187, 367
Democratic Republic of Korea 14, 76, 81, 113, 346
Democratic Republic of Vietnam 14, 113, 116, 236, 239, 244, 346
Denmark 346
Diem, Ngo Dinh 235
Dillon family 29
Dixiecrats 40, 280
Dominican Republic 14, 18, 153, 177, 193, 212, 215ff, 218, 271, 277
Dubcek, Alexander 172f, 175, 180, 183, 186
Dubinsky, David 217, 219, 236, 278
Dulles, Allen 88, 346

382

Soviet Union 48, 60, 65, 73, 75, 77,
80ff, 105ff, 112f, 124, 129, 166f, 176,
180, 182ff, 203ff, 230ff, 239, 245,
252, 257, 259, 261ff, 266ff, 272ff,
287, 295, 299, 315, 319, 323, 330,
340, 357, 362, 377
Spellman, Francis Cardinal 227
Spain 12, 18, 20, 153, 256, 271, 296, 346
Standard Oil of New Jersey 56, 210
Stimson, Henry L. 213
Sudan 20, 301, 358
Sukarno, President 52
Supka, F. 185
Supreme Court, U.S. 146, 160, 280
Svitak, Ivan 185, 341, 343
Sweden 370
Sweezey, Paul 315
Syria 69, 161f, 218

T

Taiwan 76, 88, 131, 153, 218, 259, 345
Taled, Ahmed 223
Texaco 53
Thailand 76, 229, 338
Thieu, Nguyen Van 236
Thompson, James C. 116
Tibet 346
Tito Broz, Marshall 231ff
Togliatti, Palmiro 182, 323
Torres, Jose 199
Truman, Harry S. 80, 224
Trotskyism 159, 296, 325, 339
Tugwell, Rexford 192
Tunisia 14,

U

Union Oil Co. 53
United Fruit Company 214
United Nations 18, 340

United States Steel Co. 337
Uruguay 311

V

Valverde, Eduardo Mora 311
Vance, Cyrus 209
Vatican 225ff
Venezuela 210f, 336f
Vietnam 13, 17, 69, 89, 111, 132, 140,
217ff, 225f, 231, 235ff, 263, 279
Vietnam War 36, 44, 62f, 81, 109, 115ff,
118, 120, 122ff, 126, 156ff, 162f,
240ff, 271, 292, 296f, 301, 307, 317,
330, 338, 343, 347, 353, 369
Vodslon, F. 183
Volman, Sacha 177

W

Wallace, George 148, 241
Warsaw Pact 38, 178ff, 303
Washington, George 280
Welch, Robert 89, 218, 282
Westinghouse Electric Corp. 46
Westmoreland, Gen. William C. 111
Wilson, Woodrow 108, 280
White, Byron 280
Whitman, Walt 280
Whitney, Eli 280
World War I. 13, 26f, 38, 251, 295
World War II 13f, 19, 26, 30, 35, 37f,
41, 43ff, 50, 62, 64ff, 73f, 80, 82, 87,
99, 112, 125, 158, 188f, 277, 297,
327, 333, 357, 374f

Y

Yemen 14
Young Americans for Freedom 175
Yugoslavia 228, 231ff

Z

Zionism 165, 169

ABOUT THE AUTHOR

Gus Hall, General Secretary of the Communist Party. U.S.A. since 1959 was born in 1910 in Iron, Minnesota, and has spent his entire lifetime in the working-class and Communist movements.

Since the age of 15, he has worked as a logger, a miner, a construction worker, a skilled mechanic and a steel worker. He was a leader of Little Steel Strike in 1937 in Ohio, and one of the founders of the United Steelworkers of America. He served in the U.S. Navy in World War II and was the leader of the Communist Party in Ohio.

Soon Hall became a member of the National Board of the National Committee of the Communist Party, and the National Secretary of the Party. Together with eleven members of the National Board, he was sentenced to prison in 1949 for his thoughts as a Marxist-Leninist. He served an eight-year federal prison term at Leavenworth under a Smith Act frameup and a vindictive contempt citation.

After his prison term, he returned to his responsibilities of Communist Party leadership and was elected General Secretary of the Party at the 17th National Convention and was unanimously re-elected at succeeding conventions. He became a popular speaker and broke the McCarthy barrier on the college campuses across the country. Through a series of press, radio, and television appearances, he brought the Communist Party viewpoint to millions of Americans.

After winning the fight for his passport and the right to travel, he visited Latin America, the Soviet Union and the Socialist countries, Cuba, and the countries of Western Europe. He attended the funeral of Ho Chi Minh at Hanoi and again visited the Democratic Republic of Vietnam when U.S. imperialism renewed the criminal genocidal bombing of the heroic people and the dikes of Vietnam.

Gus Hall has become recognized in all parts of the world as an outstanding Marxist-Leninist leader, theoretician and activist. His writings have been translated into the languages of the world and have contributed to the struggle against U.S. imperialism. This struggle goes beyond the writings of this book, to the field of constant activity. Gus Hall writes from the partisan point of view—as an anti-imperialist and Communist Party spokesman, with a conviction that the understanding and appreciation of the Communist viewpoint is an essential feature of any struggle against imperialism and for peace and socialism.